THE PEOPLE OF LERNA

THE PEOPLE OF
LERNA

ANALYSIS OF A PREHISTORIC AEGEAN POPULATION

BY

J. LAWRENCE ANGEL

AMERICAN SCHOOL OF CLASSICAL STUDIES AT ATHENS
PRINCETON, NEW JERSEY
AND
SMITHSONIAN INSTITUTION PRESS · CITY OF WASHINGTON
1971

Published simultaneously by the American School of Classical Studies at Athens as Volume II,

The People, in the series *Lerna: A Preclassical Site in the Argolid*.

Distribution in the United States by George Braziller, Inc.

Distribution in Canada by Doubleday Canada Ltd.

Distribution in the United Kingdom and Europe by

David & Charles (Publishers), Ltd., South Devon House, Newton Abbot, Devon, England

Library of Congress Catalogue Card Number: 73-139121

International Standard Book Number: 0-87474-098-3

PRINTED IN GERMANY *at* J. J. AUGUSTIN, GLÜCKSTADT

TO PEGGY MY WIFE

TABLE OF CONTENTS

TABLES

FIGURES

PLATES

(Follow page 112)

ACKNOWLEDGMENTS

For critical assistance with this monograph as well as for the chance to study the materials for it and the privilege of living and working at the American School of Classical Studies at Athens and at its field stations in Corinth and Myloi I am most grateful to Professor John L. Caskey, head of the Lerna excavations and at that time also of the American School, to Elizabeth G. Caskey, and to Tucker Blackburn. For technical field assistance in the summers of 1954 and 1957 I thank the late Tasso Pantazopoulos, Argyris Marinis, and also Nikos Thiraios and Panos Yannoulatos, students at Athens College. For technical help in enlarging photographs, making plates, and doing statistics I thank primarily Alfred Guzzetti, and also other summer students in my laboratory at the Jefferson Medical College in 1958–62 (Michael Little, Santo Longo, Judith Schermer (Hare), Jane Thomas, Richard Moy) and my technicians Alice Winnett and Dorothy Fox (Elicker). For help in transcribing and typing the tables and the manuscript I thank Judith S. Hare, Angela Margola, Bernice Chase and Dale Stephenson, and for further help with statistics and photography, Donald Ortner. For preparing the maps and plans for publication I thank Marcia Bakry.

Field work and analysis were supported by National Institutes of Health Grant A224 and continuations; Penrose Fund grants from the American Philosophical Society made possible my travel to and within Greece. I am grateful to these organizations as well as to the academic sponsors of the field work, the Jefferson Medical College of Philadelphia and the University Museum of the University of Pennsylvania, and to the Smithsonian Institution where I have completed the analysis and written the manuscript.

There are many others to whom I owe thanks for data or ideas, especially to those who criticized this monograph: Drs. T. Dale Stewart, I. G. Sohn, and S. S. Weinberg, as well as Dr. J. L. Caskey.

J. Lawrence Angel

National Museum of Natural History
Smithsonian Institution

INTRODUCTION

The chance to study the people who lived at Lerna between about 6000 B.C. and Roman times came to me through the kindness and interest of Professor J. L. Caskey. Throughout seven seasons of excavations of the salient portions of this site he saved for study all human bones, so that we would have the best material possible to reconstruct the health and lives of the successive populations buried at Lerna. He reviews details of the whole enterprise in his foreword to volume 1 of this series of reports.

SAMPLE

Under the impressive pre-Greek (Early Bronze Age) palace and town wall is an irregularly deep layer of Neolithic settlements dating from the sixth and fourth millennia B.C. These produced nine people: four infants, one four-year-old, one ten-year-old girl, two women, and one man. Four other infant burials, belonging to the very end of the Early Bronze Age (E.H. III), are included with the Middle Bronze Age cemetery sample, since they are culturally part of it. But the excavators found no burials of the typical Early Bronze Age levels either earlier or contemporary with the House of the Tiles, or Palace (E.H. II). From the full Mycenaean period, after the Middle Bronze Age, there is one man; from the Early Iron Age, three children, seven women, and five men; and from the Roman period, one grave containing two women. From none of these periods, obviously, do we have the full cemetery, only peripheral or scattered burials which are not cross sections of the populations of these periods.

In contrast to these, the Middle Bronze Age people buried their dead beside their houses or under the floor (children), so that excavation of these houses, which the people built around the mound over the burnt palace or big house, has given us a truly cross-sectional sample: about 235 graves, some multiple, have yielded 234 people. Only 24 graves, about 10%, lacked identifiable pieces of human bone. This record shows two things: first, that the excavators took truly extraordinary care in saving skeletons, and second, that soil conditions are better at Lerna than at most Greek cemeteries. Usually not more than 10 to 15% of graves produce skeletons.

Infants make up 35%, children 21%, and adults and subadults 44% of this Lerna sample dating from the first half of the second millennium B.C.; this 8:5:10 ratio is quite typical of the population profile of prehistoric and medieval sites. Many of the skeletons are very incomplete; only about 65% of adults, 24% of children, and 21% of infants gave skull and bones which provided a useful reconstruction of the individual. The rest were fragmentary. Some fragments of human bone from the first phases of the Middle Bronze Age occupation were undoubtedly scattered by later burials and included with the animal bones sent to N-G. Gejvall for analysis. He notes (1969, p. 3) only a few, fortunately, mostly of newborn infants.

DATES

The approximate dates which I will use for the Lerna skeletons are: Early, Middle, and Late Neolithic during the sixth, fifth, and fourth millennia B.C.; Early Bronze Age during the third millennium (with Early Helladic III starting *ca.* 2200 B.C.); Middle Bronze Age people *ca.* 2000 to 1600 B.C.; Late Bronze Age (Late Helladic I–III) from then to 1150 B.C., with L.H. I–II occupying at least the first two centuries and full Mycenaean (L.H. III) starting before 1350 B.C.; Early Iron Age 1150 to 650 B.C., with at least the last two centuries for the Geometric ceramic period (then Classical or fully historic, then Hellenistic); and finally the Roman Empire period, after the first century A.D.

SITE

The ancient town where these people lived and died is at the southeast corner of the Argolid (plain of Argos) on the western shore of the Bay of Argos directly across from Asine, Nauplion, and Tiryns on the eastern shore. As can be seen from a glance at the map (p. 11) the Argolid is in touch by land with Corinth, the Isthmus, and the west. The Bay of Argos is the southernmost of the series of diagonal southwest-northeast gulfs biting into the eastern, or Aegean, coast of Greece. North of it are a series of gulfs: the Saronic Gulf (on which lie Athens and Eleusis), with the Isthmus of Corinth separating the Saronic from the Corinthian Gulf to the west, the Euripos-Atalante Straits (between Euboea, Attica, Boeotia, and Locris) ending in the Lamia Gulf, the Thessalian Gulf (with Iolkos, and present-day Volos), the Macedonian Gulf (with Thessaloniki), and the two gulfs between the three fingers of Chalcidice on the north Aegean shore. On the southern Peloponnesian shore the Gulfs of Messenia and Laconia face south. All these deep bays have fertile plains at their heads and sides rimmed with mountains or defensible hills, inviting settlement by fisherman-farmers from earliest Neolithic times (7th millennium) onwards. Lerna has Mt. Pontinus behind as a refuge, a beautiful shelving beach less than a hundred meters in front, and to the north two springs of fresh water, similarly close, forming the famous marsh where the Hydra was supposed to live. For people living at Lerna there were wide possibilities. Lerna guards the route over the mountains into Arcadia. Sea contact is easy with the Peloponnese and with the Peninsula of Argolis, which separates the Gulf of Argos from the Saronic Gulf. Open-sea sailing, involving dependence on winds and seasons, as described later, gives less easy contact with Keos, Melos, Thera, the other Cycladic Islands, and by this means either with Crete to the south or with Anatolia to the northeast.

I studied the remains of these people in late July and early August of 1954, and June of 1957 after Tassos Pantazopoulos and Argyris Marinis, respectively, had mended them under my close supervision. In 1954 Nikos Thiraios acted as recorder and in 1957, Panos Yannoulatos. I photographed the material with their assistance, using a Leica with 13.5-cm lens and reflex attachment. Alfred Guzzetti enlarged the pictures and made the plates. Judith Schermer Hare, Bernice Chase, and Angela Margola helped with statistics and typing. The work was made possible by National Institutes of Health Grant A-224, with continuations, by travel grants from the Penrose Fund of the American Philosophical Society, and through the help of the American School of Classical Studies at Athens and the Greek Archaeological Service. This help included use of facilities at Myloi (Lerna) and at Old Corinth.

TECHNIQUE

The logical way to describe all these ancient people is by periods, with an individual description of each skeleton as well as photographs and measurements. (In this work, all measurements are assumed to be in millimeters unless otherwise noted.) The photographs of skulls (Plates I–XVII) are all to a single scale and in standard positions with the Frankfort plane (eye-ear) either parallel to or perpendicular to the lens axis of the camera. These were taken at a standard distance of 66 inches from the center of the skull. Measurements, which are recorded in the Appendix, I made in accordance with the techniques used by the Harvard school of anthropologists; these are defined by the numbers from Martin's *Lehrbuch* (1959), except for such new measurements as the slope of the alveolar plane relative to the Frankfort horizontal (eye-ear) plane that defines the position of the head usual when looking at the distant horizon.

Parietal thickness is the average of three thicknesses measured about 1 cm. from the front, middle, and back of the squamous suture. Jaw thickness is perpendicular to the vertical axis of the left first lower molar tooth. Acromion a-p is the front-to-back extent of the acromion process measured perpendicular to the scapular spine. Pubic and ischium lengths use for their central point of origin the carefully estimated junction of the three parts of the hipbone (acetabular point) marked on its medial (inner) surface. Capitate length and breadth are maximum diameters.

For angles, I orient the pelvis with anterior superior iliac spines in a vertical plane with the symphysis pubis. The upper sacral angle uses the upper edge of S_1 and lower edge of S_3 relative to the horizontal. The lumbosacral angle is the difference between the sagittal angles made by the upper surface of S_1 and the upper surface of L_5 relative to the horizontal.

The proportions of the front-to-back length of the ilium, a-p from acetabular point to posterior superior iliac spine, made up by brim and by sacroiliac joint surface plus back muscle area, differ according to sex and are measurable in children and infants. The brim, or anterior iliac segment, I measure from acetabular end to front of auricular surface; the muscular, or posterior, iliac segment I measure from front of joint surface to back of ilium (at or near posterior superior iliac spine).

Such measurements, the indices or ratios between measurements, and standardized observations on skeleton and skull describe each bone's reflection of the physiology, life history, and genetic background of each person in the sample, at least as far as we currently can understand the mirror of physiology which the skeleton is. Lengths of bones, the thickness diameters of their shafts, the size of braincase, skull base, and face—these define growth and size, as determined by diet, climate, living habits and heredity; in this respect, lines of growth arrest at joints or on tooth enamel are likewise important. Lengths of leg compared with thigh, forearm compared with arm, lumbar (waist) vertebrae compared with estimated stature, bi-iliac (pelvis) breadth compared with stature, clavicle and scapula compared with upper arm, and thickness of femur shaft compared with thigh length (robusticity index)—these describe body build as set by both environment and heredity, though fat is almost impossible to guess at. Sizes and angles of joints, relative flattening and crest developments on bone shafts (platymeric and cnemic indices), ligament grooves and special facets at joints, and such arthritic changes as erosion under joint cartilage or hypertrophic lips or crests around ligaments—these reflect use of the body, muscle development, gait, habitual posture, and in the female, childbirth. Size and ruggedness of the skull, the breadths of forehead, cheeks and jowls relative to braincase, the relative narrowness (linearity) or breadth (laterality) of braincase, face, jaw, palate, nose, and orbits, the relative height of skull vault (braincase), the depth of chin and mouth, the profile protrusion of mouth, nose, cheeks, and chin, the slope of chewing plane, the size and details of the skull (and other bones, too)—these reflect heredity more than environment, although inadequate nutrition does affect growth (e.g., length of skull base or breadth of face) and remodelling (e.g., prominence of growth centers or bosses on frontal, parietal and occipital bones which cover the brain). Skull details are clues to genetic relationships, to evolutionary changes, and to migrations.

Any disease which produces a major physiologic reaction affects bone. The signs of an acute disease or injury in childhood may heal to the point where they are invisible or at least quite difficult to read correctly, although fractures, severe wounds or bruises (e.g., on the head), abscesses, and growth arrests are usually clear. Progressive or chronic diseases, such as tuberculosis, cancer, tertiary syphilis, the anemias, osteomyelitis, or any arthritic process, are all clear in severe degree and usually discernible, although precise cause and diagnosis may be obscure. For example, I am concerned over anemia from genetically caused abnormal haemoglobins, discussed later. But we cannot yet consistently distinguish the resulting bone marrow increase from that resulting from iron-deficiency anemia. Also, people differ in their metabolic response to the same disease organism or parasite.

In childhood, the changes in ossification at the growing ends of long bones or the edges of flat bones (epiphyses) and the eruption of teeth give good estimates of age, with individual variation of two years or so. But in adulthood, after epiphyses have fused and teeth erupted, the progressive changes at such joints as the pubic symphysis, shoulder, skull sutures, and intervertebral disks, and the remodelling of bone surface of skull, scapula, and pelvis are all increasingly variable and inaccurate when used for any one person, because there are big differences in the rate of aging, and estimated age (physiological) may deviate from chronologic age by 5, 10, or even 20 years. These deviations, of course, cancel out in group averages. Sex differences, on the other hand, are almost impossible to evaluate in skeletons of children and become increasingly clear until complete adult skeletons permit accurate sex determinations in 90% of most populations. In comparison with males, females have a relatively larger true pelvic inlet and outlet (birth canal) with a longer pubic bone, wider sciatic notch, bigger preauricular sulcus, smaller ischium and smaller posterior ilium, relatively smaller joints and lessened muscularity throughout, smoothness or absence of browridges on skull, and relatively smaller face and jaws (with tooth size less reduced and orbits not reduced). Naturally, the accuracy diminishes for all the criteria for sex, age, disease, injuries, skull form, heredity, posture, nutrition, growth, and body size as we deal with increasingly incomplete skeletons.

In the part of this monograph which presents individual descriptions of each skeleton, I shall say, for example, that *196 Ler* is "the partial skeleton of a small woman who died between ages 40 and 45," rather than, "this incomplete skeleton has 10 of 15 sex criteria that indicate it is female, age criteria that indicate a range from 28 to 54, and, based only on a humerus with upper end incomplete, a stature that I guess is between 142 and 160 cm." I ignore the range of inaccuracy of estimates. But the uncertainties are still there. From an incomplete skeleton no one can pinpoint adult age at death, or state with certainty the sex, exact body size, facial features, disease status, or, usually, the cause of death. All measurements from which one terminus is missing but which still can be estimated fairly closely I list in parentheses and omit from calculation of averages or other constants. I expect the reader to remember these uncertainties of determining all facts about each individual from an excavated skeleton.

In working out the genetic relations between populations and those changes within a population not caused by plastic growth response to environmental forces, a proper technique would be to list frequencies of skeletal and dental traits which we know to result from fairly direct action of single genes. There are a few such traits so far known, such as the Carabelli cusp (Plate XXI) or metopic (forehead) suture persisting *after* early childhood (Plates V, VI, IX, XII, XIV). Berry and Berry (1967), elaborating on the trait comparisons of Hooton (1930), Laughlin and Jorgensen (1956), and others, have used a trigonometric transformation of percentage frequencies of 30 "epigenetic" traits, mostly normal variants in skull sutures or foramina, to measure population divergences and to show that trait intercorrelations are surprisingly low. Their results are reasonable and helpful in the light of evolutionary theory, and largely avoid the danger of exaggeration which occurs in comparisons of form and measurements when a single growth trend, such as extra growth around the nose-forehead junction, influences a number of traits and measurements. The "epigenetic" trait, or minutial, approach avoids this danger of trait and measurement intercorrelation by omitting the major growth variations which respond to microevolutionary forces and have clearly polygenic, pleiotropic, and also environmental causation. Yet these characters are important to include.

In other words, an attempt to get back to the reality of fairly direct gene effects at this time cannot succeed because of the interaction of gene-enzyme chains (genes are always potential rather than real) during all phases of growth: each gene may produce many effects, just as each phaenotypic detail or total skull or bone form must depend on many genes (as well as on nutrition, climate, disease). Furthermore, the fragmentary state of many skulls makes comparison of epigenetic traits especially difficult.

For evolution the phaenotype, the actual functioning individual, is just as critical a reality as the gene frequencies: each reality is a product of the other and their interaction is the essence of evolution. But it is actual individuals who mate and produce the next generation and respond to culture and environment. Hence, a shorthand method of describing whole individuals as well as describing genetic traits or growth complexes does have value, as long as we realize that combinations of growth complexes are not fixed.

To describe individuals briefly I shall use skull types (or skull form tendencies) based in a general way on local population averages (see Table 1, p. 36): for example, Mediterranean (B) or Alpine (C) or Iranian (D4). To describe trait complexes I shall use measurements, e.g., angle of alveolar plane (palate), or angle of projection of the nasal bones (nasalia angle), or simply words and photographs. This is a visual classification and approach of the sort which we all use in everyday life in appraising or responding to beauty or skill, in recognizing friends, or in choosing a mate. In fact it is precisely the factor of social selection in mixing populations which makes use of type tendencies valid within a given breeding group. For this reason I use visual appraisal (see Plates) and not the arbitrary, though objective, combinations of indices which Dixon (1923) and then Hooton (1930) used. Nevertheless, the history of anthropology shows typologies to be dangerous; as oversimplifications, they have been used for the worst purposes of generalization and racism. The semantics of types is especially tricky. Hence, when I note that a particular trait complex, part of a type tendency, occurs frequently in Early Neolithic Macedonia and also in Bronze Age Lerna, and that another complex occurs frequently in both Neolithic and Bronze Age Cyprus and Bronze Age Lycia, the inference of connections in each case is tentative—a suggestion to be tested by further comparison and by the total logic of possible demographic, archeological, and historical data. The reader must remain properly skeptical and remember the principle of parsimony: the simplest explanation for concentration of a given skull peculiarity or for a change in heterogeneity of many skull combinations is most likely to be right.

FIVE AIMS

As a physical anthropologist studying an ancient population I aim to analyze: (1) demography, (2) health and disease status, (3) body build and posture, (4) microevolution, and (5) genetic relationships or connections with other populations. In the past a standard analysis of human skeletal material has dealt with body build and group connections, and has sometimes mentioned age at death and available observations on paleopathology, with the hope of relating these to living habits, diet, and environment (cf. Hooton, 1930). But the fourth aim, study of the processes of human evolution at the population level, is seldom attempted. It is high time to study an ancient population functionally, to relate it to its physical and cultural environment in such aspects as numerical density, composition, birth and death rates, longevity, general health, specific diseases and injuries, selective and other forces for evolutionary changes, migrations and mixtures, similarities with other groups, physical appearance and processes of growth, and habitual body movements. All these things are important as results of a multitudinous complex of both environmental and cultural forces—nutrition, climate, bacteria, geography, custom, breeding pattern, games, warfare, to name a few. But the demographic and physical aspects of a population also greatly affect the performance of individuals and hence influence the culture and its control over environment, both qualitatively and quantitatively.

I came to Greece as a graduate student hoping to unravel the social biology of this area, partly in answer to Nazi racist interpretations. As a staff member of the Athenian Agora Excavations I have tried to study all skeletons excavated in Greece. Since autumn 1937 I have worked intermittently on ancient population samples in mainland Greece, some of the Ionian and Aegean islands, south Cyprus, and parts of Western Anatolia covering the time span from the Mesolithic period (8th millennium, B.C.) to modern times. In relation to the growth, fluctuation, decline, and very recent revival of civilization during this time span I have been able to pick out some of the interactions of human biology with culture change (Angel, 1946, 1951, 1960, 1969)—the positive feedback relations between cultural advance, population density, increasing longevity, taller stature, and race fusion, the inverse relation between population density and speed of microevolutionary change, the heterogeneity of isolates under certain conditions of population reduction, and the wavelike spiral of genetic change. But although my total sample of about 2,000 seems impressive when compared to other areas, the separate site samples are usually well under 50, skeletons are incomplete, and so many key places are left blank that my time map of the social biology of the eastern Mediterranean is like an airplane pilot's picture of the New England coast seen through cumulus clouds. For this reason I particularly value my present chance to make a deep analysis at one particular site— the Lerna excavated by Caskey—and to analyze successively the demography, state of health, posture and build, evolutionary responses, and apparent genetic connections of its people.

BACKGROUND

Since this monograph will appear separately from Professor Caskey's full report on the excavations, my fivefold analysis will make sense only against a background of the ecology and general prehistory of Greece and surrounding areas. Within one environment the ecologic forces affecting Paleolithic hunters were completely different from those affecting the demography, health, growth and posture, microevolutionary change, and genetics of a successful Bronze Age or even modern farming population. At any one cultural period the forested mountain, the stony hillside, the rich-soiled plain, the marshy delta, the sandy or rocky cove, and the sharp volcanic island each affected differently the people living on it. The environment limits and restricts rather than directly creates a cultural or a biological change. Yet the interaction between environment and people never ceases. Hence the fullness of life for the people of Lerna and their near and distant neighbors and ancestors will become clear only if we can picture and can savor the environments in which these people lived.

ECOLOGY: THE ENVIRONMENTAL CHALLENGE

Throughout recorded history, the geography and people of Greece have shared as their keynote diversity. Greece is neither entirely a region of mountain-valley isolation, in which the cultural tone of one community is scarcely heard in the next, nor is it entirely a fertile river plain across which a single cultural tone resounds. It is, instead, a land in which a moderate number of both extremes occur—and one where, during periods of adversity and stress, the tone of its culture has been as a chime of many bells, and during good times as the peal, laden with overtones, of a single great bell.

Geographically, Greece is a partly submerged and tilted net of mountains, between the meshes of which are caught deep sea gulfs and new plains, forcing separation on people in the high valleys and on some islands but bringing to those in the lowlands unity through the ever-present sea. To the Aegean peoples the sea has been what the steppes have been to the peoples of Central Asia, Iran, Anatolia, or the Ukraine—an access route for new influences and new peoples, and a highroad for local intercommunication. Although the whole area around the Aegean Sea lies, except for the highest altitudes, within the Mediterranean climatic zone (Koeppen's Csa), it contains a sharply contrasting juxtaposition of biotic regions that range from rocky seacoast with small bays, beaches, and marshes, through broken-up silt-rich plains, both dry and marshy, to intermontane valleys, upland pastures, and rocky mountain ridges— all often lying within an area of a few square kilometers (Myres, 1930).

The soils of Greece are equally varied chemically and are often rocky, supporting varied but limited crops, trees, and vines. Today an ever-present maquis of scrub and thorns replaces the former extensive forests of live oak and pine (Michell, 1940, p. 80; Butzer, 1964, p. 60).

The adjustment of each different cultural group in this almost unlimited variety of environments depended on rainfall just as critically as did those of the arid zone to the south, but even more slenderly because of the smaller and less certain rivers. The eastern Mediterranean, which lies on the geographic fringe of Atlantic Ocean weather, as we shall see later, also lies on the chronological fringe of rainfall belts in relation to glacial retreat (Brooks, 1926, 1949; Butzer, 1964, pp. 425–6). Between latest Paleolithic and Medieval times the annual rainfall decreased in this area to such sparsities that the country offered continual challenge to survival on a really effective level, and with a much narrower margin of safety than in the riverine civilizations of the Near East. But while constant water supplies for irrigation, like the Tigris-Euphrates flow or the annual Nile flood, were lacking in the Eastern Mediterranean littoral, including Greece, water was supplied in some areas by mountain streams or coastal marshes. Even here, however, there was danger of loss when cultural misuse caused erosion or lowered the water table, or when a change in sea level shifted both the water table and the coastline, altering the marsh and delta ecology vital for a marine food supply. Such a multiplicity of mountain, plain, and maritime ecologies demanded individualistic and variable cultural adjustments, a flexibility almost the opposite of the rolling cultural inertia underlying the river-valley civilizations of the fertile crescent. Hence, in Greece, the Aegean, Anatolia, and the Levant human ecologic opportunism paid off in the attractive possibilities of exploiting the larger supplies of clay for pottery and stone for building, as well as the limited natural supplies of such necessities as good timber, flint, obsidian, ores of copper, tin, iron, silver, lead, and washings of gold, all of which were either lacking or in scant supply in the more stable fertile crescent. I will clarify the human meaningfulness of these ecologic variables after discussing geology, soils, and climate for Greece, and for Lerna in particular.

ECOLOGY: GEOLOGY, GEOGRAPHY, AND WEATHER

In flying over the eastern Mediterranean, or glancing at a relief map of it, three things strike the eye: (1) the encroachment of the sea on the land masses which rise progressively higher and higher from the southern Aegean toward the north-northwest and toward the northeast; (2) the great bent sweep of the Dinaric-West Greek-Cretan-Lycian-Taurus-Armenian mountain chain surrounding the entire land area on the west and south, in contrast to the northwest-southeast diagonality of ranges in the Cyclades and Central Greece, with sea gulfs between them; and (3) the very small scale of the land masses in contrast to the continental plateaus of Anatolia, Arabia, Iran, or the steppe country of the North European Plain from the Tarim Basin to the North Sea. This geographical condition results from a very complex process of recent mountain-folding and vulcanism, with much local sinking, superimposed on much older geological processes occurring in three successive stages.

According to Maull (1922, pp. 6–20), in the first stage a basic shell of pre-Paleozoic igneous and metamorphic rock was formed. This later was broken into four massifs against which still later sedimentary and folded formations were laid: (1) a Lydian massif, including eastern Lydia and northern Caria west to Samos, with an uncertain southern border, (2) a big Cycladic massif under the southern Aegean as far over as southern Attica, meeting (3) a big Thracian massif in Euboea and Skyros, with (4) a western Macedonian massif west of the Vardar Valley.

In the second stage, two sets of mountains were piled up: (1) eastern Greek ranges that ran across the future Aegean during the Mesozoic to Eocene, a folding of older rocks and sedimentary formations including Paleozoic slate, Pennsylvanian and Permian limestone and serpentine, and schist and sandstone; and (2) an irregular semicircle of Triassic and later rocks folded around the edges of the original four massifs from western Greece to southern Anatolia. This semicircle consisted of an outer Western or Ionian section of Triassic limestone and dolomite continuing in Crete and Anatolia, and an inner eastern section (Pindus and Taygetus) of schist, hornstone, and flat limestone partly overlying Eocene shale plus sandstone.

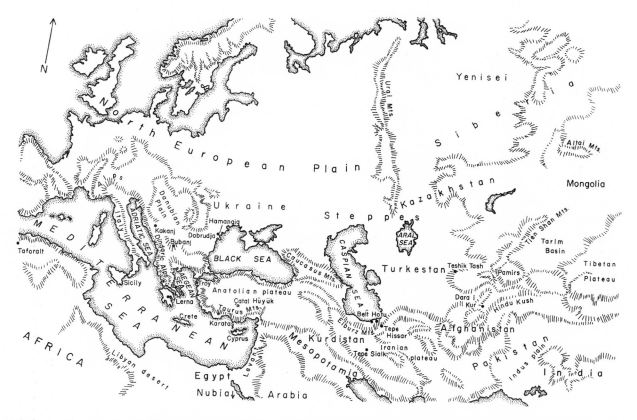

Figure 1. Map of Western Eurasia centering on the Eastern Mediterranean, showing principal archeological sites; plains, plateaus, and seas as potential routes and mountain ranges as filters, barriers, or refuges in relation to prehistoric movements and settlements of people over the time span covered in the text. I do not try to show possible changes in sea level.

The third stage began with a general uplift of original mountains and peneplains of Oligocene to early Miocene time, with much erosion and even sea-covering during the late Miocene to Pliocene, followed, in the late Pliocene, by quick uplift and violent faulting in the west and sinking in the southeast. The uplift raised the late Tertiary peneplains as much as 1,800 m., with the highest peak in the Peloponnese now 2,405 m. above the present sea level. It produced river-basin plateaus (with later Karst formation), steep valleys, and a supply of sediment for new, narrow coastal plains; and it resulted in the cutting of new river valleys (such as the Vardar), in flooding, and in the formation of marshes and deltas. The faulting produced the sea gulfs and associated plains that run north and south in the southern Peloponnese, and that north of this run diagonally southeast and northwest, as can be seen on the map (Fig. 3). Across the Aegean the Anatolian gulfs and plains run east and west, and the rivers flow to the west. The sinking is most marked in the Cretan Sea and the southeastern Aegean, which have depths of 2,000 m., less than half those in the Ionian Sea, Black Sea, or western Mediterranean.

The geography of the whole Aegean shore of Greece, with its many dividing land barriers, makes the sea vitally important for travel, depending always on seasonal winds and local weather. As a sea site on the eastern coast of the Peloponnese and on the southern extension of the Plain of Argolis Lerna lies on the gulf opposite Nauplia, just off the sea approaches to the general Isthmian area of Greece. Its successive populations formed part of the relatively dense and successful settlements in this geographically critical part of Greece. The possible sea routes between Lerna and Egypt, the Levant, Anatolia, or the Black Sea regions are without

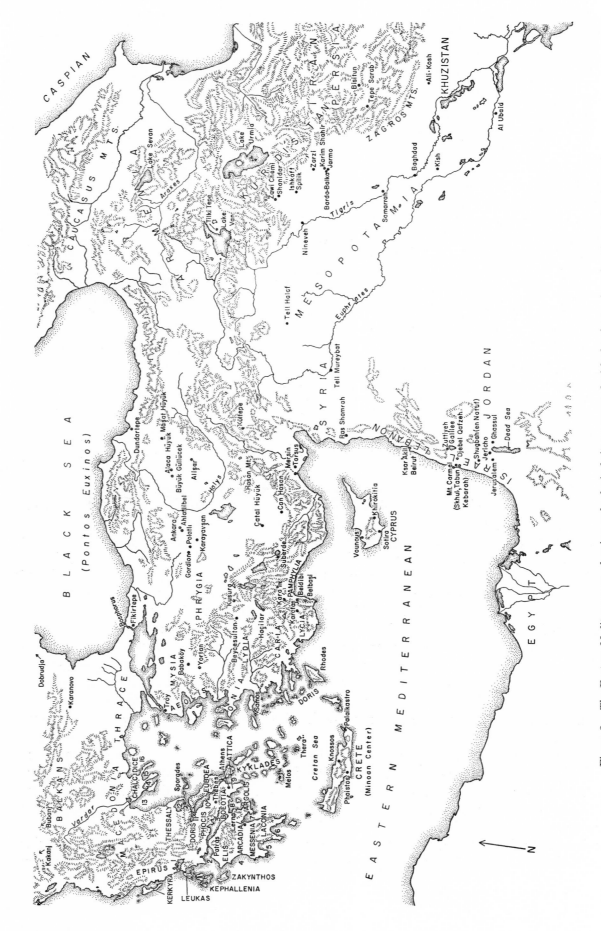

Figure 2. The Eastern Mediterranean, showing archeological sites connected with the change from hunting to farming and subsequent cultural changes. I omit sites not mentioned in the text, even including some from which skeletal material is available. Connections with places shown on Figure 1 indicated by arrows.

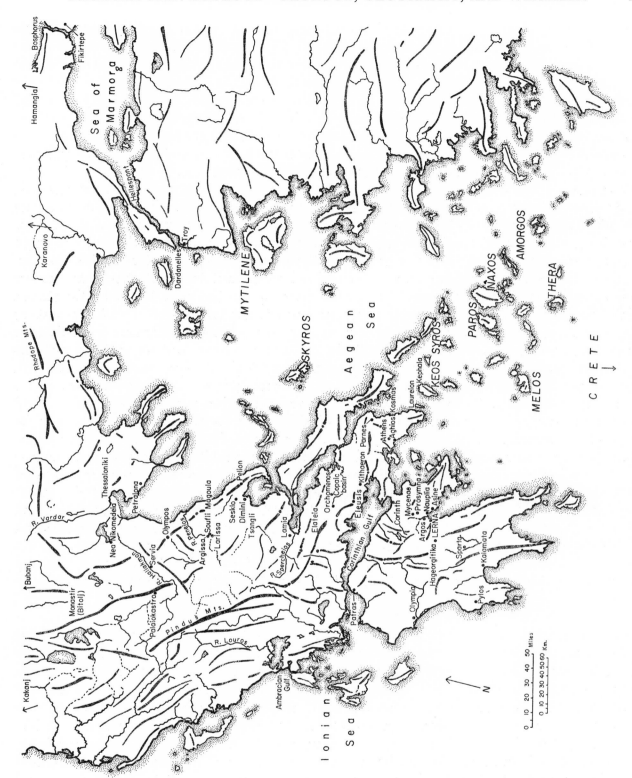

Figure 3. Greece and the Aegean coasts and islands, showing relationship of Lerna to other sites mentioned in the text, and to show directions of mountain ranges (heavy dark lines), and of rivers. These, as well as islands, harbors, and winds, are important in relation to trade and migration. Connections with places shown on Figures 1 and 2 are indicated by arrows.

number, though all are made difficult by the prevailing winds and would have been impracticable for Neolithic or even Bronze Age boats without use of the Cycladic Islands and the Sporades as way stations (Jardé, 1923, pp. 44–46; Myres, 1930, pp. 5, 7, 217). In the wet season (winter) the prevailing winds are from the west, though north winds may interrupt these rain-bringers in the coldest days of winter, especially in the northeastern Aegean. After a fairly brief period of equinoctial storms a south wind blows fairly persistently during April and May. Throughout the long dry summer the etesian winds (Meltemi) blow from the north or northeast, and these are modified from the regular northeast trade-wind pattern by the heat and low-pressure area over the Libyan and Sahara deserts. These etesian winds would have been most useful for sailing ships which could beat into the wind. In the Neolithic, and even in the Bronze Age, boats probably used oars more than sails, the use of which perhaps was limited to going before the wind, and they travelled coastwise or from island to island, always within sight of land. For these, the daily alternation of land and sea breezes, resulting from wider day to night temperature changes on the land as compared to those over the sea, is significant. For example, an Early Bronze Age vessel from Amorgos could sail north until dawn with the night offshore breeze, be driven southwest or south during the morning into the lee of Naxos by the etesian winds, row for a period, and then sail northwest again during the afternoon, with the onshore breeze to Paros (see Fig. 3). Other stretches of sea, such as the Ionian or Tyrrhenian, would have been much riskier to cross, so that Neolithic and Early Bronze Age sea contacts with the Anatolian coast, Crete, and eventually the Levant would logically have been closer than with the western Mediterranean, though evidence of the megalithic cults and the amber and tin trades shows that the latter had developed by the third millennium B.C. Islanders could control sea trade; hence, the very early importance of Melos with its obsidian and Paros with its marble, and especially of the Bronze Age thalassocracy of Crete. Land routes tend to be channeled by mountains; hence, Neolithic and later strongholds were located near narrow passes. But in the region around the Isthmus of Corinth coalitions between strategically located ports and inland towns could control trade and travel both by land and sea; Lerna, for example, controls the easiest, coastal road between Argos (or Nauplia or Mycenae) and the rolling and dissected plateau country of Arcadia, where this road begins its twisted and rocky climb across the passes to the southwest. The strength of such a town would depend on its population size and health, as well as on its location and culture. Population density, in turn, would depend on climate, rainfall, soils, crops and food, and other ecological factors, as well as on trade.

ECOLOGY: CLIMATE

Climate, in the Aegean areas, even more than in most Mediterranean areas, is conditioned by the sea. The sea prevents that intense continental winter cold typical of the plateaus of Anatolia, Iran, or Turkestan or the Ukraine or trans-Caucasic steppe grasslands, and during the winter the Mediterranean lets the wet west winds from the Atlantic bring rain to the west coast and, via the Patras and Corinthian gulfs, as far as snowy Mt. Kithaeron or even Mt. Parnes, as well as to the lower mountains behind the plain of Argolis and Lerna (E. Huntington, 1910, p. 660). But while the sea acts as a temperature control to coastal Greece in winter, its cooling effect in summer is less obvious: in the mountains of Epirus and Macedonia January temperatures average —1 to +5°C. compared to 8.6°C. at Athens and 10–12°C. in the Mycenae-Nauplia-Lerna area and the Islands. July temperatures show less contrast, from 22.2–24°C. in the northern mountains to 26–27°C. in the coastal and island region (Maull, 1922, p. 25). Etesian winds balance the summer heat. Thus in recent times central Greece has a mild winter and hot summer in contrast to a much more continental climate to the north toward the Balkan area.

From what is known of the fauna and from limited pollen data it appears that temperate woodland conditions prevailed in the Mediterranean during the Würm glaciation (Butzer, 1964, pp. 285–296), with glaciers in the mountains and snow lines at 1,800–2,500 m., and that conditions nearer those of continental cold prevailed in the Balkans. Equally important for Middle and Upper Paleolithic East Mediterranean populations and for later soil and vegetation situations were the rainfall and sea-level changes during this period. During the Early Würm period, true pluvial conditions existed in the Mediterranean (Butzer, 1964, pp. 332–333) with "intensive sheetflood erosion and deposition of a heterogeneous class of colluvial silts and alluvial gravels ..." (Butzer, 1964, p. 297), including red clay, silt, sand, and gravel, and these actions were influenced by steeper stream flow as the sea level dropped. During the coldest periods rainfall was probably no greater than now, and increased only slightly during periods of glacial retreat and in postglacial times.

Eustatic lowering of the sea level by about 100 m. and temporarily by perhaps up to 150 m. would have united most of the coastal islands to Anatolia and Greece; it would have united the central Cyclades and would have produced waterfalls at the Dardanelles and Bosporus farther out than the present locations of these straits (to drain the combined Caspian plus Black Sea lakes); and it also would have eliminated the northern Adriatic, although it would not have produced a land bridge from Italy to Tunisia. In other words, an easy dry land route between the Near East and Greece never existed in earliest Neolithic, Upper Paleolithic, or even Mousterian times.

Interpretations of postglacial climatic changes (C. E. P. Brooks, 1949) depend heavily on von Post's pre-World War I pioneer pollen studies for northwestern Europe. These changes are represented by eight zones (Butzer, 1964, p. 407). After three phases—Arctic (1), Temperate (2), and Arctic-Dryas (3)—from about 12,000 to 8300 B.C. of the terminal Pleistocene, the Preboreal (4) warming-up led to the Boreal (5) warmer and fairly dry climate, followed by the still warmer Atlantic wet (6) phase from 5500 to 3000 B.C., the Sub-Boreal (7) drier (but perhaps equally warm in the Mediterranean) from 3000 to 800 B.C., and after that the Sub-Atlantic (8) cooler and irregularly wetter climate. From the Temperate phase (2) onward, extensive oak and beech forests grew over Europe, and the successful hunting regime based on large herds of mammoth, horse, and later reindeer was fragmented into many Mesolithic cultures, except, apparently, in the loess and steppe country of the east. But there was less sharp change in the Near East, where the change to aridity had already largely occurred during the Würm glaciation; and after the Arctic-Dryas cold phase, in the ninth millennium, conditions during the period of early agricultural experimentation were clearly wetter and warmer than today (Butzer, 1964, pp. 425–426). In Greece and the Mediterranean, during the Neolithic, the sea level was about 2 m. higher than today and the climate 2°C. warmer (Butzer, 1964, p. 443) but by the second millennium Bronze Age the sea level had dropped 3 or 4 m., so that Mycenaean coastal settlements are now only 1 to 2 m. below sea level (Higgins, 1966), and the temperature was down to its present level at least by the first millennium B.C. (Maull, 1922, p. 25). The Bronze Age climate at Lerna, therefore, was probably only slightly warmer and no wetter than today.

Modern climate in the eastern Mediterranean, at least south of a line from the Ambracian Gulf to Mt. Olympus and the Bosporus, has three seasons (Maull, 1922, p. 30): A winter rainy season that lasts from October to March and is like a New England autumn with occasional colder stretches, ending in expanses of wild flowers over rocky hills; several spring months of warm growing season from April to June; and a summer dry season during which plants aestivate, for the air is as dry as in the American Southwest, and towns rely on water stored in cisterns or reservoirs. This winter-summer rainfall contrast is demonstrated in the Athens area, where 78% of the precipitation falls in the wet season and 8% in the driest months, with the Aegean Islands even drier in summer (87% and 0.8%) and the extreme northwest wetter in winter as a result of the far heavier rainfall on the western mountains, the rest of the Aegean being in their rain shadow (Maull, 1922, p. 24). In terms of annual rainfall the west to east contrast in north Greece is 136 cm. in Kerkyra, 73 cm. at Monastir, and 43 cm. at Thessaloniki; in central Greece it is 86 cm. in Kephallenia, 68 cm. in Patras, and 34 cm. in the Argolid near Lerna, 49 cm. on Syros, and 36 cm. on Thera. These contrasts make for very different ecologic conditions for the mountainous northwest as compared to the isthmian or island areas and for the Anatolian coastal valleys as compared to the plateaus and mountains of that area. This environmental diversity is particularly significant during the period of intrusion of first farmers into an area probably occupied by Mesolithic hunters. But from the standpoint of farming, the rain-holding properties of the soils in much of the alluvial plains of the east enabled these areas to support larger populations than the west, although in modern times the extreme west (Kerkyra to Messenia) has a slightly denser population than the east, except for the Athens trade center (Maull, 1922, p. 58).

Huntington's (1910) theory—that increasing aridity after Roman Empire times was what produced erosion and silting (as at Olympia), and thus reduced Greece's farming potential—is dubious. Classical period descriptions indicate aridity and treelessness about the same as at present; and the distribution of palm trees and agricultural products indicate lack of change in mean annual temperature (Jardé, 1923, p. 25; compare Michell, 1940, pp. 47–59, with Maull, 1922, pp. 32–46); although the total arable area has shrunk, and there have been several alternations of climate, with wet phases in the second to fourth centuries and in the eleventh and seventeenth centuries (Brooks, 1949, pp. 330–350), as well as an apparent rise in sea level after the Middle Ages.

ECOLOGY: SOILS, VEGETATION, AND FAUNA

The population capacity of different regions of Greece and the eastern Mediterranean, particularly after the invention of farming, depended in the first place on the fertility of the region. Soil fertility, in turn, is influenced by the processes of erosion, deposition, and formation, all of which depend on the bedrock geology of the region. Maull (1922, pp. 15–20) divides the geological bases for vegetation and farming into five groups: (1) limestone, (2) Flysch, (3) igneous plus metamorphic rocks, (4) marls plus conglomerates, and (5) silts. The interaction of these geological structures with Pleistocene weather plus vegetation determines soils.

Karst formations are typical in the extensive mountainous areas of western Greece. Here the soluble limestone weathered quickly during the Pleistocene to form a terra rossa which collected in small plains or in pockets (poljens), and at the same time to form gorges and to produce underground water tunnels (katavothroi) which extend down to the less pervious rock, slate or igneous, underlying the limestone. The underground streams, very characteristic of Greece, may reach the sea directly by their subterranean channels. They may, as at Lerna, form swamps at the shoreline, or, if dammed, may form inland swamps. The terra rossa is a red clay paleosol with a usually shallow A_1 horizon (mineral humus) over the (B) horizon of clay or clayey soil, and is colored by anhydrous iron compounds such as hematite and goethite derived from limonite through dessication in the hot-dry summers of the interglacial periods (Butzer, 1964, p. 90), and also colloidal silica. This palaeosol (the product of a seasonally humid and hot-dry climate) is fairly acid unless secondary calcification occurs, and is chemically quite stable; it was generally washed down into lower valleys and plains, for example eastern Arcadia or Attica, away from the original limestone C horizon. Brown earths are similarly formed, but with less iron dehydration. These red-clay soils are poor for agriculture and not good for forests, and the acids they contain dissolve human skeletal remains buried in them.

The Flysch areas of hard but fairly porous rocks are easily eroded into regular valley formations and allow the formation of a more crumbly brown-earth type of soil (A_1(B)C type) varying in alkalinity according to the water supply and providing the main plant-growing and agricultural soils around Karst areas.

Still better for farming are soils formed from the metamorphic and igneous rocks—schist, shale, gneiss, granite—that are more frequent in eastern Greece and the Islands. But the general landscape of these parts is steeper and often more sharply dissected than in the Flysch regions, though the soil absorbs and holds surface water better than the Flysch or Karst areas.

Marls, conglomerates, and sandstones of late Tertiary age, formed before the final upthrusting of limestone in the western mountain zone, are good for farming only if there is enough rainfall. On all these formations mountain growths of pine, oak, chestnut forests will make the grey clayey podsolized soils (A_{2e}BC), fairly acid, in contrast to drier coastal areas, where these soils are very stony and thin (Rendzina) and where dry evergreen scrub has replaced entirely the original open woods of small pines and live oak (Butzer, 1964).

The best agricultural regions are the silted gulfs, from Macedon and Thessaly south to Argolis and Laconia, and the smaller alluvial plains. This often stony and clayey alluvium is frequently too rich in soluble lime brought down from recent mountains, hence there is inadequate replacement for phosphoric acid or potassium as crops deplete these. Likewise frequent manuring and fallowing and planting with legumes are necessary to fix nitrogen, with frequent plowing-under, which is not in general good for cereal crops (Dorigny *in* Daremberg-Saglio, 1908, p. 903; Jardé, 1923, p. 59). But in spite of the burning over of fields there was no adequate replacement for potassium, and this may have been a critical factor in limiting population density in the Bronze Age and later.

Equally critical from the standpoint of population density was, as it now is, the limited total area of arable land: 22% today (Michell, 1940, p. 40) and at the height of Classical prosperity perhaps the same or as much as 25% (Jardé, 1923, p. 59). These environmental limitations alone, in prehistoric times, would have put a premium on fishing or hunting and later on trade (oil, pottery, and silver in Classical times) for grain from the Pontic regions or Africa. Likewise quite critical, even in the Bronze Age, would have been the skill used in farming and the variety of crops and animals raised.

The original vegetation of latest Paleolithic and Early Neolithic times (Boreal (5) into Atlantic (6) climates) was pine and mixed forests in the north and in the mountainous areas of the Peloponnesus, as it was in south Anatolia, and in the lowlands a dry, open forest of live oak, of umbrella, Aleppo, and maritime pines, and of evergreen scrub, or thorny maquis, including shrubs like laurel and rhododendron, bulb plants like asphodel, spring-blooming flowers like anemone, wild grasses burnt brown in the dry season, with occasional abrupt local changes to stretches of marshland and meadow (Butzer, 1964, pp. 66, 422; Maull, 1922, pp. 32–42).

The fauna included plentiful deer, wild boar, chamois, wild goat, bear, wolf, lion, wildcat, fox, weasel, many rodent and insectivore species, seal, dolphin, and a very rich variety of birds and fish (Stéphanos, 1884, pp. 401–406). No one has yet reported the onager or antelope, common on the plains in the Near East, and the cave bear found at Petralona (Kokkoros and Kanellis, 1960) was apparently extinct as was the wild horse *Equus hydruntinus*.

Since there were no large herds of game, this ecologic setting favored small bands of ingenious Mesolithic hunters (Jacobsen, 1969), and the first farming groups could have found convenient sites in open areas near streams, marshes, rivers, or the sea (Milojčić, 1956; Theocharis, 1958;

Rodden, 1962, 1964). After the slightly increased vegetation growth of the Atlantic period, the chief changes in the Bronze Age and later were the reduction of game and the cutting down of forests for farming, ship-building, winter heating (charcoal braziers), and mining. Wild olive, figs, and vines are part of the Mediterranean flora and wild barley and einkorn occur in the northern high country, but we have no clear evidence yet that any of these were first domesticated in Greece rather than farther east.

ECOLOGY: SEPARATIVE VERSUS UNIFYING FORCES—FARMING

In the Bronze Age and in Classical times the average farmer needed great skill and effort, using every bit of cultivable ground on a fairly small holding (perhaps 10 acres), with irrigation, to raise enough cereal, tree, vine, and garden crops plus domestic animals (Michell, 1940, p. 40) on which to subsist. Light and heavier varieties of the scratch-plow (without spreader) were available, having been introduced by Middle Bronze times (Angel, 1946, p. 501), and I strongly suspect that the threshing-sled (*tribulum* or *douyenni*) was used on circular threshing-floors, since typical backed blades of flint or obsidian occur at many prehistoric sites, though Dorigny (1908) says the sled was introduced in Roman times. Cereals included barley, 28-chromosome wheat (*Triticum durum*—for σεμιδαλίτης), emmer (*T. dicoccum*), and rarer 42-chromosome wheats, spelt, and eventually bread-wheat (*T. aestivum*—for σιτανίας) grown only in the north as spring wheats (Jasny, 1944; Jardé, 1925, p. 95). Barley was the chief crop because of the soil limitations, with wheat making up only 10–20% of the total grain harvest (Jardé, 1925, p. 97; Michell, 1940, p. 47). Grain crops made up about 50% of the harvest before World War I (Maull, 1922, p. 44) but Jardé (1925, p. 101) thinks that cereals were very much more important during the Bronze Age, with the percentage of other crops steadily increasing during the first millennium B.C. After fallowing, the farmer ploughed three times, deeply in March, more lightly in the dry season, and again at the setting of the Pleiades in September, immediately before sowing; but even the heavier plough pulled by oxen was not efficient in turning the clayey soil enough for full use of minerals (Dorigny, 1908). Cereals stayed in leaf during winter and the grain was harvested with sickles in mid-May.

By Classical times olives had become the most valuable single crop. In the Mediterranean climate olive trees thrive in a dry and calcareous soil on stony hill slopes and valley bottoms, though not at any great height above sea level. But they are very delicate and need much care: five years in nursery beds, often grafting, and after they are planted in groves (often among cereal crops), they need much irrigation, turning of soil, manuring, and pruning. The labor involved was considerable, for in addition to this cultivation, the farmer had to harvest and crush the olives in presses for oil. Preparing soil for vines and fruit trees was likewise laborious; the farmer has to turn the soil with the fork as well as the plough and then has to irrigate and manure each plant or tree carefully, with special hand-fertilization for figs and protection of grapes from the sun during ripening (Maull, 1922, p. 44; Dorigny, 1908). Before World War I olives occupied 21% of the cultivated land and vines 12%, and figs and other fruit trees, including pomegranates, almonds, quinces, plums, pears, and apples, accounted for 2%. All these non-cereal crops, which have roots using the deep-soil water supply during the hot-dry season, were probably of equal importance to the farmer in Classical and prehistoric times. As supplements the farmer grew such vegetables as beans, lentils, asparagus, cabbage, lettuce, celery, cucumbers, leeks, onions, turnips, radishes, chickpeas, and a wide variety of wild greens and herbs such as garlic, horseradish, mint, parsley, rue, amaranth, and sunflower.

Then, as now, the plains of the Aegean area were too dry in the summer for grazing, and sheep, goats, and pigs were pastured on mountain slopes in a cycle of transhumance. Of these the most important were sheep, which, according to Michell (1940, p. 59), were from a trihybrid cross in the Bronze Age: the big Argali, the curly-horned, maned Merino from North Africa, and the fat-tailed yellow-fleeced sheep of Anatolia and Syria. The Armenian Mouflon may also have been added. I know of no testing of this hypothesis from the study of animal bones in Greece, but the parallelism with human hybridization there is intriguing. Sheep gave not only wool and meat but also milk for cheese. Goats, which can forage anywhere and are well adapted to the many steep rocky areas on islands and mountains, got much less care. They furnished meat, cheese, and also horn for composite bows. Pigs, adapted to wooded areas, may have declined as the trees were cut off and as sheep increased in importance. Several breeds of cattle, both long-horned (Minoan, Anatolian) and short-horned, gave meat, hides, subjects for sacrifices, and a little milk, as well as draught service and wealth. This multiple usefulness is in clearcut distinction to that of the aristocratic horse, used by knights for fighting or racing, which was a small and thick-bodied animal with slender legs, not unlike the modern Greek and Turkish horses. Cattle and especially horses needed marshy or meadowland pastures, as in the north or in Boeotia, Elis, Messenia, Arcadia, and Argos. Asses and mules were vital as transport in a countryside with few good roads for wheeled vehicles (cf. McDonald and Simpson, 1961), and they also provided meat. Domestic ducks and pigeons were probably present in the Bronze Age, but chickens were rare until the end of the Early Iron Age, when hen's eggs became an important addition to Classical Greek diet (Vickery, 1936) and occur in sixth-century graves (Shear, 1928), apparently as an immortality symbol. Many varieties of fish, oysters and other shellfish, and octopus were as important in the diet then as today, and the tunny was a chief trade product of Greek colonies along the Black Sea and in Anatolia. Michell thinks that the summer migration routes of the tunny from the Black Sea to Italy helped to determine Greek Early Iron Age colonization. Finally, the raising of bees for honey added a further important dietary element.

Stone-plus-adobe houses, with gabled or flat roofs of baked-clay tile, which increased in complexity only slightly from prehistoric to Classical times (Robinson and Graham, 1938, pp. 223–316), served only as family sleeping places and work centers for women, and had few fireplaces built for heat (Markham, 1947), normally without true chimneys, though chimney pots exist from the Bronze Age onward. In towns the central courtyard and orientation to the winter sun helped to warm houses. Woolen shirts (Chiton) and cloaks left arms and legs bare so that the people adapted hardily to much greater seasonal and daily temperature shifts than we do. Later reaction to this custom may explain the popularity of Roman and Central Asiatic (Finno-Turkish) sweat-baths heated with a hypokaust, or true chimney fire, like a pottery kiln. Mycenaean-period Athenians had used enormous timber baulks to shore up the spiral staircase leading down 30 m. to the siege-spring inside the north part of the Acropolis (Broneer, 1939). By Classical times wood needed for ships and mines was used very sparingly for houses; and the conservative form of stone-pillared temple was a copy of the barnlike, wooden megaron of earlier times. The Attica described by Plato, like that seen today, was treeless.

Long before the first Hellenes entered Greece the straitness and uncertainty of the ecology had led to extensive trade, and by Classical times the pressure of population forced importation of grain from Pontus and Libya, of wood from Macedonia, of iron from Acarnania and many of the Cyclades, of copper and tin from Cyprus and via the Adriatic from Central Europe, of gold from Macedonia and Egypt, and of obsidian, emery, and marble—items whose import dates back to early prehistoric times—from the islands and other regions over the old igneous massifs. This was almost all sea trade and Θάλασσα (salt sea) is a word from the pre-Indo-European Aegean language of the people with whom the intruding Greeks mixed; seaports were the original centers of growth.

To balance these needed imports, the chief exports were pottery from the plentiful clay deposits, shaped into vases or massive amphorae to hold wine or olive oil and often stamped with the producer's name, so that Virginia Grace (1961) has been able to plot the full extent of this successful trade; wool and fruits were early export items. This was not enough, and a few generations after the invention of coinage to facilitate exchange (instead of the old iron-bar obols and silver talents) the Athenians exploited to the full their silver-plus-lead mines discovered at Laureion (Michell, 1940, p. 89 ff.). This particular advantage led indirectly to local jealousy, warfare, seapower versus piracy, and complicated shifts of population, including the immigration of non-citizen traders (metics) and slaves. Trade was vital to Greek survival, and migration followed the trade routes.

An obvious force behind migration was population growth. Density increased from a level of perhaps 5 per km.^{2} in the late Neolithic to probably about 30 per km.^{2}, in Classical times. This was followed by an irregular decline during the Roman, Medieval, and Turkish periods to about 10 per km.^{2} 150 years ago (Angel, 1946, 1951a; based on Gomme, 1933, and Stéphanos, 1884). By contrast Athens, with a population of about 320,000 in the fifth century B.C. (Gomme, 1933), had a density of 80–90 per km.^{2}, almost a third that of modern times. Thus, there were big local differences in density, and sometimes quick changes; soil-poor islands and isolated mountain valleys, unless they had some particular trade advantage, obviously tended to overflow sooner than the richer farming areas.

Class divisions between aristocrats, citizens, and foreigners and slaves tended to widen as an indirect reaction to the military attacks by the Persians (Diller, 1937, esp. 153–158; Glotz, 1926). Similarly the peculiar Classical isolation of married women and the rise of homosexuality (Gulick, 1902; Renault, 1956) added to social divisiveness, which had been very much less in the Bronze Age, when strangers were welcomed, although by Iron Age times some prejudice existed against foreign wives (Seymour, 1908, pp. 113–114, 274; Diller, 1937, p. 77). Such social attitudes affect selection and fertility, particularly in a culture which is split between farming and industry in the peculiar urbanism of the Greek city-state. Fertility and population growth depended more on endemic disease (Angel, 1966; Jones, 1909), plagues, and warfare than on social divisiveness and selection; but the psychological effect of class feeling combined with economic stringency seems to have been a factor in the one-boy families and infanticide of the first century B.C. (Tarn, 1930, pp. 92–94) and the accompanying decline in population. I think that this social divisiveness is a psychological and then cultural breakdown product of the intense individualism in farming, in trade, in crafts, which developed originally as a creative response to ecologic stress. To analyze the political, military, literary, and scientific effects of individualism and then divisiveness is beyond the purpose of this sketch and is well covered in available popular sources (Burn, 1966; Kitto, 1951; Farrington 1944, 1949). The obvious economic effect was competition, at first intensely stimulating, later increasingly diverse and confusing.

In summary the ecologically separative forces (the mountainous terrain and the relative difficulty of land travel, soil and climatic conditions, and crop specialties) and the unifying forces (the interlocking of sea with land in drowned mountain valleys, the predictability of winds, and the spotty distribution of mineral resources) are so narrowly interposed in the small area of the Aegean that such cultural values as extreme care and effort in farming, conservatism, antipathy for the next town or city-state have to exist in some sort of harmony with others arising from wide intergroup trade and social contacts, and extreme curiosity. As long as a stable and loving family structure allowed healthy growth, the Greek of Bronze Age or later could meet these dual stresses only by developing extreme individualism, self-reliance, and a widely varying but sometimes democratic attitude in matters of local self-government. Thus the effects of population overgrowth in infertile highland valleys or on islands was to produce migration to, and extreme mixture in, more fertile gulfs or port areas (such as Lerna). When these became too crowded the individualistic colonizing of the Mycenaean period and Early Iron Age developed. Minoans, Phoenicians, and Etruscans reacted quite similarly. But the river-valley civilizations of the Near East, with equally turbulent military histories, show a contrast in personality reaction and population development.

PREHISTORY: CULTURE SEQUENCE AND ECOLOGY

Acheulean hand axes and flake tools occur at a few of the stratified open sites thus far excavated in the Near East, like Barda Balka in the eastern Iraq highlands (Braidwood and Howe, 1960), in the lower layers of such cave sites as Mt. Carmel in Israel and apparently also Kara'In in Pamphylia, and in many surface finds. In Greece, Higgs (1964) reports a trachyte hand ax from Nea Palaiokastro in Western Macedonia, and there are a few surface finds farther south. But Levalloiso-Mousterian and Mousterian flint tools occur more plentifully, stratified at Asprochaliko in the Louros River gorge in Epirus (Higgs, 1963; cf. Vanderpool, 1965), along the Peneios River banks near Larissa in Thessaly (Theocharis, 1958; Milojčić, 1960), and in blowout and surface finds in Elis and Argolis (Bialor and Jameson, 1962). The peculiar huge-faced Neanderthal skull from the Petralona cave in Chalcidice extends the Middle Paleolithic population range north to Eastern Macedonia (Kokkoros and Kanellis, 1960). In the absence of flint tools, the bones of cave bear and deer with the Petralona find suggest Würm I (70,000 B.C.) as strongly as Riss (120,000 B.C.) as plausible dates for the Greek Neanderthal population and Mousterian culture. I do not know of links with the Hungarian plain or South Russian (Crimean) Mousterian, but Mousterian sites are plentiful all through the Near East from Kara'In (Kökten, 1963) in Turkey to et Tabun, es Skhul, and Ksar 'Akil in the Levant, at Ishkaft Spilik (Braidwood and Howe, 1960) and Shanidar (Solecki, 1963) in Iraq, at Bisitun in Iran (Coon, 1951), and east to Dara i Kur in Afghanistan (Dupree, personal communication) and Teshik Tash in Uzbekistan. Presumably there was a link with Greece across the old Black Sea lake outlet north of the present Dardanelles. The Mousterian time range is from before 100,000 down to about 35,000 B.C., when transition to the Upper Paleolithic Baradostian culture occurs not long before the Würm II maximum (Solecki, 1963). In human evolutionary terms this covers the change from the primitive Neanderthal of Petralona via the non-"Classic" forms of Galilee (Keith, 1931), early Shanidar at 60,000 B.C. (Stewart, 1959a), and Teshik Tash (Hrdlička, 1939; Weidenreich, 1945) and the less extreme but still gerontomorphic forms of Tabun I (McCown and Keith, 1939) and Shanidar I (Stewart, 1959), about 40,000 B.C., to the final variable Skhul and Djebel Qafzeh populations (McCown and Keith, 1939; Howell, 1958). The Israel Mousterian populations are possible evidence for absorption of a Neanderthal group by intrusive groups of *Homo sapiens sapiens*, if in fact this form had recently evolved from *Homo sapiens neanderthalensis* in some area farther to the east or south.

Solecki (1963) feels that the first Upper Paleolithic Baradostian blade-and-burin cultures in the Near East may be intrusive (from the steppe area?), and were then forced out of partly glaciated highland areas such as Kurdistan during the Würm II maximum. When hunting cultures started to expand again during the preliminary and fluctuating warm-up in the latest Paleolithic (15,000 to 9000 B.C.), there was increasing local differentiation, as at Franchthi cave in Argolis, at Kara'In and Beldibi caves in Pamphylia, at Mt. Carmel and Ksar 'Akil in the Levant, at Zarzi and Karim Shahir in Iraq, at Hotu in North Iran, and at Kara Kamar in Afghanistan. There was probably some exchange of influences with latest Gravettian to Mesolithic in the steppe area and certainly increasing control of flint and obsidian working

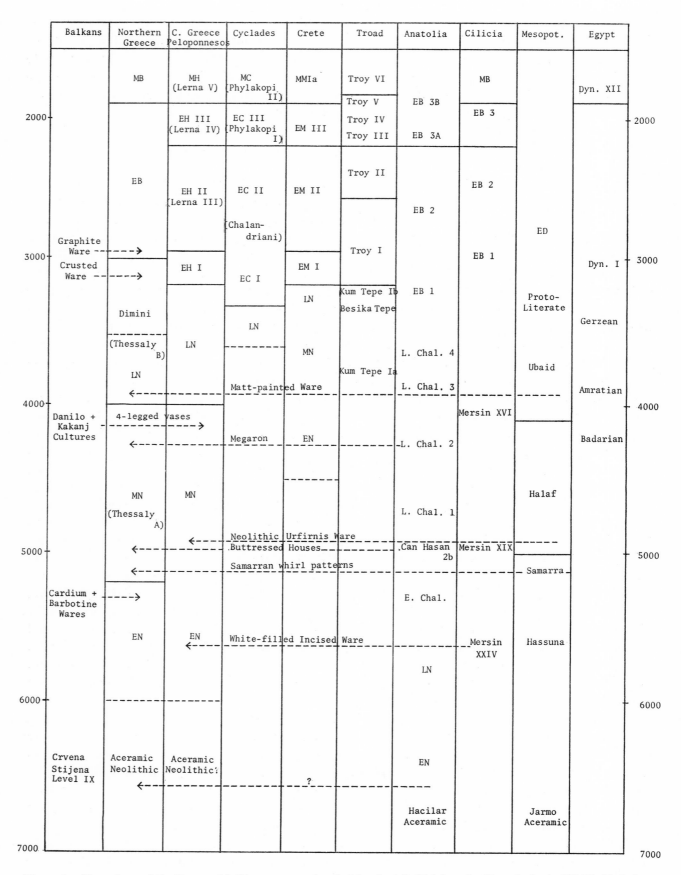

Figure 4. Chronology of the Eastern Mediterranean as sketched by Saul S. Weinberg in *Chronologies in Old World Archaeology.* (Robert W. Ehrich, ed., University of Chicago Press, 1965, p. 313; reproduced by permission of the author and the editor)

as seen in microliths and composite tools (Solecki, 1963; Coon, 1951; Mellaart, 1965), as well as experiments with new mollusk and especially vegetable and wildgrass foods. These local cultures seem a far cry from the successful and populous hunters of mammoth, horse, and reindeer and the artists of Aurignacian to Magdalenian and Gravettian times in western to eastern Europe. But cave art and carved art of high quality do occur in Pamphylia (Mellaart, 1965) and in Israel-Jordan; and these relatively impoverished highland experimenters were the inventors of grain cultivation and animal domestication, which, next to the control of fire, comprise perhaps the greatest economic revolution of human history. By the time of the latest Paleolithic, after Würm II, the physical varieties of man are modern, as at Hotu (Angel, 1952) and a little later among the Natufians (Vallois, 1936; McCown, 1939) and in Argolis (Angel in Jacobsen, 1969), paralleling the Upper Paleolithic to Mesolithic populations of Europe.

In Greece, Theocharis (1958) and Milojčić (1960) have excavated Upper Paleolithic tools at sites along the Peneios Valley and in Boeotia in 1914 Stampfuss excavated the Seidi cave on the edge of the old Copaic lake basin (Bialor and Jameson, 1962), revealing a blade culture like the Gravettian. In caves in the Kaki Skala near Megara and in the Argolid near Nauplia blades and microliths, usually of Melian obsidian, which must belong to the very end of the hunting period ("Mesolithic"), or perhaps later, were excavated by Marcovits (1929). Jacobsen's excavations (1969) at Franchthi Cave near Porto Cheli in Argolis show an Upper Paleolithic stratum followed by a 4-m. thick sequence of Mesolithic cultures (first deer hunting and later fishing) dated (C^{14}) through the eighth millennium, followed immediately by Early Neolithic farmers. Since obsidian tools of latest Paleolithic form have been excavated also on the islands of Zakynthos and Skyros (Theocharis, 1958; Weinberg, 1965), it would seem that the last hunting populations in Greece when sea levels began to rise, about 9000 to 7000 B.C., were using boats (dugouts or coracles) for Aegean trade and surely for fishing, just as their contemporaries were doing in the Baltic lake and on the Atlantic coasts of western Europe (Clark, 1952). Perhaps because these late hunters tended to occupy campsites in the open or along sea or lake shores rather than in caves, there are too few human and cultural remains of Upper Paleolithic date in Greece or Anatolia to clarify either the phase of migration and mixture with Neanderthal survivors or the relations with the steppe-country peoples living in earth lodges.

From site E in the Peneios River terraces Theocharis (1958) has excavated a somewhat mineralized apparently female occipital bone (*1 Pen*), and from various sites came upon an apparently unmineralized occipital (*3 Pen*), two broken right parietals (*2 Pen, 5 Pen*), and a female calvaria of type E 3 Mixed Alpine form (*4 Pen*). *1 Tso* is the broken face, and temporal and frontal areas of the skull of a child almost 5 years old found by Theocharis on the floor of Tsouka cave with a broken small flint blade and an unusually large (28-cm.) but immature bear skull (*Ursus arctos*), all covered with a thin (1-mm.) stalagmitic deposit; the cave is near Monressi on the slope of Mt. Pelion. All of these skull remains are modern in morphology. I cannot now exclude the possibility that *2–5 Pen* might have been shifted by river action and hence might be Neolithic or later in date; *2 Pen* is thickened to 10.5 mm. by porotic hyperostosis probably resulting from anemia, as in Neolithic and Bronze Age skulls to be described. Yet they had Paleolithic associations, so these remains suggest continuity of physical traits from late Paleolithic to later populations. The Mesolithic population at Franchthi Cave includes 8 people: very complete and less complete male skeletons (*1 and 2 Fr*) each showing marked porotic hyperostosis and wound scars, three less complete females (*3, 4, and 5 Fr*), a 3-year old child (*6 Fr*), and fragments of a male and female (*7 and 8 Fr*) showing slight calcining from hearth-fires. *1 and 2 Fr* have skulls like European Upper Paleolithic (A 2), except a little smaller. Stature, based on four skeletons, is extremely short, 157 cm. for males (*1 and 2 Fr*) and 138 cm. for females (*3 and 5 Fr*), with body build very robust and troll-like.

The Roddens (1962, 1964) have C[14] dates of about 6000 B.C. (earliest 6220 B.C.) for the beginning of the Early Neolithic farming village of Nea Nikomedeia in the western part of the Macedonian Plain, probably at that time on the somewhat marshy shore of a bay linked with the Haliakmon River. Milojčić (1956, 1960, and *in* Milojčić, Boessneck, and Hopf, 1962), and Theocharis (1958) at Argissa and Soufli Magoula on the Peneios River at Sesklo in the Thessalian Plain have excavated a Neolithic sequence starting with a relatively thin pre-ceramic stratum which clearly begins considerably earlier than the Macedonian farming site. Weinberg (1965, 1965a) points out that the Nea Nikomedeia C[14] dates put the whole southeastern European sequence very early—well back into the seventh millennium.[1] The sixth millennium, then, fits the pottery-diffusion ideas of Edmunson (1961), allowing a period of a millennium or less of farming to develop a solid economic base. Where did these first farmers come from? Where did they get their cultivated cereals, their domestic animals, their stoneworking techniques, their house styles, their art (and religion), their pottery, and their dress? Who were they? Partial answers come from a rapid survey of western Asia.

PREHISTORY: WESTERN ASIA

The latest Paleolithic of the Near East is apparently less unified than that of Europe. It includes Zarzian in the highlands of Iraq, Kebarah in the Levant, and related cultures from Pamphylia (Kara'In and Belbaşi, Oküzlü In), eastward to the Hotu and Belt caves on the Caspian, to Dzebel Peshtara in Turkestan, and to Afghanistan (Braidwood and Howe, 1960; Mellaart, 1965; Kökten, 1963; Coon, 1951). There is even more local differentiation during the Proto-Neolithic period from about 9000 to 7000 B.C. Such cultures as Karim Shahirian in Iraq (Braidwood and Howe, 1960), Natufian in the Levant (Kenyon, 1959, 1959a), Beldibian in southwestern Anatolia (Esin and Benedict, 1963; Mellaart, 1965), and the microlithic layers from the caves at Hotu, Belt, Peshtera Dzebel, and Dara-i-Kur (Dupree, personal communication) eastward to the Hindu Kush, are alike in the increased use of microliths of locally varied form for composite tools (including arrows and sickles); in the increased number of figurines or ornaments of carved bone, ground stone, and clay, of stone grinders and querns, and of storage pits; and in a striking increase in trade, especially trade in obsidian (Esin and Benedict, 1963) and bitumen (Flannery, 1965), in dentalium and other shells (Mellaart, 1965), and perhaps in perishable food items such as nuts or wild seeds and in animal hides and horns.

The animals for hunting averaged slightly smaller than the reindeer, horse, and wild cattle of the northern steppes, and they included bezoar goat, wild sheep, pig, and cattle, onager, gazelle, and deer. At the same time people ate birds, fish, mollusks, turtles, and frogs as supplementary foods. Wild vegetable foods had certainly been most important for a long time, but by Proto-Neolithic times the presence of silica polish on some of the sickle blades from some sites shows an increased use of wild grasses and grains (Van Zeist and Wright, 1963), with indications of considerable seasonal variety. Although people lived in open sites near water as well as in caves, population seems still to have been very sparse, perhaps not over the 0.1 per km.[2] Paleolithic maximum implied by Deevey's (1960) guess of 0.4 per km.[2] on a worldwide basis. And populations were still seasonally mobile, except for a few apparently fixed sites like Natufian Jericho, which were trade centers.

At this time, the postglacial warmup was ending (Van Zeist and Wright, 1963; Butzer, 1964), probably accompanied by a slight increase in winter rainfall. During the succeeding phase of a true farming economy that was based on planting and genetic selection of wild grains native to the Levant-Anatolia-Iraq-Iran highland areas, this climate was perhaps 1°C. warmer and

[1]Jacobsen (1969, pp. 374–375), from strata at Franchthi Cave, gives C[14] dates for Aceramic Neolithic of about 6000 B.C. (apparently the end of this phase) and early and late sixth millenium B.C. for Early and Middle Neolithic.

very slightly wetter than that of today. This warmer and wetter climate, parallel to the Atlantic (see p. 13) of Europe and ending about 3000 B.C., may also have helped to spread the adaptively changing cereal crops, just mentioned, beyond the range of the wild wheats and barley found today at altitudes between 500 and 1500 m. at present temperatures (Harlan and Zohary, 1966; Butzer, 1964, p. 426), and into the dry lowland areas, such as at Jericho about 6500 B.C. (Perrot, 1962, p. 152). It is now quite clear that cultivation of wild barley, emmer, and einkorn must have begun in the Israel-Lebanon, Taurus, or Zagros highlands, with a gap in the distribution of wild emmer, at least, between the Lebanon and Taurus ranges where the winter rains sweep inland to the Zagros (Harlan and Zohary, 1966; Helbaek, 1960). Potential animal domesticates occurred in the same highland arc, with local ecologic preferences. And the fact that trade all over this area in such vital items as obsidian from Lake Van or from Hasan Dag or the Araxes regions of Anatolia (Esin and Benedict, 1963) went with highly individual adaptations of local economies meant a quick spreading and individual interpretation of any new invention in this incipience of farming.

In order to understand the change, one has to forget completely the concept of "farming" as we see it today, or as it was in Neolithic times—the cliché of peasant is particularly misleading—and one has to picture a diverse group of hunters and collectors of game and wild vegetable food moving about in fairly dry uplands which were still not crowded with people but which would not have supported really settled camps like those of the earlier Gravettian hunters in Europe (Klima, 1962).

Flannery (1965) suggests that farming began by the trial planting of seeds into the disturbed refuse heap of a fairly permanent camp like Karim Shahir or Zawi Chemi Shanidar, or into a nearby stream terrace from some less accessible spot such as the edge of a talus slope. The proto-farmer knew from a long Paleolithic collecting tradition that "wild wheat grew from seeds that fell to the ground in July, sprouted on the mountain talus in February, and would be available to him in usable form if he arrived for the harvest in May" (Flannery, 1965). He had similar precise ecologic knowledge for a wide variety of wild vegetable foods: two-rowed barley (*Hordeum spontaneum*), wild emmer (*Triticum dicoccoides*), wild einkorn (*T. boeoticum* subspecies), flax (*Linum perenne*), oats (*Avena fatua*), acorns, almonds, and pistachios, such legumes as lentils, vetch, and chickpeas, such fruits as apples, pears, cherries, blackberries, grapes, perhaps already wild olives and dates (Helbaek, 1960; Harlan and Zohary, 1966), and alfalfa (*Medicago*), capers (*Capparis*), and wild legumes (*Astragalus, Trigonella, Prosopis*) in such other ecologic zones as the Khuzistan southern steppe area (Flannery, 1965). These late hunters certainly had the same detailed knowledge of the living and breeding habits of wild ungulates and smaller carnivores and almost certainly had taken the young into camp during the spring as pets after the mother had been killed for food. A strong preference for tender meat could lead to collecting kids, lambs (and wolf-pups?) in order to extend the meat supply; the next step would be selective protection of females for breeding. The excess of immature bones in early farming sites such as Jarmo, Çatal Hüyük, or Nea Nikomedeia (Reed, 1960; Mellaart, 1965; Higgs *in* Rodden, 1962) is evidence for this extending of the hunter's food preference for young animals, a preference which existed from Mousterian times onward (Perkins, 1964). By 9000 B.C. the hunters at Zawi Chemi Shanidar were eating sheep that were very like the domestic type (Perkins, 1964); domesticated goats and pigs occur at Jarmo and other sites by 6500 B.C. (Reed, 1960); cattle were probably domesticated in this period, and the dog earlier. All are found occurring at Çatal Hüyük and in Greece at Nea Nikomedeia by the end of the seventh millennium.

The key to the shift to settled village farming, then, was the advantage of stretching the spring supply of vegetables and young meat as far as possible into the summer in order to postpone frequent moving of camp with its hazards for young children and for the sick. The advantages of permanent villages for such other purposes as trade would set up a feedback interaction involving further efforts to increase vegetable and meat crops. All through the highland areas of the Near East and southern Balkans, such avoidance of moving plus local specialization and trade during the time of slight climatic improvement (9000–5500 B.C.) allowed both the settling of villages and a large increase in both human and animal populations, as seen in several continuous cultural sequences: Zawi Chemi Shanidar (Solecki, 1963), Zarzi–Karim Shahir- ?– Jarmo (Braidwood and Howe, 1960, 1962), Jericho (Kenyon, 1959, 1959a), and in Kara 'In, Beldibi, and Belbaşi (Mellaart, 1965; Kökten, 1963). In Greece and the Balkans there is no such continuity from latest Paleolithic hunting culture to farming at any single site, except at Franchthi cave and possibly at the La Adam cave in the Dobrudja (Radulescu and Samson, 1962), although these are cave sites throughout.

During the period from about 7000 to 5500 B.C. two things are clear at true farming (Neolithic) sites such as Jarmo, Tepe Sarab, Ali Kosh, Jericho, Ras Shamrah, Mureybat, Khirokitia, Mersin, Çatal Hüyük, Suberde, Haçilar, Nea Nikomedeia, Argissa, and Karanovo: (1) a quite rapid increase in population density, perhaps up to 1 per km.^{2}, and (2) a preference for sites near a spring, small river, or marsh, both for water supply and for planting. These earliest farmers used chipped or ground stone hoes or digging sticks and necessarily would have preferred relatively soft as well as treeless areas to raise emmer and barley, legumes, and probably also fruit trees. The grains at this time were a tough-rachis, free-threshing barley (6-row) and a large-grained developed emmer (Flannery, 1965; Helbaek, 1960). Piggott (1965) suggests that fallowing probably began early. In addition to stone celts (hoes, axes, or adzes), there are found sickle blades often hafted in bone, grinding querns (mano and metate), and hearths both for baking and for roasting grain for storage, perhaps in the pits which are found in most sites. Although the most frequent house type had hand-molded clay walls (tauf) on a rectangular stone foundation (with flat roof?), houses in the Levant and Cyprus (Dikaios, 1953; Mellaart, 1965) were round, and in Europe, rectangular, with a frame of wood uprights, sometimes having wattle-and-daub walls, and usually a gabled roof (Rodden, 1965; Piggott, 1965). Burial of the dead was in the village, probably next to or under the house where the dead person lived, though a distinct sacred or ritual tie with the family or kin group is clear only at some sites such as Jericho and probably Çatal Hüyük (Mellaart, 1965). The Upper Paleolithic tradition of figurines (or paintings) in relation to a biological fertility cult must have changed conceptually: throughout the Near Eastern-European early farming cultures female figurines, with varying emphasis on secondary sex characters or fat, developed from the earlier tradition; they were presumably still connected to fertility, but in this period, to fertility of crops as well as of people and animals. Tools show the same sort of continuity, though in general gravers decline and specialized microliths, pressure-flaked arrow and spear points, and sling pellets develop. The time of appearance of first fortification varies greatly from area to area, but in general there is evidence for group hostilities before the first use of copper or bronze. There is much evidence for cordage and basketry, probably Paleolithic in tradition, and at all sites spindle-whorls suggest cloth and weaving, probably of plant fibers. Mellaart (1965) identifies wool at Çatal Hüyük, perhaps before 6000 B.C. This suggests a long period of attentive breeding of sheep, for the wild forms lack wool (Flannery, 1965); the three millennia since this apparent first domestication should be enough.

Paradoxically, the use of stone bowls or other containers rather than pottery in many of these villages seems to have continued after the time when pottery first came into use in neighboring settlements. This overlap and apparent lack of a universal pre-pottery Neolithic phase strengthens Edmundson's (1961) hypothesis that the knowledge of firing clay vessels at temperatures of 500–1000°C. diffused to the Near East from central Asia from people not yet living in a true farming (Neolithic) economy. The first pots are a coarse ware, often straw-tempered, and only after firing had been controlled to produce a buff, oxidized surface did painting in stripes and "basketry" patterns begin. Development of painting seems to belong in the last quarter of the seventh millennium B.C. (Ehrich, 1965), about one millennium before the control of heat and kiln atmosphere needed for pottery began to be further adapted for smelting ores in the Chalcolithic period of Anatolia and the Near East.

PREHISTORY: NEOLITHIC, GREECE

In this context of successive individual syntheses of new techniques in adjoining areas of western Asia, it is not surprising to find in Greece, in the seventh millennium B.C., the basic farming cultures of Europe at an aceramic stage, as seen at Argissa, Soufli, and Sesklo in Thessaly (Milojčić, 1956, 1960; Milojčić, Boessneck, and Hopf, 1962, Theocharis, 1958; Weinberg, 1965a) and probably in Attica too (Weinberg, 1965). People lived in individual houses of clay supported by a frame of wood posts, in contrast to the multiple-room pueblo style of village developing in Anatolia and the Levant (Piggott, 1965, pp. 44–46). The economy rested on grain and legumes plus domestic sheep, more rarely goat and pig, and apparently very little meat from hunting; wild pig was the commonest of non-domestic animals (Boessneck, 1956). The stone industry had produced "mesolithic" trapezes (arrowheads), borers, burins, scrapers, and large backed blades like those found in Near East sites. Bone tools are found in abundance, as are red sandstone palettes and rubbing stones and finely ground and polished steatite earplugs and beads, but none of the fine and elaborate stone bowls of this phase typical at Jericho (Kenyon, 1959a) or somewhat later at Khirokitia (Dikaios, 1953) in south-central Cyprus. People buried their dead in the settlement in this and the next (Early Neolithic) phase, but it is only in the next phase that clear evidence of religion appears. The fact that a third of the stone tools found are of obsidian is clear evidence of trade, presumably with Melos. Such trade could suggest that the first extension of pre-pottery Anatolian farmers to Thessaly was a sea venture, probably in open boats like the much later ones known for the fourth to third millennium B.C. in the Cyclades (Renfrew, 1967).

The next wave of settlers apparently came immediately after pottery-making had developed and spread through Anatolia in the second half of the seventh millennium B.C., as seen in levels X–VIII at Çatal Hüyük and, after a hiatus, in the Late Neolithic at Haçilar (Mellink, 1965, p. 124). There have been as yet no coastal Anatolian (only surface finds have been reported) or Thracian sites to indicate whether the route was land or sea; Fikirtepe on the Bosphorus is later in date. The similarities between Nea Nikomedeia in Macedonia, the Thessalian sites of proto-Sesklo times, and the Bulgarian sites northeast of the Rhodope Mountains (Rodden, 1965; Piggott, 1965) might suggest a land route; but a colonization by sea is equally possible on the basis of the distribution of Early Neolithic sites in Greece during the sixth millennium B.C. Weinberg (1965, p. 287) points out that of the 28 excavated Early Neolithic sites and 10 more known from surface finds, most are "not only in the eastern part of the country but on the coast and up the valleys leading from it, giving a distinct orientation both eastward and seaward." These sites cover the whole of Greece from the island of Skyros in the east to Messenia in the west and from Macedonia south to Laconia, giving a picture of cultural unity—"a 'koine' not achieved again in Neolithic times" (Weinberg, 1965)—which includes Lerna I, the first settlement at the well-watered spot on the western shore of the Bay of Argos (Caskey, 1956).

These settlers lived in separate rectangular houses of comfortable size (8 m. long) with clay walls around timber uprights and perhaps gabled roofs of thatched straw (Rodden, 1965;

Piggott, 1965). The economy rested on hoe cultivation of wheat, barley, lentils and other legumes, and fruits, plus sheep and goats, with less frequent cattle and pigs and less than 10 percent wild-animal meat (Higgs *in* Rodden, 1962; Rodden, 1965). Boessneck (1956) and Higgs (*in* Rodden, 1962) both note individual bones of cattle approaching the massiveness of *Bos primigenius*, and Boessneck notes that Early Neolithic pig skulls show several "wild" traits in the occipital region, though the bones as a whole are domestic in size and form. He also finds great variation in the sheep skulls, particularly regarding a hornless variety unusual in the Neolithic of Europe; this fits but does not prove my earlier speculation (p. 17) on the hybridization of domestic sheep paralleling that of people in Greece and the Near East. Dogs were already more often small, like the peat-hound, than large in size, and the mingling of their bones with those of other animals suggests that people ate them, as also later in Bronze Age Lerna. As a whole these animal bones show domestication to have been quite definite, but with some traits of wild ancestors; this may have a bearing, for example, on the difficulty of bringing domestic cattle by boat. People also ate fish and mollusks and probably frogs (the frog figurines from Nea Nikomedeia are suggestive of this, though Rodden stresses their magico-religious significance.)

The stone industry was much more specialized, and without the "mesolithic" variety or the microliths of the aceramic Neolithic. Tools included scrapers and broad blades of flint and chert, but the main form was the long blade, used for knives or sickles, sometimes of obsidian—though obsidian is absent at Nea Nikomedeia. Polished celts for hoes or axes are frequent, and stone manos and metates, pestles and mortars, hammerstones, and even stone vases occur. But the real skill in polished stonework is found in the rather slender naillike earplugs or hair ornaments, the steatite stamp-seals with geometric designs (more often of pottery), and the realistically carved frogs of green-blue serpentine, already mentioned. Most of the "sculpture" found is in clay; figurines of animals and birds are common, and some of the pots from Nea Nikomedeia have human faces in relief like those at Haçilar and Hassunna (Rodden, 1964, 1965). More striking are the somewhat stylized pottery figurines, more often female than male and made of separate sections pegged together before they harden. Heads are cylindrical with beak nose and slanting coffee-bean eyes, waists are slender, thighs plumply rounded. At Nea Nikomedeia several of these figurines occurred in a large building, perhaps a shrine-meeting house, with two serpentine celts, caches of flint blades, special askos-shaped pots, and hundreds of clay roundels (possibly spindle-whorls or loom-weights). From the standpoint of religion these are suggestive but not definitive. Clay impressions of cloth indicate weaving, and also matting. The bone industry appears well developed, and the bone belt-hooks and buckles are strikingly similar to those from Çatal Hüyük (Rodden, 1962, 1965; Mellaart, 1965). Clay slingstones and spools also occur at Elateia, and perhaps a lamp (Weinberg, 1962).

The earliest pottery found is monochrome, from dark grey to buff to near-white, depending on firing; round-bottomed bowls with pierced lugs are typical, with occasional ring bases. Painted pottery appeared early in the sixth millennium and became more frequent, with geometric designs in red on a cream slip; finger-impressed pots, for example, occur at Nea Nikomedeia. By the end of Early Neolithic barbotine and cardial-impressed wares appeared in Greece; these are like those found at Yugoslavian sites such as Kakanj on the Bosna River, in a late Starcevo-Körös context (Ehrich, 1965). The Early Neolithic must have been the chief period of absorption of Upper Paleolithic or "Mesolithic" hunting groups into the new population. In Nea Nikomedeia the 13 adult and 13 child skeletons (together with fragments of 50 more) suggest this. In Lerna the five skeletons from this period—the girl's skeleton (*220 Ler*), fragments of two adults (*221* and *222 Ler*), and two infants—are not enough evidence;

nor can we test the possibility that the Early Neolithic population was, like its culture, more of a unit than those of Middle and Late Neolithic and Bronze Age.

The change to Middle Neolithic coincided with the Atlantic climatic period (ca. 5500–3000 B.C., see p. 13) and was marked by a gradual and slight increase in wetness, continuing warmer temperatures, and perhaps slightly higher sea levels. Given the known scarcity of moisture, this increase may have been enough to stimulate population growth and local differentiation during Middle and Late Neolithic times; certainly there were some migrations and a great deal of diffusion of ideas during these periods. The three phases of the Sesklo culture in the north (what used to be called Neolithic A) begin with a new house type, rectangular and placed in a row, and sometimes with internal buttresses like houses at Can Hasan in the Konya plain (French, 1963). Beside monochrome pottery there occurs a new painted pottery style showing Samarran influence (Weinberg, 1965) and suggesting a date just before the end of the sixth millennium. In the south, evidence of the new Middle Neolithic culture is particularly clear with the beginning of Lerna II (Caskey, 1958; Weinberg, 1965), in which are found more complex rectangular houses having up to three small rooms and internal buttresses, stone foundations held together with red clay, and substantial mud-brick walls. In Lerna II the new pottery with shiny paint derives from the earliest Halaf style of the Near East, according to Weinberg (1965, 1965a), who calls it "Neolithic Urfirnis" and traces its diffusion to Thessaly well after the Sesklo culture got under way. Another culture complex diffused from the Near East was "religious" and included new and more realistic female figurines like those at Lerna (Caskey, 1958) as well as the rite of secondary burial (in the Argolid at Prosymna and in Arcadia at Hageorgitika). Evidence for this diffusion is lacking in available skeletal material. The skeleton from Hageorgitika (Angel, 1945), with its Basic White A1 skull (see Table 1, p. 36), could have derived, however, directly from the Early Neolithic population, and there are only infant skeletons of Middle Neolithic date from Lerna. Weinberg (1965) points out that Central Greece had a still different pottery (Chaeronea ware) and cultural tradition. Before the end of the Middle Neolithic period, at several sites, the Megaron house style, with porch supported by pillars, plus a new pottery style, carinated and black burnished, appeared from probable Anatolian sources (Weinberg, 1965) but not necessarily in synchrony. This new pottery style plus several grey wares continued in use in some areas, especially in the south, right down to the Bronze Age and at times showed connections with the Balkans. At Elateia in central Greece Weinberg (1962, 1965) found a special white and red crusted variety of this black ware, dating from the end of the fifth millennium B.C., in the form of peculiar tetrapod vases which compare nicely with ritual pots from Kakanj on the Bosna and from Danilo on the Bosnian coast (Ehrich, 1965). These seem to have belonged to a special water-plus-phallic cult (Weinberg, 1962, 1962a).

Weinberg (1965, 1965a) chooses a somewhat later ceramic change as the start of Late Neolithic about 4000 B.C.), i.e., the appearance of matt-painted ware similar in fabrics, shapes, paint, and patterns to the ware of the more northern province of Ubaid, as he and Perkins have established. Polychrome and other wares also appeared before the beginning of the Late Neolithic Dimini culture of Thessaly (former Neolithic B); these Weinberg (1965) regards as a special local development in response to influence from the Islands, where Late Neolithic sites on Thera and Antiparos (Belmont and Renfrew, 1964) and especially on Keos (Caskey, 1964, 1966a), are first evidence of settlement and the beginning of the Cycladic culture, a little before the start of the Early Bronze Age. Gumelnitza influence from the Balkans at the end of the Late Neolithic also seems clear. There is much local variation. This is also reflected in the skeletal material. At Lerna, for example, *237, 240,* and *242 Ler,* child and adult skeletons from the very end of the Neolithic, could have derived, like the Hageorgitika skeleton, from a basic element in the Early Neolithic population. The nine partly restorable skulls from Kephala on Keos show this type A3 element plus a minority of the short type with pinched forehead (type C5) frequent in the central Cyclades (Angel, 1951), Lycia (Angel, 1966a), and Troy (Angel, 1951) in the Early Bronze Age and perhaps derivable from the Early Neolithic population of south Cyprus (Angel, 1953). This minority type shows also in one of three skulls from the Athens Agora and one from Leukas (Angel, 1945), but not in individual skulls from Tsangli in Thessaly, from Servia in Macedonia (Angel, 1945), or from Late Neolithic Nea Nikomedeia, all of which tend to perpetuate another of the original varieties (types F1–3) in Early Neolithic Nea Nikomedeia. This degree of local variation is not evidence for a Late Neolithic invasion.

PREHISTORY: EARLY BRONZE AGE, GREECE

The beginning of the Early Bronze Age, early in the third millennium B.C., is more clearly defined than that of the Late Neolithic, for the period is introduced by the invasion of the Cyclades by a metal-using culture. This moved into the Aegean, perhaps directly from Anatolia (cf. Beycesultan) but exhibiting indirect influence from the Ghassulian culture of Israel (Weinberg, 1965) and possible links with Cyprus (source of copper; fertility figurines), then in a chalcolithic stage (Catling, 1966). This Early Cycladic I culture subsequently spread to Greece, where settlement on Late Neolithic sites involved a leveling off and complete rebuilding, in several cases with a time gap, as at Lerna, before the new people took over. The relatively long Early Helladic II phase shows an increasing prosperity most obviously based on trade in obsidian from Melos (J. L. and E. G. Caskey, 1960; Caskey, 1960; Mylonas, 1959), although Mediterranean trade in pottery and other commodities also must have been involved. The E.H. I phase introduces red and brown burnished bowls and other pottery forms, while in E.H. II glazed ware (E.H. Urfirnis) begins to appear, with such forms as askoi, saucers, and especially the characteristic sauceboat, which becomes very common. Bronze is rare and often is a copper-arsenic alloy (Charles, 1967), but includes such implements as tweezers. Long obsidian blades are ubiquitous, as are beautiful pressure-flaked arrowheads with concave bases. Aghios Kosmas, on the Bay of Phaleron near Athens and with particularly close connections to the Islands, was apparently an emporium and manufacturing center for obsidian artifacts. Weinberg (1965) thinks that a second immigration from the Islands came at the start of E.H. II, very soon after 3000 B.C., and it is clear that from then on there was an increasingly dense farming population in villages and towns extending inland from the Aegean shores of Greece. On the basis of the number of sites and burials, I have guessed (Angel, 1960), that the population density in the area south of Macedonia increased from about 5 to almost 15 per km.², a density more than three times that of Early to Middle Neolithic times. One can speculate that the immigrants were Carians, speaking dialects of the language group which spread place names and nouns having sounds in -nth and -assos or -enda, though these sounds may with equal probability derive from a language used in Neolithic times in the eastern Mediterranean (cf. Caskey, 1960, citing Haley and Blegen, 1928).

Agricultural advances had taken place that would have supported this increase in population. Evidence is good that grapes (probably of several varieties) were cultivated in E.H. II times (Mylonas, 1959; Hopf, 1962), presumably for wine. The domestic olive must also have been introduced, although farmers may not yet have pressed it for oil as they appear to have been doing in Early Minoan Crete. The people must have extended considerably the dietary base for society, not only by more fishing but also by more efficient cultivation of wheat and barley; the plow seems likely but the pottery model of scratch-plows (ards) pulled by yoked oxen, from Early Bronze Age Vounous in Cyprus (Dikaios, 1961, p. 24, pl. 5), does not prove that this was yet in ordinary use in Greece, and the first socketed bronze plow-tip, not really a share, does not occur until the Middle Bronze Age (Angel, 1946, comparing Tsountas with Drachmann). I am tempted to speculate that the sauceboat was a separator for cream, though it may simply be a drinking cup. Hopf's (1962) observation that the Lernaeans used for food several wild plants, including the thistle for oil (artichoke-like) as well as acorns, suggests that Early Bronze Age diet became less than optimal probably in part because of the increase in population which the dietary improvement at first stimulated.

The economy supported towns with large rectangular houses sometimes having tiled roofs and in some cases protected by heavy fortifications with watchtowers, as at Lerna and at Chalandriani in Syros, or by smaller walls (Caskey, 1960; Weinberg, 1965). The central chieftain's house at Karataş (Mellink, 1965, 1969) has massive circular walls. The House of Tiles at Lerna, which may have been the seat of government, measures 12×25 m., with walls nearly a meter thick, the circular tholos at nearby Tiryns is nearly 28 m. in diameter, and the contemporary great megaron of Troy II is even larger (Caskey, 1960). The large number of clay sealings found in the House of Tiles and elsewhere at Lerna III as well as at other Aegean sites point to valuables stored in various containers, including jars, baskets, and boxes; it is not clear what these were; gold jewelry occurs very rarely in graves. Female fertility figurines in the Cyclades suggest cult continuity but shrines have not been recognized except probably the early tholos which the Caskeys (1960) found at Eutresis enclosing a deep shaft; perhaps there was a difference in religion between islands and mainland. Yet the Cycladic custom of secondary burial in several varieties of cist tombs or ossuaries outside the town spread to the mainland, although single earth burials also occur (Mylonas, 1959; Caskey, 1960). Because of these customs and the attendant difficulty of locating the tombs, few skeletons have been found. The 35 adults available thus far come mainly from Aghios Kosmas and Corinth (Angel, 1959) and indicate small body size and considerable population variety. The skulls of some adults continue two of the main Early Neolithic variants (types A4 and F1) and some have the broad, purse-shaped form of the central Cyclades (Alpine types C5 and C4) and of the linear Mediterranean form (types B2 and A1) peripheral to this center (Angel, 1951). Three skulls fit the deep-vaulted and aquiline Iranian (type D4) or Corded (type D2) variety of the same date found in Anatolia and the northeast Balkans, and may foreshadow the next invading group.

Many of the E.H. II towns end in a layer of burnt debris dated between 2300 and 2200 b.c. (Caskey, 1965a, Weinberg, 1965). This is true of Aghios Kosmas in Attica, of Lerna, and of most other sites in the Argolid and Corinthia, with different dating at other sites. But this period of destruction does not appear at Eutresis and Orchomenos in central Greece nor in the north (Epirus, Macedonia, Thrace) despite the occurrence there, in the same period, of some ("northern") cordmarked pottery. This destructive result of warfare parallels similar happenings in western Anatolia at Troy II, Polatli, Beycesultan, and Tarsus and signals a major conquest by new people. Probably these conquerors were speakers of Indo-European dialects (Weinberg, 1965; Caskey, 1966). Those causing the destruction at Lerna, proto-Hellenes, were probably the first of several waves reaching Greece by different sea and land routes and with different alliances with refugees from regions east and north of the Aegean (cf. Clark and Piggott, 1965; Piggott, 1965; Gimbutas, 1963). Gimbutas (1963) sees the ultimate origin of these Indo-Europeans among the steppe farmers east of the Caspian and, later, in the Kurgan peoples dwelling north of the Black Sea during the Caucasian copper age. They apparently owed their mobility to domesticated horses (Foltiny, 1959) able to pull their solid-wheeled wagons (though oxen may have also been used, especially at the beginning) and to their knowledge of copper-smelting. Certain aspects of their sometimes princely built tombs under tumuli show diffusion from Mesopotamia (Childe, 1946; Clark and Piggott, 1965). It is not clear whether they entered the Anatolian plateau country from the east as well as the west, but both are likely, in my opinion. Hittites, Palaites, Luwians, and other Anatolian peoples with Indo-European backgrounds emerged by the second millennium B.C. as a result of their integrating and organizing abilities. Mellaart (1958, 1965) feels that an invasion across the Bosphorus in the latter half of the third millennium produced the almost universal destruction of sites in western Anatolia. Perhaps both waves met in northwestern Anatolia and spread south and onto the plateau. It is tempting to see the increasing slight dryness of the Sub-Boreal climatic phase (Butzer, 1964) as the cause of these movements across the steppes, but simple population pressure and the possession of wheeled carts are equally likely causes (cf. Foltiny, 1959). The routes just outlined are tentative suggestions, not yet established.

The proto-Hellenes (perhaps proto-Ionians) must have crossed the Aegean to land in Attica and Argolis (Caskey, 1966) and hence must have been an old blend of invaders and Anatolian natives; some of them later adopted the plateau custom of intramural (typically cist) burial brought to Greece at the end of Early Helladic III. These proto-Hellenes had gained knowledge of the sea routes as well as of the valleys of the eastern shore of the Aegean, and the E.H. II pre-Greeks and Cycladic peoples had fortified their towns in fear of attack. Clearly more of these proto-Hellenes came in the next few centuries. By the end of the third millennium their ceramic hallmark was Minyan ware, especially the wheel-made angular goblet with ringed stem and the cup, or kantharos, with two high handles. Proto-Minyan pottery appeared in the few centuries before 2000 B.C. both in west Anatolia (Mellaart, 1958) and to a minor extent in E.H. III Greece, as Caskey (1960) noted at Lerna IV. Red-cross bowls are similarly found in both areas (Weinberg, 1965). E.H. III, then, was a transitional phase during which proto-Hellenes entered and reorganized society and culture in Greece, and began to develop the Greek dialects, preparing the way for the Middle Bronze Age which began about 2000 B.C. The history of the north is quite different in detail, and in central Greece, too, the main destruction and change seems to have been later than in the south.

As typified in Lerna IV, this transitional phase, Early Helladic III, spans at least six to ten generations and four rebuilding stages after people had resettled the temporarily abandoned site (Caskey, 1960, 1965). Houses were very often apsidal, with the apse end walled off; smaller in size than before; they had pillars for a gabled roof, and a great many storage and rubbish pits or bothroi, but rectangular houses still were built. Dark glaze paint on light, rarely the opposite, was typical for painted pots; and sauceboats went out of style, while proto-Minyan cups occurred. A striking event during Lerna IV was the raising of a round tumulus with low retaining wall over the site of the burnt palace, or House of Tiles, as if the E.H. III people included many of the pre-Greek natives for whom this burnt center may have been taboo. Apsidal House A, built just to the east of this mound, first on a somewhat temporary frame of wood and later replaced by a succession of houses built of adobe on a stone foundation, might have been the house of the new ruler. Generally, throughout Greece in E.H. III and through the Middle Helladic period there was no clearly marked palace, civic center, or temple. The marketplace may have functioned as the center. A town-council democracy is conceivable, perhaps with the 3-class system supposedly basic among Indo-European-speaking peoples. The towns look poor, as if from diminished trade, although during Lerna IV there was some contact with Troy IV and the islands, and perhaps with Crete and the Balkans as well. At Lerna the economy seems to have been the same. Gejvall (Caskey, 1966) notes the presence of an equid larger than the ass but not typically *Equus caballus*. Burial customs are uncertain and may have been in flux. It is unfortunate that we have no adult skeletons dating from either E.H. II or E.H. III (Lerna III and IV) to see what happened when the proto-Hellenes arrived and settled, though I will later infer a great deal from the plentiful material from

Lerna V. Four infant burials dating from toward the end of Lerna IV are included with the Middle Bronze Age sample, since there seems to be complete demographic continuity from Lerna IV to V (and from V to VI), and these infants are probably offspring of adults who may have died after the start of the Middle Bronze Age.

PREHISTORY: MIDDLE BRONZE AGE, GREECE

The Middle Bronze Age begins probably with another invasion of proto-Hellenes and the full development of wheel-made grey-pattern and other-color Minyan and matt-painted pottery, plus the custom of family burials around the houses, though at Eleusis in Attica a cemetery was used and at Aphidna, a tumulus. Economic revival began; Caskey (1966), quoting Buck (1964), notes 160 Middle Helladic sites surveyed, 20 of these in the Cyclades. There was now no urgent need to fortify towns. Because there is no cultural break during the second millennium and because the Linear B clay tablets constituting royal palace records of late 15th to 13th centuries B.C. are in a Greek dialect (Ventris and Chadwick, 1953), archeologists and linguists agree, with proper reservations, that the language of the invaders who destroyed towns of E.H. II and E.H. III culture between 2200 and 1950 B.C. must have been Indo-European. Nevertheless, even if they were blended and allied with Anatolian groups (Mellaart, 1958), had the mobility on land given by horses and wagons (Gimbutas, 1963; Piggott, 1965, pp. 95–96), a patrilineal almost proto-feudal social organization, and an efficient language, I do not understand how they got the military strength as well as the aggressive energy to conquer large areas of western Anatolia and all of Greece and the Aegean. Early Bronze Age peoples fortified their towns; their possession of stone shaft-hole axes and copper or bronze or bone daggers as well as spears, the bow, and slings from Middle Neolithic times onward is indicated archeologically. This armamentarium is clear, especially at Troy II–V (Blegen, 1963). Perhaps the weapons of the invaders were better (their bows, for example). But it is chancey to posit this on the basis of contemporary evidence from any one site, which a relatively small band of invaders could have destroyed. The riveted bronze daggers and spearpoints of Middle Helladic times (Caskey, 1957) do not look superior, but they are usually of real tin-bronze which could be whetted to a sharper edge than copper or an "improper" alloy. Yet in central Europe as in Greece (and Crete) it is only later in Middle Bronze times, after about 1700 B.C., that a profusion of swords, rapiers, and other weapons appears in tombs, as if military prowess increased with wealth and population density, as Malthus much later observed. If not the superior arms of the invaders, what then helped to bring about the conquest of western Anatolia, the Aegean, and Greece at the end of the third millennium? I speculate that it was the ill health, including falciparum malaria (Angel, 1966) and undernutrition, of the inhabitants.

The invaders did not reach Crete. Middle Minoan civilization, in contrast to the confusion on the mainland, developed directly out of E.M. II (Weinberg, 1965) with a smooth transition during E.M. III. Early in the 20th century B.C. the distribution of Minoan pottery indicates trade again with the Aegean and southern Greece as well as the XII Dynasty Egypt (Caskey, 1966). Later, by Middle Minoan III and Late Minoan I times, the civilization of the palace phase helped to change the Greek Middle Bronze Age into the Mycenaean civilization, especially in art and in some aspects of politics, with lessening effect as the diffusion went northward: Troy VI and VIIa continued to use Minyan and local pottery right down to the time of the Trojan War in the middle of the 13th century B.C.—three hundred years after the Greeks had developed their sequence of Mycenaean painted pottery forms which the Trojans imported and imitated (Blegen, 1963).

The Middle Bronze Age of Macedonia and Thrace likewise followed a largely independent course (Caskey, 1966). It is not clear just how the Greek language reached this region; although

Minyan pottery is found in the Chalcidice, its makers need not have spoken Greek. Since the relatively few tablets written in Linear A remain undeciphered, the Minoan language is unknown, but it is probably a relative of the Early Bronze Age language groups; conceivably, according to C. Gordon, it is Semitic (Caskey, 1966).

Thus, Bronze Age Greece had a continuous and fairly rapid development during the first half of the second millennium B.C. through the Early Mycenaean culture of the shaft-grave princes at Mycenae (Middle Helladic to Late Helladic I and basically still Middle Bronze Age) up to the full Mycenaean palace feudalism (Late Helladic III) of 1375 (or 1350) B.C. This growth of Mycenaean culture depended on a much more efficient farming economy; the scratch-plow with yoked oxen had certainly spread throughout the country early in the Middle Bronze Age and the same probably applies to irrigation, olives, and domestic fowl (Caskey, 1966; Hopf, 1962; Gejvall, 1969); also the Greeks had brought in the true horse (*Equus caballus*) and by shaft-grave times used a chariot with two wheels having spokes (Piggott, 1965, pl. 15; cf. Schliemann) rather than heavy, solid cart wheels. This improvement may have originated with the Hittites. Together with new swords and shields and the rebuilding of massive fortification walls the horse-drawn chariot shows a peculiar advance in military culture and the development of the sort of aggressive and aristocratic yet creative civilization which Homer recalled for his listeners in the Early Iron Age (Seymour, 1908). In addition to farming, fishing, and raids and conquest, this society above all grew on trade that involved gold, amber, copper, tin, wine, some olive oil, pottery, wool and textiles, and livestock (Clark, 1952; Clark and Piggott, 1965; Blegen, 1963). Mycenaean pottery occurs all over the east-central Mediterranean and beyond its boundaries; the Mycenaean dagger outline on Stonehenge has become celebrated. Traders, artists, scribes, tinkers, and minstrels probably traveled far, both by ship and by land over carefully defined routes made temporarily safe by rulers who held open passes and crossroads, as at Lerna (or Tiryns or Mycenae or Corinth).

Lerna V represents prosperous Middle Helladic, but Lerna VI, the L.H. I shaft-grave phase, is lost by erosion except for two large shaft graves and other graves perhaps less spectacular than those at Mycenae. The striking thing is the amount of imported pottery found, indicating trade and perhaps immigration during the Middle Bronze Age; small objects such as bone pins show the same thing (Caskey, 1956). Middle Minoan imports are quite frequent, especially in the areas of the Southern and Marsh burial groups (Caskey, 1956, 1957). Imports from the Cyclades are less common, and it is hard to see close links with Anatolia except perhaps in the pins. Most striking is the occurrence of incised flasks imported from the Bubanj 1a culture in Serbia. Since these flasks occur only in the area around House 98a and Rooms 44 and 45, and were kept in use a very long time alongside Minyan and matt-painted Lerna pottery, it is tempting to infer a few immigrants. Possibly they, too, spoke a form of Greek. The relation of the Bubanj culture to the Baden culture and to the broader culture of cord-marked pottery is clear enough to link them with the Indo-European spread across Europe at the end of the third millenium B.C. (Piggott, 1965) and well south of and apart from its extensive interaction with the Bell-Beaker movement. Illyrians are not identifiable until later. I use the term "Northern" for this apparently intrusive group early in Lerna V in complete ignorance of its precise source or language.

Two more outside sources of cultural influences logically might occur later in Lerna V. One would be Syria, in view of the Syrian prototypes for weapons and ornaments of the beginning Bronze Age in Central Europe, about 1800 B.C., plus the Cadmus origin myth and copies of cylinder seals later in L.H. III Thebes (Piggott, 1965, pp. 102–103); but an Adriatic trade-route to Syria may have bypassed Lerna. The other influence would be Egypt, considering the extensive Egyptian interchange with Crete (Caskey, 1965a) plus the Danaus origin myth.

But there is no clear-cut archeological proof for such links at Lerna, except the general Near-Eastern source for riveted handles on hand-weapons. Crete would be a logical intermediary for both sets of influence.

Myths generally are a particularly poor basis for inferring origins of a people; although they do show the geographical or historical knowledge possessed by a period later than the one described, their unknown authors may have had political motives, like the composers of nursery rhymes. Pottery, on the other hand, shows time sequence and geographical connection, but not the motives of connection nor, often, the precise means thereof. Pottery which came through indirect diffusion might tempt us to infer migration, and if trade accompanies the pottery or fits the myth, the case for a real connection and for actual migrants is stronger.

PREHISTORY TO HISTORY TRANSITION

Even without the direct contacts with the Near East, the Middle Bronze Age at Lerna and in the Aegean was a period of absorption, both of many outside cultural influences and of human groups. It was, as well, a period marked by formation of a very stable and tenacious farming and fishing population plus the start of a more leisured class from which the shaft-grave "dynasties" and the full Mycenaean (L.H. III) aristocracies could develop. Fairly plentiful adult skeletons of Middle Bronze date ($N = 133$) from all Greece show a completely new balance of physical varieties including Nordic-Iranian and several short-headed forms in incredible heterogeneity (variation over 20% above normal), as I will show later (cf. Angel, 1946, 1951a, 1960). The Mycenaean samples ($N = 174$) show blending of this compositeness plus only a few probable immigrants. Earlier study of the Middle Bronze Age skeletons from Asine, Mycenae, and Attica (Angel, 1946, 1951) showed the probability of Anatolia (with Iran in the background) rather than only the Balkans as a direct source for intruders who might have been Indo-European in language, while in Mycenaean times maritime sources such as Cyprus or the Cyclades seem likely (Angel, 1955, p. 70).

In conformity with its blending and its reduction in population variability the Mycenaean period was one of synthesis and then population expansion and colonization rather than immigration, after farming had improved to meet slightly drier and possibly cooler (?) Sub-Boreal climate and slightly lower sea-levels (Butzer, 1964; Higgins, 1966); this last factor may have facilitated swamp drainage until rainfall increased in the Hellenistic and Roman periods (Sub-Atlantic).

The relative roles of ecologic and economic factors in the population turmoil of the "Dorian invasion" sequence two generations after the fall of Troy (Broneer, 1939) and the various Eastern Mediterranean colonizing migrations of Achaeans, Arcadians, Dorians, Ionians, and Aeolians are not closely relevant to this monograph; the Early Iron Age sample from Lerna is quite small, as is the Roman sample, and there are no Classical or Hellenistic skeletons. I might expect these late Lerna samples to reflect, respectively, the confused diversity of the Early Iron Age population and the provincial isolation of the Roman occupation (Angel, 1946, 1960). But because Lerna seems, by Mycenaean times, to have lost to Nauplia (and perhaps also to Asine-Tolon) its maritime importance and because of the likelihood of a Hellenistic-Roman-Medieval increase in endemic malaria (Jones, 1909), I am equally interested in the possibility of the genetic continuity rather than the change of the population at this site.

The key interest of this monograph, therefore, must be the Middle Bronze Age phase of formation of the Greek people (Lerna IV–V–VI), rather than later developments. Clearly this formation was extensively a process of mixture, with many of the cultural, social, psychological, and educational problems that we now have in the United States. For example, many Classical scholars have tried to show that the pre-Greek and non-Greek ethnic elements included a matrilineal kinship structure (Harrison, 1922, pp. 260–280) and probably related religous rites for agricultural and human fertility, probably including ritual sacrifice of a scapegoat king or of his substitute (Harrison, 1922, pp. 109–111), not to mention the Near Eastern political system of a priestly hierarchy under the king.

It seems probable that the invading proto-Hellenes must have destroyed, changed, or re-adapted earlier cultural structures in their development of a class system and of mainly patriarchal partial democracies. It also seems probable that the Lerna family tomb-groups (clans) would reflect kinship and class structure as well as the genetic effects of immigration and mixture. But the selective effects of housing, clothing, nutrition, endemic and epidemic diseases, medical care, and climatic and physical stresses are probably more important than social selection in determining which people and which families produced the most survivors and thus which ones actually formed the emerging Greek people of the Mycenaean period. I will therefore pay particular attention to infant and child deaths, to female and clan fecundity and fertility, to longevity, and to other evidences of physical vigor or of disease. At the same time the relative homozygosity or heterozygosity of the population is important as inferred from the variability of the group and from the actual physical features of all the individuals, autochthones, and immigrants and their descendants. To the extent that psychological traits and intellectual capacities or potentialities depend on genetic polymorphisms, the various recombinations, or heterogeneity, of a mixing population is advantageous in a flexible cultural milieu (Angel, 1946, 1960).

EVOLUTIONARY BACKGROUND—MORPHOLOGICAL TYPES

During the past 100,000 years or more, from Mousterian times onward, at least four major selective processes have determined the continuing change through Neanderthal to modern man (cf. Coon, 1939, p. 28; Brace, 1964; both quoting Hrdlička): (1) paedomorphism, (2) tooth reduction, (3) somatic response to climate, and (4) physiologic response to disease.

1. Paedomorphism, the maintenance into adulthood of childhood features such as a relatively large and curled-up brain mass and a lightly built skeleton, had already played some part in producing *Homo sapiens neanderthalensis* because, in my opinion, paedomorphism was one growth-control channel for the selection effects of tool-manufacture and speech versus brain-complexity feedback in earlier Pleistocene evolution (Angel, 1964b) and because of social selection for adaptability.

2. Reduction in size of teeth and the folding of teeth, especially front teeth, were part of the selective adaptation to well-cooked food and to the increasing use of improved cutting tools, starting before Mousterian times (Brace, 1964) and greatly accelerated by the growing use of vegetable food at the end of Paleolithic times. Obviously, in this process of mainly negative selection, there was a big time-lag: it is worth considering that the beginning development of flint-blade knives in the Near Eastern Mousterian, as at Barda Balka (Braidwood and Howe, 1960) and at Shanidar (Solecki, 1963), is linked with increasing proportions of vegetable food in the diet, in contrast with the almost Eskimoid bone-using Mousterian of Europe; and that this beginning vegetable diet helped to trigger the Neanderthal to modern transition in the Near East.

3. Somatic response to a desert climate tends to select a linear body structure, often with a less massive and less massively wide skull than usual among European Neanderthals. Both Shanidar I (Stewart, 1959) and the Skhul skulls (McCown and Keith, 1939), at 40,000–35,000 B.C., show effects of all three of these selective processes not long before the second

maximum of the Würm glaciation, although it is possible that the final transition to modern man took place in the partly desert areas east of the Jordan and that the Skhul population is a mixture, anticipating what probably happened very soon afterward throughout Europe as Upper Paleolithic cultures developed.

4. Physiological response to disease, and to parasitism by such organisms as bacteria, plasmodia, treponemes, and amoebae (Cockburn, 1963), may have been as critically important during the absorption of Neanderthal man in Europe as it was in the recent absorption of many American Indian populations; it certainly had an increasing effect after 9000 B.C., with the spread of farming villages. I am not arguing that any one disease or, for example, a great epidemic of smallpox, wiped out all Neanderthal populations. Rather I am applying to the Neanderthal-to-modern demographic change the hypothesis that, after invaders have entered with new bacteria, selective increase in population sizes will tend to favor larger groups in which better hunting provides more food, more time for individual adaptation to the new bacteria, and more "modern" type invaders in the mixture. Isolated small groups of unmixed Neanderthals would be more affected by deaths and would tend to become less fertile. Although we do not have enough specific finds to give a detailed picture of demography in the period around 25,000 to 15,000 B.C., the fairly short longevity of Upper Paleolithic groups shown in Table III indicates that selective forces were strong.

Disease, climate, and other selective processes and mixtures gave rise to at least a half dozen different skull-form options in the Near East (and Europe) during and after the Upper Paleolithic—all of them lacking the extreme browridges, the huge face and mouth, the smallish mastoids, and the large paramastoid and nuchal prominences of Neanderthal man—as follows:

A. Linear rugged skull forms with reduced and sometimes wide upper face but strong jaws (Basic White, Cro-Magnoid, Eurafrican, etc.), as in latest Paleolithic South Russia (Debets, 1955) or Hotu 2 in North Iran (Angel, 1952) or in North Africa from Nubia to Morocco (Anderson, 1968; Ferembach, 1962; Briggs, 1955), as well as in Central Europe (Coon, 1939).

B. Extremely gracile paedomorphic, linear, pinch-faced forms (Classic Mediterranean) clear only late at Wadi en Natuf and elsewhere in the steppe-desert edge from Anau in Turkestan westward to Morocco (McCown, 1939; Angel, 1951; Ferembach, 1962).

C. Paedomorphic forms with reduced and rounded face but keeping the wide Neanderthal skull base and brain and hence a wide skull (Alpinoid), as at Solutré, Ofnet (Coon, 1939), and elsewhere in Central Europe or in the unknown source, perhaps northern Syria or Pamphylia, of the first Neolithic colonists in South Cyprus (Angel, 1953).

D. Forms with reduced massiveness, linear and deep, keeping Neanderthal anterior face downgrowth and nose strength to resist oblique forward chewing stresses (Nordic-Iranian, Irano-Afghan, Corded, etc.), as in Hotu 1, later at Sialk (Vallois, 1939) and Hissar (Krogman, 1940) in northern Iran, in the adjacent steppe country to the north (Ginsburg, 1956), and as with Corded culture in Europe (Coon, 1939).

E. Direct paedomorphic transformations—large, high-vaulted, mesocrane with big forehead and reduced face (Mixed Alpine), as in Hotu 3, at Jericho, or at Ofnet and Téviec in central and western Europe.

F. Forms with long-nosed big face, vaguely neanderthaloid like forms D or even like B, and comparatively short and high vault (Dinaroid, Dinaric-Mediterranean), as in Central European Mesolithic at Hohlenstein and Kaufertsberg and considerably later in the Near East (Angel, 1951).

These six types or trends (and a number of subtrends within each) do not exhaust the possible combinations of interaction between paedomorphism in braincase or face, jaw reduction, increased linearity of braincase or face in evolution from an already variable Neanderthal base. In the strict sense these six reference points are abstractions; no single modern population has ever been homogeneous enough to conform to any one such trend. But they are useful as reference points and I shall so use them in the descriptions of individual skulls and skeletons which follow. A tabular exposé of the six types with the subtrends of each is presented in Table 1.

I adopted these reference directions in skull form for shorthand descriptions after seeing hundreds of skulls from the Eastern Mediterranean, and while they accommodate the trends of variation I observed in them, they do not always precisely conform to what earlier workers may have had in mind.

The *Basic White* type A1, for example, is close to the British Megalithic form and to the Atlanto-Mediterranean of Deniker and others, and it is longer-faced, more linear throughout than A3. Type A2 is a smaller version of the Upper Paleolithic norm and is broader-based and

TABLE 1. DESCRIPTIVE MORPHOLOGY OF SKULL TYPES

KEY: Horiz.—horizontal   Rel.—relatively
      Pent.—pentagonal   Sl.—slightly
      Progn.—prognathous   Trapez.—trapezoidal
      Rect.—rectangular   V.—very

Type		Muscularity	Vault form	Angularity	Occiput
A	Basic White	Rugged	Linear, long	Strong	Prominent
A1	Atlanto-Mediterranean	Rugged	V. linear	V. strong	Hausform
A2	Upper Paleolithic	V. rugged	V. linear	Strong	Scaphoid
A3	Basic, cf. Eurafrican	Rugged	Linear	Medium	Prominent
A4	Basic, Eastern	Rugged	Linear, low	Strong	Prominent
A5	Basic, Royal	Average	Massive linear	V. strong	Angular
B	Classic Mediterranean	Gracile	Linear, small	Strong	Projecting
B1	Mediterranean	Paedomorphic	Ovoid, small	Slight	Projecting
B2	Mediterranean Angular	V. paedom.	Linear, small	V. strong	Proj., hayrick
B3	Desert, Classic	Paedomorphic	V. linear	Slight	V. prominent
B4	Desert, Eastern	Med. paedom.	Linear, long	Medium	Prominent
C	Alpine	Medium	Lateral	Slight	Rounded
C1	European Alpine	Medium	Round	Slight	Rounded
C2	Small Alpine	Slight	Round, small	Slight	Rounded
C3	Upper Paleolithic Alpine	Rugged	Wide, large	Medium	Rounded
C4	Eastern Alpine	Medium	Sphenoid, high	Medium	V. deep, flat
C5	Low Eastern Alpine	Medium	Byrsoid, low	Slight	Sl. flat
D	Nordic-Iranian	Rugged	Linear, high	Slight	Deep, rounded
D1	Nordic	Rugged	Ovoid, low	Medium	Rounded
D2	Corded	Rugged	Ellipse, high	V. slight	Deep, prominent
D3	Iranian-Mediterranean	Medium	Linear, high	Medium	Deep, prominent
D4	Iranian	Rugged	V. linear, byrsoid	Slight	V. deep, prom.
D5	Danubian-Hallstatt	Rugged	Linear, high	Slight	Upswept, rounded
E	Mixed Alpine	Medium	Intermediate, big	Medium	Rounded
E1	Mixed Alpine	Slight	Massive, high	Medium	Flat lambda
E2	Nordic-Alpine	Rugged	Large	Slight	Flat lambda
E3	Mediterranean-Alpine	Medium	Intermediate	Medium	Rounded
F	Dinaric-Mediterranean	Medium	Byrsoid, lateral	Medium	Upswept
F1	Dinaric-Mediterranean	Slight	Byrsoid, high	Strong	Hayrick
F2	Dinaroid	Rugged	Sphenoid, big	Medium	Sl. flat
F3	East Balkan Dinaroid	Medium	Byrsoid, low	Slight	Rounded
F4	Eastern	light	Sphenoid, small	Medium	Sl. flat

more rugged than A3, the central Basic White, which approximates the Eurafrican of the literature and is a smaller version of Cro-Magnon. A4, a squat-faced and low-headed version of A3, being more Eastern than African; and A5 is a fuller, more massive version.

The *Classic Mediterranean* type B1 is a generalized Mediterranean, whereas B2 is the more angular form, as often found in Egypt. Types B3, more linear and "Classic" in Sergi's sense, and B4, with the long face, approximate the desert-belt Mediterranean versions in the range from North Africa and Siwah to Hissar and Kazakhstan.

The *Nordic-Iranian* type D1 lies between Anglo-Saxon and Keltic area norms, and D2 is the earlier pre-Bronze Age Corded form which Coon identifies. Type D3, lighter and more hawk-nosed, is transitional to the Mediterranean type B4 and to type D4 (Iranian), which is the Proto-Iranian of Vallois, Irano Afghan of others, and Proto-Nordic of Krogman, and which is more linear and more rugged than D3 and has a more tilted chewing plane, more nasal convexity, and deeper occiput. Type D5 approximates Coon's Danubian-Hallstatt and successor Central European forms.

The *Dinaric-Mediterranean* type F1 is the lighter more Mediterranean version found in Lower Egypt or Anatolia; F2 is the broader bigger-faced more Dinaroid version, rarely with less curved occiput; and F3 is the low-headed East Balkan version with some Iranian face features. Type F4, with its more Iranian face and short vault and with little occipital bulge,

Forehead	Face, outline	Jaws	Nose	Orbits
Rel. wide	Low, square	Long, mouth deep	Med. thick	Low rect.
Rel. wide	Med. linear	Long, mouth deep	Med. thin	Low rect., sloping
Rel. wide	Wide, square	Long, mouth v. deep	Coarse	V. low rect., horiz.
Rel. wide	Low, square	Long, mouth med.	Med. thick	Low rect., sl. sloping
Rel. wide, low	Squat, trapez.	Angular	Med. thick	Low rect., sl. sloping
Rel. wide	Med., square	Angular	Med. thick	Rectangular
Steep	Pinched, tapers	Shallow, chin pointed	Med. thin	Square
Steep	Pinched, tapers	Shallow, chin pointed	Med. thin	Square, tilted
Steep	Pinched, tapers	Sl. progn.	Med. thin	?
Steep	Pinched, tapers	Sl. progn.	Med. thin	?
Steep	Long, pent.	Long, chin tilted	Beaky	Rhomboid, tilted
Rel. pinched, full	Short, hex.	Short, chin strong	Med. wide	Square or rounded
Rel. pinched, full	Slightly flat	Short, chin strong	Med. wide	Square or rounded
Rel. pinched, full	Round	Small	Rel. wide	Rounded
Wide, slope	Wide, square	Angular, mouth deep	Coarse	Low rect.
Pinched, steep	Hexagonal	Angular, tilted	Beaky, thin	Rhomboid
V. pinched	Squat	Shallow	Beaky, short	Low, tilted
Wide, sloping	High, rect.	Angular, chin deep	High, beaky	Rect., tilted
Wide, sloping	High, rect.	Angular, chin deep	High, beaky	Low rect.
Rel. wide	High, rect.	Angular, chin deep	Thin, beaky	Low rect.
Rel. wide	Med., rect.	Angular, chin prom.	Prominent	Rect., tilted
Rel. wide	High, rect.	Tilted, chin deep	High, v. beaky	Rect., tilted
Rel. wide	Linear, rect.	Angular, proj.	High	Rhomboid, tilted
V. wide, high	Short, taper	Shallow, chin proj.	Short, big root	High
Capacious, steep	Small	Shallow	Med. wide	Rhomboid
Wide, sloping	Square	Angular	Strong root	Rectangular
Big	Intermediate	Medium chin	Medium	High, tilted
Pinched	Long, hex.	Long, chin deep	Long	High
Pinched	Linear	Long, chin tilted	Thin	Rhomboid
Rel. pinched	Big, hex.	Angular, deep	Beaky	Rect.
Rel. pinched	Big, hex.	Angular	Long	Square
V. pinched	Med. small	Light, chin pointed	Thin, beaky	Rhomboid

diverges toward the Armenoid of Bunak and others. Note that type F never has the "flat" occiput of Dinaric and Armenoid types; this occiput is probably artificial (head-binding) in any case.

The *Mixed Alpine* type E1 has the A3 form puffed out and more paedomorphic (cf. Alpine), whereas E2 is Nordic-Alpine and E3 Mediterranean-Alpine.

The *Alpine* type C1 is the typical Central European Alpine form, C2 a smaller trend of this, and C3 is the Upper Paleolithic to Mesolithic form (cf. Borreby). Type C4, short-faced but narrow-nosed and with an almost flat occiput, is an Eastern but not Armenoid form; and C5 is a low-headed and squat-faced version of C4, perhaps frequent in Hittites. These two may be pre-Armenoid.

INDIVIDUAL DESCRIPTIONS

NEOLITHIC

EARLY NEOLITHIC

221 Ler (west skeleton, next to burial J6 in area JA-JB) consists of the right forearm and pieces of the hand of an adult male plausibly about 33 years old (Plate XXVI). Stature was tall (almost 172 cm.) and the shafts of radius (245 mm.) and ulna (268 mm.) appear somewhat sinuous and slender compared to the joints: upper and lower epiphyses of radius measure 24 and 32 and of the ulna, 33 and 19 mm. But forearm breadth of 48 mm. is not small and the man appears to have been muscular and to have used his bony frame at top capacity, since wrist and elbow joints show slight lipping around their rims; slight periostitis on the flexor surface of the middle third of the ulna likewise suggests hard use of the thumb, probably in pronation, conceivably in pressure-flaking or in producing obsidian sickle blades such as occur with silica polish in this layer. Metacarpals 1 and 2 measure 47 and 68 mm.

222 Ler (central bones from burial J7 in area JA-JB) consists of the incomplete left forearm and hand of a young woman (25–35 ?). The incomplete radius (195 mm.) and ulna (222 mm.) suggest a stature of 147 cm. and have slender, pinched, and strongly bowed shafts (forearm breadth about 36 mm.) with relatively large joints; proximal ulna and radius epiphysis breadths 25 and 19 mm. The hand was not small, measuring 147 mm. in length without the missing lunate and distal phalanx of the middle finger. Metacarpals 1 to 4 measure 44, 65, 65, and 55 mm. Fragmentary trochlea of the humerus shows perforation of the olecranon fossa. Small osteophytes occur on the arches of some lumbar vertebrae.

220 Ler (burial JA-JB-6, west skeleton) is the skeleton of a child of about 10 (dental age 9.5) with milk canines still in place and permanent second molars visible in crypts). It appears to be female according to appearance of skull and pelvis with wide sciatic notch. The long bones tend to have flattened shafts, with strong bowing of forearm and femur. Deep or wide fossae for attachments of soleus, gastrocnemius, and gluteus maximus suggest strong muscles for climbing hills. Flexion facets are absent at the ankle, but the retroversion angle of the upper tibia is very marked (22°) indicating frequent use of knee bending in climbing hills. There is a definite erosion fossa on the femur neck produced by strong extension of the hip, as in running downhill (see Plate XXVI). Clavicles, scapulae, and the ilium suggest a fairly stocky build, and stature was in the range of 125 to 130 cm., probably one standard deviation below modern American stature for a 9-year-old girl. There are minor signs of malnutrition in three striations across the enamel of the incisors and molar teeth (Plate XXII). These suggest interferences with nutrition at about 14, 26, and 36 months. This might mean seasonal periods of partial starvation if confirmed by other evidence.

The skull is complete except for missing parts of the left frontal bone (Plates I, XXII). The skull vault is intermediate in linearity and pentagonoid in top, side, and rear views because of the sharply curved bosses. The vault has a marked depression behind bregma, with rising profile behind it, and a long and rather deep occipital region with a strong cerebellar bulge and pit rather than crest at inion. A striking individual feature is a complete metopic suture, with the expected extra width of forehead. The face is small and pentagonoid rather than square, with slight prognathism, rather projecting nasal bones over a thick nose, and low rhomboid orbits. The mouth region is wide, with a marked overbite. The teeth show strong wear, very marked on the milk molars, pronounced on milk canines, and already through the cusps of the permanent first molars after only four years in the mouth: Neolithic diet wore down teeth three to five times faster than that of the Middle to Late Bronze Age (Plate XXII). The dentition shows no lesions, and roots of the unerupted permanent canines and premolars are about half grown (Plate XXII). Traces of rays around the parietal bosses may perhaps represent healed porotic hyperostosis, and cribrous areas of medium degree mark the orbit roofs; these conditions might represent thalassemia in heterozygous form. The skull as a whole is Basic White (A1) and is comparable to earlier skulls from Nea Nikomedeia.

222a Ler (burial JA-JB-7) consists of unmeasurable fragments of the right scapula and left mandible (unfused). These point to a fetus or premature infant (6–7 fetal months) associated with the woman *222 Ler;* both adult and fetus are so incomplete that the association may be accidental.

224 Ler (burial 1.5 m. west of AX 2.8 in area JA-JB) is the skeleton of an infant which died soon after birth. It is probably female, since the brim portion of the ilium (16+ mm.) exceeds the posterior breadth (15— mm.). There is no skull.

237 Ler (grave BD-29) is the incomplete skeleton of a child of about four, perhaps female. Vertebral arches are not united to their bodies and the lower first permanent molar, visible in its crypt, has a crown formed almost down to the neck of the tooth. The preauricular part of the ilium (brim 26 and 27 mm., left and right) measures as large as the combined areas for sacral attachment and muscles (posterior iliac segment 27 and 29 mm.); the sciatic notch is wide and preauricular sulcus average; these observations suggest female sex. The femur at midshaft measures 12×12 mm. and the tibia 12×10 (a-p $\times$ transv.). The only noteworthy thing about the skeleton is an erosion fossa on the neck of the femur. The skull (Plate I) shows only slight raying around parietal bosses which are prominent enough to make the top view pentagonoid; there are no other signs of suboptimal nutrition because milk teeth are formed before the childhood phase of nutritional stress and show no cross-striations on the enamel. The skull vault is notably linear and high, with bulging forehead and sharply curved and deep occiput. The mouth area shows incipient prognathism, deep chin, and probably rather tilted chewing plane. In general the skull shows more Basic White (A1) than Iranian (D4) tendencies; these latter may be confused with infantile traits in a notably narrow skull (deep occiput and jaw tilt).

Late Neolithic

240 Ler (grave HTN-1) is the broken skeleton of a woman about 26 years old. The part from the knees down is missing because of wall foundations of Early Helladic date. Estimated lengths of femora, left humerus, and right radius suggest a stature of 158 cm. Long-bone shafts tend to be flattened and not thickened, compared with a femur head of full male

size. Femora show marked bowing and deep gluteal fossae. Other muscle markings are sharp, especially for pectoralis major and extensors of hand. The ilium shows a wide sciatic notch and deep preauricular sulcus. The iliac crest is well fused, but there are no signs of bony outgrowths or lumbar facet lipping; the sacral promontory does show incipient lipping. The skull (Plates I, XXII) consists of major parts of the parietal bones, the lower half of the frontal bone and right cheekbone and the mouth region. The vault seems to have been robust and linear, in top view pentagonoid, with small browridges, marked constrictions behind the orbits and behind bregma, and average mastoids and supramastoid crests. The jaw is strong and wide, indicating relatively wide skull base. The tringular chin is not projecting and the mouth region as a whole is rather squat, with no prognathism and a wide and high palate. Teeth are robust, with an edge bite and in general a pronounced degree of wear, except on the second and third molars, as expected in a young person. Only four teeth were lost in the ground after death; there were no lesions during life. The dentition is perfect. For the face we can say only that the orbits were low and depression of the nose root at nasion almost lacking. The skull as a whole was probably an adult version of *220 Ler*, type A3, roughly comparable to Neolithic skulls at Hageorgitika in Arcadia (Angel, 1945) and at Nea Nikomedeia and to the important Basic White element in the pre-Greek population in the Early Bronze Age in Corinth and Attica (Angel, 1959).

242 Ler (burial JC-1) is a relatively complete skeleton of a rather small but muscular woman in her mid-twenties with the flattening (but not bowing) of long-bone shafts, tilt of tibia head at knee, ankle flexion facets (tibia and talus), and gluteal and heel exostoses expectable in an active person in a hilly place. Strongly flanged pubic pecten and many irregularities in the attachment areas of sacroiliac ligaments suggest many pregnancies, but the pubic symphyses crucial for this estimate are missing. Slight "arthritic" lipping occurs only on the sacral promontory, lower neck vertebrae, odontoid process, foot bones, and shoulders. Humeri are sinuous, with perforation of the olecranon fossa only on the left. The hand was apparently about equal in size to that of *222 Ler*, measuring 126 mm. without carpus and distal phalanx; capitate measures $22 \times 13 \times 16$ and left metacarpals one, two, four, and five measure, respectively, 43, 66, 54, and 49 mm. Sex criteria of the pelvis are very strongly female but the skull has well-developed browridges and nasion depression, and like *240 Ler* a more massive mouth region than in modern females.

During skull restoration, I succeeded in correcting the moderate warping, so that measurements are reliable. The ovoid vault (Plate I) has an exceedingly strongly rising profile (auricular-bregma height is almost 8 mm. less than vertex height), with average side-wall rounding and average mastoids. The face is angular in outline, rather squat except for long jaw and quite deep pointed chin. Shallow cheekbones bound rectangular orbits, and the extremely salient nose is not at all narrow. Teeth show pronounced wear and edge bite. Incisors are strong but not shovel-shaped. The upper first molars and lower right first premolar have central crown caries, leaving only shells. In life, 5 lower molars were lost, the right first molar just before death, with an abscess above it; an abscess occurs also above the diseased lower premolar. Altogether, 8 of the 30 preserved alveolar spaces show lesions, more than the 5 modal in this general period (table 5); but surprisingly, there is no paradontal disease. Striations on the enamel indicating growth arrests are absent, in contrast with *220 Ler* and many of the Middle Bronze Age skulls. But a striking disease sign appears in the skull vault: thickening of the blood-producing diploë, so that the

parietal boss and vertex region measures 10 mm. in thickness (normally 5–7 in females), with a sagittal groove at obelion. This is porotic hyperostosis, generally a result of strong anemia, sometimes from hookworm or severe iron deficiency, often from thalassemia in a place where falciparum malaria is endemic. The skull as a whole is closer to Basic White (A3), like *240* and *220 Ler* than to the Dinaric-Mediterranean varieties (F1, F2, F3) common in Neolithic Macedonia, though its high ovoid vault fits the latter trend.

223 Ler (Area JA-JB, with pot J6.44 between JBK, JAA at 9.30) consists of skull fragments only of a late fetus; chin height is 10 mm.

225 Ler (Grave HJT-1) is a fairly large infant who died soon after birth, probably female according to the iliac proportions; brim is 19 mm., posterior segment 15 mm. (Plate XXVI). There are no signs of defective ossification, and chin height is 13 mm.

MIDDLE BRONZE AGE

Broadly defined: Late Lerna IV (Early Helladic III), Lerna V (Middle Helladic), and Lerna VI (Middle Helladic, end, and Late Helladic I)

Since the people of this period follow the custom of burying their dead either next to or under the floors of their houses we can assume that neighboring groups of graves usually form family units. The excavators provisionally identified 27 such family groups. I have combined these into 13 clans, named according to their site or location (Fig. 5) and to be described in order from west to east (landward to seaward) across the excavated part of the site. Since the original numbering follows the order of trenches as excavated between 1953 and 1957, it does not correlate neatly with the order of description by clans. From archeological inference the Middle Helladic period includes the migrations of many people, both in groups and as individuals, among which is the entry of the first speakers of Greek perhaps in more than one wave from more than one source. In these circumstances clan differences and biological exchanges will reflect ethnic differences, intermarriages, fertility differences, and social plus biological selection. In the biological sense these are the raw materials of microevolution (Dobzhansky, 1951; Simpson, 1958), and from the social standpoint they form source groups from which the class structure and somewhat specialized societies of Mycenaean and Homeric Greece could have evolved.

1. WESTERN CLAN: Trenches C, H, M (Middle Bronze Age, early to middle phases)

18 Ler (grave C-L) consists of a somewhat broken skull of a male almost 50 years old (Plate II). No useful pieces of the skeleton survive. The vault is extremely linear, ellipsoid in three views, high with deep occiput and continuous browridges. The face is long and rectangular, with long jaws below a very

prominent and thin nose which had been broken and healed with a 3 mm. shift to the right. There is also a wound depression on the frontal bone close to bregma. Only three teeth were lost (one third molar is suppressed) and incisor teeth show enamel striations from growth interference. Traces of porotic hyperostosis appear on parietals. This skull is basically Iranian (D4) with Mediterranean (B4) influence.

19 Ler (grave C-M) is the skeleton, broken, of a robust man about 42 years old, not really tall (170.4 cm.) with relatively large hands and muscular limbs. Lumbar vertebrae are arthritic and cervical vertebrae markedly so. The byrsoid skull vault (Plate II) is notably high and deep, with definite lambdoid flattening. The rectangular face has median proportions except for the low ellipsoid orbits. The nose is sharply angled and is recessed under continuous browridges. Seven teeth were lost, probably following abscesses, and an eighth is abscessed. The incisor teeth are deeply worn and the rest only markedly worn. This skull fits Coon's (1939) Corded type (D2).

31 Ler (grave H-1) includes the skeleton and much broken skull of a subadult girl almost 18 years old, with elbow and hip epiphyses fused and knee, wrist, and shoulder open. She is not short (154.2 cm.) and not especially muscular. Long-bone shafts are flattened and femur neck shows an erosion fossa. Hands and feet are not small. The warped and incomplete skull (Plate II) is long and ellipsoid. The face was probably long and rectangular, quite prognathous, with sloping mouth, prominent nose, and high rhomboid orbits. Two teeth are carious, enamel striations appear, and a Carabelli cusp on the upper first molar; third molars are just erupting. The skull appears to be Iranian (D4).

59 Ler (grave M-1) is the relatively complete skeleton of a woman who died at about age 26 (closure of sagittal suture beginning). She is short (152.5 cm.) with slender bones and small hands and feet. There is no arthritis. The ellipsoid skull vault (Plate II) is linear and high with deep-bulging occipital region and some lambdoid flattening. The rectangular face has a tilted chewing plane and a slight alveolar prognathism, but relatively wide palate, nose, and orbits. Teeth are excellent. There is a sharp wound depression just to the right of vertex. The skull fits type D3 (Iranian-Mediterranean).

16 Ler (grave C-F) is the very fragmentary skeleton of an adolescent apparently female, age about 15¼ because the elbow epiphyses are fused, metatarsals fusing, and knee, hip, ankle, and shoulder open. According to the preserved left half (Plate II), the skull vault was sphenoid and short, with full temporal squama. The face appears square, with triangular chin and sloping mouth region. Teeth are excellent, with third molars still in crypts. This skull approximates Eastern Alpine (C4) as in both early Cyprus and Anatolia (Angel, 1953).

17 Ler (grave C-H) is the partial skeleton, probably of a girl, about 8 years old, since the lower lateral incisors are just erupting. Skull fragments are too few to study. Femur is markedly bowed and just below the modern norm for this age. Long bones are well developed. There is a wide sciatic notch and preauricular sulcus.

Graves C-J and C-K produced no skeletons.

2. SOUTHERN CLAN: Areas AD, G, GP, GQ, J, JA, JB (Middle Bronze Age, very early to middle phases)

212 Ler (grave JA-J2B, lower skeleton) consists of a fragmentary male skeleton of average stature (167.3 cm.), robust build, and age about 33 (phase 6). The preserved part of the skull vault (anterior) and upper face suggests a byrsoid or ovoid shape and narrow forehead, whereas the face is wide with low rectangular orbits; in general fitting Basic White (A3) norms.

216 Ler (Grave JB-J4A, upper skeleton) is a more fragmentary male, probably older than *212*, to judge by some exostosis development at the knee, and probably smaller (between 160 and 168 cm. in stature). Face fragments show strong cheekbones, wavy nose profile, and average tooth wear, with edge bite and bilateral but not prominent or deep chin.

217 Ler (grave JB-J4B, lower skeleton with Middle Minoan jar), a male, has an almost equally fragmentary skeleton, younger (*ca.* 24?) than the foregoing, to judge chiefly from the open skull sutures, but with slight lumbar arthritis and slightly more slender long bones and taller stature (between 163 and 170 cm., guess) than *212 Ler*. The skull vault (Plate III) is strikingly linear and angular in profile, with a flat rise to a high vertex. The hexagonal face has sloping orbits, wide nose, and long and rather prognathous mouth region. Tooth wear is barely medium and there is a slight overbite. One tooth is carious and there are slight enamel grooves. This skull fits Basic White (A1) norms, with resemblance to the Greek Neolithic skull from Hageorgitika as well as to Cretans.

207 Ler (grave GP-G2) is a fairly complete but much broken skeleton of a female, about 30 years old (Todd's late phase 5 pubic symphysis), short in stature (148.2 cm.), of average build, and with pubic exostoses indicating many pregnancies, although there is no arthritis of neck or lumbar vertebrae. A Colles fracture of the right radius with a spiral fracture of the right ulna, plausibly in adolescence, has resulted in a slight dorsal deviation at the wrist and shortening of about 5 mm. of the forearm. The linear, high, and rounded angular vault has a deep occiput and flat sides (Plate III). The square face has a wide but rather high-bridged nose, small cheekbones, and long but only slightly prognathous mouth region with edge bite and marked tooth wear. There is a slight porosity on the occipital and adjacent right parietal, and medium arthritic change of the left temporo-mandibular joint, with some flattening of the jaw condyle. The skull type is Basic White (A1), rather than Iranian or Mediterranean, much like *217 Ler* and resembling also *91 Ler* and *189 Ler*.

208 Ler (grave GQ-G3) is the upper half of a female skeleton about 38 years old, of low average stature (151.2 cm.), with slight arthritic exostoses on thoracic vertebrae. The skull vault (Plate III) is sphenoid and quite high, rounded in rear view, and not small for a female. The square face is low, with low and rectangular orbits and a short but projecting nose. The squat mouth region has an edge bite with marked tooth wear and slight enamel grooves on the teeth. In addition to the loss of 8 teeth in life, 5 of the remainder are carious and 2 of these show abscesses. The skull type is Eastern Alpine (C4), with similarities to *48 Ler* and *89 Ler*.

210 Ler (grave JA-J1) consists of the right upper extremity and fragmentary femur and mandible of a woman about 30 years old, of medium size (stature between 150 and 160 cm.). The jaw has a triangular chin, 31 mm. high, of medium prominence, and with only slight alveolar prognathism. Tooth wear is medium and loss and caries absent.

211 Ler (grave JA-J2A, upper skeleton) is the partial skeleton of a woman slightly larger (158.7 cm.) but of about the same age (early phase 6 symphysis) as *210 Ler*, and lacking arthritis on the few vertebrae preserved. The frontal, occipital, temporal, and face pieces suggest a full vault and fairly wide face somewhat like *208 Ler*, but with higher orbits and longer face and possibly type F2 Dinaric-Mediterranean norms. The chin shows medium prominence and the teeth are only slightly worn, without loss in life.

213 Ler (grave JB-J3A), compared to *210 Ler*, is a taller (160.5 cm.) and younger (late phase 4 symphysis) and less complete female skeleton, with marked signs of childbirth at the symphysis but no arthritis on preserved vertebrae. The spheroid skull vault (Plate III) is more capacious than that of the average woman and is striking because of a complete metopic suture on the wide frontal bone. The wide jaw has a deep chin and tooth wear is slight, loss absent, and enamel grooves slight in the left half of the jaw, which is all that remains for study. This skull is of massive Alpine type (C3).

218 Ler (grave JA-J5), compared to *210 Ler*, is an older (about age 38) apparently shorter (149–159 cm. stature, guess) female, with a jaw fragment showing a triangular chin of medium prominence and 32 mm. height; the incisors show extreme wear. No other teeth are preserved.

53 Ler (grave J-1) consists of fragments of an adolescent, probably about 13 years old, since the second molar and the premolars have erupted but the elbow epiphysis is still open. The fragmentary skeleton is perhaps female. The incisors are to a medium degree shovel-shaped.

214 Ler (grave JB-J3B, cist) is the partial skeleton of another adolescent of about 13, perhaps male according to pelvic and skull criteria, and with stature about 146 cm. The elbow epiphyses and acetabulum are about to fuse and the second permanent molars have just erupted. The left clavicle shows a foramen for a branch of the middle supraclavicular nerve of the cervical plexus. Skull fragments show small browridges; the first molar has a small Carabelli cusp.

215 Ler (grave JB-J3C, cist) is the partial skeleton of a child (possibly male) about 4 years old, since the unerupted first permanent molar is starting root formation and the cervical arches are still separate from their vertebral bodies.

60 Ler (grave, AD-1, in cut 3) is the remains of a small infant, with bones more porous than usual, apparently female (ilium).

209 Ler (grave GP-G4) is an infant skeleton, full-term newborn and perhaps female (iliac proportions). The edges of the epiphyseal ends of long bones seem unusually "sharp," but there are no signs of disease on skull fragments or teeth crowns. The chin height is 15 mm.

219 Ler (bones at 11.28, area J) consists of the extremely broken remains of a newborn infant, perhaps full term, possibly male, not measurable.

3. FOREST CLAN: Areas B, BA, BB, BC, BD (Middle Bronze Age, very early to middle phases)

33 Ler (grave BA-1) is the skull and axial skeleton, lacking limbs (except for right hand) of a youth about 22 years old, with wisdom teeth almost completely erupted. Left clavicle measures 137; right metacarpals I and III 46 and 65; L4 25 and 23, L5 26 and 20?; sacrum height 103; left iliac brim 50; and posterior segment 61 mm. The vertebrae and hand and scapulae are rather small and lack arthritis. The ilium shows an average sciatic notch and brim length, the epiphyses of ilium and vertebral bodies are just fused, but medial end of clavicle is unfused.

The skull (Plate V) is small, linear and delicate, with ovoid and rather high vault, and a long oval face having a somewhat prognathous mouth region and sloping rhomboid orbits. Teeth are excellent, with slight enamel grooves, only one caries, and fully developed Carabelli cusps (Plate XXI). This skull is Mediterranean type B1. The striking thing about it is, however, the crudely cut opening of the right frontal region, 40 by 60 mm., with edges cut with a scalloped bevel from periphery toward the center as if the two trephined fragments had been raised with the scalp at the time of death. The instrument must have been blunt. The muddy earth in this area seems unusually adherent to the bone; did blood facilitate this? This operation contrasts with that on a slightly later Mycenaean prince (Plate XXII). Could this youth have served as a scapegoat (pharmakos)?

73 Ler (grave BA-4) consists of fragments of skull and skeleton of a male perhaps 50 years old (coronal suture almost closed), and medium tall (170.1 cm.). Long-bone fragments are robust and the talus large. Extensive arthritic exostoses overhang two adjacent lumbar fragments. The right forearm shows a healed compound fracture at the junction of the lower quarter, with proximal parts of the bones and injury extensive enough to produce a complete bony bridge fusing the bones in a position of moderate pronation (Plate XXVI); this suggests a wound rather than accident. Skull fragments show large cheekbones, alveolar prognathism, and marked tooth wear.

76 Ler (burial BC-4) consists of teeth and badly broken skeleton of a man about 40 years old (symphysis early phase 8), of medium stature (167.9 cm.) and rather slender build. The vertebrae show a disc injury between T9 and T10 and fusion with possible fracture between T11 and T12 on the right: marked arthritic changes accompany this. The teeth are average in size and show medium wear.

12 Ler (burial B-2) consists of the fragments of the skeleton and fairly complete lower jaw of a small woman (150.2 cm.) about 45 years old. The lambdoid suture is closed. The jaw is quite robust, wide-jowled, with deep chin and little prognathism. Three teeth were lost, one is carious and another is abscessed, for a total of five lesions. Like *33 Ler* she shows a trace of transverse grooves in the enamel. Tooth wear is not marked. Skull fragments and jaw suggest Basic White.

13 Ler (grave B-3), includes the extremely fragmentary skull, humerus (23 × 18 mm., midshaft), talus (48 length, 28 height, flexion facets +), and sciatic notch area of a woman about 25 years old. The skull (Plate V) was long, large, and probably long-faced, with square orbits and average nose. Teeth are excellent, with only one tooth carious, slight wear, and an overbite. The skull seems to be Basic White type A1.

14 Ler (grave B-3A) includes the right foot (talus 46 × 36 × 26 mm., facets slight) and ankle and fragments of ischium and femur head (43 mm.) of a young adult female (20–30 years old). Metatarsals I–V are not large (56, 69, 62, and 54–62 mm.).

74 Ler (burial BC-1) includes skull fragments and 6 teeth of a subadult, probably female. The third molar is just erupting(?); tooth size is average and wear slight.

77 Ler (burial BC-5) is the skeleton, lacking skull, of a woman of about 28 years old (phase 5 symphysis) of almost average stature (153.2 cm.) and rather slender build. Femora are much bowed with strong pilaster but lack an erosion fossa. There is no sign of arthritis.

35 Ler (grave BA-3) consists of unmeasurable fragments of a 3-year-old child, aged by the loose teeth.

75 Ler (burial BC-2) includes skeletal and skull fragments of a 12-year-old, apparently male (short brim segment of ilium). The skeleton is rather small. Milk molars, which are being replaced by premolars, show medium wear. Molars are of Dryopithecus pattern and shovel incisors are medium.

78 Ler (grave BC-6) includes skull fragments, right radius of rather small size (95) and clavicle (62 mm.) of a 3-year-old, perhaps male, in which the roots of the second molars are finishing growth and the permanent first molar crowns are rather large (upper 11.6 × 12.4, lower 11.4 × 10.7 mm.) and wrinkled.

15 Ler (grave B-4) comprises the fragmentary remains of a newborn infant whose left clavicle measures 44 mm.

34 Ler (grave BA-2) is a full-term infant with humerus, tibia, and scapula at United States norms: 66, 67, 39 × 30 mm.

79 Ler (grave BC-7) includes the smaller humerus (61?) mm. and left temporal bone and jaw shell of a newborn infant, possibly premature.

84 Ler (grave BD-4) is the upper part of an average infant, probably a boy, about 7 months old, with upper incisors starting eruption (root one-third formed), and radius length 69 and clavicle length 55-mm.

36 Ler (grave BA-5) E.H. III, is the skeleton of an infant born just before term, perhaps female, a little below average size (iliac brim 14, posterior segment 15 — mm.

58 Ler (grave BB3, E.H. III) is the skeleton of an infant perhaps born just before term, apparently female (brim 15, posterior 16 mm.).

Grave B-1 appears to be that of an adult with bones completely eroded; grave BC-3 is that of an adult.

4. Central Clan: Areas B7, B8, BB (Middle Bronze Age, very early to middle phases)

37 Ler (grave BB-1) includes skull fragments and slender (17 × 15 mm.) humeral shaft of a man about 32 years old. The vault was not long and had full temporal regions with large mastoids and a rather flat occiput with very small crest. The jaw is deep-chinned, wide, and notably thick. There is slight prognathism and notable chin projection. Twenty-three alveoli with teeth show no loss or other lesions and a plus degree of wear. The skull appears to be Alpine, probably type C4.

40 Ler (grave B7-9) is a man about 48 years old, medium tall (169.7 cm.), broad-shouldered, with average muscularity and only a trace of arthritic exostoses on vertebrae and on the thumb. All long bones are markedly flattened; there are slight flexion facets at the ankles and medium tibial retroversion at the knee (rough-country adaptions). The very linear ellipsoid vault (Plate IV) is very high, with deep occiput and smooth profile. The edentulous palate and jaw make difficult a proper estimate of the apparently long and rectangular face with beaky nose. The temporomandibular joint shows medium arthritis (Plate XXIII), involving pitted absorption on the anterior surface of the articular eminences and marked absorption on the posterior surfaces of the greatly thinned mandibular condyles; jaw motion must have been limited and probably very painful. The skull is Nordic-Iranian, type D4.

43 Ler (grave B8-12B) is the skeleton of a young man 21 years of age (pubic symphysis phase 2, beginning fusion of epiphyses of vertebrae and pelvis). He was not big (166.5 cm.), but was fairly robust with rather flat humeral shaft, strong femoral pilaster and crest for soleus muscle, definite retroversion of tibia at knee, and flexion facets at ankles. The ovoid skull (Plate IV) is fairly wide and not high,

although the occipital region is deep. Below continuous browridges the face is extremely long, elongated-hexagonal in outline with thin nose, rectangular orbits, and relatively large mouth, slightly prognathous and showing a peculiar crowding of upper lateral incisor teeth, which deviate lingually and produce a modified cross bite, A third lower molar is missing and a second molar carious. The first upper molars show small Carabelli cusps (Plate XXI), and enamel grooves show trace development. The skull is Dinaric-Mediterranean, type F3.

44 Ler (grave B8-13) includes the skeleton without skull of a man, 25 years old, whose stature was of medium size (166.5 cm.) but robust, with rough-country limb changes and without arthritis.

32 Ler (grave B-5) consists of a number of unmeasurable bone fragments or scraps plausibly from a middle-aged female.

38 Ler (grave BB-2) includes scapular, clavicle and rib fragments and the jaw and back half of the skull of a woman about 44 years old. The skull (Plate IV) is wide, with short occiput, perhaps Eastern Alpine, type C4, and shows a shallow "wound" depression 12 × 23 mm., just to the right of obelion. One tooth is carious, five were lost in life, wear is marked, and the incisor enamel is slightly grooved. No upper teeth were recovered.

39 Ler (Grave B7-7) is the partial skeleton without skull of a woman about 30 years old, quite tall (165.9 cm.) and robust and lacking limb arthritis (no vertebrae preserved).

42 Ler (grave B8-12A). The skeleton of a female about 20 years old, with epiphyses of the medial clavicle, a conjoined ramus just fusing, and a rather deep, "anthropoid" true pelvic brim (Plate XVIII), nevertheless shows in the pubic area definite signs of childbearing, including an unusual spike formation of the pubic tubercle. Stature is shorter than average (149.9 cm.). There are only four lumbar vertebrae, the lumbosacral joint area is normal, and there is no arthritis. The skull vault (Plate IV) is ovoid, not compressed, with wide forehead above a low, heart-shaped face having ellipsoid orbits and a short nose with pointed spine. One third molar was lost in life and four molars are carious. A peculiar crossed version of a slight overbite results from lingual diversion of the upper left second incisor and upper right canine, like *43 Ler*. Major features of the skull are Basic White, type A3.

56 Ler (grave B8-14), the skeleton of a female about 37 years old (symphysis phase 8), shows very marked childbearing changes in the pelvis (Plate XVIII) and has a spiky pubic tubercle very much like that of her daughter(?) *42 Ler*. She is also short (150.7 cm.). She does have the normal number of lumbar vertebrae, however, and these show beginning arthritis, as do the occipital condyles. The second metatarsal shows shaft thickening from extra stress. The pentagonoid skull vault (Plate IV) is larger as well as more angular than that of *42 Ler*, with more pinched forehead and low and square face having more sloping orbits, narrower nose, and more prominent chin; but in profile and in shape details of pyriform aperture and jaw ramus the skulls are very similar, though *56 Ler* is more Mixed Alpine (E2) than Basic White. Nine teeth were lost in life, three are carious, and another abscessed; tooth wear is pronounced in the front of the mouth but the slightly worn lower molars (without opposition from the six lost upper molars) bring the average wear to medium. This is accompanied by an edge bite. There are slight enamel grooves on teeth. Medium porosity is present and there is a small frontal osteoma to the left of the midline.

241 Ler (grave B-8, ?) is a full-term infant, possibly male, about 5–10% smaller than United States averages, with some raying on the frontal bones, especially externally (anemia?). Scapula height is 37 and 36 mm. (left and right). The iliac a-p measurement is 29 and 30, the brim 13+ and 14+, posterior segment 16 and 16, and auricular height 12 and 12+ mm. Chin height is 13, gonion-chin length 31, and bigonial breath 40 mm.

41 Ler (grave B7-10, E.H. III) is the average-sized skeleton of a full-term infant, apparently male, since the preauricular or brim part of the ilium is only 42% (brim 13 vs. 17 mm. posterior).

Grave B-6 is uncertain and grave B-11 produced no skeleton, but is apparently an adult grave. It is curious that this "clan" group includes no burial of a child.

5. MARSH CLAN: Areas A, B9, B10 (Middle Bronze Age, middle to late phases)

1 Ler (grave A-1, north body), is the broken skeleton of a young man about 26 years old. He was medium tall (170.1 cm.), of average muscular development but broad-shouldered and platycnemic, with strong crests for soleus and for peroneal tendons on heel bone. There are traces of arthritis only on the axis vertebra facets and some lumbar facets. The pelvis appears rather flat from back to front, android, with short pubis and big sacrum, having six vertebrae and a sacral hiatus up as far as S1 (Plate XXI). This is a common form of spina bifida whose genetic determination may be either dominant or sex-linked recessive (Falls *in* Sorsby, 1953, pp. 265–266). The ovoid (almost byrsoid) skull vault (Plate VI) is long, smooth, and high with sloping forehead and deep occiput. The extremely orthognathous face has a high bridged but not projecting nose, low and elliptical orbits and a wide and deep mouth region, giving the face a rectangular outline. The triangular chin is exceedingly prominent and the teeth are very good, with only one caries. Third molars apparently were suppressed, and there is remarkably little tooth wear, accompanied by slight overbite. Traces of porosity mark the occipital. This skull is morphologically Nordic-Iranian, type D1.

2 Ler (grave A-1, south body) is a strongly built and broad-shouldered man of average height (166.3 cm.) who died at about age 34 and is probably a brother or cousin of *1 Ler*. They are alike in platycnemia plus the strong crests for soleus and peroneal tendons combined with a lack of erosion fossa on the neck of the femur; but *2 Ler* has more robust bones. Lumbar and thoracic vertebrae do not show arthritis. The byrsoid skull vault (Plate VI) is larger, broader, and broader-based than in *1 Ler*, but is otherwise similar. The long hexagonal face, with its drooping orbits, thin and beaky nose, and very deep, rather protrusive mouth region is well set back in relation to the strong browridges. Lower first molars lost and two molars carious; upper third molars suppressed; and there is slight tooth wear, with slight overbite, as in *1 Ler*. The skull type is F2, Dinaric-Mediterranean, with D1 traits also.

66 Ler (grave B10-20, outside, close to area A, excavated in 1955) is the isolated skull cap and right orbit of a small male about 33 years old, showing a medium degree of healed porotic hyperostosis and on the right parietal bone a transverse groove which appears to be a wound. The vault is ellipsoidal, and intermediate in proportions and the face, probably broad, has a wide nose and low orbits; the skull is Mixed Alpine, type E3.

68 Ler (grave B9-23) is the incomplete skeleton of a male 25 to 35 years old and of average height. There is no scrap of the skull. The long bones are robust and hands and feet, not small.

69 Ler (grave B10-24) is the fairly complete but broken skeleton of a short, stocky, robust, bandy-legged, and arthritic man who died at about age 40. Hands and feet are rather small and ankle flexion facets occur. There is lipping at the edges of most joints including lumbar, thoracic, and cervical facets (Plate XXV). Signs of Schmorl herniations occur

(Plate XXV) on T10, C5, and C6. There is hyperostotic arthritis on the anterior surfaces of the sternal ends of the clavicles. Round holes in the outer table of the left side of the skull vault are probably postmortem and not metastatic lesions. The skull vault (Plate VI) is a broad ovoid in profile, rising to a high vertex. The squat hexagonal face is small, with narrow and beaky nose, low orbits, and horizontal mouth area. Teeth are poor, with 17 lesions out of 25 alveoli preserved; 15 are lost and 2 carious, with 5 abscesses active at death. The skull is Alpine type C4 and could be duplicated in east or south Cyprus or Antiparos or southwestern Anatolia.

72 Ler (B10-Shaft, Late M.H.) is the partial and broken uppermost trunk and skull of a man about 40 years old, probably not big. The short and squat skull vault (Plate VI) is wedge-shaped, with pinched forehead and profile rising to vertex placed far back. The square face is small and very low, with extremely wide nose, but the striking feature is extreme alveolar prognathism. Teeth are poor, with 20 lesions (13 lost, 6 carious, 6 abscessed). There are traces of porotic hyperostosis. The skull is Alpine, type C5, approximating certain neolithic Cypriots or early Anatolians (Karataş, Troy).

3 Ler (graves A2, -3, -4) is the isolated and broken skull of a woman about 33 years old (Plate V). The ovoid vault is short and low, with wide forehead showing a complete metopic suture. The rather squat face has a narrow nose, horizontal orbits, and a rather long and sloping palate. Teeth are only fair with 12 lesions (9 lost, 2 caries, 2 abscesses). Premolars are extremely worn. She had slight porotic hyperostosis, with cribrous orbit roofs. The skull is Small Alpine, type C2, like *126 Ler* in the Northern clan (8).

7 Ler (grave A-8) is the incomplete skeleton, lacking femora, of a woman about 45 years old, whose skull is represented only by a single cheekbone. She was of just over average height (158 cm.) with rather broad shoulders, flattened long-bone shafts, and marked ankle flexion facets. The pubic symphysis is early phase 9 and there is medium arthritis of the lumbar vertebrae, which are average in height. Hands and feet are not small and the right fifth metacarpal is fractured, with very slight twisting and angulation, rather unexpected in a woman.

61 Ler (grave B9-16) is the very fragmentary skeleton, lacking skull and vertebrae, of a subadult girl about 19 years old. The iliac crest is fusing and epiphyses of long bones are already fused. This was a small and slender-boned person, rather short (150 cm.), with very deep pilastric index of the femur.

62 Ler (grave B10-17) includes fragmentary bones, lacking skull or vertebrae, of a woman of medium height (156 cm.), about 45 years old (buckling on scapula, exostoses on pelvis). The preauricular sulcus is very deep and the ilium thick. Toes show arthritis.

65 Ler (grave B10-20) consists of fragments of a rather small(?) woman about 45 years old. Skull fragments show a chin rather pointed, a carious upper first molar, and a closed lamboid suture. There are marked bony outgrowths on the ilium, wide notch, and very deep preauricular sulcus (seven pregnancies?). Metacarpals and right hand bones show slight arthritic exostosis, though none appear on thoracic vertebral facets.

67 Ler (grave B10-21) is a woman about 30 years old, rather small (151 cm.), with relatively flat humeri. Vertebrae and hands lack arthritis. Warped pieces of the skull suggest type F1. The jaw is narrow and deep-chinned, with doubling of the left mental foramen, as in *95 Ler* in the Spring clan (6).

4 Ler (grave A-5) includes the non-restorable fragmentary bones of a child about 6½ years old (upper permanent incisors and lower first molars erupting), perhaps female.

5 Ler (grave A-6) includes unrestorable fragments of a child about 18 months old (second molar crowns completely formed).

8 Ler (grave A-9) is the partial skeleton and skull fragments of a child about 5½ years old (permanent first molar about to erupt), perhaps male (small sciatic notch). The skeleton is scarcely below modern size averages, and is notable only for the occurrence in the temporal region of the left parietal bone of three peculiar round holes with edges rounded and diameters 13, 8, and 6 mm.

9 Ler (grave A-10) includes the skeleton and unrestored skull of a child about 6½ years old (first molar in place, first permanent upper incisor about to erupt), probably female (wide sciatic notch), who was apparently at about the 5-year-old standard for modern Americans (cf. Maresh, 1955).

63 Ler (grave B10-18) is a child about 8 years old (incisor teeth almost erupting), probably male. Long bones seem well developed, but rather small for this age. Mandible is relatively wide and thick, with little chin projection.

6 Ler (grave A-7) is the complete skeleton of a newborn infant or late fetus, not small in size, probably female (iliac brim and muscle area measure 16 and 17.5).

6a Ler (grave A-7) consists of a few fragments of a newborn infant, sex unknown.

10 Ler (grave A-11) is the skeleton and partly restorable skull of an infant just over 12 months old (incisors in place, first molars about to erupt), apparently male (the short iliac brim measures 15 and posterior segment 21 mm.). The skeleton does not seem to be small and looks normal except for a puffed appearance of the lower femoral shaft. The skull vault (Plate V) is short and pentagonoid, with strong bosses and very narrow base. It looks inflated, and the bregmatic fontanelle is still wide open (over 3 cm. wide). This fits the marked degree of porotic hyperostosis (Plate XXII) in parietals, occipital, alisphenoid, and orbital roofs. This is only partly healed, and the parietals show striking raying and thickening (Plate XXIII). This infant boy may very well be homozygous for thalassemia (cf. Angel, 1964, 1966). The skull appears to be Alpine, type C1.

11 Ler (grave A-12) is the incomplete skeleton and skull of an infant about 10 months old (lower incisors in place, first molar visible in crypt) probably female (the long iliac brim measures 22 and posterior segment 21 mm. The metopic suture is closed and the fontanelle about to close. This girl is relatively large, and much larger than *10 Ler*.

64 Ler (grave B10-19) consists of the femur (69? mm.), ulna (58? mm.), and right jaw shell of an infant, without signs of prematurity.

71 Ler (grave B9-28) an apparently premature but not small infant female, shows pitting and raying (Plate XXIII) on the internal surface of the frontal bones (anemia?). Iliac brim is 12, posterior segment 14, femur 69 mm.

Grave B-22, possibly that of an adult, failed to produce a skeleton.

6. SPRING CLAN: Trench BD west and central (Middle Bronze Age, early to middle phases)

95 Ler (grave BD-19) is the quite complete skeleton of a man about 39 years old buried with a pot of Cycladic manufacture (island of Melos). He is average in stature (168.5 cm.) and build, with slight lumbar arthritis. The left big toe is arthritic; instead of showing usual ankle flexion facets, the neck of the left talus shows a strong ridge with a separate facet of medium size; and the left femoral shaft is flattened in an anteroposterior direction by about one-third, although it appears to be longer than the right; both tibiae are bowed, with pronounced popliteal crests, and both gluteal crests are pronounced; the cruciate

ligament attachments on the left are pronounced. Possibly this represents quadriceps femoris paralysis or weakness (poliomyelitis or a wound?), with a tendency for unexpected flexion at knee and ankle. The ovoid skull vault (almost byrsoid) is small (Plate VII) and not high, robust, and with sharply curved occipital producing lambdoid flattening and constriction. The rectangular and fairly long face has compressed cheekbones, beaky nose, and long mouth region, with a strong chin and flaring jaw angles. There is an extra mental foramen on the left, as in *67 Ler* (Marsh clan). The upper third molars are suppressed, a lower one is carious, and four teeth were lost in life. Medium tooth wear accompanies a medium overbite, and the lower incisors are slightly crowded and rotated. There are enamel grooves of medium degree and areas of possible periostitis (not porotic) on the parietal bosses, plus some calcareous incrustation on the right. The skull type is Iranian-Mediterranean (D3), comparable to Coon's "Cappadocian" and resembling *91 Ka* from Karataş in southwestern Anatolia (Angel, 1910).

92 Ler (burial BD-15) is the much broken skeleton of a woman of medium size, about 30 years old (late phase 5) with enough pubic roughening and pecten sharpness to indicate a good number of pregnancies. The wide but posteriorly incomplete skull vault (Plate VII) was probably ovoid, with steep forehead surmounting a low and heart-shaped face, with a beaky, convex nose and pointed chin. An upper third molar is carious, five teeth were lost in life, one recent enough to still show an abscess, and there is an abscessed premolar. Medium tooth wear accompanies a slight overbite, enamel grooves are absent, and there is light hypertrophic arthritis of the left temporomandibular joint. The skull features appear to be Mixed Alpine (E1).

97 Ler (grave BD-21) is of a woman 29 years old, fairly complete except for sacrum and feet, tall (163.0 cm.), with signs of arthritis beginning only on vertebral arches (not on the bodies) and occipital condyles, and with pronounced irregular exostoses on the pubic bone indicating many childbirths (Plate XXI). The small, short-ellipsoid vault (Plate VII) is round in side and back views and has a wide forehead above a relatively large heart-shaped orthognathous face with narrow nose and pointed chin. The upper incisor teeth (lost in the ground after death) apparently protruded somewhat, and medium to marked tooth wear was apparently accompanied by a slight overbite. There are seven carious teeth, of which the upper right canine and premolars have apical abscesses, and from the lower first molar and adjacent premolar abscess drainage spread into the inferior alveolar canal as far forward as the mental foramen.

Two other abscesses of premolar sockets, from which the teeth dropped out in the ground, make six abscesses in all. Since 5 teeth were lost in life, a total of 15 teeth were diseased out of 29 alveoli preserved for study. There is no proof, however, that this severe infection was connected with the unknown cause of death. This skull approximates the small-headed (type F4) version of Dinaric-Mediterranean.

80 Ler (grave BD-1) consists of fragments of skull and leg bones of a child 2 years old (milk first molar fully erupted); left tibia approximates 105 mm.

93 Ler (grave BD 16) is the partial skeleton, probably of a boy 12 to 13 years old, with second molar erupted but acetabulum open, and stature about 141 cm. Iliac brim measures 31? and posterior breadth 45 mm. There is an erosion fossa on the femur neck.

98 Ler (grave BD-22) is the partial calvarium (Plate VII), probably of a boy about 11 years old, with canine and first premolar erupting and second molar and premolar about to erupt. The short, almost rhomboid vault is spheroid in rear view and is marked by a complete metopic suture. The face appears short, with square orbits and broad nose, and the apparent skull type is Alpine, type C1.

99 Ler (grave BD-23) is the broken skeleton of a boy (narrow subpubic angle and notch) 7 years old (upper lateral incisors about to erupt), in whom both milk and permanent first molars show a clear Carabelli cusp (Plate XXI).

103 Ler (grave BD-27, transitional from E.H. III) is a child between 2 and 3 years old, possibly female, with complete milk dentition but incomplete closure of bregmatic fontanelle and lack of fusion of vertebral arches to bodies. The girl is small for an age over two, and the skull shows strongly marked cribra orbitalia (Plate XXIII) and traces of cribrous change and thickening of diploe also on the vault bones (thalassemia?). The vault (Plate VII) is a wide rhomboid, with the bosses prominent and persistent metopic suture. The heart-shaped face and the skull base seem unexpectedly narrow and the bregmatic fontanelle still showing an opening 11 × 31 mm. also suggests developmental retardation compared to the extent of tooth eruption. The molars show Carabelli cusps. The type is Basic White, type A5.

90 Ler (grave BD-13) is a fetus, not yet full term, possible female, with striking raying and cribrosity on the inner surfaces of the frontals and partly on the parietals also (Plate XXIII).

94 Ler (grave BD-18) consists of skull fragments of a newborn infant, apparently full term and without noticeable pathology.

96 Ler (grave BD-20) is an infant, possibly a girl, born just short of full term. Iliac brim is 15 and posterior segment (16) mm.

100 Ler (grave BD-24) is an infant, possibly a girl, who died within days or weeks after birth, certainly before eruption of any milk teeth. The iliac brim is 18, posterior segment 19— and a-p 36+ mm.; skull bones are not pitted.

102 Ler (grave BD-26) is a full-term infant possibly a girl, showing traces of raying on the inner surfaces of the frontal bones (Plate XXIII). Left and right iliac brim and posterior diameters are 19—, 18; 18, 18—; and a-p 34, 34 mm.

104 Ler (grave BD-28) is an infant, possibly a boy, virtually full term.

7. RIVER CLAN: Trench BD, Area BF (Middle Bronze Age, middle phase)

82 Ler (grave BD-3, lower body) is the extremely incomplete skeleton of a man, about 43 years old, of stature not above medium. The humerus (300+) measures 24 × 21 mm. in the midshaft and the clearly robust femur suggests a length of over (420) mm. The long and high ellipsoid skull vault (Plate VIII) has flat sides and a straight forehead above a wide and angular face with beaky nose and some alveolar protrusion. Five teeth are carious, one with an abscess, three were lost in life and marked tooth wear is accompanied by an edge bite. The skull morphology matches Coon's Corded type D2, Nordic-Iranian.

83 Ler (grave BD-3, upper body) is the much broken skeleton of a man about 33 years old, of medium stature. The high and short ellipsoid skull vault (Plate VIII) has a wide forehead above a fairly large face, which tapered somewhat from top to bottom. A slight overbite accompanies slight tooth wear in an excellent dentition, lacking lesions but showing slight enamel grooving. The type resemblance of the skull is Dinaric-Mediterranean, type F2, and a family resemblance with *82 Ler* shows clearly in the jaw (ramus form, chin) and forehead.

85 Ler (grave BD-5) consists of blackened fragments of an adult with medium tooth wear (three teeth) and open skull sutures, possibly about 30 years old, and femur shaft measuring 31 × 28 mm. in the middle, giving a pilastric index of 110.7 that suggests male sex.

87 Ler (grave BD-9) is a relatively complete skeleton of a robust man about 29 years old and of medium-tall stature (169.6 cm.), showing rough-country specializations and no arthritis on the facets of two remaining lumbar vertebrae (bodies not preserved). The notably massive and long ellipsoid skull vault (Plate VIII) has flat sides and a high forehead above a long rectangular face with rectangular orbits, long jaw, triangular chin, and some alveolar protrusion. Two teeth are carious (with incipient caries in three others); wear is slight, with a slight overbite, and enamel grooving is medium. There is considerable vault and facial resemblance to *82 Ler*, except for the long jaw ramus and chin which are comparable to *50 Ler* (clan 12). The skull type is Nordic-Iranian Corded (D2).

88 Ler (grave BD-11) is a relatively complete and robust skeleton of a man about 34 years old and rather short in stature (164.5 cm.), with a "male" sciatic notch and average to muscular build. There are slight arthritic exostoses on the facets of lumbar vertebrae (bodies not preserved), a healed fracture of the right seventh rib, and periostitis and arthritic changes of right thumb and little finger, including fusion of the last joint of each (distal phalanges fused to basal or middle phlanges respectively (Plate XXIV). This may be the end result of a wound, with subsequent spread of infection via the flexor tendon sheaths and radial and ulnar bursae at the wrist ("V-phlegmon"). A partial hiatus of the sacral part of the vertebral canal is comparable to those in *91 Ler*, (clan 7), *1 Ler* (clan 5), and *48 Ler* (clan 12), and is important as having a genetic origin (Plate XXI). The rather small and gracile ellipsoid skull vault (Plate IX) has a rounded forehead above a small, angular and slightly tapering face, with rhomboid orbits, wide but projecting nose, and slightly projecting alveolae. Two teeth were lost in life (one with abscess still active), five are carious (in three with active abscesses), while another abscess marks a socket emptied after death; eight alveoli exhibit lesions. Pronounced tooth wear accompanies an edge bite, and there is slight temporomandibular joint arthritis. The field of incisor-canine junction shows disturbance; the lower canines remain unerupted in the jaw, the left upper lateral incisor is absent (a recently lost milk tooth?), and the canine tooth next to it has a sharp white spike next to its posteriolabial corner which may be the root of a milk molar or an aberrant extra tooth. This skull is a representative Classic Mediterranean, type B3.

89 Ler (grave BD-12) is the skeleton of a stocky, muscular, and notably short (158 cm.) man, age about 42, with medium arthritis on bodies and facets of cervical and lumbar vertebrae, slight arthritis of the elbow, and destructive arthritis at the base of the fifth metatarsal, perhaps as a sequel to trauma. The high and wide sphenoid skull vault (Plate VIII) is full enough to appear spheroid from the rear, and has an extremely pinched forehead about a squat hexagonal face (round when alive) with strikingly salient nose and cleft chin. The upper part of the occipital is cut off by a transverse suture to form an interparietal or "Inca" bone, and the inion projects sharply. Though the palate is not preserved, the jaw shows clearly that pronounced tooth wear accompanied an edge bite. Two teeth are carious, there is an abscess in the vacant right first molar alveolus (loose before death and lost in the ground), and three teeth were lost in life. There are traces of enamel grooving. This skull morphology agrees nicely with the Eastern Alpine (C4) trend in the central Aegean and areas to the east and southeast.

91 Ler (grave BD-14) is the reasonably complete skeleton of a robust man of medium size (168.8 cm.) and build, age about 45 (symphyseal phase early 9), with marked arthritis of vertebral bodies. In the cervical region the whole vertebral facet column on the left side is affected, and there is extreme mushroom distortion of facets of cervical vertebrae 4, 5, and 6 (Plate XXV). On the right scapula immediately medial to the glenoid surface is a large perforation, 18 × 22 mm., with edges rounded with inflammation (Plate XXVI). This is clearly the effect of trauma (spear or sword thrust?) most likely from behind, since a thrust through the armpit from the front would have destroyed or severely injured the brachial plexus and axillary blood vessels; the right hand, forearm, and arm show more muscularity than the left and no atrophy as a result of the wound. Sacral fragments indicate a hiatus like that of *88 Ler*.

The strikingly long pentagonoid skull vault (Plate IX) shows a rising vertex slope, flat plane above lambda, and sharp occipital curve. There is a complete metopic suture. The rectangular face, with its low orbits under forbidding browridges, appears virtually square because of the loss of at least 7 mm. of height through marked tooth wear, accompanied by edge bite. There is some alveolar protrusion like that of *82 Ler* and *87 Ler*, and the nasal saliency resembles that of *89 Ler*. Six teeth are carious and seven were lost in life, including, surprisingly, three upper incisors; only the left central one remained and this has dropped out in the ground. The adjacent lateral incisor root in life was replaced by an immense cyst, 12 × 13 × 12 mm. in size, which eroded the alveolar bone through to nose floor, palate, and incisive canal (Plate XXII). In addition to this area of infection there are eight tooth-root abscesses, all at spots where teeth are carious or had been recently lost in life or, in three cases, where caries had reduced teeth to a mere shell or stump. In spite of this extensive infection only 15 alveoli actually show lesions. Medium enamel grooves occur, as do slight cribrous areas in orbit roofs. There is a small osteoma just to the right and in front of bregma. A semicircular break just to the left of obelion looks as if it was made while the bone was still fresh but seems too irregular to be a sword or axe wound at the time of death. This cantankerous skull fits the Upper Paleolithic trend (A2) within Basic White, including the expected parallels with Corded (D2).

The lack of burials of women in this group is surprising.

57 Ler (grave B8-15) is a child between 3 and 4 years old (first molars still in their crypts) probably a boy and not large for his age. The skull vault is unrestorable but the jaw shows a chin height of 21, bigonial 67, bimental 37, and corpus thickness 13 mm. The triangular chin shows neutral projection. Iliac brim is 28, posterior segment 32, and a-p 58 mm.

81 Ler (grave BD-2) is the skeleton of a child just over 2 years old, since the second milk molar has just erupted with its roots still not fully grown. But the limb bones are almost a year behind in size (right humerus 107?, ulna 92, femur 122?, left tibia 107 mm.). This retardation agrees with the clearcut cribrous orbit roofs and pathological thickening of the skull vault (porotic hyperostosis) which may signal homozygous thalassemia.

86 Ler (grave BD-6) is the more complete remains of a somewhat small male infant about 9 months old, in whom the upper milk incisors have erupted and lower incisors are erupting in a jaw whose chin had still not fused. Chin height is only 16, bigonial (58), ramus height and breadth 24 × 19, and corpus thickness 10 mm. Iliac brim (left and right) is 17 and 17, posterior segment 25 and 25, a-p 41 and 41 mm.

236 Ler (burial BF-1) is the very complete skeleton of an infant who died soon after birth, probably female, according to iliac measurements (brim 19, posterior segment 17 mm.). Chin height of the measurable mandible is 11, bicondylar 67, bigonial 50, c-s length 40?, ramus height 17+, ramus breadth 14— mm. The frontal bone shows no signs of pitting, raying, or other indications of pathology.

Grave BD-8 had bones (adult?) too decayed for removal. Grave BD-6 had adult metatarsal bones within it.

8. NORTHERN CLAN: Trench BE (Middle Bronze Age, early to middle phases)

106 Ler (grave BE-2) is the extremely scanty skeleton of a man about 35 years old, fairly robust but rather short, to judge by guessed left radial length of (220 mm.). Left metacarpals 1 to 5 measure (mm.), respectively, 47—, 70—, 68—, 56, and 55; the right talus length is 52; metatarsal 5 measures 73 and 71 mm. on left and right. The frontal fragment shows heavy browridges, the nose root morphology is average, and the minimum frontal breadth, 101?mm., is wide. The cheekbone is large, with strong marginal process. The broken mandible has a chin height of 32; bimental breadth is 34 and corpus thickness, 18 mm.; there is marked gonial angle eversion and a median chin. Tooth wear is pronounced. The right first molar was lost in life, with evidence of an abscess, and a left premolar was also lost. These observations indicate a rugged but rather low face beneath a broad forehead, fitting general Alpine tendencies, possibly type C3.

115 Ler (grave BE-11, late early phase) includes a well-preserved skull and broken skeleton of a medium-sized (164–174 cm.) and fairly robust man about 38 years old, with pronounced arthritic exostoses on bodies of the lumbar vertebrae and arthritic facets also. The ellipsoid skull vault (Plate X) has a deep occiput below slight lambdoid flattening. Strong browridges surmount a big, long hexagonal face with tilted mouth region and the expected drooping orbits and strong aquiline nose, fitting the distribution of chewing forces. Four teeth are carious and five were lost in life, mostly right molars. Of the five abscesses, three occur with carious teeth on the right and two in alveoli of upper left teeth lost in the ground after death. The total of eleven lesions would have been greater if the left side and symphysis of the jaw had been preserved. Marked tooth wear accompanies an apparent edge bite. The skull is Nordic (D1), with personal resemblances to *125, 127,* and *128 Ler,* and to other males in the "early" part of the Northern clan.

70 Ler (grave BE-18) is the skeleton with small skull fragment of a 35-year-old man who may have been the victim of gout. A yellow-purple deposit marks the left elbow and the right big toe is markedly arthritic, with interphalangeal space medially (Plate XXIV) for an inclusion mass such as a tophus. But arthritic hyperostoses occur in all joints around the right talus (Plate XXIV), which shows possible signs of an old neck fracture. Stature was probably tall (171 cm.) and the sacrum has six vertebrae with incipient lumbarization (Plate XVIII).

124 Ler (grave BE-18, early phase) includes the fragmentary right lower extremity and right third metacarpal and capitate of a man, probably short, about 38 years old. The partial talus shows flexion facets and the navicular has a deformed lateral extension with porous surface facing the cuboid.

Femur midshaft a-p and transverse are 28 and 26+ mm.

125 Ler (grave BE-19, first body, early phase) is the fairly complete skeleton of a 44-year-old man (symphysis phase 8) of average build and size (167 cm.) with quite shallow android pelvis (Plate XVIII) showing very strong pubic pecten and marked eversion of the conjoined ramus. The lumbar curve is quite sharp and medium lipping occurs on the lower vertebrae; elsewhere the vertebral arthritis is slight, but there are medium exostoses on the left patella. The basal and middle phalanges of the right second and third toes are fused. The ovoid skull vault (Plate IX) is smoothly curved and rather high, with full forehead surmounting a fairly small and square face, non-projecting, with almost horizontal chewing plane and an unexpectedly salient nose, quite thick in its lower part. An edge bite accompanies marked tooth wear. The left upper first molar is carious and its right partner was lost in life, with two clear abscesses at this and the next alveolus, making three lesion sites in all. But there is marked paradontal disease along the whole right side of the mouth, with lack of tooth wear there, arthritic change of the eminence of the right temporomandibular joint, perhaps from chewing hard on the opposite side, and unusually heavy deposit of tartar on the right tooth rows, as if the man had used some poultice habitually to relieve pain. Third molars were suppressed. Enamel grooving is absent, but the vault shows slight cribra orbitalia and traces of porotic hyperostosis. The skull is Mixed Alpine, type E2.

127 Ler (grave BE-20, early phase) is the quite complete skeleton of a 43-year-old man of average build and stature (167 cm.), with relatively long forearms and six sacral vertebrae marking a sacrum in which the promontory is at the top of S2, and in which S1 appears lumbarized. The pelvic brim is not deep and the lumbosacral angle is large. There remain five lumbar vertebrae showing slight arthritis, with slight exostoses occurring also on the thoracic arches. But the striking pathological change is a peculiar deformity of the right foot (Plate XXIV) accompanied by a 2 to 3 cm. shortening of the right lower extremity; the right talus is rotated laterally and downward in the mortise of the ankle joint so that the medial malleolus contacts its upper surface, and the normal ridged trochlea formation is completely wiped out and replaced by a plain convex surface, as if the ankle joint were completely unstable. The navicular, cuneiforms, and metatarsals seem underdeveloped and the remnants of the calcaneus suggest a healed fracture; the instability may be the end result of complete dislocation with fracture in adolescence. The linear ellipsoid skull vault (Plate X)

has a long vertex and lambdoid planes in profile, a deep occiput, and relatively wide and high sloping forehead above a linear pentagonoid face with high aquiline nose, retreating cheekbones, full mouth, and little chin prominence, producing a convex profile and a total match with Iranian (D4) features. Seven alveoli on the right are lost through breakage, and of the remaining spaces, four on the left show loss of teeth in life; one lower median incisor is both carious and abscessed. Medium tooth wear accompanies a slight overbite; slight enamel grooving occurs.

128 Ler (grave BE-22, early phase) is the skeleton, less complete than *127 Ler*, of a medium-sized (167.4 cm.) man about 44 years old (symphysis phase 8 to 9), probably relatively slight in build. There are slight arthritic exostoses on the bodies of the last two lumbar vertebrae, ossification of the cartilage of the first rib, and a fusion (traumatic?) of the right fibula to the tibia below the knee. The ovoid, almost byrsoid and rather short skull vault (Plate XI), is high enough to be almost circular in profile and ellipsoid in rear view, with deep occiput. The square face has a strong chin and full mouth region below an average nose, with especially high root (suggestion of "Classic Greek" profile) and drooping orbits with retreating cheekbones. Third molars are suppressed, except the lower left, which is carious. There are no other dental lesions at all except slight paradontal inflammation around the second molars and right lower first molar. The teeth show pronounced wear, although a slight overbite is indicated. There are a number of detail resemblances to *127 Ler* and *125 Ler*, but the general skull morphology is European Alpine (C1).

129 Ler (grave BE-23, early phase) is the skeleton of a fairly robust, tall (170.3 cm.) and broad-shouldered man about 38 years old (symphysis phase 7), with high-arched feet (Plate XXIV) and slight arthritic exostoses on lumbar bodies and facets. The large, ovoid and high skull vault (Plate X) is sphenoid in profile, with rising vertex slope and well-marked lambdoid flattening. Below a capacious and sloping forehead the low face is trapezoid in outline because of flaring jowls. A strong triangular chin goes with a rather sloping chewing plane and prominent but short nose. Nine alveolar spaces were lost in the ground through decay, but of the remaining teeth only one (a lower second molar) is carious; enamel grooving is absent. Tooth wear is only medium, but an edge bite was developing. Basic White and Eastern Alpine traits interlock in a Nordic-Alpine (E2) compromise, with considerable resemblance to the less rugged *125 Ler*.

131 Ler (grave BE-25, very early phase) is the skeleton of a very large (178 cm.) youth not over 24, without lipping of lumbar vertebral bodies, but with some extra sharpness of outline of joints of the feet. The pubic pecten is sharp and the iliac crest only just closed. The rather low, linear ellipsoid skull vault (Plate X) is even more warped by earth pressure than the others in this group, but was probably ellipsoid in rear as well as side view, with deep occiput. The rectangular face below the wide forehead has a thin aquiline nose with high root and sloping chewing thrust only for the second and third molars, markedly drooping rhomboid orbits with retreating molars, and a strong triangular chin. One carious tooth, the right first lower molar, is the only dental lesion. Slight tooth wear accompanies slight overbite; enamel grooving is absent. The upper second incisor on the right is congenitally suppressed and a slight Carabelli cusp occurs on the first molars. The orbital roof surface is slightly cribrous. With resemblances to *115 Ler* and to *127 Ler*, the skull morphology fits Danubian-Hallstatt Nordic (D5).

132 Ler (grave BE-26, early phase) is the skeleton of a rugged man of medium size (165.7 cm.) who died at about age 48 (symphysis phase 9) with medium arthritic exostoses on bodies of lumbar vertebrae and facets and on bodies of neck vertebrae, as well as exostoses on the tibia and a definite plaque at the reaction area under the ligament-crossing spot on the femoral neck (Plate XXVI). There are six sacral vertebrae. The ellipsoid vault (Plate XII) is high enough to be ovoid in profile, with bulging cerebellar region and some lambdoid flattening. The relatively broad skull base and forehead anchor the rugged square face, with its flaring jowls and deep square chin. The orbits are rectangular, with little droop, but the nose is thick and heavy and also high, in consonance with a sloping chewing plane. Third molars, except the right lower one, are suppressed and the only lesion is at the left upper second molar, which is destroyed by caries on the medial side, giving rise to a double abscess. Tooth wear is only medium, with edge bite developing. The right articular eminence is slightly arthritic. Enamel grooving is medium. A healed depressed area 8 mm. in diameter and 2 mm. deep lies 3 cm. to the left of bregma on the frontal bone, just where an oppontent's blow might land. Although the general morphology of the skull fits the Upper Paleolithic version of Basic White (A2) there are facial resemblances to *115 Ler*, *127 Ler*, and *131 Ler*.

140 Ler (grave BE-30D, near room 45 containing possible Bubanj pottery, very early phase) is the fairly complete skeleton of a small (161.3 cm.) man of average build, about 27 years old (symphysis phase 5). The true pelvis is shallow and the hips not narrow (Plate XIX). The subtalar joints show medium

lipping, there are flexion ridges on the talar necks matching the facets on the anterior edges of the ankle surfaces of the tibias, and there is a reaction area plaque (Plate XXVI) on the femoral neck, all mountain-country specialties. The lumbar vertebrae show slight arthritic lipping. The broad ovoid skull vault (Plate XI) has a rounded occiput and a steep but pinched forehead above the short hexagonal face, which would have been round in life. The nose is inconspicuous and non-projecting between sloping orbits. Two molar teeth were lost in life, each recently enough to show persisting abscesses, and one molar is carious. Tooth wear averages medium, but is extremely marked on the upper incisors in relation to the edge bite. There are slight enamel grooves. The skull type is Alpine (C3), almost of Mesolithic Borreby form, with some resemblances to *115 Ler*, e.g., in the regions of browridge and the lambdoid suture.

121a Ler (grave BE-17) is the upper central incisor of an adult, possibly female, probably middle-aged since it shows marked wear, and not assignable to any adult in nearby grave 30. The crown measures 8×8, the root 19, and the total height 26 mm.

126 Ler (grave BE-19, second body, early phase) is the skeleton of a girl of age 19 (to 20), with shoulder and skull base mature but iliac crest and vertebral rim epiphyses still completing fusion (Plate XXV), and symphysis still phase 1; there are, however, signs of pregnancy stress at the symphysis (1–3 births?). She was small (142.7 cm.) and slender but not weak. The fifth lumbar transverse process articulates with a 16×29-mm. area of the sacral wing on the right (Plate XXV) and this slight unbalance goes with a notably sharp lumbar curve (indicating a pelvis tilted more than usual) and definite erosion of the bone cortex as a "fossa" at the reaction area of the femoral neck (Angel 1964a) under stress of the joint capsule when the thigh was moved backward, as in running downhill (Plate XXVI). The well-filled skull vault (Plate IX) is small and almost cubical, with deep cerebellar region and with large vertical forehead above a heart-shaped face. Although all four third molars appear to be suppressed, the mouth region protrudes and the chin is neutral; in consonance with this, the chewing plane is tilted. One lower molar is carious and the socket for the left upper premolar shows disease, with an extensive abscess opening into the maxillary sinus which is also irritated; presumably the tooth was carious and started this infection, but it dropped out in the ground. Slight tooth wear accompanies medium overbite; the lateral incisors show slight shovel formation, and enamel grooving is absent. The skull type is Alpine (C2); there are no clear resemblances to *125 Ler*, who shared the burial with her, but there are with *3 Ler* (Clan 5) and *97 Ler* (Clan 6).

137 Ler (grave BE-30, body A, near room 45 containing possible Bubanj pottery, very early phase) is the fairly complete skeleton of a rather short (150.3 cm.) but not too lightly built woman of about age 28 (symphysis phase 5), with broad shoulders and hips and severe enough exostoses and eroded areas on the pubic bones next to the symphysis to indicate many pregnancies, perhaps nine. The quite complete pelvis (Plate XIX) has an adequately large but shallow inlet and large outlet of the birth canal. The sacral angle of 32° and upper sacral angle of 16° indicate a sharper than usual setting of the lumbar vertebrae on the sacrum; and the lumbar vertebral rims, recently fused, show beginnings of arthritic exostoses, as do the arches of the thoracic vertebrae. The femoral neck reaction areas show marked fossae, with erosion of the cortex (Plate XXVI), the tibial plateaus are tilted, and flexion facets on the tibias match neck ridges on the tali at the ankles. Together with platycnemia and strong crests for gluteus maximus, soleus and adductor magnus, these fit rough-country locomotion. The right shoulder joint shows slight arthritic erosion of the lower quarter of the glenoid surface on the scapula and a roughening of the lesser tuberosity and biceps tendon groove on the humerus, as if from some activity involving abduction and then sharp internal rotation of the shoulder, such as throwing the shuttle through the shed of warp on a loom. This might explain the extraordinarily heavy marking for insertion of the scalene muscles (especially the anterior scalene) on the upper surface of the first rib. The smooth ellipsoid skull vault (Plate XI) is quite high, with deep occiput, and a flatter forehead and fuller temporal regions than *127 Ler*, which otherwise is very similar. The wide forehead makes the face heart-shaped with pointed chin, prominent nose, and drooping orbits bounded by large but compressed cheekbones. The teeth are excellent, lacking enamel grooves, with only slight wear and a marked overbite; this is a mechanically "civilized" dentition, but it shows only two carious teeth, both lower molars, and definite tartar deposits near the entrances of parotid and submandibular gland ducts in cheeks and anterior mouth floor. There are big Carabelli cusps on the first and third upper molars (cf. *131 Ler*). Despite some Mixed Alpine traits, the most apt type is Danubian-Hallstatt (D5), with some resemblances to *127 Ler* and *131 Ler*.

138 Ler (grave BE-30, body B, near room 45 containing possible Bubanj pottery, very early phase) is a less complete skeleton of a girl of average stature and light build and age of 18 or slightly less; shoulder and wrist and iliac crest epiphyses are still unfused, knee recently fused, vertebral ring epiphyses starting to join, and symphysis is phase 1. The quite complete pelvis (Plate XIX), has a capacious but strikingly flattened birth canal (platypelloid inlet), and is more tilted than usual (upper sacral angle 15°?), resulting in the expected sharp lumbar curve. Pubic changes indicate perhaps one pregnancy. The talus shows a definite plaque as response to ankle flexion. The fragmentary vault appears to have been short, with bulging temporal regions and low forehead. The facial fragments indicate a tapering form (heart?), with wide mouth and pointed chin. The ramus is short and wide with a very obtuse jaw angle, suggesting a rather tilted chewing plane. The excellent teeth show slight wear and are accompanied by medium overbite. There is a trace of enamel grooves. Third molars have not yet appeared. The preserved parts resemble *139 Ler* and the skull morphology fits Dinaric-Mediterranean (F1), or possibly Alpine (C1), patterns.

139 Ler (grave BE-30, body C, near room 45 containing Bubanj pottery, very early phase) is a woman of about age 28 (symphysis phase 5), short (151.6 cm.) and fairly slender, with pubic indications of about four pregnancies. The lumbar curve is sharp, tibial plateau tilted, and ankle flexion facets clear, but the femur neck reaction area is smooth and unmarked. Arthritis has begun only on the arches of cervical vertebrae. There is an extra facet in the sacroiliac joint just as in *137 Ler*. The small skull vault (Plate XI) is notably short, not low, and rhomboid in top view, with prominent bosses and occiput, and five or six Wormian bones along the lambdoid suture. The rather squat hexagonal face has prominent cheekbones, low orbits, and narrow but non-projecting nose above a mouth with clearcut alveolar projection and such a tilt of the chewing plane and whole mandibular body that there is no chin projection. A slight overbite is accompanied by slight to medium tooth wear and complete lack of dental disease. The left upper first premolar is rotated slightly and there are definite enamel grooves, two on the incisors and one on the canines, suggesting some metabolic disturbance (nutritional?) in late infancy and again in early childhood. There are slight shovel incisors and a peglike upper third molar. The skull morphology tends toward Dinaric-Mediterranean, type F4, with resemblances to *138 Ler*.

243 Ler, *244 Ler*, and *249 Ler* are fragments of young adult female skeletons from BE-443, above grave BE-30 and adjacent to room 45, in which was found possible Bubanj pottery. *249 Ler* includes a left malar and fragmentary skeleton, including left pubic bone indicating a number of pregnancies (five to seven?), vertebrae lacking arthritis, ribs, a left foot with ankle lacking flexion facets, right metatarsals, and hand fragments including a thumb metacarpal (40 mm.). The talus length, breadth, and height measure 46, 38, and 25 mm., respectively, with diversion angle 28°. *243 Ler* includes parts of leg (fibula) and metatarsals, and nasal area fragments. *244 Ler* includes a left rib and metatarsals, and parts of the left hand.

110 Ler (grave BE-6, fairly late early phase) includes fragments of a young child, possibly a boy, 16 to 24 months old (lower second milk molar visible in its crypt and arch of axis vertebra still unfused) with femur length about (130) and humerus (103) mm.

122 Ler (grave BE-18) is the headless skeleton of an adolescent male about 15 years old, not large or tall, and with striking deformity of the left foot (Plate XXIV), apparently talipes valgus, which may be the cause of reduction in shaft thickness of the left femur. The left femur head is starting to fuse ahead of the right one, although the acetabulum and calcaneus tuberosity are still unfused, as are the medial humerus epicondyle and radius head at the elbow.

123 Ler (grave BE-18), probably a girl about 10 years old, with unerupted premolars and second molars and a big Carabelli cusp on the upper first molars (Plate XXI), is small for her apparent age.

130 Ler (grave BE-24) is a young boy about 3½ years old, with complete milk dentition and first molar crown and neck formed, with chin height 21, right humerus length 133, and midshaft diameters 9 × 12, and right ulna 108 mm. These lengths fit modern United States norms for about a year younger. The three pieces of the atlas vertebra are unfused. The striking thing about the partial skull is an eroded area with sharp borders penetrating the inner table of the left temporal bone to join the cells of the left mastoid process (Plate XXIII). The groove for the sigmoid sinus is not apparent, but there is a groove across the petrous base and along the petro-squamous fissure: possibly the blood flow through the main exit on the left side was blocked through infection (of mastoid origin?), producing first thrombosis and then development of collateral channels through the normally minuscule petro-squamous sinus into the middle meningeal veins and through the superior petrosal sinus. There are many lambdoid Wormian bones; it is tempting to speculate that mastoid infection and venous blockage, perhaps with recurring meningitis, may have raised in-tracranial pressure for some time before death. Unfortunately the right side of the skull could not be put together.

133 Ler (grave BE-27) is a young girl 24 to 32 months old, with second milk molar erupting, arches of sacral vertebrae just starting to fuse, and right radius length 72 and right clavicle 61 mm. There is a small Carabelli cusp on the permanent first molar crown. But the striking thing about this undersized girl is the marked porotic hyperostosis (Plate XXIII) of the skull and skeleton. In addition to the thinning, pitting, and raying on the outside of the parietals and occipital, these bones are thickened to about 5–5.5 mm. with unusually porous diploë, as are also the frontal, malar and wing of the sphenoid (10.5 mm. thick). The shaft of each femur, which measure 10 a-p and 10.5 mm. transversely at midshaft, shows some bowing and has a notably thin cortex. The upper ribs are thickened, but the lower ribs and other long-bone fragments do not appear to show thickening. There are no transverse grooves on the teeth. The simplest explanation for these appearances is hemolytic anemia, most probably homozygous thalassemia.

245 Ler (BE-443, above grave 30) is the partial skeleton of an adolescent youth of age 12 to 13 whose upper first molar already shows a large carious lesion filling the crown. The palate and nose are average in size but the long bones are small for the stage of dental development (second molars and premolars erupted) and bone growth (metatarsal heads just fusing). Iliac brim is 39, posterior segment 42, and a-p 79 mm.

246 Ler (BE-443, above grave 30) consists of the lower leg bones of an adolescent, possibly a girl, with epiphyses just fusing (age 14–15).

247 Ler (BE-443, above grave 30) consists of skeletal parts of a child, possibly a boy, about 3 years old, with left fibula 94 mm. long, left and right ischia 30 and 29 and pubic bones 27 and 27 mm.

107 Ler (grave BE-3, late early phase) is a quite large full-term infant, possibly a female, with right clavicle and humerus measuring 46+ and 74 and left femur and tibia measuring 86— and 71 mm. Skull fragments lack pitting, raying, or other signs of disease.

108 Ler (grave BE-4, late early phase) is an infant about 8 months old, including skull fragments without erupted milk teeth and femur shaft 10 × 11 mm.

109 Ler (grave BE-5, late early phase) is an infant, possibly male, with erupted milk incisors, about 11 months old but almost 5 months behind the modern United States norm in size (Plate XXVI).

111 Ler (grave BE-7) is a full-term infant, possibly male, with left and right tibiae 61 and 62, iliac heights 27? and 30, breadths 31?, 34, brim 14? and 20, and posterior breadths 18 and 16 mm.

112 Ler (grave BE-8, late early phase) is a full-term infant, possibly male, with right iliac height 31, breadth 32, brim 14, and posterior breadth 19 mm·

113 Ler (grave BE-9, late early phase) is a full-term girl, slightly below the modern United States norm, with iliac brim and posterior measurements 16 and 17 mm., respectively, and iliac height 31 mm.

113a Ler, from the same burial, is an infant, slightly smaller than *113 Ler*, possibly a girl, with humerus, radius, and tibia lengths of 66, 54, and 64? mm., respectively.

114 Ler (grave BE-10) is the relatively complete skeleton of an infant, possibly a girl, apparently full term but small by modern American standards. Iliac brim and posterior breadths are 16–17 and 17–18 mm., respectively. Chin height is 13+ bicondylar and bigonial 66+ and 53+, bimental 29, gonion-symphysion and condylo-symphysion lengths 30 and 47, ramus breadth and height 17 and 19, and corpus thickness 10 mm. The jaws show thin bone but there are no traces of pitting on vault bones.

116 Ler (grave BE-12) is a fetus probably seventh month and possibly male, with medium raying on the inner surface of the frontal bones and jaw scarcely a shell of bone. The brim and posterior breadths of the ilium are 15— and 16, the ischium 18, and innominate height 45 mm. Humerus and femur lengths of 58? and (69) mm. are about 12% below United States norms for a live infant.

117 Ler (grave BE-13) is a full-term infant, possibly a boy, slightly small, with traces of raying and pitting on the inner frontal surface. Brim and posterior breadth segments of the ilium 14+ and 20 mm. Scapula height is 35— mm.

118 Ler (grave BE-14, double cist) is part of a virtually full-term infant, possibly male, with humerus and femur lengths of 65 and 74 mm., which is average in size by the modern American norm.

119 Ler (grave BE-15) is a premature seventh-month infant, possibly a girl, with traces of raying on the frontal bone and shell-like jaw, and about one-quarter smaller than the United States norm for a live infant. Brim and posterior iliac breadths are 14 and 13 mm.

120 Ler (grave BE-16) is the partial skeleton of a full-term infant, possibly male, its size comparable to United States norms, without sign of pathology on the fragmentary skull.

121 Ler (grave BE-17) is a full-term infant, possibly a girl, large in size, with slight raying and pitting on the inner frontal surface. Brim and posterior iliac breadths are 15 and 17 mm. Scapula height is 37+ mm.

125a Ler (grave BE-19) is the right femur, 76 mm. long, of a newborn infant.

134 Ler (grave BE-28) is a slightly premature (eighth-month) infant, possibly a girl, its size 10% below the United States norm for a newborn infant, the frontal bone shows medium raying and pitting, brim and posterior iliac breadths are 17— and 16 mm., and scapula height is 35 mm.

135 Ler (grave BE-29) is a full-term infant, possibly male, fragmentary, with medium pitting on the inner surface of the frontal bones.

136 Ler (grave BE-30, near room 45 containing Bubanj pottery, early phase) is an infant, probably a boy, about 6 to 9 months old with lower second molar crown complete, and slight thickening of the vault fragments, apparently without osteoporotic thinning of the outer table. Brim and posterior iliac breadth segments are 22 and 24, (24), and 23 mm., respectively, for left and right sides. The femur shows a medium gluteal fossa and medium erosion fossa of the neck (Plate XXVI). The size approximates the United States norm for this age.

248 Ler (BE-443, near grave 30) includes the humerus and tibia, 63 and 64 mm. long, of a newborn infant, somewhat small by United States norms.

Graves BE-21 and BE-31 contained infants whose bones had dissolved.

9. BRIDGE CLAN: Trench DE south end, next to Northern clan (Middle Bronze Age, early middle phase)

174 Ler (grave DE-28) is a man about 34 years old (symphysis phase 6–7), not big (165 cm.) but not weak, with strong pilasters on bowed femora, deeply flanged fibula shafts, somewhat flattened long-bone shafts, and slight ankle flexion facets. The feet have metatarsal shafts concave on the lateral side, especially the fourth and fifth metatarsals, marked erosion at the adjacent lateral ends of the third cuneiform and navicular for insertion of the bifurcating ligament at Chopart's joint, and an 8° lateral angulation of the talus on the line of the rest of the foot (Plate XXIV), as if the man tended to toe in and to walk somewhat on the outer edge of the foot (compare fibular marks for peroneal muscles). There are slight arthritic exostoses on feet, knees, and vertebral arches and medium arthritis of the neck vertebrae. The large and high ovoid skull vault (Plate XII), with big forehead, surmounts a deep-jawed hexagonal face having a high-bridged and big nose and tilted jaw with surprisingly obtuse angle and lacking good markings for the chewing muscles. The cheekbones similarly are shallow and have deep canine fossae probably as a result of maxillary sinus inflammation caused by diseased teeth.

At the time of death there were three active abscesses and definite paradontal disease. In life 13 teeth were lost, mostly molars but including also the upper lateral incisors, left canine, and an upper and a lower premolar; 5 of the remaining teeth are carious, including the lower incisors and upper right canine. Tooth wear is pronounced except where teeth are unopposed, indicating the very early loss of some teeth. The bite has clearly shifted from an edge bite to an underbite. Enamel grooving is absent, and there is no apparent reason for this peculiarly poor dentition. The skull as a whole approaches the type E2 Mixed Alpine norm, with many Dinaroid (F2) traits.

238 Ler (grave DE-71, room AR, early middle phase) is the fragmentary skeleton of a man about 39 years old (symphysis early phase 8), very small (159.7 cm.) but with unusually strong pectoralis major and deltoid insertions and perceptible flattening of humerus and tibia shafts. The ankles show flexion facets, and the feet show slight and the lumbar vertebrae medium arthritic exostoses. There are large eroded areas on the calcanei beside and behind the subtalar joints (Plate XXIV). The long ovoid skull vault (Plate XII) has a prominent and sharply curved occiput and strong browridges. The face was probably small, cheekbones shallow, and teeth poor; the 17 preserved alveolae show 5 teeth lost in life and 3 (upper lateral incisor, canine, and adjacent premolar) with both caries and periapical abscesses of good size. Tooth wear is very marked. This skull fits the Mediterranean (B1) norm.

239 Ler (grave DE-72, room AR, adjoining DE-71) is a man about 36 years old (symphysis phase 7), not tall (165.8 cm.) and average in build. There is a good femoral pilaster but the long bones are not flattened except for the tibia, which also shows retroversion at the knee and ankle flexion facets. The humerus is bowed inward. Vertebral arches show beginning arthritis, the metacarpo-phalangeal joint of the left thumb is flattened and arthritic, probably as a result of injury (dislocation?), and the feet show inflammation on the calcanei near the subtalar joints, as in *238 Ler*. The small, short ellipsoid skull vault (Plate XII) is rather boxlike, with a steep but pinched

forehead above strong browridges and complete metopic suture running along a strong median frontal crest. The face is hexagonal in outline, with deep mouth region, sloping jaw with open angles, prominent nose, and shallow cheekbones, rather like *174 Ler*. The teeth are in better condition than in *174 Ler*; only five teeth (molars) were lost in life, of which one lower molar alveolus still shows the abscess which loosened the tooth, with one carious molar above this. Enamel grooves are perceptible. Tooth wear is medium, as is the degree of overbite. The skull form is Alpine type C1 with minor Dinaroid (F2) traits.

176 Ler (grave DE-30) is a child, probably a boy, about 2 years old (second milk molars just level with gumline) but in body size nearer to American norms for 1 year than to those for 2 years. Brim and posterior iliac breadths are 23 and 27 mm., and the notch is medium. The pentogonoid skull vault (Plate XIII) shows asymmetric flattening of the right occiput and left frontal and parietal, so that the skull leans toward the right; this is exaggerated by some postmortem distortion. The skull vault has a low forehead and prominent occiput, and the face is long-jawed, suggesting Mediterranean type B2 norms; it would be easy to argue relationship to *174 Ler* and *238 Ler*. There are no clear signs of disease. The first permanent molar crown is formed down to the neck.

186 Ler (grave DE-41) is the partial skeleton of a child, possibly a boy, about 2½ years old (second milk molars erupted but roots not yet complete), but almost a year behind the modern American norm in size. Brim and posterior iliac breadths are about 23 and 30 mm. Chin height is 21 and ramus breadth and height, 24 and 27 mm.

205a Ler (grave DE-68a) is the central part of a frontal bone of a child between 5 and 10 years old.

174a Ler (grave DE-28) consists of the ilium of a child, probably a girl, about 2 years old. Brim and posterior breadth segments are each 23 mm., the sciatic notch is wide, and iliac breadth (from anterior to posterior superior spine) 59 mm.

165 Ler (grave DE-18) is a nearly full-term infant, possibly female, only slightly below modern American norms in size. Brim and posterior iliac breadths are 15+ and 17— mm., with wide notch.

179 Ler (grave DE-33) is a full-term boy baby, of average size by modern American norms, and without raying or pitting of the preserved frontal bones. Brim and posterior iliac breadths are 15 and 17+ and scapula height 33 mm. Chin height is 14, bicondylar and bigonial breadths 71 and 57, and ramus breadth and height 16 and 17 mm.

193 Ler (grave DE-50, early middle phase) is an infant, possibly a boy, about 1–2 months old, and apparently large for this age; the mandibular symphysis is fused and milk-tooth crowns formed, but with no signs of eruption. Brim and posterior iliac segments are 17 and 21? mm. The pentagonoid skull vault (Plate XIII) is relatively wide, with full temporal regions and forehead and typical infantile bulging of forehead and cerebellar regions; the bregmatic fontanelle is still wide open (42 mm. along the sutures and 18 mm. across the angles). A very prominent pointed nasal spine and rather light jaw mark the face, and the typical infantile skull morphology inevitably fits the Mixed Alpine type E1, with little indication of the direction of divergence with growth.

195 Ler (grave DE-52) is an infant, nearly full term, possibly a girl, about the same size as modern American infants at birth. Brim and posterior iliac segments are 16— and 15 mm. Chin height is 12, bicondylar and bigonial breadths 60? and 46, bimental 26, condylo-symphyseal length 43, and jaw ramus breadth and height 16 and 20 mm.

204 Ler (grave DE-64) is an infant, possible male, between 8 and 11 months old, with the incisor teeth erupted and the first molars ready to erupt, and slightly larger than the modern American average for 6 months. Brim and posterior iliac segments are 19 and 26 mm., and the sciatic notch is of medium width. Chin height is 19, bicondylar and bigonial breadths 78 and 63, bimental 32?, corpus thickness 11, and jaw ramus breadth and height 20 and 25 mm. There is striking pathological change; the long bones in general are thicker than normal by about 10% and in particular the right humerus (Plate XXIII) is thickened and contains an inner shell of bone representing the original unremodelled shaft and joined to the outer bone cortex by fine trabeculae which span a space of 1–2 mm.; the parietal bone fragments are slightly thickened and show irregular granulation on the internal surface, and the frontal bone shows cribra orbitalia. These are indications of a hemolytic anemia (or other blood disease), most plausibly thalassemia; scorbutic rickets (Barlow's disease) is less likely in a Mediterranean context.

205 Ler (grave DE-68) is an apparently premature (seventh month) infant possibly a boy, small, with medium sciatic notch, femora lengths 72?, and tibia 62 mm., a little below the American norm.

206 Ler (grave DE-70) is an infant of average size by modern American standards and possibly a full-term boy, with ischial length 17+, radius 53+, and tibia 66 mm. Raying and pitting occurs on the internal surfaces of parietal and occipital, on the orbits, and outer surface of the cheekbones (anemia?).

Graves DE-49 and DE-69 contained adults; graves DE-65, DE-66, and DE-67 contained infants.

10. EASTERN CLAN: Trench DE northeast (Middle Bronze Age, middle to late phases)

164 Ler (grave DE-17) includes only parts of the skull and jaw of a massive man, about 30 years old. The chin height is 40+, corpus thickness of the jaw 16, and the length of the lower molar tooth row 35 mm.

175 Ler (grave DE-29, early middle phase) is a man about 35 years old, of average size (165.7 cm.) and build, with strong thigh and leg muscle attachments, shaft flattening of humerus and tibia, retroversion at knee, and flexion facets at ankle. The vertebral arches show slight exostoses, but arthritis is particularly clear on the bodies of the lower cervical vertebrae, with signs of injury to the disk between C6 and C7. The left fibula shows medium periostitis on the outer aspect of lower half of its shaft, most marked about the middle, possibly a result of infection (wound?). The ovoid skull vault (Plate XIII) apparently was linear and smooth, surmounting a heart-shaped face that is small and tapering, with prominent pointed chin below a small mouth with definite overbite, compressed cheekbones, and a notably wide, coarse nose. In life, 2 lower molars were lost; 6 teeth are carious (2 of these with abscesses), including 2 upper incisors reduced to stumps and an upper first molar reduced to a mere shell. This illustrates graphically the process of tooth infection, periapical abscess formation, subsequent paradontal inflammation, and loss. Despite the marked degree of wear, medium overbite has persisted, lower incisors have fairly heavy tartar, and paradontal disease with absorption marks the alveoli. Enamel grooves are slight. This skull is Mediterranean in form (B1) with Basic White type A3 traits.

181 Ler (grave DE-35, late early phase) is a small (163.5 cm.) but fairly muscular man about 42 years old (symphysis phase 8), average in body build, with particularly strong pectoralis-major markings and big clavicles, and with ankle flexion facets. Noteworthy are the pathologies of the vertebral column: separated neural arch of the fifth lumbar vertebra, with some indication of spondylolisthesis (sacrum incomplete, however); pronounced exostoses of vertebral bodies (almost certainly from disk collapse) in lumbar (Plate XXV), lower thoracic, and cervical regions, with pancake deformation of the cervical facets especially, arthritis of the odontoid process, and fusion of the axis with C3 and of C7 with T1 vertebrae (Plate XXV). Taken with the arthritic exostoses on the sternum and on the hand (thumb especially), this suggests a smith or other occupation, not necessarily servile, involving the heavy use of the torso and arms. The almost byrsoid, rather small, smooth, heavy, and very high skull vault (Plate XIII) surmounts a squat face with low orbits, rather shallow but prominent chin, and extraordinarily prominant, beaky, thin nose. In life, 19 teeth were lost, with 5 active abscesses still clear at sites of loss and considerable paradontal disease and alveolar absorption. The 5 remaining teeth in apposition show pronounced wear and 3 others less wear (5 dropped out in the ground after death). The bite was originally a medium overbite, but strong wear facets on the lateral (distal) side of the right upper first incisor, on the outside (labiomesial) of the right upper canine and on the inside (linguodistal) of the corresponding lower canine indicate a peculiar crossbite with the jaw pushing out and to the right. This developed as the teeth were lost; the teeth in the left premolar region seem to have dropped out very soon before death. But dental infection seems a less likely cause of death than violence. A gap in the right parietal bone 3 × 6 cm. in size (Plate XXII) extends down in a vertical stripe from the top over the right parietal boss and has a 1 cm. vertical "crease" at the upper posterior end as if from a heavy blow when the bone was still fresh; one of the loose fragments is 26 × 31 mm. in size and the inner table is split off and slightly curled as if by an imploding force. The type is perhaps a little closer to Basic White type A3 than to the Iranian-Mediterranean (D3) variant that approximates the so-called "Cappadocian" type which is as much at home in Anatolia (cf. Karataş, Angel 1968) as in the Aegean.

178 Ler (grave DE-32, late middle phase) is a medium-short (156.2 cm.) but stocky and wide-hipped woman about 33 years old (symphysis phase 6), with flattened long-bone shafts, normal feet with slight ankle flexion facets (Plate XXIV), and marked stress-erosion fossae on the femoral neck. But in spite of this indication of stress in hip extension and the wide pelvic inlet (Plate XX), the preserved lower part of the pubic symphysis has only traces of exostoses from pregnancy stress (one or two births?). There are likewise only traces of arthritic exostosis on lumbar and cervical arches. The acromial process was separately ossified. The low and broad ovoid, almost byrsoid, skull vault (Plate XIV) has bulging cerebellar and temporal regions combined with narrow skull base and heart-shaped face having a prominent, pointed chin and rather thin nose; the face slightly

resembles that of *175 Ler*. In life, 9 teeth were lost, all molars, and 3 of the rest are carious, including an upper second incisor with developing abscess; 6 dropped out after death. Heavy tartar along the right upper cheek teeth (lowers lost) and on the lower incisors is accompanied by paradontal disease. Slight tooth wear accompanies a slight overbite. A depressed rounded area 16 mm. in diameter and 3 cm. to the left of bregma shows periostitis and contains a small absorption hole through the inner table; this may be traumatic, or more plausibly the result of pressure from a sebaceous cyst in the scalp. The skull is Alpine type C1 with some Mediterranean face traits.

182 Ler (grave DE-36) is a fairly tall (163 cm.), robust, and wide-hipped woman of about 36 (symphysis phase 7) with some long bone flattening, tibial retroversion at the knee, and ankle flexion facets. A rather tilted pelvis goes with arthritis of the lumbosacral joints, a sharp lumbar curve, as well as medium arthritic exostoses of lower lumbar and cervical vertebrae, a Schmorl herniation pit in the upper surface of L_4, and arthritis of the atlas-odontoid joint. The pelvic inlet is fully as deep as in healthy modern Americans (Plate XX) and very marked "pregnancy exostoses" suggest many births (up to 10?). The attachment for the adductor longus is strong and comes up high on the symphysis, as in *178 Ler*. The large, low, relatively wide skull vault (Plate XIV) is ovoid-byrsoid in form, with full temporal regions, and prominent occiput. The forehead shows a completely retained metopic suture. The long hexagonal face has an extremely prominent chin below a wide mouth and thin, high, beaky nose which follows down the line of the forehead almost in the unreal "Classic profile." In life, 8 teeth were lost, 1 with a still active abscess; 7 teeth are carious, of which 3 with abscesses have become reduced to mere shells, showing the next stage to loss. Marked wear accompanies an edge bite. Slight enamel grooves occur, the molar roots are preculiarly bowed, and the remaining upper third molar is diverted labially and backward. Both temporomandibular joints are arthritic, including the condyles, but with little deformity except for a marked forward extension of the joint, with an accompanying porous inflammation reaction. A sharply depressed groove just above the outer rim of the right orbit, a depressed circle 7 mm. in diameter just medial to and above the right frontal boss, and a shallow depression 9 mm. in diameter on the left parietal 4 cm. diagonally behind bregma all appear to be healed scars from blows and led to "the Amazon" as a nickname. The skull is type F3 Dinaroid with obvious Iranian (D4) and Eastern Alpine (C5) traits.

196 Ler (grave DE-53, middle phase) is the partial skeleton of a small woman who died between age 40 and 45 (sagittal suture closed and slight acromial age plaque) with medium arthritic exostoses at acromio-clavicular and coraco-clavicular joint attachments, lumbar and cervical arthritis (C4 has mushroom-shaped facets), and true osteoporosis with signs of Schmorl herniation and disk atrophy in lower thoracic region. Skull fragments show a very full temporal region, divided browridges, low face, pointed chin, and big and pointed nasal spine. With 28 alveolae preserved, 10 teeth were lost in life (one upper incisor still showing its abscess of exfoliation) and 5 were carious (2 mere shells, 1 with abscess). The lower incisors are crowded and tartar-encumbered, and the canines, in particular, show sharp enamel grooves suggesting growth disturbance (malnutrition or illness) at age 4 to 5. Medium wear accompanies medium overbite, and, as in *182 Ler*, the temporomandibular joint shows medium arthritis, with pitted erosion of the articular eminence. Many of the traits of this skull are Alpine; type E1 (Mixed Alpine) seems closest.

200 Ler (grave DE-59, middle phase) is a stocky little woman of about 25 or less (skull sutures just starting to close) with tilted tibia head and well-marked flexion facets at the ankle. There is no arthritis. The linear ovoid and high skull vault (Plate XIV) is ellipsoid in rear view, with very deep occiput and flat sides. The face appears to have had compressed cheekbones and a rather long jaw with deep and pointed chin. With 24 alveoli present and 5 teeth lost in the ground, there are 3 carious teeth and no loss or abscesses at all. A medium overbite accompanies slight tooth wear, and there are no enamel grooves. The skull trait grouping is Iranian-Mediterranean (D3).

201 Ler (grave DE-60, early middle phase) is a medium-short (154.2 cm.) 31-year-old (symphysis just phase 6) woman with broad pelvis, flattened shins and ankle flexion facets. A rather low angle of sacral tilt (almost horizontal) accompanies a relatively straight lumbar curve and consequent drastic lumbosacral angulation, with the L_5 transverse process articulating with the left sacral ala, and with arthritis of lumbar facets and bodies. There is also medium cervical arthritis, with the axis fused to C_3 by their facet joints and laminae. The arthritis appears to be a result of breakdown of the disk between T_{11} and T_{12}. The unexpectedly deep (anthropoid outline) pelvic inlet (Plate XX), as in *182 Ler*, goes with pubic signs of a number of pregnancies (at least 4?) and a lateral spiking of the left pubic tubercle suggesting stress on the inguinal ligament (femoral hernia?). Small vault fragments suggest open coronal and sagittal sutures and a medium mastoid process. The relatively more com-

plete mouth region shows a pointed chin and slight overbite, with medium tooth wear. In life, 10 teeth were lost (mostly molars), and 2 are carious, out of 32 preserved alveoli, with no teeth lost after death. Chin height is 28, bigonial 90, bimental 44, and gonion-symphysion length (73) mm.

154 Ler (grave DE-5) includes the broken skull and partial skeleton of a young child about 14 months old, possibly female. There are no clear pathologic signs. Bimental breadth is 34, ramus height 26—, and corpus thickness of the jaw 11 mm. Femur length is about (120), and a-p and transverse diameters are 9 and 10 at subtrochanteric level and 8 and 8 + mm. at middle level, indicating a rather slender and small bone.

157 Ler (grave DE-9) consists mainly of skull fragments of a child, possibly a boy, about 2 years old.

158 Ler (grave DE-10, late phase) is a child not large in size, 12 to 14 months old, possibly female, with incisors completely erupted.

167 Ler (grave DE-21, middle phase) includes only skull fragments of a child, possibly a boy, about 2 years old or more, with second milk molars erupted. Chin height is 20, bigonial 67, and ramus breadth and height 19+ and 26 mm. Upper and lower permanent molar crowns are not small (10.8 × 11.4 and 12.0 × 10.8 mm.).

168 Ler (grave DE-22) is a child, probably a boy 18 to 20 months old and comparable in size to modern American standards for that age. The arches of the vertebrae have fused at the spines, and the second milk molar is visible in its crypt. Iliac brim and posterior segments are 22 and 29 mm. There is no pathology.

170 Ler (grave DE-24) is a child about 24 to 27 months old, possibly male, quite small by American standards for this age, and lacking the skull. Brim and posterior iliac segments are 23 and 30 mm.

173 Ler (grave DE-27, late middle phase) is a child about 5 years old, probably male, with first molars erupted (roots incomplete), unfused odontoid and open atlas vertebra, but cervical arches fused to bodies and lumbar and thoracic just fusing. The brim and posterior iliac breadths are 29? and 36? mm., and the general dimensions are about two years smaller than those of the apparent age, without any obvious pathology. There are peculiar pocklike pits, fairly regularly spaced, eroding the inner table on parietal and frontal bone fragments; these may be from some peculiar soil action after death.

177 Ler (grave DE-31) is probably a girl, about age two but small by United States norms for this age, with second milk molar just erupting, a wide sciatic notch, and brim and posterior iliac breadths 25 and (25) mm. Chin height is 20 and bimental 35 mm.

180 Ler (grave DE-34) consists of skull and other fragments of a child about 16 months old, possibly female, with the first milk molar erupted and the crown of the second formed.

203 Ler (grave DE-63), is probably a girl, almost 4 years old, with the crown of the first permanent molar visible in its crypt, the lumbar vertebral arches fused to their bodies, but the thoracic and cervical unfused. In size she is about at the American standard for 2 years old. Brim and posterior iliac segments are 28+ and 31 mm., the sciatic notch is wide, and there is a visible preauricular sulcus. The pentagonoid skull vault (Plate XIV) is high and very well filled, with a deep occiput and broad and bulging frontal above a heart-shaped face, with straight profile and the beginning of a strong chin. The teeth show slight wear and there is a huge Carabelli cusp on the upper milk molars. The parietals show raying and traces of healed porotic hyperostosis, much less than in the other Lerna children who appear actually thalassemic; this might be a heterozygote, or the cause may be different. The striking pathology is a circular exostosis developed in the right auditory meatus, almost closing it; this is most unusual in a child, and its cause is unknown. The skull has enough fullness to approximate Mixed Alpine (E1) more than Basic White, type A1.

150 Ler (grave DE-1, L.H. I–II) is a boy about 7 months old (crowns of milk molars completely formed) and average in size by American standards for this age. Brim and posterior segments of the ilium measure 21 and (25) mm.

150a Ler (from the same grave as *150 Ler*) is the right frontal bone of an older infant, plausibly about 12 months old.

151 Ler (grave DE-2, late M.H.) is a baby 6 to 10 months old, probably female, lacking skull parts, average in size by modern American standards. Iliac brim and posterior segment breadths are 19 and 22+ mm., and the sciatic notch is wide.

152 Ler (grave DE-3) is a full-term infant, possibly male, average in size. Only fragments of skull exist. Brim and posterior iliac breadths are 12 and 15 mm.

155 Ler (grave DE-6, late phase) is a baby possibly male, with the crowns of canine and first molar formed, suggesting an age of 3 to 6 months. The left femur is 92— long, and the a-p and transverse subtrochanteric and midshaft diameters are 8+ and 9, 7+ and 9— mm., respectively. Brim and posterior iliac segments are 19+ and (17) mm., and the sciatic notch is medium.

156 Ler (grave DE-8) is a full-term infant, possibly male, not small. Humerus length is 72, clavicle length 45, and scapula height and breadth (36) and (30) mm.

159 Ler (grave DE-11) is a newborn infant, possibly female, of good size. Brim and posterior iliac segments measure 17 and 19+ mm. and the sciatic notch is wide.

160 Ler (grave DE-12, late middle phase) is a full-term baby, possibly male, without obvious pathology though rather small. Brim and posterior iliac segments are 15 and 15 mm.

161 Ler (grave DE-13) is an almost full-term fetus or infant, possibly a girl, with iliac brim 13?, total breadth 32 mm., and medium notch. Right humerus and femur measure 62—? and 73 mm.

162 Ler (grave DE-14, late middle phase) is a baby about 1 month old, possibly male, of normal size by American standards, noteworthy for a swelling 7 mm. thick at the junction of middle and outer thirds of the right clavicle, apparently from the healing process of a fracture (at birth?). Brim and posterior segments of the ilium are 16 and 18 mm. Chin height is 16, bicondylar and bigonial 73? and 63?, and ramus height and breadth 21— and 16— mm.

163 Ler (grave DE-15, late phase) is a slightly premature infant, possibly female, not strikingly small or pathological. Brim and posterior iliac breadths are 16+ and 16 mm.

166 Ler (grave DE-19, late middle phase is a full-term infant, possibly male, fairly large. Brim and posterior iliac segments are 16— and 18 mm.

169 Ler (grave DE-23, rather late phase) is a full-term infant, possibly male, fairly large in size, with slight raying on the inner surface of the fragments of vault bones. Brim and posterior segments of the ilium are 14? and 20 mm.

202 Ler (grave DE-62, middle phase) is a newborn infant, possibly male, of a size about equal to the American average for this age, with chin starting to fuse and molar crowns formed. Both radius and tibia are more bowed than usual and the ends of the leg bones show extra lipping, as if from some growth disturbance (antigenic blood reaction or thalassemia or jaundice?). Brim and posterior iliac segments are 16 and 19 mm.

Graves DE-7, DE-20, and DE-61 contained infants; the contents of graves DE-16 and DE-58 are uncertain.

11. PLAIN CLAN: Trench DE central part (Middle Bronze Age, late phase)

185 Ler (grave DE-40) is a rather short (160.4 cm.) man about 30 to 34 years old and average in build, without flattening of long-bone shafts but with tilted tibial head and ankle flexion facets strongly developed. Slight arthritic exostoses occur on vertebral facets and on metacarpal bases. But the striking pathology is a tumor of the head of the left fibula; this measures $12 \times 17 \times 21$ mm., projects postero-medio-inferiorly, and is composed of fairly normal spongy trabeculae under a very thin cortex. It appears benign and may be a reaction to trauma, possibly myositis ossificans. The corresponding tibia has an unusually deep groove for the middle insertion of the semi-membranosus ("deep goosefoot") on the medial side. The small, ovoid, rather high skull vault (Plate XV) has a prominent and sharply curved occiput and is more linear than the photograph shows because of post-mortem warping on the incomplete left side. The rectangular and rather small face has a thin nose above a relatively large and toothy mouth with somewhat tilted chewing plane and short ramus. The teeth are perfect; three dropped out in the ground and two alveoli are broken away. A medium overbite accompanies slight tooth wear, and enamel grooves are absent. The skull is morphologically Mediterranean (B1) with Iranian (D3) traits.

189 Ler (grave DE-45) is a man about 38 years old, of short-medium stature (165.7 cm.) and average build except for sacralization of L_5, with medium exostoses on lumbar vertebral bodies, arthritic mushrooming of some articular facets in the neck (right C_{3-4} and left C_{4-5}), and slight ulnar arthritis at the wrist. With this goes a cauliflower exostosis on the radial side of the base of the left fifth metacarpal, fitting an area of periostitis on the fourth, and suggesting trauma some time before death. There is a gaping split which runs across the back of the head just above lambda, with an area of crushing above and in front of this on the left parietal and a punched-in area, over 1 cm. across, behind the right parietal boss. The rather sharp, "woody" appearance of the broken edges suggests a blow from the right while the head was resting on the ground on its left side,

either soon after or just before death. The long and high, smooth ellipsoid skull vault (Plate XV) has a deep occiput and a high forehead above a small rectangular face with rugged but non-projecting cheekbones, small nose, and toothy and relatively large mouth region. In life, 3 teeth were lost (1 alveolus abscessed), and 3 are carious, 1 of these being only two root shells with a periapical abscess. Enamel grooves are slight, the right upper incisors are slightly rotated, and a slight overbite accompanies medium tooth wear. The left temporomandibular joint shows slight arthritis. The skull morphology is Basic White, type A2, with Iranian-Mediterranean (D3) details.

198 Ler (grave DE-55, late middle phase) is a man of about 35 (symphysis phase 6–7), medium tall (170 cm.), robust, and broad-shouldered, with non-flattened bone shafts, rather sharp lumbar curve, and very marked flexion facets at the ankle joints. There is no arthritis on vertebral column or hands, but the right clavicle is thickened and arthritic at the sternoclavicular joint. The ovoid skull vault (Plate XV) is not large but has relatively flat sides and deep occiput, ellipsoid in rear view, with sloping forehead and pentagonoid outline in profile. The long rectangular face has cheekbones compressed laterally but prominent anteriorly in support of the high-bridged, long nose probably beaky in profile (nasalia lost). The lower face has a retreating profile, with a toothy but tilted mouth region and related short jaw ramus. The dentition is perfect, with slight (to medium) tooth wear accompanying a slight overbite. Transverse grooves mark the enamel of canines, incisors, and first molars at intervals suggesting growth disturbance (malnutrition?) at age three and probably also at four and five. The skull form is Iranian (D4), with some Mediterranean (B1) gracility, a trend also occurring at Karataş.

192 Ler (grave DE-48, late phase) is a short (150.9 cm.) but fairly robust woman about 27 years old (symphysis phase 5—) with flattened bone shafts, tibia tilt at the knee, and definite ankle flexion facets. Lumbar and sacral curves are fairly sharp and exostoses occur on lumbar facets and on the upper bodies of L_4 and L_5 but not elsewhere on the column. Indications of pregnancy are equivocal. The pentagonoid skull vault (Plate XV) has a deep occiput, ellipsoid in rear view, and rather sloping forehead and pentagonoid vault profile. The long hexagonal face has tilted orbits and very wide and rather coarse concave nose above a prognathous mouth with pointed chin, and a long jaw with short ramus. The right lower third molar was lost in life and two others are carious; one of these, a second molar above the lost tooth, is a mere shell. Medium wear accompanies a slight overbite, and enamel grooves are slight. The morphology is Mediterranean Angular (B2) with Iranian and Alpine traits; she could be the offspring of one of the Eastern clan (e.g., *178 Ler*).

184 Ler (grave DE-39, very late phase) is a child about 6 years old, probably a boy, with first permanent molars showing roots about one-third formed and the crowns of upper incisors also formed. Browridges are small. The right femur length is 208 mm., and a-p and transverse diameters at subtrochanteric and midshaft levels are 13 and 18, and 12 and 13 mm., respectively, indicating a size less by two years than the American norm for that age.

187 Ler (grave DE-42) is a rather small infant, possibly female, about 14 months old, with the first upper milk molar about to erupt and the crown of the second formed, and the bregmatic fontanelle about to finish closing. The iliac brim measurement is (18) mm. and the sciatic notch appears medium wide.

190 Ler (grave DE-46) is a child, possibly a boy, about 2½ years old, with second milk molar erupted (roots almost complete), small browridges, and chin height 22 mm. Jaw length is 78?, bigonial breadth (67), and ramus breadth and height 25 and 30 mm. Brim and posterior iliac segments are 24 and 30 mm., with medium notch. Long bones are slender and almost a year behind the modern American size norms.

101 Ler (grave DE-37) is an apparently premature (eighth month?) infant, possibly female, with humerus length 64+, radius 51, tibia 63+, iliac breadth 36, posterior segment 17 mm., and the sciatic notch wide.

153 Ler (grave DE-4) is a full-term infant, possibly male, about average in size by modern American standards, with only fragments of skull. Brim and posterior iliac segments are 14 and 18 mm., and the sciatic notch is medium.

171 Ler (grave DE-25, late phase) is a full-term infant, possibly female, of average size, by modern American standards, with slight raying and markings for blood vessels on the internal surface of the frontal bone. Chin height is 12, bigonial breadth 50, and ramus breadth 15 mm. Brim and posterior iliac breadths are 16 and 16 mm., and the sciatic notch is wide.

172 Ler (grave DE-26, late phase) is an almost full-term (eighth month?) infant, possibly a boy, whose skull fragments seem very thin, though normal. Chin height is only 11 and ramus breadth and height 15 and 16 mm. The left humerus and femur lengths are 62 and 76, iliac breadth is 36, pubic length 13?,

and scapula height and breadth 35 and 29 mm. Brim and posterior iliac segments are 14 and 16 mm., with the sciatic notch medium.

183 Ler (grave DE-38) is a newborn infant, possibly a boy of average size without raying or pitting on skull fragments, though some long bones have flaring ends and tibiae seem more bowed than usual. Chin height is 11, bicondylar jaw breadth 65, and ramus breadth and height 15 and 19 mm. Brim and posterior iliac breadths are 13 and 16 mm., with sciatic notch medium.

188 Ler (grave DE-43, late phase) is an almost full-term (eighth month?) infant, possibly male, not small and without pathology though the vault fragments are thin and the jaw a shell. The brim and posterior iliac breadths are 14 and 17 mm., and the sciatic notch medium.

191 Ler (grave DE-47, late phase) is a virtually full-term infant, possibly a girl, of average size by modern American standards, with wide sciatic notch and brim and posterior iliac segments 14 and 16 mm.

194 Ler (grave DE-51, late phase) is a full-term infant, possibly male, of good size. Brim and posterior iliac segments measure 16 and 21 mm.

197 Ler (grave DE-54) is a full-term infant, possibly male, normal in appearance. Brim and posterior iliac breadths approximate (13) and 20 mm.

199 Ler (grave DE-57) is a full-term infant, possibly female, of normal size. Brim and posterior iliac breadths are 17 and 14 mm.

Grave DE-44 had two or three tiny fragments of skeleton not saved, together with Late Helladic sherds; grave DE-56, although it produced no skeleton, is apparently that of an infant.

12. Sea Clan: Trench D (Middle Bronze Age, middle to very late phase)

20 Ler (grave D-1, late middle phase) consists in a partial right humerus and a warped skull of a 30-year-old male. The well-filled, spheroid, and large vault (Plate XVI) has a steep wide forehead above a notably short hexagonal face, very orthognathous, with projecting median chin and an edge bite accompanying worn teeth. The nose is not wide and the skull as a whole (type C1) resembles both Neolithic Cypriote and Mesolithic European Alpine varieties. Teeth show a trace of transverse enamel grooves and third molars are suppressed, except for upper right, lower left first molar was lost in life. An edge bite accompanies marked tooth wear.

23 Ler (grave D-4, late middle phase), an old man of rather short stature (162.3 cm.) and stocky build, has somewhat flattened long-bone shafts, small hands with slight arthritis, (e.g., exostoses at quadriceps insertion), and disk breakdown with more cervical (medium, Plate XXV) than lumbar arthritis. The large, thick-walled, and long pentagonoid skull vault (Plate XVIII) has a rising vertex profile, pentagonoid in side view, a short square face, fairly deep jaw with wide ramus, horizontal orbits, and average nose with high root. He resembles *52 Ler*, who could be his grandfather. In life, 25 teeth were lost and some paradontal inflammation and absorption surrounds the remaining teeth. The skull type (A4) is comparable with Minoans but also with some Basic White elements, as in the Neolithic population at Nea Nikomedeia and at Hageorgitika. A "wound" depression shows clearly on the forehead, 4 cm. above the left orbit.

28 Ler (grave D-9, late middle phase) is a middle-aged (symphysis phase 8, late) man of medium-tall height (169.7 cm.) with average bone shafts and medium arthritis of hands and of lumbar vertebrae. The ovoid and fairly rugged skull vault (Plate XVII) surmounts a broad hexagonal face with horizontal orbits, average nose, and shallow mouth in which nine teeth were lost in life (mainly upper premolars and canines), one is abscessed (lower central incisor), and several show paradontal disease (upper molars). Third molars are suppressed. There is a trace of enamel striation. Tooth wear is pronounced, except on upper molars without lowers to oppose them. The skull type (A3) could be from the Early Bronze Age.

29 Ler (grave D-10, L.H. I) is a middle-aged skeleton (possibly age 35) too incomplete for measurement.

48 Ler (grave D-18, middle M.H.) is a short and stocky male about 21 years old (symphysis phase 2; pelvic epiphyses fusing, medial clavicle unfused) with typical male pelvis (Plate XXI) flattened leg bones, ankle flexion facets, tilted knee, femur reaction area at hip, as signs of rough-country living or very active use. A disk injury produced slight cervical arthritis, absent elsewhere, and a slight sacral hiatus occurs (S_2 downward, Plate XXI) as in the Marsh and River Clans (5 and 7). The byrsoid skull vault (Plate XVII) is notably wide, low, and laterally well-filled, with relatively pinched forehead above a rather small square face with rectangular orbits, intermediate nose, and toothy mouth with squat jaw. The left parietomastoid suture shows premature fusion, there is a slight porotic hyperostosis along the sagittal suture, and two small osteomas occur in front of bregma. There are no enamel grooves. Three lost teeth (one abscessed) and four carious teeth (two mere shells) may be linked with a trace of temporomandibular arthritis. Average tooth wear accompanies edge bite. The skull type (C5) matches the low-headed Eastern Alpines of Cyprus, southwestern Anatolia (Karataş), and the Bronze Age Aegean (as at Asine).

50 Ler (grave D-20, middle phase) is a tall and perhaps rather slender young man about 27 years old (pubic symphysis phase 5), average in robustness, and without arthritis. The long and very high skull vault (Plate XVI) is ellipsoid in all three views and has a wide forehead above a linear hexagonal face with elliptical orbits, beaky nose, and large deep mouth region, with strong chin; impressive enough for the nickname "the chief." The left upper central incisor is missing, perhaps knocked out in the violence which fractured the nose slightly to the left, and adjacent teeth have moved over. The lower canines are rotated laterally 60°, with slight crowding; a slight overbite accompanies the slight tooth wear. Enamel grooves are perceptible, and the labial caries in the lower second molars look like primary enamel defects, the lower third molars are suppressed. The skull type (D2 or 3) is close to Coon's "Corded" as well as to skulls at Hasanlu and Hissar (Iran), and Karataş (southwestern Anatolia), with resemblance to *1 Ler* (Marsh clan) and *87 Ler* (River clan). This may reflect one element in the Greek-speaking (Ionia?) immigrants.

52 Ler (grave D-22, early middle phase) is a medium-tall (168.5 cm.) broad-shouldered, and fairly robust man in his middle fifties (pubic symphysis phase 10), whose leg bones are extremely bowed. He has slight arthritis of the vertebral column (especially C_{6-7} fused [Plate XXV] and at L_{1-2}), of knees, and of right foot (ball region) which has hammertoes (Plate XXIV). A transverse fracture through the middle of the left ulna (radius intact) was healing at the time of death, with active formation of a callus (Plate XXVI). The very long, low, byrsoid, and slightly gabled skull vault (Plate XVII) has very heavy browridges over a short and wide square face, rhomboid orbits, thick and concave nose, and squat and orthognathous mouth region with a strong chin. Edge bite is accompanied by marked wear of incisors only, that of other teeth is average. There are three abscesses—of the upper first molars and of the right central incisor—resulting in the two teeth on the right side being lost and the left first molar being reduced to a carious shell; there is a carious left lower third molar also, and slight paradontal disease. The nasalia show signs of a slight healed fracture. In details of nose and mouth this skull resembles *23* and *28 Ler* (see above) and could be ancestral to them; its Basic White type (A4) suggests Early Helladic or Minoan parallels.

45 Ler (grave D-15, late phase) is a 33-year-old (pubic symphysis phase 6) wide-hipped and medium-tall (159.9 cm.) woman, with pubic exostoses indicating many childbirths, possibly about 6, although the pelvic brim is wide (Plate XX) rather than deep. A long lumbar region is accompanied by incipient lumbarization of S_1 and medium arthritis. Hip joint reaction area, knee tilt, and ankle facets occur, but the long-bone shafts are not flattened at all. The relatively wide ovoid skull vault (Plate XVI) shows lambdoid flattening and a well-filled forehead and cerebellar region. The fragmentary face has rectangular orbits and a slightly toothy mouth. The three right lower molars (left alveoli destroyed) and left upper first molar were lost, and the left third molar and first premolar are carious shells, with abscesses at the latter and at the first molar. Tooth wear averages slight and exceeds this only in the incisors, where an edge bite developed. The incisors and canines show deep grooves, indicating growth disturbance (possibly illness or malnutrition) in childhood, although the skeleton as a whole is healthy and well developed, except for a shallow pelvis. The Mixed Alpine skull type (E1) should not hide resemblances to *20* and *50 Ler.*

141 Ler (area D, section V, cleaning area between southwest side of well 2 and east face of wall Vc; this spot produced Late Helladic pottery) is the frontal bone of a young adult female with small browridges and almost no nasion depression, strong bosses and median crest, fairly wide (95 mm., estimate), with a high (37 mm.) and vertical (?) forehead, suiting Alpine or Mixed Alpine trends. This may be the latest person included in the Middle Bronze Age series.

55 Ler (grave D-14) is the relatively complete, though broken skeleton and skull of an adolescent girl about 15 years old (wrist epiphyses still not fused, spheno-occipital synchondrosis open, third molars in crypts). She was slender-boned and short (150.9 cm.), with a sharp lumbar curve and flexion facets at ankles, but without an eroded area on the femoral neck. The brim segment of the ilium is relatively long, 48 and 49 mm. compared with 49 and 48 mm. for the posterior segments. There are six sacral vertebrae, with S_1 becoming lumbarized. The very linear pentagonoid skull (Plate V) has a long and sharply curved occipital, flat sides, rectangular face with long, toothy mouth, short and rather concave nose, and excellent teeth showing a slight overbite. This skull morphology fits Basic White type A1 as a continuation of the autochthonous Neolithic population.

24 Ler (grave D-5, late phase) includes unrestorable fragments of a child about 6, with lower first molars and incisors just erupting.

46 Ler (grave D-16, early middle phase) is probably a boy, 4+ years old, with lumbar and sacral arches fused and thoracics fusing, and with first molar visible in its crypt. Lumbar curve is sharp and the femur neck reaction area shows slight erosion. Long bones fit American size norms for age 3. The low and narrow skull vault is too warped to measure, but the orthognathous mouth with wide jaw ramus resembles *20, 23, 28,* and *52 Ler,* and the type is possibly Corded (D2) but with Basic White features. Iliac brim is (27) and posterior breadth 38 mm. There is no apparent pathology.

47 Ler (grave D-17, early middle phase) is a slightly larger child than *46 Ler,* probably a boy, about the same age, with lumbar arches fused and first molar visible in its crypt. There is medium erosion at the hip joint reaction area on the femur neck.

51 Ler (grave D-21) is a slightly younger child (3–4) with first molar crown formed and right humerus length 114 mm.; otherwise fragmentary.

21 Ler (grave D-2) includes unmeasurable bones of a full-term infant.

22 Ler (grave D-3) is a full-term infant with long bones scarcely below the modern American size norm. Humerus is 65, femur 71, and tibia 61? mm.

25 Ler (grave D-6, late), a similar newborn infant, shows radius 48 and tibia 61.

26 Ler (grave D-7) is a newborn a shade smaller than *25 Ler,* with clavicle 40 and femur 68 mm.

27 Ler (grave D-8) is an older infant (perhaps 6 months old) with milk incisors erupting. Measurable bones are lacking.

30 Ler (grave D-11) is a full-term infant with clavicle measuring 42 and radius 50 mm., scarcely below modern American size norms.

49 Ler (grave D-19) is an infant (6–8 months old), fragmentary except for left femur 102 and tibia 86 mm., almost up to modern American norms for six months.

13. Bay Clan: Areas DC, DB (Middle Bronze Age, very late phase)

145 Ler (grave DC-1, skeleton 1, L.H. I) is the partial skeleton of a man about 50 years old, fairly tall (170 cm.), and linear in build. The rather low, ellipsoid skull vault (Plate XVI) has a sloping forehead and is Classic Mediterranean, type B3, with Iranian traits.

144 Ler (grave DB-1-2) is a rather short (152.9 cm.) and fairly thick-boned individual, possibly a young woman, with open lambdoid suture and no skeletal exostoses. A partial jaw and mouth region (21 alveoli) shows 4 of 19 teeth carious, with none lost before death and no abscesses. Tooth wear is slight. Upper first and third molars show clear-cut Carabelli cusp. The ramus breadth is 30+ mm.

146 Ler (grave DC-1, skeleton 2, L.H. I) is the partial skeleton of a woman about 49 years old (pubic symphysis phase 9), not tall (stature, guess, about 153 cm.), not especially robust, with pubic exostoses suggesting many childbirths and with slight arthritic exostoses on lumbar, cervical, and thoracis bodies. The ovoid vault with its deep cerebellar region has a complete metopic suture (almost closed now), and with it a rather narrow and shallow jaw; gonial angles are inverted; both third molars were lost in life, and a first molar is carious. The skull morphology suggests Basic White (A3) with Mixed Alpine and Iranian influences. Marked parietal thinning (3 mm. thickness) above the bosses (7 mm.) goes with a general deepening of all meningeal grooves, perhaps partially from a general inner table hyperostosis resulting from aging; on the right side the groove for the middle meningeal artery's anterior branch just above pterion is 4 mm. wide and 2.5 mm. deep (possible arteriosclerosis with hypertension?).

147 Ler (grave DC-1, skeleton 3, L.H. I), is the quite fragmentary remains of a woman of about 40,

fairly short (153.1 cm.) and lightly built, with slight lumbar and cervical arthritis. Suture closure is medium. Skull fragments show a sharply curved occiput, medium-deep chin (31) mm., and relatively wide jaw ramus (32—× 58) mm. high, with only slight eversion of gonial angle; its type is possibly Basic White or Nordic-Iranian.

148 Ler (grave DC-1-2, transitional L.H. I) includes fragments of a child, possibly male, almost three years old, with second milk molar roots nearly complete and first molar crown formed. The atlas vertebra is still unfused. The femur (165?) has midshaft diameters of 12 and 12+ and the left tibia (130?), of 15 × 11 mm.

142 Ler (DB-1, cut 3) is a full-term infant, fragmentary.

143 Ler (grave DB-1-1) is a newborn infant, perhaps dying a short time after birth, slightly larger than United States norms for the newborn and possibly male. Iliac brim and posterior segment on left and right are 16 and 19, 18 and 19, with total a-p measurement of 33 and 33? respectively, and auricular heights of 15? and 14 mm. The left scapula total and inferior heights are 36 and 32 mm. Raying and pitting are absent from the existing skull vault bones.

Grave DC-3 is that of a child. Grave DC-4 contains one bone, uncertain.

MYCENEAN
Late Helladic III

54 Ler (grave 1 in area K) is a young man about 28 years old (pubic symphysis phase 5), surprisingly short (159 cm.) and robust and probably stocky. The femur neck reaction area shows slight erosion and the

platymeric index is 76.5, but other bone shafts are not flattened. Arthritis is lacking on vertebrae. There is no skull.

EARLY IRON AGE
Geometric: Trench BE and Areas PA, PB

105 Ler (pithos 1, trench BE) consists of lower extremity fragments, probably of a female (age, in the fourth decade). Femur upper shaft diameters 26 × 30 mm. give a platymeric index of 86.7; tibial shaft diameters of 38 × 29? mm. give a cnemic index of 76.3, neither of them "flattened." The first, third, and fourth metatarsals measure (60), 69?, and 64 mm.

226 Ler (grave PA3-2a, Mt. Pontinus) is a man of average size (stature 167.8 cm.; radius 235 mm.) whose tibia (360) mm. has a compressed shaft (35 × 23.5) of rhomboid section, with average ankle bones (52—× 42 × 29.5 mm., diversion angle 31°)

lacking flexion facets. First metatarsal measures 61 mm. There is no skull.

228 Ler (grave PA3-5, partly destroyed by a later grave and by a "Fortress Europe" trench) is a fragmentary male, age about 34. The left clavicle measures 143, the humerus shaft 21 × 20, femur midshaft 27 (a-p) × 29 and first left metacarpal 41 mm. Browridges are divided and of medium size, postorbital constriction is marked, the marginal process is medium, and the skull impression is Alpine, type C1. Tooth wear is about medium, there are slight shovel incisors, the sagittal suture is closed (inner surface) and the coronal advanced.

229 Ler (grave PA4-1, early pithos, probably second half of ninth century B.C.) is a man about 33 years old (pubic symphysis phase 6), tall (176.3 mm.), massive and robust in build, with sharp pubic pecten, and considerable lumbar curve, but without arthritis. Knee tilt and flexion facets (ankle) occur, but shafts of long bones are not flattened. The mouth region shows no dental lesions, average tooth wear, and suppression of the lower third molars. The jaw is broad, with deep and strongly projecting chin. Mastoids are large and cheekbones massive, but too little of the skull vault remains to determine its morphology, which is Alpine, possibly type C3.

232 Ler (grave PB1-1) is a fragmentary male about 25 years old (coronal and sagittal closure beginning), short (about 159 cm.), with average muscle attachments, femur neck plaque, and rhomboid tibial shaft, quite platycnemic.

234 Ler (grave PB1-4) includes very fragmentary remains of a man about 38 years old (symphysis phase 7), with femur midshaft measuring 30 × 30 and calcaneus 79 × 49 mm., and with slight lumbar arthritis.

226a Ler (grave PA3-2b) is a fragmentary female, about 30 years old, with traces of arthritic lipping on the preserved lumbars (three and four). The femur head measures 44 mm. and the neck shows an eroded reaction area. The platymeric index is 89.66 (26 × 29 mm.) and pilastric index 112 (28 × 25 mm.). Ankle flexion facets are well marked and the talus measures 49 × 36 × 28 mm., with diversion angle of 36°.

226b Ler (grave PA3-2c) is a female, smaller than *226a Ler*, about 25 years old, with bowed tibia prismatic in section and not platycnemic (75 index, 24 × 18 mm.), flat oval femur shaft (pilastric index 91.3, 21 × 23 mm.), and small talus (44 × 38 × 25 mm., diversion angle 26°). It is not clear why three adults occupy one cist grave.

227 Ler (grave PA3-3) is a woman about 25 years old (iliac crest fairly recently fused), short (146.9 cm.), with slight tooth wear and average skull muscularity (nuchal area, mastoid), small browridges, pointed and prominent chin measuring 27 mm. in height. The jaw

looks narrow but too little remains of the skull to determine its type, which is possibly Basic White.

230 Ler (grave PA5-1a) is a 24-year-old woman of average muscularity and short stature (about 153 cm.). The skull (Plate I) is somewhat angular, long, and very high, with deep occiput and high forehead. The broken face is rectangular and narrow, with square orbits and narrow nose. The mouth shows no lesions and slight tooth wear. Skull type is Corded (D2).

230a Ler (grave PA5-1b) comprises fragments of a female smaller than *230 Ler*, young, with platymeric index 77.8 (21 × 27 mm.), pilastric index 104.2 (25 × 24 mm.), and tibia plateau with only slight retroversion.

233 Ler (grave PB1-2) includes fragments of a woman about 32 years old (phase 6) of average height (156.8 cm.), with pubic signs of many childbirths (4–6?), and rhomboid tibial shafts. Skull fragments show the lambdoid and coronal sutures open, average mastoid, molar teeth lost in life, and other alveoli destroyed in the ground. Chin height is (25), bigonial breadth 104, bimental 45?, jaw thickness 16, and ramus breadth 28? mm.

230b Ler (grave PA5-1c) includes fragments and jaw of a child 7 to 8 years old, possibly a boy, with lower first molar and first incisor erupted and second incisor about to erupt. Ramus breadth is 26—, chin (25), bigonial (84), and condylo-symphyseal length (55) mm.

231 Ler (grave PA6-1) is the occiput of a very young child (age possibly 18 months) together with a first molar crown (permanent) just formed.

235 Ler (grave PB2-2) is the headless skeleton of an early adolescent probably age 12–13 and probably a boy, with acetabulum almost ready to fuse. The long bone lengths fit a modern norm three or four years younger. The femur neck reaction area shows slight erosion and the tibial shaft is convex posteriorly. The iliac brim measures 41 and 48 (left and right), the posterior segment 55 and 51, the total a-p 96 and 98, and the auricular height 37 and 41+ mm.

ROMAN PERIOD

Area DD

149 Ler (grave DD-1) is a small and lightly built woman about 33 years old. The ovoid mesocrane skull (Plate I) is quite large and low, with low fore-

head, projecting occiput, and definite lambdoid flattening. The face is squat hexagonal, wide, with rhomboid orbits, strong jaw, and pointed chin. With

24 alveoli preserved the mouth shows 8 teeth lost in life (1 alveolus shows an abscess), 1 carious, and 1 abscess (of a tooth lost after death). There is definite paradontal disease. Tooth wear is average, pronounced only on the lower incisors. There are traces of healed porotic hyperostosis on the occiput. A double tubercle or third condyle occurs near basion, as in several Classical Athenians. The type is Basic White, type A4, with Mediterranean-Alpine (E3) fullness.

149a Ler (grave DD-1a) is a very short (149.2 cm.) and light-boned woman about 30 years old or less (iliac exostoses, trace). Right iliac brim and posterior segments are 53 and 56 and the total a-p is 106 mm. The skull is missing.

INTERPRETATION

SAMPLING PROBLEMS

The Middle Bronze Age sample I have just described is laughably small for the following essays on its social biology and ecology, especially when I extend these data and interpretations to apply to the Eastern Mediterranean as a whole. The sample of 234 people from Lerna IV, V, and VI—the Middle Bronze Age continuum—spreads over about 25 generations; the three earliest burials (Lerna IV) are those of infants (some early burials were destroyed by later ones) and only about ten burials date from the very last phase (Lerna VI) partly because the Shaft Graves at Lerna had been robbed in ancient times. Yet even over 20 generations or less the resulting samples of 11 people per generation are far too small to be really representative of a population of over 500. Thus, for demographic purposes I have had to use the sample as if it represented a single cohort. This, the standard oversimplification of paleodemographers, would be entirely valid had the biosocial conditions been static, which, of course, they were not. Yet, on the other hand, this Middle Bronze Age sample of 234 is, as I have already pointed out, uniquely large and representative, for Professor Caskey and his teams excavated only 24 burials (9 infant, 8 adult, and 7 uncertain) which did not produce bones. By comparison, the 275 Early Neolithic house-burial skeletons from Çatal Hüyük (Mellaart, 1965; Ferembach and Angel, unpublished) and 540 Early Bronze Age pithos-buried skeletons which Mellink currently (in 1969) has excavated at Karataş (Angel, 1966, 1970) lack true representation of newborn infants; and the much larger samples from Egypt (e.g., the E series), Israel (e.g., Lachish), and British plague-pits include only adults. Hooton's (1930) demographic sample of 501 over the time span of a millennium at Pecos—the basis of his analysis that stands as the pioneer one in paleodemography as well as in microevolution—is larger (actually a selection of 973 skeletons from 1823 burials), but the number per generation is about the same as at Lerna. Indeed, most ancient cemetery samples range from no more than 5 or 10 to 150 skeletons, yet have supported broad conclusions.

Thus, it is clear that in attempting to understand the interrelations among the population at Lerna and its ecologic, social, and disease pressures, its genetic sources, and its changes, I shall be forced to use speculation as well as inference, but I will explain each step used in reaching my conclusions.

LONGEVITY AND DEMOGRAPHY

Data on length of life depend on accurate estimation of the age of each skeleton. For non-adult skeletons, I judge this by the degree of ossification of bones and closure of epiphyses (Krogman, 1939; Mainland, 1945, Appendix IV, based on Western Reserve data; McKern and Stewart, 1957), and by the stage of eruption of teeth (Robinow et al., 1942, Klein, Palmer and Kramer, 1937; Hurme, 1957; Garn et al., 1958). For adults I use the phase of the pubic symphyseal face (Todd, 1920, McKern and Stewart, 1957), the degree of closure of sutures of

TABLE 2. DEATHS AT LERNA COMPARED BY AGE GROUPS WITH SAMPLES FROM PALEOLITHIC TO MODERN TIMES

Age at death spans columns 0–1 through 85+.

Sample	N (male / female / total)	Sex and %	0–1	1–4	5–9	12.5	17.5	22.5	27.5	32.5	37.5	42.5	47.5	52.5	57.5	62.5	67.5	72.5	77.5	82.5	85+
Final Paleolithic Old World[a]	303	M.	83	52	33	6	10	28	28	14	25	6	12	3	2	1					
	248	F.	60	42	22	6	17	40	30	20	8	2	1								
	551	%	26.0	17.0	10.0	2.2	4.9	12.3	10.5	6.2	6.0	1.4	2.4	.5	.4	.2					
Early Neolithic Greece: Nea Nikomedeia[b]	54	M.	15	3	8	7	1	4	5	5	4	0	2								
	51	F.	12	3	8	5	2	4	7	2	5	3									
	105	%	25.7	5.7	15.2	11.4	2.9	7.6	11.4	6.7	8.6	2.9	1.9								
Middle Bronze Age: Lerna	130	M.	46	18	6	5	1	5	5	12	13	11	4	2	1	1					
	104	F.	38	12	4	3	7	2	12	12	6	3	5	1							
	234	%	35.9	12.8	4.3	3.4	3.4	3.0	7.3	10.3	8.1	6.0	3.8	.9	.4	.4					
Estimate alive		%	3.4	13.0	14.1	13.0	12.4	11.9	11.3	8.4	5.1	3.4	1.7	1.1	.6	.3	.3				
Late Bronze Age: Athens, Agora[c]	96	M.	32	7	12	2	2	3	3	6	5	10	6	5	3		1				
	76	F.	24	5	6	4	4	5	5	2	8	6	4	4							
	172	%	32.6	7.0	10.5	3.5	3.5	4.6	4.7	7.6	9.3	5.8	5.2	1.7		.5					
Classic Greece: Athens (Agora) & Corinth[d]	82	M.	22	9	5	2	1	3	8	8	3	7	12	3	4	4	1	1			
	62	F.	17	6	4	1	3	6	2	5	8	2	3	4	1						
	144	%	27.7	10.6	6.4	2.1	2.8	5.0	3.5	9.2	7.8	6.4	10.6	5.0	3.5	.7	.7				
A.D. 200–600, Rome[e]	11,607	%	31.6	10.8	10.5	6.5	9.0	7.9	6.0	4.4	3.3	2.5	1.5	1.2	.7	1.2	.5	.7	.4	.5	.8
A.D. 1928, Greece	101,839	%	17.7	18.1	3.8	1.9	3.2	3.6	3.8	2.8	3.2	2.7	3.2	3.5	3.7	4.5	5.2	5.3	4.9	4.1	4.8
A.D. 1960, U.S.A.	Census	%	2.3	.4	.2	.2	.4	.5	.6	.6	.9	1.5	2.4	3.8	5.4	7.7	10.2	12.9	15.1	15.7	19.1

a Includes Upper Paleolithic and Mesolithic. Paleolithic deaths are adjusted to coincide with infant and child frequencies at Predmost, Lautsch, Téviec, Ofnet, and Taforalt.

b Frequencies of infants (9) at Nea Nikomedeia tripled to adjust proportion to 1:2 ratio of skeletons to fragments at other ages.

c Late Bronze Age infant frequency adjusted as mean of infant: child and infant: adult ratios at Lerna and at Mycenae (18 infants: 18 children: 15 adults of age 15 and over). This adjusted frequency may be an overestimate.

d Classic infant and preadolescent frequencies based directly on observations on type of burial, size, and skeleton in 644 graves at Olynthus in Macedonia.

e Infant frequency for the city of Rome estimated at average of infant: child and infant: adult ratios at Olynthus.

NOTE: These adjustments have to be made because of the generally rather careless disposal of infants: I am assuming that the infant frequencies at carefully excavated sites are valid, but even in these sites there is possibility of underestimating the frequencies. Note that percentages are all interdependent. Estimates of the age composition of the living population at Lerna depend on the estimate of 5.0 births per woman (5.55 per fertile woman) derived from pelvic signs of pregnancy and birth.

the skull, especially on the endocranial surface (Todd and Lyon, 1924), the appearance of exostoses at sites of tendon attachment (McKern and Stewart, 1957), and the development of atrophy and shrinkage in both spongy and compact bone (Graves, 1922, Stewart, 1968, Nemeskeri et al., 1960). Since there is great individual variability in the absolute and relative timing of processes of growth, maturation, and aging, no individual estimate is "accurate" within a decade each way in adult skeletons, and this potential divergence between individual physiological age and actual age in years appears to increase as people grow older. But the errors introduced by this variable will cancel out.

Two other sources of error in estimating age at death, both serious, are the effects of ecology and nutrition and the decay of bone in the ground. For example, largely because of changes in ecology and nutrition over the past century, menarche has shifted from about 17 to about 13; the age at which epiphyseal closure occurs likewise has become earlier by several years, and stature has increased (Tanner, 1962): so that use of today's age standards possibly results in some underestimation of age when applied to ancient populations, especially in the adolescent-subadult range. I have made some allowance for this in grouping subadults (15 years and over) with adults; the actual chronological age of many of these skeletons (15–18 years old, aged by modern norms) may have been 17-20, but I cannot assume this growth lag to be a fact. As for the second source of error, decay of bone in the ground, this simply means for many skeletons the only valid age criteria left are the closure of the skull sutures and the surface appearance of other bones. Bone in extreme old age and in infancy, especially, survives poorly and in the ground the bones of females survive less well than those of males.

To be fully useful, data on demography must include an accurate determination of sex as well as of age, together with all available cultural data. For sex I use pelvis (Washburn, 1948, Stewart, 1968), robusticity and size of joints (Thieme and Schull, 1957; Krogman, 1962), and skull (Borovansky, 1936; Krogman, 1939, 1962; Giles and Elliott, 1963; Giles, 1964). Guessing at sex in adolescents, children, and infants becomes increasingly uncertain with lessening age; although Reynolds (1945) shows quite clear-cut pelvic contrasts between male and female infants, there is considerable overlap, and when one has only the ilium, looking like a bent fifty-cent piece, plus, sometimes, minute ischium and pubic bones, differences are hard to assess. I have relied largely on the openness of the sciatic notch together with the ratio between the iliac segment of the pelvic brim (as measured from acetabular end to auricular surface) and the posterior, or combined joint and muscle, segment of the ilium (auricular edge to posterior surface of posterior superior spine): the proportion of the iliac brim segment to the posterior segment is about 5 percent less in male than in female infants, but there is a very large overlap. In general, then, the sexing of infants and children involves a large amount of judgment.

Table 2 shows (third series down) the distribution of the Middle Bronze Age population of Lerna by age at death and compares the frequencies with those at some other sites in Greece, ranging from 6,000 B.C. to the 1920s, with frequencies for the Upper Paleolithic plus Mesolithic cemeteries, and with census frequencies for the United States in 1960. The very high proportion of infant deaths, the high proportion of child deaths, the excess of female over male deaths in the chief childbearing age range from 15 to 35 years, and the small proportion of survivors after age 50 are all striking features of these death frequencies, not only for Lerna but for all human populations before the recent industrial and atomic revolutions. Thus, these data show immense human wastage, particularly at birth and involving some mothers as well as infants, but also throughout life as a whole. At Lerna there were more infant deaths (36%) and fewer child deaths (21%) than in the Paleolithic hunting populations or in the very first farming populations in Greece, and this shift is probably nicely linked with disease patterns, perhaps involving malaria, as I will try to show in the next section. Up through Classical times infant and child loss lessens slightly, and in the same time span adult longevity rises from 33 and 27 years (male and female) at the end of Paleolithic times to 37 and 31 years at Middle Bronze Age Lerna and to 45 and 36 years in Classical times. Living conditions were not good in Imperial Rome for the actual city population; the proportion of infant and child deaths was high, and adult longevity was only 36 and 30.5 years (male and female), whereas in the Roman province of North Africa adult longevity was 53 and 50 (MacDonnell, 1913, tombstone data) and in Greece at the same time it was 40 and 34 years (skeletons). In Greece adult longevity had decreased by Turkish times (1400–1800) to 34 and 28, and then increased sharply during the past century. But even in the past generation in Greece female longevity, at 54.5 years, was less than male (56.1), in consonance with high infant mortality there, and in contrast with recent United States adult longevity of 70.1 and 76.7 years for males and females, with infant deaths only 2% of the total.

I must stress that all these statistics are simple statements based on frequencies of deaths; in no sense do they represent life expectancy nor proportions of deaths in relation to those alive at a given age (death rates). We have become accustomed to the latter, more sophisticated type of statistic (life expectancies, birth rates, death rates) because of the necessary application to the living population (Dublin, Lotka, and Spiegelman, 1949), such as for actuarial purposes. It is the activities and nature of the living population which interest social scientists, including archeologists. We have seen from the list of deaths (Table 2) that its complement, the curve of survivors, shows very few old people in the Lerna population. But one cannot, for at least two reasons, deduce logically from the curve of deaths or survivors the distribution by age of the living population: first, because death rates are different at different ages; and second, because these differences and the birth rate are constantly changing, so that no population is actually stationary but is always increasing or decreasing.

How can we, speculatively, get a better comparative picture of the living population at Lerna and perhaps even a guess at age distribution of the living? One critical piece of evidence is the number of children actually born.

Certain changes in the pelves of adult females, as Stewart (1957) has suggested, signify parity. The stresses of pregnancy and childbirth pull at the rectus and external oblique tendons (inguinal ligament), they tear ligaments at the pubic symphysis and stretch those at the sacroiliac joints, possibly subjecting the latter also to the wear of unusual motion. Thus anterior exostoses, posterior pits, and erosion of different degrees of the pubic symphysis give a good clue to the number of children a given woman has produced—that is, to her fecundity. This, of course, is realized fecundity rather than a woman's genetic fecundity (her production of 400 or more eggs) or her potential fecundity were she to bear children every 18 months for her reproductive life span (at Lerna, 8 children). This realized fecundity, or average parity, is in fact fertility at birth. But this is an ambiguous phrase and I here use "fertility" to mean average number of living children, i.e., either alive just after birth or reaching adulthood.

To set up a means for estimating this fecundity, I arranged a scale of ancient Greek, Eskimo, Indian, and modern American parous female symphyses in order of bony pits, grooves, erosion and exostoses, assuming 12 births as maximum. (The available American autopsy symphyses of known parity—no more than a dozen—cover all of this range.) Subtracting from this estimate of average fecundity the number of children dying at birth gives the average fertility. Out of the 20 Lerna pelves where an estimate is possible, 3 suggest 1 child (*31, 138, 178 Ler*, 1 suggests 2 children (*126 Ler*), 1 suggests 3 children (*42 Ler*), 2 suggest 4 children (*139* and *201 Ler*), 1 suggests 5 children (*213 Ler*), 3 suggest 6 children (*45, 92, 249 Ler*), 2 suggest 7 children (*65* and *97 Ler*), 2 suggest 8 children (*56* and *207 Ler*), 1 suggests 9 children (*137 Ler*),

1 suggests 10 children (*182 Ler*), and 1 suggests 12 children (*146 Ler*). There are 2 pelves showing no signs of childbirth (*14 Ler, 77 Ler*). Thus, 18 women may have produced 100 children, or about 5.5 children per fertile mother (perhaps 5 per average adult woman in the population). The *average* age for first childbirth may have been about 19, (as indicated by the estimate of 21 years as the age at death for those with one to three births); the difference between this average age, and the average female adult age at death gives an average childbearing period of 12 years. During this period the fertile women might have borne a child every 2.2 years (2.4 years for the average adult female, assuming that 10% were infertile). But less than half the children born may have survived to adulthood: there are 132 non-adults in the cemetery and 47 adult females, or 3 dead children per fertile female (N=42) and 2.81 (132/47) per average female. Thus, there would be 2.19 surviving children per average woman per generation (or one every 5.5 years) and 2.4 per fertile woman.

On this basis, if, to correct for poor preservation of female skeletons, we assume 49 women and 51 men among every 100 living adults, there would be 245 children (5 × 49) per generation, of whom 138 would die and 107 would survive to grow up—a rate of increase of at least 7% per generation. How many of these (2.19 × 49) living children would be infants? In relation to 100 living adults 88 infants would die out of 245 born (84 of the 132 Lerna skeletons under 15 are infants). Hence 157 children would survive the first year, i.e., infancy; over a 24-year "generation" this means 6.5 infants alive in any one year. In the group aged 1 through 4 only 31 out of the total 138 would die, or about one per year, so that there would be 23 live children in this age group (6+ × 4−1). Similarly 25 children might be alive in the group aged 5 through 9, and 23 in the group aged 10 through 14. The infants and adults alive in any one year are prorated as follows by five-year age groups (Table 2 shows these figures as percentages):

1–12 months	6.5	15–19 years	22	35–39 years	9	55–59 years	1
1– 4 years	23	20–24 years	21	40–44 years	6	60–64 years	.5
5– 9 years	25	25–29 years	20	45–49 years	3	65–69 years	.5
10–14 years	23	30–34 years	15	50–54 years	2		

This is a useful place to outline my demographic assumptions and deductions in tabular form. In the first data column of Table 3 I show the basic data uncorrected. In the second column I correct for the greater fragility of female skeletons by arbitrarily adjusting the sex ratio. In the third column I use the sex ratio corrections demanded in Tables 4 and 5, where the data are set out by clans. In the text I am following the direct sex-ratio adjustment of the second.

By the method of estimation followed above (cf. column 2 of Table 3) there would be 77 children alive per 100 adults at any one time, although over their total lifetime these 100 adults would produce, as I have noted, 245 children, 138 of whom would die before the age of 15 and 107 of whom would survive beyond that age. The figures for those alive at different ages would have been somewhat different if I had used female life span (31 years), or the average life span of both sexes (34 years), or the maximum childbearing period (15 years to about 45 years), as the time during which 100 adults would raise their children. Also I have made no specific allowance for the 7% increase per generation, nor for the average gap between end of childhood taken arbitrarily here at 15 years and the beginning of childbearing, nor for the stillbirth rate. Further speculation regarding marriage, family size, fertility, and generation length will be necessary to check the internal consistency of these estimates.

First child at age 19 suggests marriage at 17 (or even 16) for girls and perhaps 19 for men. Over the age period from 18 to 34 (average age at death, both sexes) the above estimates show 62 living adult parents. To divide 77 living children between 62 parents gives 2.5 children per couple, more than the 2.2 surviving children per woman by a fraction of the 1.0 child (per woman) who dies during childhood. If we assume that virtually all adults married, we might expect a grandparent or widow or widower to live in the household of a child or sibling; the 38 adults of middle age or older who probably had become grandparents or are in that age grade would increase the size of the average household from 4.5 to 5.7. Thus 177 people might live in 31 households, each containing between five and six people. This estimate assumes monogamy and avoids consideration of remarriages after death of one spouse, of possible unmarried adults, and of infertility. If we assume 157 living infants for the total 49 females this would mean 3.2 live infants per female (of whom about one per female would die before adulthood) or one live infant each 3.75 years (12/3.2). Between ages 19 and 31 there would be about 24 (48/2) childbearing women, and they would produce 6.4 live infants in any one year.

TABLE 3. THE LIVING POPULATION AT LERNA IN THE MIDDLE BRONZE AGE, AN EXTRAPOLATION BASED ON DEMOGRAPHIC ANALYSIS OF CEMETERY REMAINS

Observation	Skeletons found		Corrected for decay of females		Corrected by clans (cf. Table 4)	
Length of generation (years)	24		24		24	
Childbearing period (19–31 years)	12		12		12	
Male adults in graves	55		51		55	
Female adults in graves	47	102	49	100	52	107
Offspring born (5.0 per female)	235		245		266	
Offspring dead (infants)	84		88		85	
Offspring dead (children)	48	132	50	138	48	133
Total dead (female-child ratio)	234		244 (or 238)		240	
Offspring living (2.19 per female)	103		107		133	
Excess over parents	1		7		24	
Surviving infants	151 (235−84)		157 (245−88)		181 (266−85)	
In any one year of generation:						
Living infants	6		6+		8−	
Living children	68	74	71−	77	80	88
Living parents	63		62		67	
Living older adults	39	102 176	38	100 177	40	107 195
Living offspring per household	2.4		2.5		2.6	
Living parents per household	2+		2.		2.	
Living older adults per household	1.2+	5.6+	1.2	5.7	1.2−	5.8
Male life span (years)	37		37		37	
Female life span (years)	31		31		31	
Average (years)	34		34		34	
Births per 1000	$1335 = \left(\dfrac{235 \times 1000}{176}\right)$		$1384 = \left(\dfrac{245 \times 1000}{177}\right)$		$1364 = \left(\dfrac{266 \times 1000}{195}\right)$	
Births per year of female life span (31) = birth rate	43.1		44.6		44.0	
Deaths per 1000	$1329 = \left(\dfrac{234 \times 1000}{176}\right)$		$1378 = \left(\dfrac{244 \times 1000}{177}\right)$ (or 238×1000)		$1231 = \left(\dfrac{240 \times 1000}{195}\right)$	
Deaths per year of life span (34) = death rate	39.1		40.5 (or 39.6)		36.2	
Infant mortality per year	$357 = \left(\dfrac{84 \times 1000}{235}\right)$		$359 = \left(\dfrac{88 \times 1000}{245}\right)$		$320 = \left(\dfrac{85 \times 1000}{266}\right)$	
Natural increase per year (per 1000)	4.0		4.1 (or 5.0)		7.8	

This fits the original estimate of 6.5 and suggests that to use the average female life span (31 years) to give five live infants (157/31) is less plausible than to use the 24-year "generation," though the effects of infertility and of miscarriages would be hard to gauge. In this case it seems possible that the figure of 3.2 living infants per female is high, rather than low, and that infertility should be set at more than the 10% assumed in the above estimates.

Length of generation is a factor of less importance to the previous discussion than it is to an attempt at estimating the rate of population growth. Length of generation is the average age at which mothers produce their children, and for the Lerna sample it must lie between 25 years (19 + 12/2) and 23 years (15 + 16/2); the latter figure uses the earliest beginning of childbearing and both figures use the mean female age at death (31) as the upper limit. Assuming that the actual generation length was probably about 24 years, the survival of 107 children per 100 adults would mean an increase of about .3% per year or three per thousand; it is not practical to use the more accurate method of calculating the percentage excess of daughters over mothers. Thomas Malthus long ago showed that population growth is geometric (Notestein, 1960). If the rate of increase were steady at 7% per generation the population would have doubled in four or five years more than ten generations, or about 250 years (i.e., 500 to 1,056, at .3% annual increase); likewise it would have been half its observed size almost 250 years earlier. If for the Middle Bronze Age cemetery at Lerna the middle period was about 1700 B.C. and the living population at that time was 500, the living population in 2,000 B.C. would have been 170, in 1450 B.C. 1050, and in 1200 B.C. 2161. This, however, is only a statistical exercise, because the actual rate of population growth would certainly have fluctuated considerably from the 7% rate over the period of 25 generations of the Middle Bronze Age.

In all probability, however, the absolute size of population could have been slightly larger. In the first place, the assumptions that each of the 13 clans or family burial groups represent two households, and that these cover one-quarter of the area in use during the Middle Bronze Age, would give 104 households or 593 people at 5.7 people per household. Moreover, Dr. J. L. Caskey (personal communication) estimates that not more than 20% of the Lerna V, Middle Helladic, housing area was excavated and that within the area excavated between 20 and 25 houses may have been occupied at any one time. Extrapolation from these estimates gives a range of from 570 (5 × 20 × 5.7) to over 800 people for the Middle Bronze Age population at Lerna. This figure is better than that based on the 13 clans, since not all these burial areas were in use at any one time.

Rate of increase is the difference between the birth rate and the death rate, both very important parameters in any outline of the demography of a group. According to the apparent data on the female pelves, five births per woman was the average (5.55 per fertile woman), or 245 births per 100 adults plus 77 children per female life span. This would be 138.4 births per 100 population per 31 years, or 4.46 annually. Thus the birth rate would be 44.6 per thousand. Since the cemetery shows 234 dead per 47 females per life span, the death rate would be 243.96 per 177 people (including 49 females) per 34 years (average life for male and female), or 137.83 per 100 per 34 years, or 4.05 annually. Thus the death rate would be 40.5 per thousand, and the rate of natural increase just over four per thousand, agreeing only roughly with the direct inference of 7% per generation made above. An estimate of conventional infant mortality might be 88 deaths during the first year as a proportion of 245 births, or 35.9 per thousand. I have no reliable data for estimates of stillbirths, abortions, and miscarriages. Out of the 84 dead infants in the cemetery 15 appeared slightly premature, 16 appear to be from one to twelve months old, and the rest "newborn," that is, of a size reached a few days or more after birth. Thus a fraction of the infant mortality estimate should represent still-births—possibly 30 to 60 per thousand births—and the fact that no bones of early fetal age occur by no means negates the existence of early fetal deaths or miscarriages: perhaps all fetal deaths were about the number found today in the Punjab and in New York, 130–140 per thousand pregnancies (Potter et al., 1965).

In comparison with recent census data (Thompson, 1942; Dublin, Lotka, and Spiegelman, 1949) the estimated rates for Lerna of 44.6 (birth), 40.5 (death), 4.1 (natural increase), and about 300 (infant mortality) are all high, and are comparable with early-19th-century Russia or with modern Egypt. While the rate of natural increase is lower than that during the industrial revolution in western countries or that during the current population explosion in non-western countries, it nevertheless doubled the population in from 7.5 to 10 generations and was vastly higher than the rates which must have prevailed throughout the Paleolithic period in general. It was accompanied, moreover, by a female life span shorter than that of the male by six years and an infant mortality about ten times greater than necessary, by modern standards.

Such a heavy biological load on the average Middle Bronze Age female implies interesting social conditions and values, psychological forces even more vital and purposeful than the extremely loving valuation of children usually found in successful hunting bands (Service, 1965) and in farm families where many hands speed and lighten the work and large families bring prestige. The extra motive already may have been the need for fighting manpower, and I think that the extra psycho-biological strength came from race mixture, whose stimulating effect I will discuss later. The result, in any case, was the excess of deaths of infants and of their mothers noted above.

ECOLOGY, HEALTH, AND SOCIETY

What hazards of life killed so many infants and other people? How healthy or how diseased were the people of Lerna while they were alive? To answer these questions we need a quite specific ecological sketch of the western shore of the Bay of Argos, an enumeration of diseases as indicated by the bones, and a series of links between the diseases and the deaths.

Bronze Age Lerna, as I have noted earlier (p. 9), lay on the southwest edge of the Plain of Argolis, a few kilometers from the steep mountains guarding Arcadia, on the lowest slopes of acropolis-like Mt. Pontinus over a hundred meters west from the beach on the Bay of Argos and immediately south of the swampy and spring-lined estuary from which the place took its ancient name. Both north and south along the coast lay well-watered and plentiful farmland for barley (common and naked forms), wheat (einkorn and emmer), fava beans, peas, olives, grapes, figs, plums and other fruit-trees (Hopf, 1962), demanding only a careful control of streams, and drainage in some areas, to distribute irrigation water and to prevent the development of marshes. Grazing land for sheep, goats, cattle, and horses was available inland; the sea, with a convenient place to beach fishing boats, was a few steps away from the town; and the mountains, with deer and boar as well as smaller game, were likewise close at hand. Forests probably extended closer to town than today, they included pine, spruce and other conifers and also elm, ash, chestnut, poplar and especially several varieties of oak, whose acorns probably fed both man and pig. Among domesticated-animal bones from Lerna V, N.G. Gejvall (1969, p. 12) finds pigs most frequent (43.4%) then sheep and goats (38.9%), then cattle (17.7%) at a high enough frequency so that people ate more beef than pork or mutton. Gejvall notes that only 7–10.5% of animal bones are from wild animals and that some of the plentiful dog bones show signs of gnawing. Horse bones are scarce and begin to appear only in Middle Helladic times, though donkeys appear first in Lerna III (E.H. II). The town itself, built around the tumulus erected over the ruins of the Early Bronze Age House of the Tiles (palace?) about seven meters above present sea level, was on a low mound less easily defensible than Mycenae or

Tiryns or Argos or Nauplia or Asine. In other respects it was apparently ideally placed for a flourishing life based on a good diet and easy trade by sea or by land, but it had one major disadvantage—marshiness.

POROTIC HYPEROSTOSIS AND MALARIA

In addition to Karst basins with red clayey soil, described on page 14, the edge of the Tertiary limestone blocks forming the mountains of the Peloponnesus are in many places interleaved with clay formed from earlier schists and with marl and sand deposits, so that underground streams may suddenly come to the surface in strong springs which form basins or pools (Maull, 1922, Stephanos, 1884, pp. 390–395), especially at the edge of the major fault that runs along the western side of the Argolid and the east coast of the Peloponnesus. One of these springs, draining into the sea, is next to the town of Lerna and was plausibly the focus for Neolithic settlement there. Along this coast are several others, and consequently a number of marshy spots where mosquitoes can breed. Primitive farming methods from Neolithic times onward would have tended to leave water standing in the irrigation ditches radiating from such springs, and would thus have extended the breeding areas for such malarial mosquitoes as *Anopheles superpictus* and *A. sacharovi* (Balfour, 1936, Jardé, 1925, Jones 1909). For a very long time, according to Stephanos (1884, p. 494), this was one of the malarious areas of Greece. Stephanos points out that the Lernaean Hydra was one of the plausible personifications of malaria, while Jones (1907) establishes that malaria was frequent in Hellenistic times, was known to Hippocrates, and probably was described by Theognis. Before the recent eradication campaigns against mosquitoes, Greece was one of the most malarious regions of the Mediterranean (Hackett, 1937) and the disease affected at least one-third of the population, with *Plasmodia vivax* (tertian), *P. malariae* (quartan), and *P. falciparum* (aestivo-autumnal) occurring in about equal frequencies in the blood of sufferers, and, of course, with great local variation (Balfour 1936). When did malaria start in Greece? Did it affect the Greeks of the Bronze Age or even the pre-Greek populations of areas such as Lerna, which have mosquito-breeding places nearby?

Although malaria stands as a classic case of interaction between a parasite (*Plasmodium*) and its human and mosquito (*Anopheles*) hosts, and hence should represent a balance, most authorities consider malaria the most fatal disease of man (Fiennes, 1965) as well as one of his oldest, presumably deriving from a malaria affecting his primate ancestors (Dunn, 1965, Bruce-Chwatt, 1965). Man has adapted to this parasite both as an individual, by antibody formation and resistance, and as a population, by genetic means. Several recessive variants of normal human hemoglobin, such as hemoglobin S (sicklemia) and alpha and beta chain variants of thalassemic (sometimes fetal) hemoglobin, occur in extra frequency in malarious regions (Allison, 1955, 1964; Motulsky, 1960; Neel *in* Sorsby, 1953; etc.), although children who are homozygous for either of these genes (one inherited from each parent) develop hemolytic anemia and often die. This anemia is sufficiently severe to cause gross enlargement of blood-forming marrow in the long bones and especially in bones of the skull vault and face, so that if such children are kept alive long enough they develop great widening of bone spaces, improper remodelling of long bones, and porosity and thinning of the outer table of the skull strikingly visible in X-rays (Caffey, 1937; Wintrobe, 1951; Pendergrass, Schaeffer, and Hodes, 1956, pp. 333–337). Even in less developed form these changes are quite identifiable in dry skulls and skeletons (Angel, 1964, 1966, and in the discussion of Neel, 1951).

Lehmann (1959), Moulder (1962), and others have shown that people heterozygous for sicklemia and thalassemia have extra resistance to *Plasmodium falciparum*, and Moulder has shown the probable mechanisms: hemoglobin too viscous for the plasmodium to ingest into its food vacuole. This extra resistance seems to be typical also of G6PD deficiency (lack of the enzyme Glucose-6-Phosphate Dehydrogenase) which also produces favism and primaquine sensitivity. Thus the extra viability of heterozygotes in a malarious ecologic setting causes, through natural selection, an increase in the frequency of these rather harmful genes until, against the background of reduced viability and of deaths from malaria among individuals having normal hemoglobin and lacking sicklemia, thalassemia, or G6PD deficiency, a balance occurs between deaths or non-reproduction of homozygotes from anemia and the extra fertility of heterozygotes. These genes form balanced polymorphisms and may reach frequencies in which they are carried in heterozygous form in over half the total population and produce anemic homozygotes in four to ten percent of it. This is true of Greece, Cyprus, and some Mediterranean islands and parts of Italy where thalassemia is especially frequent; it is also true of the farming areas of West Africa, where sicklemia is the usual disease, and throughout the Middle East and Far East (Bruce-Chwatt, 1965).

Throughout this whole area, and in the Americas among some Indian groups, a manifestation or disease, once called "osteoporosis symmetrica" occurs in ancient skeletons. It is a porotic hyperostosis of the skull and other bones (Angel, 1964, 1966); and Hamperl and Weiss (1955) in Peru have described it as hyperostosis spongiosa. In the Mediterranean porotic hyperostosis probably represents thalassemia or sicklemia, although observers must take care to distinguish the bony effects of these or other types of anemia from those of any deficiency disease, such as rickets. In the Americas, before malaria was introduced from the first colonists, porotic hyperostosis must have been caused by another form of anemia since many anemias, (e.g., that caused by hookworm) may produce this bony change (Moseley, 1965).

According to my observations, porotic hyperostosis occurs in fully developed form in one-quarter of the 45 skulls of all ages from the Neolithic site of Nea Nikomedeia (sixth millenium B.C.) in the Haliakmon estuary on the formerly marshy Macedonian plain (Rodden, 1964; Angel, 1966), and a further 40% of skeletons show some slight development of the process. I observed this also at Çatal Hüyük (seventh millenium B.C.), near marshes in the Konya plain, where among 143 of these early Neolithic skulls the bone change is marked in 8 and it is slight in 50 more (cf. Angel 1966). On the other hand, at early Neolithic Khirokitia, situated in a rocky and seasonally dry valley in south-central Cyprus, hyperostosis, in incipient degree only, occurs in but 4 out of 36 skulls (Angel, 1953); at Kephala, a rocky headland on Kea island (Caskey, 1962), among 42 Late Neolithic skulls it occurs in only 1 infant and slightly in 2 adults (Angel, 1966); and among 416 Early Bronze Age skulls excavated at Karataş by Mellink (1965, 1967) in a mountain valley of Lycia, this thickening markedly affects only 9 skulls, with 37 other skulls slightly affected. Early Bronze Age Corinth, on the other hand, located on a well-watered, fertile plain below a limestone slope, with tiny arroyos eroded through the limestone, has 11 out of 21 skulls affected, although of these only 1 shows medium hyperostosis and 1 medium orbital roof porosity. Similarly, Late Bronze Age Bamboula, located above coastal salt-marshes in southwestern Cyprus, shows 2 children and 2 infants with clearcut hyperostosis out of 44 skulls of all ages; and these 4 are from a single family tomb. Hence, in early Eastern Mediterranean sites, at the very beginning of settled agriculture, porotic hyperostosis as a probable result of thalassemia is especially frequent in sites near marshes, it is absent or only incipient in sites separated from marshes, and it occurs in 10–20% of skulls found in Bronze Age sites near marshes which were later foci for malaria. It is not surprising to find porotic hyperostosis earlier, in two out of five Mesolithic adult skeletons at Franchthi Cave diagonally across the Bay of Argos (Angel in Jacobsen, 1969).

At Lerna, well-developed porotic hyperostosis occurs in 3 out of 73 adults, 3 out of 30 children, and 4 out of about 54 infants in which skulls are complete enough for good judgment of this pathology. This is an overall rate of 6.4%. Slight and trace degrees of the trait occur in 8 adults, 1 child, and 13 infants, or 14% of 157 individuals. Thus about one-fifth of the Lerna population show this lesion in some degree, and the 7 children and infants (8.3%) with well-marked bony changes (*10, 71, 61, 103, 133, 136,* and *204* Ler) very likely show results of homozygous thalassemia, the typical anemic form in which inheritance of thalassemia genes from each parent results in severe anemia and death (Neel *in* Sorsby, 1953). The upper part of Plate XXIII shows the extent of these bone changes, including interference with remodelling and persistence of an "inner shell" in the marrow cavity of long bones of affected children.

The above figure of 8.3% is the proportion out of 84 dead juveniles, i.e., 4.7% of 149 live births. The occurrence of homozygous thalassemia (recessive) in the population taken as .047 ($= q^2$) indicates a gene frequency of .22 for the thalassemic gene (q) and .78 for normal hemoglobin (p) with .61 ($= p^2$) for normal homozygotes. Heterozygote carriers of the thalassemic gene ($2pq = .34$) will then occur in 34% of the population, using the Hardy-Weinberg formula ($p^2 + 2pq + q^2 = 1.00$) for gene-trait relations. Trace and slight degrees of bone change occur in 20% less than the 34% frequency; probably many carriers show no bony change, since different forms of thalassemia show different clinical as well as molecular effects. This is about the frequency one might expect in a malarious environment about like those of modern Greece in the 1930s. Thus Lerna confirms the expectation based on deduction from earlier series and from modern distributions, that endemic malaria occurred there at least as early as the Middle Bronze Age and probably before; and it is tempting to assume that its frequency among the pre-Greek population was somewhat higher, in line with that at Nea Nikomedeia and Corinth.

From this standpoint it is important to note that in Greece all the adult frequencies of hyperostosis change thus: Mesolithic 40% (5), Early Neolithic 60% (20), Late Neolithic-Early Bronze 28% (56), Middle Bronze 13% (124), Royal Graves 8% (23), Late Bronze 8% (210), Early Iron 4% (92), Classic 1% (114), Hellenistic 10% (121), Roman 24% (95), Medieval 12% (83), Turkish 45% (51), Romantic 37% (200). If we had data for children and infants from all these periods the trends might be clearer; for example, the unexpectedly large number of child deaths at Nea Nikomedeia may reflect more malaria there than at Lerna. But a steady decrease in thalassemia (and in malaria too) from first farmers to the 4th century B.C. would fit the probabilities expected from increasingly efficient use of farmland and swamp-drainage as suggested by several of the Labors of Herakles, including his legendary control of many hydra-like springs at Lerna. The subsequent rather quick increase would fit the evidence, amassed by Jones (1907, 1909), Stephanos (1884), and their successors, showing that malaria became endemic and then fluctuated somewhat in severity down to modern times. Lerna fits this pattern, being apparently more thalassemic (malarious?) than other Middle Bronze Age sites but perhaps less so than it had been during the Neolithic and Early Bronze Age. Probably the intrusion of Greek-speakers, and others, at the start and during the Middle Bronze Age would have introduced some people previously unexposed to malaria, and others with *falciparum* malaria who would then have married into the local population. Analysis of this situation, and of the fertility factors which would produce further microevolutionary changes and would also be necessary to maintain the frequency of genes for thalassemia or other balanced polymorphisms, requires a study of the data in Tables 4 and 5, showing the deaths and plausible births for each of the thirteen cemetery clans.

In these tables the families have been divided into four groups, depending on the absence or type of incidence of porotic hyperostosis, on the assumption that this is thalassemia and depends on recessive genes for full expression: in three clans there is no hyperostosis; in three it appears in infants and children only, so that parents may be mildly affected heterozygotes; in five it occurs among infants, children, and adults, suggesting more heterozygous parents

TABLE 4. DEATHS, FECUNDITIES, AND FERTILITIES BY CLAN AS RELATED TO POROTIC HYPEROSTOSIS (THALASSEMIA OR SICKLEMIA)

Clan number and name	Dead in cemetery — Infants (0–12 months)	Child. (1–14 years)	Adults M.	Adults F.	N	Juv. pct.	Graves with no bones Inf.	?	Ad.	Births N	Births Per F.	Survivors N	Per F.	Pct.	Tr. Sl.	+ and ++	Porotic Adult Pct.	N	Juv. Pct.	N	Probable genetic makeup for thalassemia vs. falciparum malaria
A 3 Forest	6	3	3	5	17	52.9	0	0	2	13	2.6	4	.8	30.8			(Absent)				Child deaths from falciparum malaria since no protection by thalassemia.
11 Plain	10	3	3	1(+1)	18	72.3	1	1	0	13	6.5	0	0	0							
13 Bay	2	1	1	3	7	42.9	0	2	0	22	7.3	19	6.3	86.4			0	9	0	14	
Subtotal	18	7	7	10	42	59.5	1	3	2	48	4.8	23	2.3	47.9							
B 6 Spring	6	5	1	2	14	78.6	0	0	0	13	6.5	2	1.0	15.4	1	1	(In juveniles only)				Both parents mildly affected carriers; anemia and malaria, plus infections.
9 Bridge	7	4	3	0(+2)	16	68.8	3	0	2	11	5.5	0	0	0	0	1					
10 Eastern	14	10	3	5	32	75.0	3	1	1	27	5.4	3	.6	11.1	2	1					
Subtotal	27	19	7	9	62	74.2	6	1	3	51	5.7	5	.6	9.8	3	3	0	13	22	36	
C 1 Western	0(+1)	1	2	3	7	28.6	0	2	0	6	2.0	4	1.3	66.7	1	0	(In male adults)				One parent carrier anemia and malaria.
12 Sea	7	4	7	3	21	52.4	0	0	0	12	4.0	1	.3	8.3	0	1					
Subtotal	8	5	9	6	28	46.4	0	2	0	18	3.0	5	.8	27.8	1	1	15	13	0	5	
D 2 Southern	3	3	3	6	15	40.0	0	0	0	37	6.2	31	5.2	83.8	0	2	(In people of all ages)				Both parents severely affected heterozygotes; anemia cause of juvenile deaths, plus infections, perhaps dysenteries, hookworm, etc.
4 Central	2	0	4	5	11	18.2	0	1	1	30	6.0	28	5.6	93.3	0	1					
5 Marsh	6	5	6	6	23	47.8	0	0	1	34	5.7	23	3.8	67.7	2	0					
7 River	2	2	7	0(+2)	13	30.8	0	(1)	1	10	5.0	6	3.0	60.0	1	0					
8 Northern	19	7	12	8	46	56.5	2	0	0	38	4.8	12	1.5	31.6	5	3					
Subtotal	32	17	32	27	108	45.4	2	2–	3	149	5.5	100	3.7	67.1	8	6	24	38	45	29	
Hyperostosis Subtotal	67	41	48	42	198	54.5	8	5–	6	218	5.2	110	2.6	50.5	12	10	17	64	30	70	Partly resistant to malaria.
Grand Total	85	48	55	52	240	55.4	9	8–	8	266	5.1	133	2.6–	50.0	12	10	15	73	25	84	

NOTE: To compensate for destruction of bones in the ground I have added 5 females (in Plain, Bridge and River clans) and 1 infant (Western clan). I have estimated fecundity for the 27 females lacking pelves by taking the norm of 5 births found for 20 females (including 2 with 0 births, and so allowing 10% of sterility) who died at age 30 and modifying this according to the age of the skeleton: I assumed 1 birth each 2.5 years between 17 and 30, 1 birth each 5 years, 30–40, 1 birth each 10 years, 40–50, and 1 birth for each late adolescent dying between 15 and 17.

TABLE 5. DEATHS, FECUNDITIES, AND FERTILITIES OF INDIVIDUALS WITH SKULLS COMPLETE ENOUGH FOR DEGREE OF POROTIC HYPEROSTOSIS (THALASSEMIA OR SICKLEMIA) TO BE JUDGED

Degree of porotic hyperostosis	Dead in cemetery							Births		Survivors			Porotic hyperostosis				Probable genetic status of thalassemia or sicklemia and selective effect
	Infants (0-12 months)	Child. (1-14 years)	Adults M.	Adults F.	N	Juv. pct.		N	Per F.	N	Per F.	Pct.	Abs.	Tr.	Sl.	+ & ++	
Absent [a]	37	26	35	27	125	50.4		127	4.7	64	2.4	50.4	125				Mainly homozygous normal: malaria deaths
Trace [b]	5	1	6	0(+2)	14	42.9		14	7.0	8	4.0	57.1		12+			Heterozygous for thalassemia and sicklemia: protection against malaria
Slight [c]	8	0	1	1(+2)	12	66.7		17	5.7	9	3.0	52.9			10+		
Moderate [d]	2	2	1	2	7	57.1		12	6.1	5	2.5	41.7				7 }	Heterozygous affected and few homozygous
Pronounced [d]	2	1	0	0	3	100.0										3 }	Homozygous affected: anemia deaths in childhood
Total	54 } 84	30	43 } 73+4	30(+4)	161	52.2		170	5.0	86	2.5	50.6	125	12	10	10	

[a] Fecundity derives from 15 females averaging 5.2 births less 10% allowance for sterility = 4.7 → 127.

[b] Fecundity derives from subtracting 127+17+12 births from 170, assuming 5.0 births for the total group.

[c] Fecundity derives from 207 Ler (8) +2 unknowns (at 5.6) less 10% allowance for sterility = 5.7 → 17.

[d] Fecundity derives from 56 Ler (8) +1 unknown (at 5.6) less 10% allowance for sterility = 6.1 → 12.

NOTE: As in Table 4, I have had to add females (4) arbitrarily to compensate for destruction in the ground. Obviously the homozygous children (++ and some of +) must have come from matings between Trace, Slight and adult categories and hence the survivor categories as listed may be biased. Nevertheless, the extra fertility and protection conferred by the heterozygous state is clear in the Trace and Slight groups and not in the homozygous thalassemic or sicklemic group as expected. The balance between deaths presumed from falciparum malaria (some of the Absent category deaths) and deaths from anemia is complicated by loss of fecundity from malaria and protection by thalassemia; the fecundity data from 17 of the 20 pelves available are hardly enough.

more severely affected; and in two clans it occurs in just a single adult per clan, leaving children unaffected and suggesting matings never involving more than one heterozygote. The calculation of number of children born derives directly from the numbers deduced from 20 female pelves, with two special provisos: (1) females whose fecundity was unknown (inadequate pelvic fragments preserved in the ground) were credited with one child each 2.5 years up to 30, each five years to 40, each ten years to 50, unless they had died as late adolescents (15–17 years) when they were assigned one child; (2) where the number of female skeletons (zero) was clearly inadequate for the number of dead children found in that clan's cemetery, one or two females were added arbitrarily to the statistics. There is one such family each in groups A, B, and D of Table 4; I hope that the irregularities from this source, and from the fact that the clans (family burial groups) span many generations, will tend to cancel out in each grouping. But

---

The 34 hypothetical matings (with clans in the sequence of Table 4, starting with group B) are given below. An asterisk (*) marks each of the 20 females whose fecundity I estimated from the pelvis, and a dagger (†) marks an adult of assumed heterozygous status, since not all sicklemia or thalassemia heterozygotes in modern populations show overt anemia which might produce even a trace of porotic hyperostosis. The italics identify the individuals.

	Heterozygous parents		Porotic hyperostosis (thalassemia) in offspring born				
Clan	Female	Male	Absent	Trace	Slight	Medium	Pronounced
6 Spring	*97†	95†	3	2(102)	1(90)	1(103)	0
9 Bridge	DE69†	174	3	1	1(206)	0	1(204)
10 Eastern	*182	DE58†	5	3(169)	2(202)	0	0
1 Western	CK	18(tr.)	3	1	1	0	0
12 Sea	*45	48(sl.)	3	1	2	0	0
2 Southern	*207(sl.)	217	4	2	2(60)	0	0
4 Central	*56(med.)	44†	4	0	3(241)	1	0
5 Marsh	3(med.)	66(med.)	0	1	1	2(71)	1(10)
5 Marsh	*65	1(tr.)	3	2	1	0	0
5 Marsh	62	72(tr.)	4	3	1	0	0
7 River	BD8	91(tr.)	1	1	2	1(81)	0
8 Northern	*126	125(tr.)	1	1(121)	0	0	0
8 Northern	*249†	131(tr.)	2	1	1(134)	1	1(133)
8 Northern	*137†	124	5	2(119)	1	1(136)	0
8 Northern	243†	115	2	2(117)	1(116)	0	0
8 Northern	*139†	140	2	1	1(135)	0	0
Total matings	16 heterozygous	18 homozygous (absent)	45⎫ 115 70⎭	25	20	7	3

Hypothetical homozygous mothers in the porotic-hyperostosis-absent category assumed mating with homozygous males (also lacking porotic hyperostosis) follow (with numbers of offspring in parentheses):

3 Forest	*14(0)	13 Bay	144(2)	1 Western	*31(1)
	*77(0)		*146(12)		59(4)
	74(1)		147(8)	12 Sea	141(5)
	13(4)	6 Spring	*92(6)	2 Southern	*213(5)
	12(8)	10 Eastern	*178(1)	4 Central	*42(3)
11 Plain	192(5)		*201(4)	8 Northern	*138(1)

it is at once obvious that the selection of group C as one lacking hyperostosis in children has within it one clan, the Western, with one child burial; the cause of this might as well be archeological accident (see Figure 5) as good child health.

Groups B and D, the most fecund, are the ones where many parents are presumably heterozygous for thalassemia and sicklemia and hence protected against *falciparum* malaria. The least fecund is group C, with slight hyperostosis in adult males only (*18* and *48 Ler*), and hence with mothers less protected against malaria, including two girls dying as early subadults (*16* and *55 Ler*). Groups B and D with mildly and definitely affected heterozygous parents, respectively, are more fecund than group A only because of the low fecundity of the Forest clan in the latter; this clan is the only reason that fecundity is lower in the group (A) lacking hyperostosis. But this "unprotected" group does indeed show more juvenile deaths and lower average fertility than the whole hyperostotic group, although the "unprotected" group (A) includes the Bay and Plain clans, which are opposite poles with regard to fertility.

Although Group D, with 24% of adult hyperostosis, fits expectation in being the most fertile and has fewest juvenile deaths, groups B and C are both notably lacking in fertility, possibly because of child deaths from anemia (*103, 204*, and perhaps *90 Ler* in group B may be homozygous for abnormal hemoglobins) as well as from possible malaria. If some other disease such as infant diarrhea or tetanus or possibly infanticide accounts for excess infant deaths during one particular time period in that part of the cemetery (Trench DE) containing the Bridge, Eastern and Plain clans, this would bias the abnormal hemoglobin statistics.

The data in Table 4 suggest a slightly greater viability of the hyperostotic (thalassemic or sicklemic) families as compared to "normal" ones: 2.6 versus 2.3 fertility. But because of the possibility of sampling accidents, this difference is too small to trust. I cannot conclude that selective fertility in favor of the hyperostosis (thalassemia) heterozygote was strong enough to continue to cause actual increase in Th or S gene frequency during the Middle Bronze Age at Lerna, even though two females with hyperostosis (*56* and *207 Ler*) have pelves indicating many births. But Table 4 does show how such natural selection maintains a fairly high frequency of the hyperostosis (thalassemia or sicklemia) gene, since child deaths presumably from malaria in Group A are balanced by deaths, presumably from anemia in groups B and C, and deaths from both causes are counterbalanced by childhood resistance to malaria and anemia in group D.

Table 5 shows the 157 people with skulls complete enough to judge porotic hyperostosis. Adding 4 females in the heterozygous categories (trace and slight) enables me to estimate the demographic situation on the limiting assumption of matings and offspring within each category. This assumes a balance between segregation of offspring of heterozygous parents into pronounced and absent categories and the addition of heterozygous offspring from matings between homozygous (absent) and heterozygous categories. Hence the apparent extra survival of heterozygotes in this table needed checking. A careful reconstruction (on the basis of 30 + 4 females with usable skulls) of possible matings within each clan produced the number of offspring (170) found in Table 5. I find a total of 16 matings involving heterozygous parents and 18 matings in the homozygous absent category. The results of the 34 hypothetical matings (see opposite) are summarized as follows:

	N	Absent	Trace	Slight	Medium	Pronounced
			Porotic hyperostosis categories			
Offspring	170	115	25	20	7	3
Dead as children (Table 5)	84	6	66	8	4	3
Survivors	86	52	19	12	3	0

This summary suggests that the proportion of heterozygotes could increase dramatically within the Lerna clan setup through selectively better survival, though I think that this hypothetical reconstruction exaggerates the situation.

Another check is to estimate by the Hardy-Weinberg formula the trait frequencies expected with a thalassemia or sicklemia gene frequency of 22% and the trait frequency of 4.7% found earlier (see p. 79). The trait frequencies are .61 absent (p^2), .34 slight to medium ($2pq$), and .05 pronounced (q^2), giving the following expectation for the offspring: 104 normal (absent), 58 heterozygote carriers (trace, slight, and medium), and 8 homozygous affected (pronounced) who would not survive to reproduce.

Both Table 5 and these hypothetical mating estimations suggest a fecundity and fertility higher enough among the matings producing slightly hyperostotic children (in contrast to deaths of those with moderate and pronounced hyperostosis) to show how a balanced polymorphism works as a selective force to protect against a disease to which the heterozygote is somewhat resistant. These data, admittedly inferential, show clearly the high cost, in terms of infant deaths and shortening of maternal life span, of maintaining a balanced polymorphism resistant to malaria; but it is undoubtedly this resistance which allowed the extra fertility for the Bronze Age expansion of population in malarial parts of Greece. Please note that excess of births over deaths indicated by Table 4 is inflated by the effects of having to allow for clans with no female skeletons. Also note the slight suggestion in Group A that hyperostosis and malaria may have been declining in frequency; two of the clans (Plain and Bay) belong to the end of Middle Bronze.

Other diseases as well as malaria probably burdened the lives of the people of Lerna. The most obvious of these are the dysenteries, infant diarrhea, probably hookworm, tetanus, and many infections (cf. tooth abscesses on Plate XXII, and venous dural sinus infection on Plate XXIII), as well as childhood diseases and possibly smallpox. There are no bony signs of tuberculosis, venereal syphilis, or clear-cut cancer.

NUTRITION, GROWTH, AND BODY BUILD

Diet at Lerna must have been varied, with cereals supplemented by deer, fish, and seafood as well as including milk products (cheese, etc.) and flesh from domestic cattle, pig, sheep, goat, and probably dogs, to judge by animal bones excavated. Olives and grapes as well as beans, peas, figs, and other vegetable foods (e.g., thistles) antedate the Middle Bronze Age (Hopf, 1962), by which time the plow, or ard, had replaced the stone hoe of "shoe-last" form (Drachmann, 1938; Angel, 1946; Clark 1952, pp. 100–102). Sharp flint and obsidian sickle-blades had been in use since Neolithic times and some form of the threshing-boat set with flint blades may have developed by this time. The potential food supply was excellent, although there may have been problems with storage to compensate for a poor harvest. Malnutrition was probably not severe but may have occurred during winter months. Lines of temporary arrest of tooth-enamel formation during childhood (cf. 220 Ler on Plate XXII) occur in clear-cut form in 18% of 60 adult dentitions and in slight degree in another 43%. Clear-cut enamel lines decrease to 4% by Mycenean times and rise again to 11% in the Romantic period sample. The inference is that childhood growth disturbance affected a good proportion of the Lerna adults, even though the causes are unclear. It is impossible to implicate malaria more than other infections or the occasional poor nutrition: enamel striations are not linked positively or negatively with hyperostosis. In addition to the 13 out of 54 who show clear-cut raying and pitting of the inner surface of the frontal or other vault bones, presumably the preliminary hyperemic phase of hyperostosis, several infants (183, 202, 209 Ler) show "lipping" at the ends of long bones, suggesting prenatal growth disturbance.

Further effects of disease and perhaps of variable nutrition appear in stature and body build. Average adult stature of 166.3 cm. in males and 154.2 cm. in females is over 5 cm. less than that of the ruling families at Mycenae at the end of this period and 4–5 cm. less than that in Classical and Hellenistic times. Even at Early Neolithic Nea Nikomedeia the stature is perhaps taller (167.8 cm. for 9 males and 155.4 cm. for 12 females), though there was probably a lower point in the third millennium B.C. (161.5 and 149.3 cm., respectively, for 7 males and 6 females). Much of this relative shortness at Lerna must be environmentally caused, if a 5 cm. change can occur because of a social class difference within the newly formed Greek population of Argolis. As we will see later, both commoners and rulers during the first half of the second millennium B.C. were extraordinarily heterogeneous, with signs of *past* isolation, so that the heterozygosity from mixture should have raised stature and vigor throughout the population.

Pelvic inlet proportions correlate with stature, and confirm this conclusion. Greulich and Thoms (1938) and Nicholson (1945) have shown that a lower to upper class difference or a wartime to peacetime dietary improvement like that following World War I in England can deepen the adult pelves of those women whose childhood occurred under better conditions (upper class or peacetime diets) by at least 5 mm. or about 4 units of the depth-breadth index. At Lerna this index, 80.6, is 4 units below the Classical average and about 15 units below that of healthy modern Americans. Although the absolute cross-sectional area of the pelvic inlet is more vital, individual shallowness of the birth canal probably plays some part in infant-maternal death rate as a selection factor operating against the birth of large babies, and in relative infecundity. But at Lerna the more fecund women may not have had relatively deeper pelves, index: 82.9 (3) vs. 79.2 cm. (5), and were only 8 mm. taller, 154.7 (6) vs. 153.9 cm. (9) than the less fecund, although signs of childbirth strain clearly should be greater in women with shallow pelves.

ENVIRONMENT, ACTIVITY, AND GAIT

Body build (Tables 6 and 7) is fairly stocky and muscular, with relatively broad shoulders and hips and otherwise usual European proportions of limb segments and vertebral column. It is the build shown in Classical sculpture and typical of mainland Greeks from the Bronze Age to the present day. The daily stresses for men in such activities as farming, fishing in boats, hunting afoot or on horseback, and probably warfare, and for women of gardening, weaving, or water-carrying, demanded the observed toughness of body structure despite the handicaps disease placed on child growth. As a result of the mountaineer's gait needed on Greek hillslopes, a third of the males, half the females, and most of the children of Lerna show an actual erosion at the reaction area of the femur neck produced by tightening of ligaments at the hip joint in going downhill (Angel, 1964a); a slight extra backward tilt of the plateau of the tibia at the knee, facilitating strength when flexed; frequency of ankle flexion facets on talus and tibia 72% and 94%, respectively, as opposed to 50% and 30% in modern America; extra shaft flattening of the upper femur (platymeria) by stress from gluteal and other hip-balancing muscles, of the middle femur (pilaster formation) by quadriceps attachments, of the upper tibia (platycnemia) by stress from the soleus and deep plantar-flexors of the feet; an extra forward reach of the neck of the femur; and a slightly greater lumbar curve and pelvic tilt. All these postural conditions, when compared with those of average modern Americans, differ in the direction of providing greater joint flexibility and muscular strength of the body below the thorax and are an adaptation to walking and running in rough country, although possibly the flattening of long-bone shafts may also reflect an

THE PEOPLE OF LERNA

"economy" of bone in relation to hard muscular use. This overall development is a little less than that present in Neolithic peoples, and less than that in Paleolithic hunting peoples.

STRESS AND ARTHRITIS

The usual joint responses to hard use are (1) capsule, cartilage, and bone hypertrophy, and 2) cartilage thinning and bone sclerosis that leads to hypertrophic arthritis, with bony lipping and exostoses (Tobin and Stewart, 1953). Various degrees of this response affect the vertebral column (usually primarily the lumbar region) of 75% of Lerna males and 50% of females, in

TABLE 6. MALE AND FEMALE SKELETONS FROM LERNA: MEAN MEASUREMENTS, BODY PROPORTIONS, INDICES, AND ANGLES

Measurement (mm.), index, or angle (For definitions, see p. 3 and Martin and Saller, 1959)	Males				Females			
	Left	N	Right	N	Left	N	Right	N
	A—MEAN MEASUREMENTS							
Measurement:								
Humerus: Max. length	302.5	18	309.7	13	277.5	11	287.8	12
Max. midshaft diam.	21.6	37	22.7	29	19.7	27	20.4	26
Min. midshaft diam.	17.7	37	18.1	29	14.8	27	15.2	26
Epicondylar breadth	60.9	30	61.1	19	52.7	10	54.0	19
Radius: Max. length	233.4	20	237.8	15	209.5	11	209.9	10
Ulna: Max. length	251.7	18	260.3	15	229.5	6	236.4	5
Clavicle: Max. length	144.7	15	143.5	10	125.0	9	132.8	9
Scapula: Breadth	98.7	7	–	–	85.3	3	84.7	4
Acromion a-p diam.	46.9	16	47.1	8	36.6	5	38.2	6
Femur: Max. length	434.6	19	434.4	11	395.5	11	395.5	8
Max. head diam.	46.0	24	45.3	13	40.3	24	40.2	15
Subtrochanteric a-p diam.	25.8	32	25.4	30	28.9	21	22.8	16
Subtrochanteric transv. diam.	33.7	31	33.0	30	28.6	21	28.8	16
Midshaft a-p diam.	29.4	36	29.5	34	25.0	24	24.7	18
Midshaft transv. diam.	27.3	35	27.1	35	23.7	24	23.9	18
Tibia: Length	359.1	16	354.2	9	331.0	9	334.0	5
Nutr. foramen level a-p diam.	35.6	23	36.3	24	30.8	19	29.4	16
Nutr. foramen level transv. diam.	23.6	21	24.3	23	21.4	18	20.9	17
Fibula: Max. length	344.1	7	338.2	4	311.7	4	305.3	3
Lumbar vertebrae anterior height	132.5	15	–	–	127.5	11	–	–
Sacrum height	110.7	9	–	–	102.7	6	–	–
Sacrum breadth	112.8	10	–	–	110.1	3	–	–
Innominate: Height	209.8	6	206.3	10	192.2	5	190.2	9
Iliac breadth	145.0	4	150.8	5	148.0	4	148.8	6
Ischial length	80.7	10	82.6	9	74.5	11	72.4	12
Pubic length	67.4	7	67.7	4	74.7	7	75.8	13
Pelvis: Inlet a-p diam.	99.0	5	–	–	104.7	8	–	–
Inlet transv. diam.	121.6	5	–	–	130.6	8	–	–
Interspinous breadth	79.7	4	–	–	103.2	6	–	–
Talus: Length	51.0	26	52.1	27	47.9	19	48.0	19
Max. breadth	43.4	26	42.9	27	37.8	18	37.6	18
Mid-trochlear height	30.0	26	30.1	27	26.4	18	26.7	18
Calcaneus: Max. length	80.7	22	79.7	17	68.9	10	71.6	15
Max. breadth	43.7	17	44.9	16	39.5	10	40.6	15
Metatarsal: I	61.3	22	61.4	25	58.4	16	59.4	18
II	74.6	20	74.7	21	68.6	14	70.2	12
V	60.3	21	60.6	20	56.0	14	55.3	13
Metacarpal: I	44.6	21	45.7	22	41.8	9	43.0	12
II	67.4	25	67.7	23	62.2	10	63.0	16
V	52.3	21	52.6	16	49.8	11	48.7	11
Capitate: Length	25.1	16	25.8	12	22.8	9	22.9	8
Breadth	17.9	17	19.4	9	16.8	9	17.4	8

Measurement (mm.), index, or angle (For definitions, see p. 3 and Martin and Saller, 1959)	Males		Females	
	Mean	N	Mean	N
B—Body Proportions and Other Indices and Angles				
Stature estimate (cm., Trotter)	166.8	38	154.2	27
Indices:				
Relative hip breadth	16.3	3	17.0	8
Claviculo-humeral	47.2	16	45.1	11
Brachial (radio/humeral)	77.8	23	74.1	14
Crural (tibio/femoral)	81.5	15	83.0	9
Robusticity (femur)	13.1	22	12.5	15
Humerus (midshaft)	81.6	42	75.5	32
Pilastric (femur midshaft)	107.4	43	105.2	27
Platymeric (femur subtrochanteric)	76.8	37	79.2	26
Cnemic (tibia)	66.6	34	70.3	25
Lumbar curve	96.7	9	97.1	8
Pelvic brim (inlet a-p/transv.)	80.8	6	80.6	8
Calcaneus (breadth/length)	55.3	21	57.3	16
Talus (height/length)	58.6	32	55.5	23
Angles:				
Femur, neck-shaft	127.3	16	133.7	9
Femur, torsion	13.5	17	6.1	8
Tibia, retroversion	10.9	26	11.0	13
Tibia, torsion	30.0	9	22.2	5
Talus, diversion	28.5	34	28.6	25
Talus, torsion-head	38.4	31	41.8	23
Talus, posterior facet	46.3	34	44.5	23
Pelvic brim	54.0	5	58.9	8
Upper sacral	29.4	5	22.2	8
Lumbo-sacral	29.5	4	26.0	2

comparison with under 50% of males in Classic to Roman times and under 19% of males in the same age group in modern America (Runge, 1954); only Eskimos have vertebral columns as arthritic as those of the people of Lerna at this age (20–40 years). In addition to frequent arthritis of facets and lipping around intervertebral disks, with signs of disk breakdown, there are a few examples of herniations of disk material into vertebral bodies (Schmorl and Junghanns, 1957), as in *69, 182,* and *196 Ler,* indicating sudden pressure from lifting or other movement, but no wedge fractures of vertebral bodies. It is interesting that *182* and *196 Ler,* are in the same part of the cemetery as *181* Ler who shows marked signs of disk destruction and of arthritis of facets in the cervical, lower thoracic, and lumbar regions, ending in the fusion of C_2 and C_3 and of C_7 and T_1 in the neck area and in a separation of the neural arch and lower facets of L_5. This separation, perhaps a form of fatigue fracture (Nathan, 1959) from excessive bending strain, may occur in as much as half of certain Eskimo isolates (Stewart, 1956) and almost certainly has a genetic background. At Lerna *181 Ler* is the only example (2.2%) among 28 males and 17 females. The human lumbosacral joint often shows other unstable variations which may predispose it to arthritic breakdown, as, for example, the tendency for the fifth lumbar vertebra to become incorporated with the sacrum, or for the first sacral vertebra to become lumbarized. The sacralization is complete in *42 Ler* (5.9%), who thereby has only four lumbar vertebrae, and is beginning in *126* and *201 Ler* (11.8%); all three are females. Incipient lumbarization occurs in three males, *70, 127, 189 Ler* (10.7%), all thereby having six sacral vertebrae, and in one female, *45 Ler* (5.9%). In three males (*1, 23, 132 Ler*) and one female (*182 Ler*) the first coccygeal vertebra has been added to the sacrum without the first sacral vertebra having started to lumbarize. Taking both sexes together, in 45 lumbosacral columns there are 7 examples of complete or beginning vertebral shifts, but only 2 of these (4.4%) show real instability. This incidence is not an excessive amount of transitional shift. Also predisposing to lumbar stress and arthritis, are exceptional sharpness of the lumbosacral angle or exceptional pelvic tilt, but here again the people of Lerna are not exceptional; 9 exhibit a lumbosacral angle of 30.3⁰, and 13 a pelvic brim angle of 58⁰.

But if almost all the lumbar arthritis at Lerna is attributed to simple wear and tear and exposure to weather, how then do we explain the comparatively high incidence of arthritis of the neck? Here, 29% of 25 males and 12% of 22 females show marked breakdown of neck joints, with probable subluxation; in some cases paresthesias of hands and arms and even muscle weakness must have resulted. This cervical arthritis includes breakdown and mushrooming of some articular facets, usually more on one side than the other and usually in the midcervical area, and the breakdown of disks and of Luschka joints, indicated by marked

TABLE 7. CERTAIN MEAN MEASUREMENTS, INDICES, AND ANGLES OF MALE AND FEMALE SKELETONS FROM LERNA COMPARED WITH THOSE OF MODERN UNITED STATES SAMPLES

Measurement (mm.), index, or angle	Male				Female			
	Lerna		Modern[a]		Lerna		Modern[a]	
	Mean	N	Mean	N	Mean	N	Mean	N
Measurements:								
Humerus, max. length	309.7	13	336.2	1445	287.8	12	304.3	63
Radius, max. length	237.8	15	251.7	1364	209.9	10	222.1	63
Ulna, max. length	260.3	15	270.4	1382	236.4	5	239.9	63
Clavicle, max. length	143.5	10	154.1	50	132.8	9	134.6	15
Femur, max. length	434.4	11	472.5	1171	395.5	8	429.6	63
Tibia length, lat. cond. to mall.	354.2	9	385.6	1240	334.0	5	340.3	63
Fibula, max. length	338.2	4	383.2	1125	305.3	3	343.4	63
Stature estimate (cm., Trotter)	166.8	38	175.1	1288	154.2	27	160.7	63
Lumbar vertebrae height, ant.	132.5	15	143.1	39	127.5	11	134.7	16
Iliac breadth	150.8	5	162.4	100	148.8	6	157.0	20
Calcaneus, max. length	79.7	17	83.8		71.6	15	78.7	
Metatarsal II, length	74.7	21	77.2	84	70.2	12	73.3	21
Metacarpal II, length	67.7	23	70.7	80	63.0	16	66.4	28
Indices:								
Claviculo-humeral	47.2	16	46.2	50	45.1	11	44.2	15
Brachial (radio/humeral)	77.8	23	73.8	182	74.1	14	73.0	63
Crural (tibio/femoral)	81.5	15	82.0	66	83.0	9	81.6	28
Robusticity (femur)	13.1	22	12.5	100	12.5	15	12.3	28
Pilastric (femur midshaft)	107.4	43	104.1	100	105.2	27	102.7	28
Platymeric (femur subtrochanteric)	76.8	37	83.5	100	79.2	26	81.1	28
Cnemic (tibia)	66.6	34	71.1	66	70.3	25	71.9	28
Talus (height/length)	57.6	32	58.8	83	55.5	23	58.9	21
Lumbar curve	96.7	9	96.2	43	97.1	8	98.6	16
Pelvic brim (inlet a-p/transv.)	80.8	6	99.2	50	80.6	8	93.9	500
Angles (⁰):								
Pelvic brim	54.0	5	57.2	50	58.9	8	57.7	500
Femur, torsion	13.5	17	8.7	106	6.1	8	14.0	31
Tibia, retroversion	10.9	26	9.3	85	11.0	13	9.1	29

[a] Data for modern U.S.A. based on American war dead (Trotter and Gleser, 1958), several dissecting room samples cited in Angel 1946a, a recent sample from the Jefferson Medical College, and radiographic pelvic brim measurements by Young and Ince (1940). Bones from the left side only were used, except for midline measurements.

lipping and inflamed porosity of adjacent surfaces of the vertebral bodies (Plate XXV) with fusion of vertebrae in at least four people. These look like the end results of modern whiplash injuries through automobile accidents. The Greek-speaking intruders presumably had introduced the horse and wagon or chariot. Gejvall identifieds horse bones in Lerna V, though the chariot does not appear unequivocally until the end of the period, on a shaft-grave stela and on a gold ring at Mycenae (Clark, 1952, p. 304, quoting Karo). But jolting on a horse (or in a cart) could scarcely produce so many injuries. Did the Lernaeans practice some type of acrobatic bull-baiting like the Minoans or the earlier Çatal Hüyük ritualists? Are these neck collapses simply the results of heavy labor of some kind? Did the men wear heavy helmets in warfare? There is simply not evidence to test these guesses or to explain the arthritis, though dental disease may possibly play a role.

Arthritis of joints in the limbs, hands, or feet occurs in 41% of males and 18% of females (Plate XXIV), very often related to some extra stress, deformity, or healed fracture, as in *52, 70, 174 Ler*. This is about twice the frequency in Classic to Roman times; data for a comparable age group in modern America are lacking. *137 Ler*, probably a weaver, with her arthritic changes in the right shoulder joint and biceps groove and her stress enlargement of scalene muscle insertions on the first rib, suggests that occupational strain had much to do with arthritis of extremity joints just as it does in the shoulder and biceps bursitis of modern western civilization; but she is the only clear example of shoulder arthritis (though *196 Ler* has clear-cut arthritis of the clavicular attachments). Gout seems likely only for *70 Ler* (Plate XXIV) because of the shape of the big toe lesion and the yellowish elbow joint deposit. The arthritic hammertoes of *52 Ler* and the fusion of phalanges in the second and third toes of *125 Ler* probably result from direct posture-stress and injury.

DENTAL DISEASE, DIET, AND HEREDITY

Table 8 shows dental disease as fairly severe at Lerna (Plate XXII), with about one-quarter of all teeth diseased (lost, carious, abscessed, or carious plus abscessed). This condition is comparable to that of other prehistoric and Medieval groups and of most populations of primitive people (cf. Brothwell, 1963), and is, of course, healthier than that of modern urban populations (cf. Sognnaes, 1950). In Greece itself, with concomitant increasing cereal diet, increasing age at death, and fluctuating decrease and increase in tooth wear, dental lesions increased from 4.8 per mouth at Early Neolithic Nea Nikomedeia to 6.5 per mouth in the Late Bronze and Early Iron Ages. With the Classical rise in level of civilization, dental health improved markedly, before returning to the previous level of disease which lasted from Hellenistic to Turkish times, when, in the Romantic period, by A.D. 1800, dental health suddenly deteriorated and half the teeth were diseased. Mouth acidity from increased dietary sugar could be a factor in maintaining this high rate into modern times. Clearly civilization has had a contradictory and inconsistent effect on dental health. The importance of adequate protein as well as phosphorus and calcium ions for enamel and dentine formation in childhood (cf. Sognnaes, 1950) is suggested by the extraordinarily good teeth of the Mycenaean shaft grave aristocrats who have only about one-fifth the dental disease rate of the Lerna common people; 11% of the rulers have perfect dentitions, as opposed to 6% of the Lerna group. Paradontal disease likewise is much less severe among the ruling families. This protein-mineral relationship remains hypothetical, however, since the only evidence for more meat in the diet of the aristocrats is their greater bodily size and robustness and the occurrence of gallstones in one of them.

Lerna women have worse teeth than men, if one makes allowance for their younger age at death, because of the pregnancy drain on health already outlined; and, because of the younger age at death, they have less tooth wear and probably did not lose teeth from abrasive exposure of pulp, as did a few males.

Apparently Bronze Age bread produced less abrasion than Early Neolithic bread and meat, since marked wear affects half the Nea Nikomedeia people but only 28% of those at Lerna. This partly explains the occurrence of edge-to-edge bite in only a third of Lerna people, as opposed to half in Neolithic times, the start of a progressive change in chewing mechanics which ends in the marked overbite, prominent chin, and relatively unworn and diseased teeth of modern times. This slow dental deterioration from Paleolithic to modern times is a mechanical, rather than a chemical plus metabolic, effect of the change in diet from wild meat and wild plants to cooked cereal products and fruits and, more rarely, domestic meat. Change in the incidence of arthritis of the temporomandibular joint, however, followed that of other arthritis; 20% of the people at Lerna were affected, compared to only 12% in Classical times.

Resistance to decay depends not only on mouth chemistry, proper enamel and dentin formation, and the stimulus of hard use on the tooth's blood and nerve supply, but also on heredity. Some individuals at Lerna have perfect or almost perfect dentition (especially *59, 138, 139, 185, 198 Ler*) and some clans, such as the Sea clan, have poor teeth. In the Northern

TABLE 8. COMPARISON OF INDIVIDUALS AT LERNA AND OTHER GREEK LOCALITIES WITH RESPECT TO DENTAL DISEASE, TOOTH WEAR, AND TYPE OF BITE, EXPRESSED AS AVERAGE FREQUENCY PER MOUTH OR AS A PERCENTAGE OF POPULATION

Observation	Early Neolithic Greece: Nea Nikomedeia	Average per Mouth			Classic Greece	Living Greek males
		Middle Bronze Age				
		Lerna		Mycenae[b]		
		Males	Females	Shaft graves		
Alveoli available [a]	30.3	29.1	28.5	27.8	30.0	31.6
Teeth: Suppressed	.2	.8	.2	.6	.7	.2
Unerupted	.1	.1	.1	0	.2	.1
Lost	3.3	4.8	4.2	.5	2.7	8.4
Carious	1.3	1.8	2.5	.8	.8	4.7
Abscessed	1.0	1.5	1.0	.2	1.1	(2.2)
With lesions	4.8	6.9	7.0	1.3	4.3	13.2
Percent with lesions	16.0	23.7	24.6	4.7	14.3	41.8
Lost after death	2.9	2.6	3.6	5.3	9.6	–
Present	24.1	24.6	24.2	26.2	19.7	23.2
Paradontal disease (percent):						
Absent	47	18	17	50	40	
Slight	26	37	57	40	20	
Medium to pronounced	27	45	26	20	40	
Tooth wear (percent):						
Absent	0	0	0	0	2	1
Slight	10	22	52	45	27	26
Medium	40	40	33	40	31	40
Pronounced to very pronounced	50	38	15	15	40	33
Type of bite (percent):						
Underbite	7	6	0	6	0	1
Edge bite	47	37	30[b]	33	44[b]	22
Slight overbite	40	40	45	50	46	35
Medium to pronounced overbite	6	17	25	11	10	42
Average age of subject	30	37	31	36	41	38
N	19	39	25	20	87	118

[a] Alveoli destroyed in ground have been subtracted.

[b] Aristocrats contrasting with commoners in physique and dental health.

clan three people show heavy tartar deposits (occurring in 9% of the general population), possibly from the use of a special herb coating over diseased and painful teeth. Yet two in this clan have excellent dentition.

Genetic influence shows also in the frequency of the extra or Carabelli cusp (Plate XXI) on the lingual side of the protocone of an upper molar (usually the first molar). This occurs in 19% of Lerna people, a higher frequency than at other Greek sites, though less than in the United States, where its occurrence is over 50% among whites. At Lerna, 6 adults and 6 children show it, 4 in the Northern clan (*123, 131, 133, 137 Ler*), 3 in the Spring clan (*98, 99, 103 Ler*), and the other 5 in five different clans, following the expected pattern of marriages between clans if the original bearers of this trait controlled by a dominant gene had been commonest in the first two groups. Tooth wear hides this trait in many adult teeth, so that the 31% frequency among 19 Lerna children may be a better estimate. Carabelli's cusp increases the chewing area slightly and must have provided a considerable selective advantage in earlier times. On the other hand, the mongoloid type of strengthening of the incisor teeth is the true shovel incisor and is rare in Europeans and perceptible only in *13 Ler*. But over 40% at Lerna have concave incisors, slightly shovel-shaped, without any folding of the side rims (cf. Plate XXI). Seven people have rotation of teeth but only one (*88 Ler*) show suppression of an upper second incisor. All four third molars are suppressed in four adults and the average number of unformed permanent teeth and their occurrence in 22% of adults are typical for Europeans.

Susceptibility to dental disease may result from the same intermittent childhood illness or malnutrition which shows in enamel arrest lines in half the people at Lerna and seems to have diminished body size and true pelvis depth. There is an added possibility that active abscesses may have sometimes helped to bring on death, especially when they caused large cysts (*91 Ler*) or invaded the maxillary sinus (*174 Ler*) or mandibular nerve and artery canal (*97 Ler*). Dental abscesses may possibly have played a role in severe neck arthritis, either directly through spread of infection via the pterygoid and vertebral venous plexuses or indirectly through inflammation, muscle spasm, and effect on general health. The association between abscessed teeth and "collapse" of neck vertebrae shows a contingency coefficient (C) of .4, significantly below the .01 level by χ^2 test ($\chi^2 = 9.9$, N = 53). A causal relationship, therefore seems to be likely, though aging certainly increases the association.

TRAUMA

Fractures, wounds, and various injuries mirror a different aspect of Lerna society (Plate XXVI). Two men (*52 and 73 Ler*) and one woman (*207 Ler*) have broken left forearms, the men plausibly from direct violence, as in parrying a blow. One man and one woman (*89 and 7 Ler* have fractures of the fifth metacarpal. This usually follows striking a misdirected blow. At least one man (*88 Ler*) has a rib fracture, and another has a fractured spine (*76 Ler*) in the susceptible region (Th_{11-12}). At least two men (*18 and 50 Ler*) have broken noses. All these are well healed except *52* (healing actively at death) and *73* (fusion across interosseous membrane). This 10% population incidence of fractures is an underestimate because of incompleteness of skeletons. But the true incidence was presumably rather less than among ourselves.

Four men (*18, 23, 66, and 132 Ler*) and four women (*38, 59, 178, and 182 Ler*) show healed scars of head wounds, and two men (*181 and 189 Ler*) show skull splits which may possibly have caused death (Plate XXII). Four of these ten are in the Eastern clan. The periostitic and arthritic fusion of right thumb and little finger phalanges of *88 Ler* points to infection spreading through the tendon sheaths and ulnar bursa probably after a wound (Plate XXIV), and *189 Ler* also has an injury on the ulnar side of the right hand. The hole in the back of the right scapula of *91 Ler* (Plate XXVI) probably represents a thrust wound from behind (and not another cyst) and *175 Ler* has a leg wound showing on the left fibula. Some of these injuries, affecting roughly another 10% of adults, as well as the fractures, could result from sword or club blows in war. There is no example of a clean bone cut, like those from Iron Age swords or axes, except perhaps in *189 Ler*. Bronze weapons are perhaps less sharp, though probably equally hard. I suspect that some of this violence was from minor fighting with staffs or clubs, possibly ceremonial, and involving both sexes. Bullfighting is not ruled out; *76, 88, 91*, and *175 Ler* may show effects of being tossed or gored.

Another class of pathology, foot and leg lesions (Plate XXIV), affects the Northern clan more than others, *122 Ler*, the subadult boy has a clubfoot (talipes equinovalgus?); *124 Ler* has a twisted right foot with arthritis of an abnormal navicular-cuboid joint; *127 Ler* has a "flail" right ankle (cf. Coutts and Woodward, 1965) with complete rounding off of the trochlea of the ankle bone, leg shortening, and possibly heel fracture; *70 Ler* has gouty arthritis; *125 Ler* merely has fused toe phalanges; *128 Ler* has tibio-fibular fusion at the knee; and *131* anp

TABLE 9. MEAN MEASUREMENTS OF INFANT SKELETONS FROM LERNA COMPARED WITH THOSE OF LATER SAMPLES

Measurement (mm.)		Middle Bronze Age: Lerna				Hellenistic Athens		Modern United States[a]			
		Newborn (7 f.m.–1 m.)		First year (1–12 months)				Fetal (JMC)	Newborn	First year	
		Mean	N	Mean	N	Mean	N	Mean		2 months	6 months
Humerus shaft length		66.0	46	84.7	9	64.9	304	57.7	63.7	72.0	87.7
Radius shaft length		53.1	39	67.2	10	–		46.6	51.1	57.8	68.8
Ulna shaft length		60.6	31	72.5	6	–		53.1	58.2	65.8	76.4
Clavicle length		44.3	22	52.8	6	–		38.7	43.9		
Scapula height		36.2	23	42.3	3	33.9	133	30.6	34.7		
Scapula breadth		29.1	26	33.8	4	28.2	133	25.4	28.8		
Femur shaft length		76.2	44	102.8	11	74.5	380	65.4	76.5?	86.5	111.8
Tibia shaft length		66.0	38	87.0	9	64.5	313	57.3	61.4	69.5	88.9
Fibula shaft length		62.1	17	73.4	5	–		53.9	58.3	66.0	85.3
Ilium length a-p[b]											
Brim	male	14.4	18	18.8	8	15.3	53	13.2	15.0		
segment	female	15.6	23	20.5	2	16.8	76	14.5	16.5		
Posterior	male	17.9	19	22.3	6	16.9	53	14.4	16.3		
segment	female	16.4	21	22.0	2	15.6	76	14.0	15.9		
Breadth	male	36.8	14	48.3?	3	–		29.9	33.9		
	female	35.6	14	47	1	–		32.0	36.3		
Stature		515[c]		630[c]		510[c]		444	504	570	664

[a] Comparative data from the United States are from Maresh (1955) for the 2-months and 6-months samples, studied by X-ray. For the newborn sample Maresh's 2-months group has been reduced by 11.6%, representing the difference between living stature at 2 months (570 mm.) and at birth (504 mm.); newborn shoulder and pelvic girdle measurements come from a sample of 11 white "full-term" foetuses at the Jefferson Medical College (with stature of 444 mm.) increased by 13.5% to adjust to living birth stature of 504 mm. (Meredith, 1943). This sample's adjusted long-bone lengths are quite close to Maresh's, being in general larger. American newborn estimates are for the day of birth.

Note that it is impossible to obtain a true modern sample of newborn bone diameters since hospitals do not X-ray normal healthy newborn babies and the small sample of apparently full-term babies dead at birth (J.M.C. sample above) must include some bias toward biological misfortune even though many nondefective infants die at birth. I excluded all clearly premature fetuses.

[b] The brim segment of iliac length (a-p) I measure from the acetabular end of the bone to the front edge of the auricular (sacral) joint surface; the posterior segment I measure from the front edge of the joint surface to the back of the bone at or near where the posterior superior iliac spine will develop.

[c] Estimate.

140 Ler have arthritic lipping of subtalar and other foot joints. These are all males. Three males and at least four females have healthy lower extremities. (Could the injuries be related to overland travel connected with the Bubanj-like pottery found in House 45?) On the other hand, the clubfoot and other congenital deformities probably have a genetic background.

In the Bridge clan, *174 Ler* has areas of periostitis indicating strain of the bifurcating ligament and probably also of the lateral ankle ligaments, as from repeated ankle sprain; and *239 Ler* has an area of erosion immediately behind the subtalar joint. The extremely slender left femur shaft of *95 Ler* in the Spring clan suggests partial paralysis, perhaps poliomyelitis. Together with the arthritis and gout mentioned earlier, this is a fairly extensive list of lower extremity pathology.

The level of surgical skill is not low; the trephination on *33 Ler* is certainly less neat than that on *51 Myc* several generations later, at Mycenae, but trephination of any sort takes skill and the difference seems largely one of improved cutting instruments (Plate XXII). If the young man, *33 Ler*, died a ritual death as a pharmakos, or scapegoat, these observations on surgery may be less relevant.

GENETICS, MICROEVOLUTION, AND SOCIETY

Evolutionary change depends on selection pressures working on the amount of variability produced and maintained by the mutation rates of all genes, plus other factors such as isolation, mixture, and change in size of breeding group (cf. Mayr, 1963, quoting works by Dobzhansky, Wright Haldane, Fisher, Neel and others). Selection pressures at Lerna include, from a negative standpoint, the infant and child death rate and the limitations on adult longevity, and, from the positive standpoint, the differential excess of fertility. The infant death rate of 359 per thousand is high enough to have a considerable selective effect. But there is no proof that the dead infants are less healthy than the survivors except the occurrence of porous skull bone of potentially thalassemic type (all degrees of severity) in 32% of infants but in only 16% of adults. Size of the dead infants is about the same as that estimated for newborn modern American infants, as shown in Table 9. We do not know the size of the surviving infants, but it is a fair inference that there was little difference between the dead and the survivors (modern stillborn American whites close to full term but still premature are shown in Table 9 to be 13.5% shorter than living infants at birth). On the other hand the older Lerna infants and several of the Lerna children seem small by modern standards, so that some negative selection by disease must have occurred. Those Lerna infants which were homozygous for the thalassemia gene and died of anemia, together with the deaths of those others lacking this or other resistance to malaria, add up to a disproportionate share of the total infant and child deaths. At Nea Nikomedeia, the excess of child deaths (a ratio of infants to children to adults of 5:8:10, as opposed to 8:5:10 at Lerna) is very probably linked to malaria severe enough both to kill older children and to reduce fecundity. This is part of the price for positive selection of heterozygous individuals resistant to malaria. It is possible that resistant individuals tend to be of a certain physique, probably linear, but our sample of 9 juvenile skulls (3 type C; 2, E; 1, D; 1, B; and 2, A) is too small to show that negative selection eliminates one variety more than another. Except for the anemia plus malaria deaths, there is no solid evidence at Lerna that a high juvenile death rate eliminated the less fit. Interestingly enough, our modern preservation of the lives of infants and children is probably doing no genetic harm either.

In any society, positive selection may have a very striking effect. At Lerna there seem to be big differences in the fecundity of women and the fertility of clans. Eighteen women (20, including the sterile ones) produce 100 children, but only 5 of these women produce 47 of these children; i.e., a fourth of the mothers produce half the next generation (cf. Neel, 1958); the 6 or 7 most fecund females are older at death (37 versus 26), scarcely taller (155 versus 154 cm.), but more linear and more thalassemic than the 11 or 12 less fecund. The more fecund compared with the less fecund show skull circumference 498 versus 486, cranial index 77 versus 81, fronto-parietal index 72 versus 69, skull height index 74 versus 71, facial index 86 versus 83, nasal index 48 versus 53, and chin height 28 versus 29 mm. The more fecund tend to have bigger, narrower and higher skulls, faces, and noses (but not deeper chins) than the less fecund, but in a total sample of only about a dozen skulls.

The more fecund versus less fecund distribute by skull type respectively as follows: A, 2:1; B, 0:0; D, 1:1; F, 2:2; E, 1:2; and C, 0:3. Given this small sample, the distribution is too even

TABLE 10. COMPARISON OF CLANS GROUPED WITH RESPECT TO FERTILITY AND CHRONOLOGICAL PERIOD

Observation	Total group		Clans grouped with respect to:							
			Fertility				Chronological period			
			Less – 8 (1, 3, 6, 8–12)		More – 5 (2, 4, 5, 7, 13)		Earlier – 6 (1–4, 6–8)		Later – 7 (5, 7, 9, 10–13)	
	M	N	M	N	M	N	M	N	M	N
Age:										
Male	36.8	55	37.9	34	35.2	21	36.1	25	37.3	30
Female	31.0	47	28.2	27	34.9	20	29.3	29	33.8	18
Stature (cm.)	166.6	65	166.5+	41	166.4+	26	167.1	32	165.9	35
Skull circumference (mm.)	519.4	54	518.0	35	521.1	21	516.1	24	521.5	32
Chin height (mm.)	33.8	70	33.2	46	34.2	28	34.4	36	33.6	37
Ramus breadth (mm.)	31.6	59	31.4	40	31.9	22	31.6	29	31.6	33
Face profile angle (°)	86.4	47	86.5	35	86.2	13	85.9	25	86.9	23
Indices:										
Robusticity	12.8	37	12.8	28	13.0	10	12.6	17	13.0	21
Pelvic brim	81.4	15	81.2	12	81.9	3	79.5	8	83.5	7
Cranial	76.5	57	76.6	38	76.8	22	76.6	26	76.7	34
Auricular height	73.0	56	72.6	38	73.4	20	73.0	25	72.8	33
Fronto-parietal	69.9	55	69.8	37	69.7	19	70.2	25	69.4	31
Fronto-gonial	98.2	39	98.0	35	97.6	19	98.8	26	97.1	28
Facial height-breadth	87.3	45	87.1	33	88.2	13	88.2	23	86.7	23
Upper facial	51.9	46	51.9	34	56.7	14	53.0	24	51.0	24
Nasal	50.9	49	50.9	37	51.6	15	50.4	25	51.8	26
Orbital	83.1	52	84.3	37	81.2	20	83.4	29	83.0	28
Porotic hyperostosis:										
Adult	15.1%	73	9.1%	44	23.3%	29	14.7%	34	15.4%	39
Juvenile	25.0%	84	24.2%	69	33. %	15	40.6%	32	15.4%	52
Deaths:										
Age 0–12 months		84		69		15		36		48
Age 1–14 years		48		37		11		19		29
Adult		102		61		41		54		48
Births		237		114		123		137		100
Births per female		5.0		4.2		6.2		4.7		5.6
Survivors		105		8		97		82		23
Survivors per female		2.2		.3		3.9		2.8		1.3

NOTE: For all measurements, I have added female to male averages, after adjusting them by the following factors (based on skulls and people of known sex): stature 1.0785, skull circumference 1.042, chin height 1.124, minimum ramus breadth 1.059, face profile angle 1.014. Indices of the two sexes I have combined directly. The data for the clans include doubtful measurements excluded from other statistics.

to prove that Alpinoid traits are being lost. Moreover, the distribution by clan is quite random and the correlation of fecundity with clan fertility, determined largely by deducing fecundity from individual female pelves, is less striking than expected (see Table 4). Thus clans 13, 2, and 4 are more fertile, but 6 and 11, because of many infant deaths, are not. Their output, in fact, is almost as low as 9, 10, and 12, where there are many juvenile deaths. The only correlation with thalassemia is the greater average fertility of the clan groups having many parents heterozygous. If we had enough pelvic fragments of the 27 women whose fecundity had to be assumed and also knew the mates of fertile versus non-fertile women we could see the direction of positive selection on a realistic individual basis. Possibly Mediterranean, Dinaric-Mediterranean, and Eastern Alpine traits (types A, B, F, and C4 and C5) are favored because of the observed fecundity differences and fertility of clans 2, 4, 5, 7, and 13: these clans have characteristics that are probably pre-Greek, largely Neolithic, and although clan 7 appears less strongly pre-Greek.

Table 10 shows that, in comparison with the less fertile group, the 5 more fertile clans (2, 4, 5, 7, and 13) have slightly larger and higher heads, more linear faces, and lower orbits. This comparison agrees with the type distribution mentioned in the last paragraph in showing the fertile clans less linear in the vault than are the fecund females. The fertile clans agree with fecund females in predicting only the larger head size of later as compared with earlier clans and, indeed, Table 10 shows almost no change in this respect during the Middle Bronze Age at Lerna. In relation with Table 12 the fertile clans predict the general change from Middle to Late Bronze Age only in head and chin size and face linearity; they fail to predict the increased prognathism, lower head with narrower forehead, relatively wider jowls, narrower nose, and higher orbits. More important distinctions of the fertile clans in Table 10 are the increased longevity of their females (35 versus 28 for the nonfertile clans) and the greater incidence of adult thalassemia (23% versus 9%), factors which, taken together, may explain their extra viability. If falciparum malaria was still the key selective factor in the first part of the Middle Bronze Age a decrease in malaria may explain much of the change in direction of microevolution by the middle of the Late Bronze Age. Mutations, isolation, and mixtures may also explain the actual change at the end of the Middle Bronze Age, where group fertility is too crude a predictor.

I cannot see any way to estimate mutation rates. Since most mutations are recessive and virtually all unmodified mutations are harmful, I must assume that in the mixing Lerna population their outward effects were minimized and there was an adequate loss of harmful mutations through inviability of homozygous embroyos. This brings me to discussion of isolation and mixture at Lerna.

The new isolating mechanism of the beginning of farming, which in Greece occurred in the seventh millennium B.C. (Rodden, 1962), was the development of the village as the breeding unit rather than the more mobile and smaller hunting band. Bands often have only three or four breeding couples and in larger and partly polygynous bands (up to 500 people) the chief and the best hunters father a majority of the offspring each generation (Coon, 1962, pp. 94–100; Neel et al., 1964). Most bands tend to exchange mates only with traditional neighbors (Service, 1962, pp. 41–109). Both conditions produce a total limitation of variability but with enough genetic recombination so that several family "types" tend to develop, as seen in pre-agricultural skeletons from such localities as Indian Knoll in Kentucky, the Sacramento Valley, Teviec in Brittany, Afalou, Mechta and Taforalt in North Africa, Hotu in Iran, Mugharet es Skhul in the Near East, and Choukoutien in China, and through descriptive data on modern Bushmen, for example (Thomas, 1958). Villages often show very similar lowering of variability combined with internal contrasts, as in Melanesia (Oliver and Howells, 1957), Peru (Lasker, 1960), or

TABLE 11. MEANS AND STANDARD DEVIATIONS OF MALE AND FEMALE SKULLS FROM LERNA

Definitions of measurements[a]		Measurement (mm.), angle, or index	Male			Female		
			Mean	σ	N	Mean	σ	N
Biometric	Martin	Measurement:						
U	23 a	Horizontal circumference	521.05	16.28	39	494.20	14.89	15
S	25	Sagittal arc	372.58	17.60	24	357.54	16.28	13
S_1	26	Frontal arc	128.56	8.36	39	122.89	6.72	18
S_2	27	Parietal arc	129.44	10.90	39	125.78	6.38	18
S_3	28	Occipital arc	118.97	14.50	31	110.72	10.42	11
—	b	Parietal thickness, left	5.56	.96	40	4.55	.75	18
L	1	Skull vault: length, max.	186.22	8.67	41	173.63	7.63	19
H′	17	Height, basion-bregma	134.36	9.08	14	128.22	4.69	9
(OH)	(21)	Height, auricular-vertex	118.70	6.24	40	112.50	4.23	16
LB	5	Base length, basion-nasion	103.17	5.21	12	95.00	5.98	9
B	8	Breadth, max.	140.46	6.97	41	136.50	7.43	18
B′	9	Frontal breadth, min.	97.81	4.72	42	93.93	4.35	14
J	45	Cheek breadth, bizygomatic	129.53	7.27	34	122.31	4.57	16
w_2	66	Jowl breadth, bigonial	97.90	5.12	29	87.47	6.45	17
w_1	65	Jaw breadth, bicondylar	119.40	4.93	15	110.92	7.82	12
GH	47	Face height	114.13	6.65	30	104.47	4.15	17
G′H	48	Upper face height, nas.-prosth.	68.22	3.78	32	62.06	3.39	17
h′	69	Chin height	33.78	2.95	41	30.03	2.54	29
ml	68(1)	Jaw length, condylo-symph.	105.33	6.72	21	98.67	4.42	9
rb′	71 a	Ramus breadth, min.	32.03	2.60	38	29.00	2.31	21
—	b	Jaw thickness	15.21	1.67	38	14.09	2.33	21
NH	55	Nose height	49.53	3.18	34	44.71	2.87	17
NB	54	Nose breadth	25.12	1.79	34	22.88	2.24	16
DC	49 a	Interorbital breadth	22.80	2.10	39	21.60	1.67	18
—	57(2)	Upper nasalia breadth	12.48	2.53	33	11.14	2.17	14
$O_1′L$	51 a	Left orbit breadth	39.06	2.05	31	37.23	2.66	13
$O_2′L$	52	Left orbit height	31.97	2.31	35	31.71	1.94	14
$G_1′$	60	Palate, alveolar length	53.70	3.49	27	50.00	2.69	11
EB	61	Palate, alveolar breadth	63.56	3.06	23	58.70	4.80	10
		Angles:						
P∠	72	Face profile	85.72	4.85	32	86.73	5.16	15
—	75	Nose profile	51.22	7.04	23	57.67	9.50	6
—	74	Alveolar profile	68.67	5.89	27	70.08	4.57	12
—	b	Alveolar plane	6.07	3.98	30	8.77	2.96	13
m∠	79	Jaw	125.21	8.26	33	126.36	5.54	14
		Indices:						
—	8 × 100/1	Cranial	75.64	5.71	41	78.54	4.85	16
—	(21) × 200/1 + 8	Mean auricular height	72.58	3.56	40	73.60	3.64	16
—	9 × 100/8	Fronto-parietal	69.81	4.09	41	69.99	4.95	14
—	45 × 100/8	Cranio-facial	92.00	4.96	34	90.05	4.07	15
—	66 × 100/45	Zygo-gonial	75.34	4.73	28	70.00	4.89	11
—	47 × 100/45	Facial	88.55	7.49	31	84.74	3.30	14
—	48 × 100/45	Upper facial	52.66	5.15	31	50.71	2.27	15
—	52 × 100/51 a	Orbital	82.45	5.47	37	84.60	7.96	15
—	61 × 100/60	Alveolar palatal	120.06	7.11	21	118.04	10.43	8
—	54 × 100/55	Nasal	51.09	5.29	34	50.40	5.04	15
—		Sigma ratio [c]	129.0			125.0		

[a] For definitions see pages 3 and Martin and Saller, 1959.

[b] See p. 3.

[c] Average variability is extraordinarily high, as seen in the Sigma Ratio (σ). This percentage figure, based on a norm of 100, results from dividing certain Lerna standard deviations ($σ_9$) by Howells' Mean Sigmas for those particular characters; Howells (1936, 1941) used for his Mean Sigmas all available skull series (about 25) with N above 50. Pearson and Davin's famous Egyptian E series (26th–30th dynasties) has a Sigma Ratio of 97.2, and medieval British are close to average (98.1–99.9), while American Indians run low (Stewart, 1943) and 17th-century Londoners (Howells, 1941) are high. In order to avoid counting the same growth force many times I have used for Sigma Ratio the following: horizontal circumference (for gross brain size), auricular height (brain height), chin height (mouth size), and minimum ramus breadth (jaw muscle

Cyprus (Angel, 1954), but with an expanding population. Thus Nea Nikomedeia, Çatal Hüyük, and Khirokitia approximate this balance of relative isolation, in which immigration may have been 15% per generation or less—the reciprocal of exogamous mating between neighbors where marriageable women make up about 15% of the population.

But during the third millennium B.C. there was a sharp enough increase in population to break village isolation through further migrations, through more trade (for example the Adriatic-Baltic amber route), and through conquest (Childe, 1946). In the second and first millennia these forces for mixture were at a pre-Medieval maximum.

Thus Lerna shows effects of both isolation and mixture. Former isolation shows up in the occurrence of partial sacral hiatus in 19% of males (in clans 7, 1, and 12); of Carabelli cusp (especially in clan 8): in 19% of males, 11% of females, and 22% of children; and of metopism in 7% of males and 19% of females. These and other traits could have spread from one clan to the rest, but really striking is the mixture and almost unbelievable heterogeneity of the group even within a clan, immediately obvious in the Plates. Variability as measured by the Sigma ratio (Howells, 1941) is 20% above normal—further above the average than Khirokitia or most American Indian groups are below average. This high variability, together with heterogeneity, indicate contributions from several diverse populations and a lack of time for intermarriage to produce blending and recombinations. By Mycenaean times enough blending between descendants of strangers had taken place so that variability is normal, at least in Argolis, Attica, and Messenia; although the range of variation then is still large, there is a definite central trend. The Early Iron Age again sees a period of heterogeneity before the phase of Classical blending and normal variability. But whereas the Early Iron Age mixing involves trait combinations already present in the Bronze Age, this does not appear to be true for the Middle Bronze Age people in general or at Lerna. Immigration from areas outside of Greece is the best explanation for the high levels of both heterogeneity and variability (Stewart, 1943; Angel 1946, 1960).

TYPES, FUNCTION, AND GENES

In order to objectify the processes of migration, blending, and internal evolution of the Lerna population and of others in the Eastern Mediterranean I developed a system of arbitrary types (see Introduction, p. 34f.), each composed of a number of growth tendencies which I suppose to be the growth effects of genes on skeleton and skull. Specific effects are still almost entirely unknown, except for such tooth traits as Carabelli's cusp. My type A (Basic White, or Upper Paleolithic) has a long and large skull vault, often showing flattened planes as if the brain expansion did not quite fill it, more than average robusticity (and excess of bone) and muscularity, and a deep-jawed face with fairly wide and coarse nose and low and rectangular orbits; some fairly narrow faces are included as A1 (these overlap with Type B and D traits) but the type A norm (A2, A3, A4, A5) is a short and wide and muscular face. Type B (Classic Mediterranean) has a fairly narrow and small skull vault, often quite angular (B2), paedomorphic and lacking in muscularity, with a narrow vertical forehead, pinched and small narrow-mouthed face with incipient prodonty and fairly high orbits, thin nose, and slender but not tall build. Type D (Nordic-Iranian) has a long, high, well-filled and muscular skull vault, with strong and arched browridges on a broad forehead, a peculiarly deep occiput (D2,

---

mass), cranial index (brain shape), frontoparietal index (face-brain junction), nasal index (mouth – sense organ interaction), and face profile angle (mouth – brain mass interaction). I have especially tried to avoid counting mere size variation many times over.

TABLE 12. COMPARISON OF PRE-GREEK WITH MIDDLE AND LATE BRONZE AGE GREEK MALE SKULL SERIES

Definitions of measurement, etc.		Measurement (mm.), angle, or index	Early Neolithic Nea Nikomedeia		Neolithic-Early Bronze Age		Middle Bronze Age						Late Bronze Age	
Biometric	Martin						Lerna		Attica + Argolis		Mycenae (royal graves)			
			Mean	N	Mean	N	Mean	N	Mean	N	Mean	N	Mean	N
		Measurements:												
U	23a	Horizontal circumference	518.2	4	512.6	23	521.0	39	518.1	19	538.2	13	522.0	93
L	1	Skull vault: length, max.	183.5	4	183.9	23	186.2	41	187.0	24	194.6	16	186.6	104
(OH)	(21)	Height, auricular-vertex	121.2	4	117.0	20	118.7	40	118.2	21	117.4	15	115.7	96
LB	5	Base length, basion-nasion	99.7	3	100.7	9	103.2	12	99.2	12	108.0	4	99.5	60
		Parietal thickness	5.8	5	5.4	24	5.6	40	5.4	23	5.1	14	5.6	108
B	8	Breadth, max.	144.8	4	139.3	26	140.5	41	141.0	24	143.9	15	141.2	106
B'	9	Frontal breadth, min.	96.6	5	95.9	22	97.8	42	96.5	21	98.5	16	96.6	96
J	45	Cheek breadth, bizygomatic	128.0	4	127.0	9	129.6	34	131.3	16	133.9	10	129.6	60
w₂	66	Jowl breadth, bigonial	95.0	5	93.0	11	97.9	29	96.0	14	99.7	10	99.2	30
G'H	48	Upper face height, nas.-prosth.	65.0	4	70.7	9	68.2	32	67.9	17	71.2	10	67.8	46
h'	69	Chin height	34.1	7	32.8	16	33.8	41	31.7	19	33.5	15	33.6	57
NH	55	Nose height	45.8	4	49.7	10	49.5	34	49.4	17	52.4	8	49.1	45
NB	54	Nose breadth	27.0	4	23.7	10	25.1	34	23.9	17	24.8	10	24.1	48
rb'	71a	Ramus breadth, min.	33.0	5	30.7	10	32.0	38	30.6	20	32.5	15	30.4	45
		Angles:												
P∠	72	Face profile	84.2	4	85.4	7	85.7	32	87.4	16	84.0	7	85.8	37
—	c	Alveolar plane	8.0	4	7.5	10	6.1	30	6.6	15	5.3	7	7.6	40
		Indices:												
—	8 × 100/1	Cranial	79.6	4	75.7	23	75.6	41	75.8	23	74.2	14	76.2	100
—	(21) × 200/1 + 8	Mean auricular height	73.9	4	72.4	20	72.6	40	72.0	20	69.3	14	70.6	96
—	9 × 100/8	Fronto-parietal	66.1	4	69.1	22	69.8	41	68.5	21	68.4	14	68.1	89
—	45 × 100/8	Cranio-facial	88.5	4	91.2	9	92.0	34	92.6	16	92.6	10	91.2	58
—	47 × 100/45	Facial	88.4	4	94.1	5	88.6	31	86.6	15	90.0	7	89.4	23
—	48 × 100/45	Upper facial	50.8	4	55.6	8	52.7	31	52.4	15	53.2	6	52.7	41
—	54 × 100/55	Nasal	59.4	4	47.9	10	51.1	34	48.4	16	46.8	9	49.1	44
—	52 × 100/51a	Orbital	80.9	4	85.5	9	82.4	37	80.1	17	84.3	10	84.9	56
—	61 × 100/60	Alveolar palate	112.8	4	117.9	8	120.1	21	116.6	15	118.4	9	117.5	38
		Sigma ratio	(105.1)		101.8		129.0		120.0		120.5		101.5	

D3, D4, but not D5) and a face with a rectangular and deep jaw, a long, high-bridged and beaky nose often linked with chewing stress from a sloping mouth plane (D4) and compressed cheekbones around sloping orbits (D5); the body build is tall and muscular. Type F (Dinaric-Mediterranean) has a byrsoid and intermediate (mesocrane) vault that is often high (F1, F2) and has a sloping vertex area and short occiput with flat cerebellar area; and a long hexagonal face with a deep chin and long nose and tendencies toward a "classic profile," and with flaring cheekbones and sloping orbits. Type E (Mixed Alpine) has a very well filled, large, wide and mesocrane vault with lambdoid flattening and with an especially capacious frontal area dominating a rather short and orthognathous face that is wide in the orbital region and palate, and has a somewhat delicate mouth region and a large-rooted but non-projecting nose. Types C1, C2, and C3 (Alpine) have a rounded, short and wide vault (brachycrane), with short parietals and base, combined with a rounded square and low face that is orthognathous and sometimes concave in profile, and that has a fairly broad, non-projecting nose and a short and horizontal chewing plane. Body build is short and lateral. Types C4 (Eastern Alpine) and C5 (Low Eastern Alpine) have a short and laterally-bulging vault (brachycrane) with short very deep and scarcely curved occiput and rising vertex profile, and a relatively pinched forehead above a broad and fairly short face that often has a sloping chewing plane and high-arched nose, the same "Iranian" trait complex often found in type D and sometimes in type F.

In the eastern Mediterranean, artificial head-shaping after birth, often by flattening the occipital area in short-headed groups was, in contrast to Cyprus, rare in ancient times in Greece. People who use it tend to emphasize rather than completely to change head form. Angularity resulting from lack of enough childhood remodelling of bone around the original vault bone centers probably reflects diet and water-balance as well as genetic factors. Obviously the eruption, placement, occlusion, bite, wear, and loss of teeth can greatly affect the form of the face as well as that of the mouth region. I try to avoid or to allow for these non-genetic factors in assessing skulls. Obviously the type-tendency system is a stopgap until the time when twin and genealogical studies will reveal actual genetic components of skull growth. For example, I find the tilted mouth plane (a retention of the present childhood condition) is 10.5° in Eskimo and it is the same in the Iranian (D4) mouth complex; this is 3–4° more tilt than in Europe, and in both cases it is accompanied by an excess of downgrowth at the junction of face and forehead in contrast to a lack of growth at the pterygoid and jaw condyle areas. But in the Eskimo, with their flat mongoloid face, the increased forward chewing thrust and forward temporal and masseter strength is largely absorbed and put in action by the extreme forward placing of cheekbones and forehead angles and by the extra muscle surface of the large marginal processes and zygomaxillary protrusions. In the Iranian face, however, it is the salient and strong upper nose and interorbital area which absorbs the thrust and the high skull and long but compressed zygomatic arches and jaws which give the extra muscle area; the chewing muscles are spread out more posteriorly. One may ask: Genes at how many chromosome loci determine the extra growth forces? Must there not be at least one each for downgrowth at the front and back of the face, one for transverse forehead convexity or flatness, and one for forward or backward displacement of chewing muscles and their bony attachments? How different is the Iranian face complex when it is attached to a short, rather than long, skull base, as in the Eastern Alpine (C4)? It is clear that general size contrast (B1 or C2 versus A2 or C3) gracility versus ruggedness (B versus A and D), general linearity versus lateral growth (A, B, D versus F, E, C), excess of bone versus paedomorphic fullness (A and D versus E and C), really short face versus high face (A2–A5, E, C1, C2, C5 versus A1, D, F), large incisors and coarse nose versus small ones (A, F2, C3 versus B2–B4, E, C2, C4) each may depend on one or two gene loci. But many critical shape traits are seemingly complex both in terms of structure and of growth. How many genes one may ask, determine the extremely bulging drooping cerebellar region of Iranians (D4), many Corded Nordics (D2), and Eastern Alpines (C4) as against the equally bulging cerebral pole projection with "upswept" occiput and usually very long mastoids found in Central Anatolia (F1–F3, A3) and the Balkans (D5 and sometimes C3)?

GEOGRAPHY, PEOPLES, AND MICROEVOLUTION

In terms of such skull types and such average measurements as are shown in Tables 1 and 11–13, Mesolithic Franchthi Cave in Argolis contained a heavy-jawed Basic White, type A2–4, of almost Upper Paleolithic head size and shape, but of extremely short stature (Angel 1969c) and Early Neolithic Macedonia centered on a Dinaric-Mediterranean type F) average but with an extremely broad nose, more prognathism, and a little more mouth tilt than expected (all, perhaps from negroid development of the incisor region); beside this modal trend (quite comparable to later Lower Egyptians) there is robust Basic White (A2, A3) and massive Alpine (C3), apparently both of European Upper Paleolithic descent, and some Iranian traits (Angel, in press). Both Starçevo-Cris and Boian phases of Balkan Neolithic populations could be slightly more linear, Mediterranean, versions of this combination (cf. Necrasov and Cristescu, 1965), and the later Hageorgitika and Lerna Neolithic skulls suggest a more linear Basic White trend (A1–A3). Early Neolithic Central Anatolia, as at Çatal Hüyük (personal data), may have

TABLE 13. COMPARISON TO SHOW GEOGRAPHICAL AND CHRONOLOGICAL RELATIONSHIPS OF CERTAIN MEASUREMENTS, ANGLES,

Observations	Nea Niko-medeia Macedonia		Greece		Lerna		Mycenae–Royal Graves		Greece		Magdalen-ska Gora North Yugoslavia		East Balkans–Ochre Graves[a]	
	Early Neolithic		Late Neolithic – Early Helladic		Middle Bronze Age		Middle Bronze Age		Late Bronze Age		Hallstatt Iron Age		Copper Age	
	6300–5500 B.C.		4000–2000 B.C.		2000–1600 B.C.		1600 B.C.		1450–1150 B.C.		500–400 B.C.		2300–2000 B.C.	
Age at death	30.4	45	31.2	64	34.0	102	35.9	27	36.5	286	38.0	32	–	–
Measurements:														
Stature estimate (cm., Trotter)	167.7	21	162.6	15	166.6	65	171.5	18	166.3	89	172.3	23	172.0	26
Skull, horizontal circumference	517.1	14	516.0	41	519.4	54	539.3	15	523.2	141	528.8	23	533 ca.	27
Chin height	35.9	18	33.1	28	33.8	70	33.9	17	33.9	87	33.1	19	++?	–
Ramus breadth, min.	33.4	16	31.9	23	31.6	59	32.4	17	30.8	73	30.4	18	+?	–
Face profile angle (°)	84.9	13	87.6	13	86.1	47	85.0	8	85.8	64	86.8	12	–	–
Indices: *	(2.4)		(1.9)		(base)		(1.9)		(1.6)		(2.4)		(?2.6)	
Robusticity (femur)	12.5	10	12.8	8	12.8	37	13.2	13	12.9	50	12.4	18	–	–
Platymeric (femur subtrochanteric)	75.2	16	76.0	10	77.8	63	82.4	13	77.0	93	81.6	29	73.4	21
Pilastric (femur midshaft)	108.3	17	103.9	10	106.5	70	107.6	16	102.7	95	108.1	33	106.8	20
Cnemic (tibia)	67.2	12	67.5	7	68.2	59	67.7	9	67.4	81	75.3	21	61.5	19
Cranial (8 × 100/1)	77.1	15	77.1	42	76.5	57	74.6	16	76.7	152	78.0	24	73.0	27
Mean auricular height ((21) × 200/1–8)	73.7	14	72.2	34	73.0	56	69.6	16	70.8	138	71.1	22	70.5	*
Fronto-parietal (9 × 100/8)	68.1	15	68.4	40	69.9	55	68.8	16	68.0	139	66.8	20	71.6	23
Fronto-gonial (66 × 100/9)	98.5	14	100.8	15	98.2	39	99.5	11	101.3	42	102.3	14	+?	–
Facial (47 × 100/45)	93.3	13	89.6	9	87.3	45	89.8	9	90.3	38	88.9	13	+?	–
Upper facial (48 × 100/45)	54.8	13	54.4	14	51.9	46	53.0	8	53.1	70	53.4	13	52.2	19
Nasal (54 × 100/55)	55.7	12	48.5	16	50.9	49	47.0	11	48.8	76	48.6	12	47.4	20
Orbital (52 × 100/51 a)	82.7	12	86.0	17	83.1	52	83.4	12	85.9	89	86.2	9	80.0	21

[a] Necrasov and Cristescu, 1959a. [b] Krogman, 1940. [c] Ginsburg, 1956. [d] Krogman, 1949. [e] Duckworth, 1910. [f] Woo, 1930. * Indices calculated from means of measurements (percent difference in 13 characters shown in parentheses). NOTE: Females have been included with males in the above averages. In the Indices and angles they have been combined

averaged somewhat more linear than Nea Nikomedeia, though closely comparable and with some well-filled vaults, as in Hotu 3 from Upper Paleolithic Northern Iran (Angel, 1952). One striking detail in several individuals consists of extremely long and slanting mastoid processes sweeping up into a protrusive upper occiput, as in the later Hamangia people of the Dobrudja area on the Black Sea (Necrasov and Cristescu, 1965) and elsewhere in the Balkans. Proto-Cilicians at Tarsus (Ehrich, 1940) were more Mediterranean-Iranian (A3 and D3). North Iranians, as at Tepe Sialk and Djamshidi and later at Hissar (Vallois, 1939, Krogman, 1940) were very much more linear, with extremely deep cerebellar region and exaggeratedly convex, rectangular, almost scroll-like faces having huge aquiline noses and tilted chewing planes (D4). The earliest Mesopotamians, known from mouth and other fragments from Jarmo, seem to have included a short-headed trend exhibiting F2, F4, or C4 traits and with mouths less extreme than the Iranians, as well as a long-faced Basic White trend (A1 and A2), dominant much later in Kish and Al 'Ubaid in Early Dynastic times (Angel, 1951, after Buxton and Rice and Keith).

Although the first agricultural inhabitants of the belt from Syria-Israel-Jordan to North Africa were mainly rugged Mediterranean (A3 and some B, in varying preponderance) the eastern end of this belt (McCown, 1939; Vallois, 1936), shows some almost Bushmen-like Basic White (A4β) as well as lateral traits (E1 and C4) as at Jericho (personal observation); (one wonders what people lived at Tell Mureybat, see map, page 10). Egypt includes an almost

AND INDICES OF SKELETON SERIES (BOTH SEXES COMBINED) FROM VARIOUS EASTERN MEDITERRANEAN LOCALITIES

Catal Hüyük, Konya Plain		Karataş, Lycia Southwest Anatolia		Tepe Hissar,[b] Northern Iran		Kazakhstan [c]		Khirokitia, South-Central Cyprus		Amuq G-O,[d] Northern Syria, Antioch Plain		Palaikastro,[e] Crete		Sedment,[f] Lower Egypt		United States, Accidental Deaths	
Early Neolithic		Early Bronze Age		Bronze Age		Bronze Age		Early Neolithic		Prehistoric		Minoan		Dynasty IX		Modern White	
6500–5300 B.C.		2100–2300 B.C.		2500–2000 B.C.		2000–? 1500 B.C.		5500–5000 B.C.		3300–500 B.C.		3000–1700 B.C.		2200–2100 B.C.		20th Century	
31.6	216	31.8	358	29.4	138	–	–	32.3	35	37.2	12	–	–	–	–	43.0	68
169.3	44	165.9	130	167.9	35	–	–	166.0	4	169.5	5	166	10	–	–	174.3	44
521.3	37	515.9	76	516.6	137	530.4	9	520.1	21	522.5	14	517.6	32	511.4	70	521.4	58
35.6	94	34.7	144	35.6	110	34.7?	11	34.0	29	33.4	10	31.3?	2	34.1	55	33.7	35
35.5	68	31.4	129	33.5	110	–	–	35.6	32	32.5	11	sm.?	–	32.8	59	29.8	46
84.8	16	87.0	48	86.2	133	86.7	14	90.0	9	–	–	83.4	15	84.9	65	87.8	34
(2.6)		(1.6)		(2.4)		(1.4)		(3.4)		(1.9)		(1.6)		(2.5)		(2.6)	
12.8	23	12.8	87	–	–	–	–	13?	4	12.9	3	–	–	–	–	12.8	36
71.9	49	74.8	266	76.8	40	–	–	–	–	78.2	4	76.0	62	–	–	84.7	42
111.8	48	106.7	264	–	–	–	–	119?	4	110.4	4	–	–	–	–	108.8	42
65.4	39	67.4	199	66.5	45	–	–	65?	5	66.7	1	66.4	65	–	–	70.5	37
76.3	47	77.4	81	71.7	138	77.3	24	87.1	21	75.5	16	73.3	67	76.6	70	77.6	58
72.6	33	73.2	78	72.2	132	73.9?	*	73.5	16	68.3	14	73.2	*	72.6?	*	72.6	57
69.3	40	69.1	79	71.1	137	69.1	21	67.3	19	68.7	15	70.2	15	66.3	*	67.9	58
98.0	17	103.7	43	100.8	108	100.9	9	96.4	12	103.1	10	–	–	98.8	*	101.7	42
92.1	14	91.4	44	90.8	91	86.4	10	83.5	10	(92.6)	2	85.2?	2	94.4?	*	91.7	27
55.2	19	54.3	47	55.3	118	50.9	16	49.8	10	52.6	3	51.2	8	56.6	*	54.9	35
52.4	19	49.8	49	50.4	131	52.4	16	48.0	10	48.9	3	49.8	14	48.2	67	46.2	51
80.9	21	82.0	59	81.9	116	80.2	20	84.8	10	82.7	4	81.8	17	86.9	61	85.6	51

directly, but for size adjustment of direct measurements the following factors have been used: Estimated stature 1.0785, horizontal circumference 1.042, chin height 1.124, minimum ramus breadth 1.059. These factors are based on samples of known sex.

Mouillian-negroid (beyond A2) early population (cf. Ferembach, 1962, Briggs, 1955), linear but with extraordinarily broad nose and heavy and deep mouth region (A2β) (Ewing, 1966; Anderson, 1968), as well as the negroid small-faced and prognathous and broad-nosed trend (B2β) in the gracile Badarians (Morant and Stoessiger quoted in Angel, 1951). Early Neolithic Cyprus had inland Khirokitians with their extremely short, broad, high and deep skull vaults, owl faces, and tilted jaws (C4), a mode often much exaggerated through artificial flattening of the occiput (Angel, 1951, 1953) and conceivably linked to the undescribed brachycrane element hinted at in Jarmo and Jericho. But two millennia later, on Cyprus, there are also Mediterranean trends with Iranian traits (A2, B4, D3) on the south and north coasts (Angel, 1961, Hjortsjö, 1947).

At the end of the Neolithic period the Central Cyclades, typified by Paros and Antiparos, center on an Eastern Alpine norm (especially C4 and C5) with Mediterranean influence, smaller as well as less lateral and lower headed than the owl-faced Khirokitians; but other Aegean areas were more typically Mediterranean, like Lesbos or Keos, for example. Many island populations are unknown, like that on Melos. By the third millennium B.C. the West coast of Anatolia ranges from very linear Mediterranean (A1, B2) with Iranian (D4) and Eastern Alpine (C4 and 5) influence in the Troad (Angel, 1951) to a Mediterranean Dinaroid blend with more Iranian (D3, D4) and more Cyprus-like Eastern Alpine (C4) around the south corner at Karataş-Semayük in the Lycian mountains. The Anatolian plateau (Lake Van, Pağnik Öreni, Arslantepe, Dundartepe, Maşat Hüyük, Büyük Güllücek, Alaca, Alişar, Ahlatlibel, Kocumbeli, Kusura) continues the disturbed and mixing Neolithic population elements (A3, B1, D3, C5) with enough strength in the Eastern Alpine elements, especially the turtle-headed variant (C5), to anticipate the dominance of a short- and low-headed, somewhat hawk-faced mode in the Hittite period (Kansu, Şenyürek, and Krogman quoted in Angel, 1951; Şenyürek, 1951; and personal observation). But the actual changes are not clear without much more data from this area, especially from its eastern end, whence must have come the Iranian element at Troy, Babaköy, Tarsus, and Karataş. Crete by the third millennium shows a rather short-statured and squat-faced combination of Mediterranean with Basic White (B1–B3, A4) (Duckworth, quoted in Angel, 1951) with indication of Eastern Alpine (C5) at Palaikastro.

Meanwhile in the area from the eastern Danube over to the Ukraine the Early Neolithic Mediterranean combination mentioned above continues with but slight Alpine (Mesolithic?) addition except for the Hamangia people in the northeast, who show Basic White (A1, A2), Eastern Alpine (C4), and Danubian-Hallstatt (D5) additions, the latter with the special upswept occiput (D4) noted at Çatal Hüyük and contrasting with the Iranian (D4) form. (Can this group have a Central Anatolian source?) It is noteworthy that their environment is marshy, but we lack data on diploic thickening (possibly a malaria response). Bulgaria also shows a Mediterranean-alpine blend, small-faced and sometimes prognathous (Jaronoff in Gaul, 1948). Early material from the western mountains of Yugoslavia is lacking, but later data from Laibach, Glasinac, and Magdalenska Gora (Angel, 1968b) shows massive Upper Paleolithic square-heads (C3) and Basic Whites (A2, A3), together with a Nordic (D2 and D1) element whose origin begins to become clear. We now know that in the Balkans (Clark and Piggott, 1965, p. 288) as much as in Greece (Caskey, 1960), in the Aegean, and in Anatolia (Mellaart, 1958, 1965; Mellink, 1966), the second half of the third millennium B.C. was a period of cultural change, migrations and intrusions. In Rumania, Necrasov and Cristescu (1957, 1959, 1959a, 1965) note that the ochre-covered skeletons of the chalcolithic tumulus-culture, or pit-grave and wagon-using people, from the steppes northeast of the Black Sea (and ultimately from Kazakhstan) bring in a new combination which the authors describe as Protoeuropoid (Basic White A2), Protonordic (Corded, D2) and Dinaroid (F2), and they note that at Holboca and at other sites many females seem to continue the earlier Neolithic type. These invaders are the earliest of the Kurgan people of southern Russia and the steppes of western Siberia (Debets, 1948, Ginsburg, 1956), and according to Gimbutas (1963) they probably brought the Indo-European language into Europe, starting by 2500 B.C. (Clark and Piggott, 1965). At the same time that they spread through the Balkans, there appears the globular amphora cist-grave culture, in which a much more Alpine trend is exhibited, and from this combination arise the people with cord-marked pottery (often beakers in shape) and stone battle-axes who spread farther westward and northward, bringing the Corded (D2) and more typical, almost mesocrane Nordic (D1) into northern Europe. Thus, it is natural to find some corded pottery in Early Helladic III Greece, as at Eutresis, and two skulls at Aghios Kosmas which are Nordic (D2).

The situation in the Balkans is much simpler than that in Early Bronze Age Anatolia (Mellaart, 1958, 1965), where the second millennium B.C. literary evidence of an Indo-European-speaking element in the Hittites, and of other Indo-European speakers (Luvians and Palaites, Gurney, 1966), suggests that Indo-European intruders from the Kuban Caucasus center, or from south of the Caspian, might be responsible for the burnings and confusion at many sites in this period. On the other hand, the Hittites and Hurrians might have been involved in these about 2000 B.C., and the westbound Indo-Europeans might be part of the Early Bronze Age people of Pağnik Öreni, Karayavshan, and Troy III–V. We have few skeletons to confirm this, and the relation of the Balkan refugee movement to the Aeolia-Ionia area, as outlined by Mellaart (1965), is a complication which present skeletal material cannot really test. But if Indo-European speakers started to travel westward in the early third millennium B.C., when the Sub-Boreal dry period started, according to Gimbutas' (1963) fairly elaborate theory, they ought to be chiefly linear Nordic-Iranian (D4, D2), with a little Upper Paleolithic of both linear (A2) and lateral (C1) varieties (Debets, 1948, Ginsburg, 1956, Krogman, 1940). In South Russia, in the Caucasus, and in the Balkans they would be increasingly changed by addition of European Alpine (C1, C2, C3), Mediterranean, and the local Mesolithic blend as at Voloschkoyo (Debets, 1955) of short-faced linear Nordic-Mediterraneans (D3, A1, A2) to produce the Kurgan people and the pit-, or ochre-grave, group and the corded-pottery makers farther west. By the route south of the Caspian, on the other hand, the influences would be first Iranian-Mediterranean (D4, B4, A3), as at Hissar (Krogman, 1940), and then Eastern Alpine (C4 and especially C5) and Mediterranean throughout Anatolia, with Mixed Alpine and Dinaroid intermediate combinations (cf. Angel, 1946). It may be significant that the proto-Minyan pottery of northwest Anatolia after 2400 B.C. (Mellaart, 1958, 1965) and some Early Bronze Age pottery of the plateau may have general parallels in the various metallic-looking stemmed vessels of northern Iranian gray ware at Hissar IIa (Schmidt, 1937) and Tureng Tepe. On the other hand the custom of intramural cist burial of the Anatolian plateau (dating back to Çatal Hüyük) does not give place to tumulus burial, and if the Indo-European intruders did adopt the custom of cist burial, it is not certain that they brought it into western Anatolia, except, perhaps, at Hanai Tepe in the Troad.

The Aeolian and Ionian coast Indo-Europeans (probably proto-Ionians and Luvians) are physically undefinable because adequate data is lacking. Troy III, it is true, does show three skulls (*9, 10, 11 Tr*) which are Iranian-Mediterranean (D3, D4, A1); and from Troy IVe, somewhat later, *12 Tr* is a low-headed, almost byrsoid Eastern Alpine (C5) like the plateau variety frequent in the Hittite area (Angel, 1951, Krogman, 1937). The Karataş Lycians (Mellink, 1965a) of about 2400 B.C. show distinct Iranian (D4) traits in their partly Eastern Alpine (C4) plus Mediterranean (A and B) blend. These Early Bronze Age Iranian traits in each area may belong to much earlier (probably Neolithic) movements, with the rugged Babaköy male (D3+A2) and Troy II adolescent (D4) as evidence (Angel 1951). But in any case we are talking about individuals from opposite areas of Western Anatolia and we can only guess that at this time an Indo-European group on the Aegean shores of Anatolia (at Troad, especially) would have been mainly Iranian-Eastern Alpine with some Mediterranean influence (D3, D4, C4, C5, A2). The strikingly Iranian (D4) skeleton (Angel 1970) of a warrior (?) from the Early Bronze Age site of Pağnik Öreni excavated by Dr. Richard Harper in the Keban region of the Euphrates River supports my hypothesis of an east-west movement involving this and other physical types.

In this setting of surrounding peoples (Angel, 1969a) the key skull changes in the pre-Greek population by 3000 or 2500 B.C. are toward a much smaller general size, much more linear nose, higher orbits, smaller and more gracile and orthognathous Mediterranean-type mouth region. These probably are in part the result of internal evolutionary and nutritional changes (smaller tooth space and decrease in stature and in part the effects of maritime intrusion of typical Mediterraneans and both varieties of Eastern Alpine from the Aegean and south-western Anatolia (or even from Cyprus, Eastern Crete, or the Egyptian delta).

In comparison with this Early Helladic norm, the average Lernaean of the Middle Bronze Age is taller, larger-headed, slightly longer-headed and higher-headed, with relatively wider cheeks, orbits, forehead, and nose and deeper chin and much greater heterogeneity, as if broad-faced Alpines from the north (or from the east) and taller and deep-jawed Nordic-Iranians from the steppes (by either route) had been added. But this is perhaps jumping ahead too fast, because the changes from the Early Helladic samples are not large, very little greater than those from the Middle Bronze Age to Mycenaean. Hence analysis of the clan composition will illuminate the process of mixture between the pre-Greek indigenous population and the intrusive Indo-Europeans, whether Luvians or proto-Illyrians or proto-Ionians. In Attica, Corinth, and the Argolid the pre-Greek population included chiefly Basic White (A3), Mediterranean (B) sometimes slightly Dinaroid (F1) and Eastern Alpine (C4) with minimal Iranian, Corded, or Alpine influence. If the intrusive Greek-speakers during Early Helladic III came chiefly from the north they would add Corded, European Alpine, and Upper Paleolithic (A2), and Mixed Alpine-Dinaric (E2, F2) characteristics; if they came from the east, with proto-Minyan pottery and possibly the custom of intramural burial, they would add chiefly Iranian (D4) and low-headed Eastern Alpine (C5) characteristics. These intruders throughout Greece south of Macedonia would have been generally a small minority. But at or during the start of Early Helladic III many sites south of Macedonia show destruction, whereas others, especially in Central or Northern Greece, show it only at the end of that period (Caskey, 1960; Clark and Piggott, 1965; Weinberg, 1965): one can conclude that individual groups or tribes of intruders varied in size and made different adjustments to and arrangements with the local peoples whom they ultimately overcame. As in Anatolia, the Balkans, and Central Europe the arrival of Indo-European speaking peoples was not the simple addition of a handful of conquering refugees at a single point in time but an extended and very complex series of military, social, and economic adjustments.

MIXTURE OF PEOPLES OF LERNA

At Lerna the first group of intruders overcame the walled defenses of Lerna III and burnt down the fairly new and very impressive Early Helladic II palace (The House of the Tiles). The people who, during the few centuries before 2000 B.C. occupied and rebuilt the site, now Lerna IV, had such respect for their conquered predecessors (Caskey, 1965), or else such fear of a desecrated center, that they built a tumulus of earth with a low retaining wall over the ruins of the burnt palace. I think that this indicates a strong element of the old population existing together with the conquerors. But we have no adult skeletons from either Lerna III or from Lerna IV to check my guess, which is based in small part on the apparently Corded type D2 males (11 *AK* and 15 *AK*) in graves 3 and 4 at Early Helladic IV Aghios Kosmas (Angel, 1959); the cemeteries at Early Bronze Age Lerna must have been some distance away from the town. Apsidal houses and wheel-made grey Minyan pottery first appear in Lerna IV (Caskey, 1965, 1966), considerably before people brought this ware to Troy VI, at the start of that Middle Bronze Age town (Blegen, 1963), and there is trade with areas of central Greece which had not yet undergone destruction, as well as with Anatolia. Near the end of Lerna IV people began to bury their dead, apparently only infants at that time, next to their houses, as if this Anatolian plateau custom had arrived a number of generations after the original conquest.

Soon after this (ca. 2000 B.C.), at about the time of further burnings of Early Helladic III sites in areas of Greece north of the Peloponnese, Lerna V begins quietly with further varieties of pottery that is fully Middle Helladic (dark Minyan, matt-painted and lustrous patterned), with the horse, with a variety of house styles, and with the custom of regular intramural cist and earth burials, all of which give evidence for possible changes in population. In Lerna V there is evidence of trade contacts more widespread than before: the appearance of possibly Bubanj-culture (certainly exotic) incised handmade pottery flasks in room 45 and house 98A (in the Northern clan area) in larger amounts than the considerably earlier cord-marked sherds in Early Helladic Eutresis; the fairly widespread occurrence of Middle Minoan pottery of several styles and dates in the Southern and then in the Marsh clan areas, including a spouted jar of Early Palace style in grave J-4 (Caskey, 1957); the occurrence of Cycladic pottery, including an import probably from Melos, in grave BD-19 (Spring clan); and the pins, stone hammer-axes, riveted dagger blades, and other small finds. All these give evidence of continuing contact with Anatolia and the East Mediterranean coasts; and if contact does not necessarily mean immigrants, it may nevertheless suggest directions to look for comparisons when a population is as heterogeneous as that of Middle Bronze Age Lerna.

In relation to the end of Lerna IV and the developments during Lerna V, six clans shown in block letters on the plan (Figure 5) seem to have earlier roots than the others. Among the graves of the Forest, Southern, Spring, and Central clans, burying around the central palace tumulus, occur Early Helladic III juvenile graves; the Northern and Western clans also have their beginnings early in the Middle Bronze reoccupation. All these tomb groups last at least into the mid-phase of the town—the Spring group perhaps longer.

The Forest clan people have skulls that are linear and Mediterranean, like the non-Dinaroid edge of the Neolithic population, and that match the Lerna Neolithic skulls (compare Plates V and I). They include the man with the crudely trephined skull and a burial (BC-3) disturbed later in the Bronze Age. There is no porotic hyperostosis, and there is a fair number of infant deaths, as if from a newly introduced disease.

The Southern clan has hyperostosis (*207* and *60 Ler*) and is both much more fertile and more varied than the Forest clan; it includes what are really two cemetery units. In this group (Plate III) a linear, coarse Mediterranean element (resembling the local Neolithic as much as the low-faced Minoan Mediterranean) is juxtaposed with Eastern Alpine (like eastern Crete or Cyprus) and with minor Balkan or Macedonian Alpine and Dinaroid elements to produce a big mesocrane and very broad-nosed average, with toothy and "primitive" mouth region; the women seem especially diverse.

The Central clan, likewise hyperostotic and fertile, is a completely different blend (Plate IV), close to the total average except for the long face and low and drooping orbits with deep prominent chin and strong coronoids. A forward reach of the mastoid process occurs. This group includes Eastern Alpine and Basic White elements of probably Early Helladic origin with Iranian and Dinaroid plus Mixed Alpine combinations, suggesting connections with both the Northwestern Ionian coast (*40 Ler*) and Macedonia (*43 Ler*). As in the Southern clan some adults (here females *56* and *42 Ler*) may be siblings or parent-child combinations, but the males are quite diverse.

The Spring clan is equally varied in form of skull vault, which averages small and brachycrane, the face is orthognathous and thin and the nose thin (Plate VII), and the stature is tall. This group combines a pre-Greek or perhaps Central Cycladic Mediterranean plus Alpine trend with Iranian-Mediterranean (D3) and Dinaroid (F2) combination rather like the Early Bronze Age Lycians (Angel, 1966a, 1970) and probably somewhat later in date than the other clans. (We have no Melian skeletons but one might ask, could Melos have approximated a blend between Lycia and Paros?) There are many child deaths. Two children are metopic and both women and one child share family characteristics of heart face, shallow cheekbones, and thin hawk nose.

The Western clan, which comes from more westerly parts of the excavated area, shows hyperostosis in only one case, a man. The central tendency (Plate II) is toward a long ellipsoid, high, and flat-sided skull with deep occiput, high and rectangular face with beaky nose and orthognathous but somewhat toothy mouth—Iranian (D4) with some Basic White traits, and with little variation. These people may be direct descendants of Anatolians since there is virtual identity with the linear element at Troy, Karataş, early Tarsus, and regions farther east; I stress, however, their Tarsus rather than Trojan resemblances since they lack an Eastern Alpine (C4) element. Nevertheless, this may well be one of the first Hellenic clans, part of the group which might have brought intramural burial, proto-Hellenic speech, and Minyan pottery to the Argolid. The girl *16 Ler* from Trench C is plausibly a local wife, but the other two women, adults from Trenches M and H resemble the men.

The Northern clan which is the largest one, is burdened with hyperostosis, infant deaths, and leg injuries; the stature is average rather than tall; the skull is mesocrane and not large, with a broad forehead and face, a full mouth with protruding chin, an intermediate nose, and a forward reach of the mastoid and coronoid processes (like that of the Central clan) and includes a wide range of varieties (Plates IX, X, XI)). One finds in these people the appearance of Alpines and Basic Whites of European Upper Paleolithic affinity, quite tall Balkan Nordics (D5) with the occiput reminiscent of those of the Danube delta Hamangia people, Nordic-Iranians (probably with Corded connections), Mixed Alpines, and Dinaroids that parallel the people of the Neolithic Macedonian Plain. These could be a combination of West Balkan paleolithic survivors with northern Indo-Europeans (probably proto-Illyrians or proto-Thracians or proto-Phrygians) and with pre-Greeks from the north (a Trojan resemblance is possible). Except for the family resemblances in the rather varied group in tomb BE-30, the males seem to resemble each other (especially *115, 125, 127, 131 Ler*) more than do the females.

Of the remaining clans, the River, Marsh, Bridge, Eastern and Sea clans begin about the middle of the occupation, while the Plain and Bay clans begin later. The Sea clan lasts through to Late Helladic II and the Bay clan survives through Late Helladic I and II.

The River clan, slightly hyperostotic and apparently fertile, exhibits considerable variety. The average (Plate VIII and IX) is large, linear and high-headed, with a broad forehead, medium face with retreating cheekbones around low orbits, long jaws with projecting teeth, and rather short stature. These people are a blend of coarse Mediterranean with Nordic-Iranian and Eastern Alpine, like a blend of Neolithic with Northwest Anatolian elements, a local plus Hellenic combination as in the Forest, Western, and Southern clans, which continues the Western clan's traits (*82* and *87* comparable to *19 Ler*, *91* to *18 Ler*) perhaps more than those of the Forest clan (comparable with *33 Ler*). There are no females to compare with the males but BD-8 is near infant burial BD-6 which contained two adult metatarsals, possibly female.

The Marsh clan is quite hyperostotic, as implied by the name I have given it, and quite fertile. The average skull (Plate V and VI), is quite small, short and high, byrsoid to sphenoid in shape, and with a rising profile, pinched forehead, an average and orthognathous, wide-jowled face, deep chin, and prominent nose. These people, Eastern Alpines of both high- and low-headed (owl-and turtle-headed) varieties combined with Nordicand Alpine, are the third- or fourth generation or later hybrids of Early Helladic pre-Greeks (plus Central Cycladic or Eastern Cretan) with Hellenic intruders.

In terms of physical traits and cemetery location, the Bridge clan stands between the Northern, Marsh, and Eastern clans. It is quite infertile, with eleven dead juveniles, two of them with hyperostosis. A lack of female adults is arbitrarily balanced by considering that the empty adult graves DE-49 and DE-69 might have been of females (three infant graves also produced no skeletons). Stature is short. The skulls average less wide, higher, and more pinched forehead than those of the Marsh clan (Plate XII and XIII); the face has a short nose, shallow cheekbones, and a long and tilted mouth region with very deep chin. These people, with puzzlingly short stature, exhibit Iranian mouth traits in a Mediterranean-Alpine combination that is apparently an Anatolian-Balkan-pre-Greek blend. The Eastern clan, a large one with a number of head injuries, is equally infertile and with hyperostosis only among the juveniles. The skull (Plates XIII and XIV) tends to be byrsoid and mesocrane, even though the forehead is relatively wide and the face wide and often heart-shaped, with a pointed and shallow chin. The nose has a high root and is beaky, though relatively short. These people, like the Bridge clan (cf. *174* and *175 Ler*), are an Iranian-Mediterranean-Alpine blend resembling Lycians and central Cycladics or North Anatolians (cf. Alişar) in a special combination of west Anatolian and pre-Greek traits. The females seem to resemble each other more than the males do.

The Sea clan is equally infertile, fairly large, and with hyperostosis absent except in one male. It covers a notably large range of heterogeneity, perhaps partly because of its long time span. The large skull vault averages mesocrane and low, but with so little uniformity that not one conforms to this average (Plate XVI and XVII). The face tends to be low, angular, and orthognathous, with deep canine fossa, low orbits, and a fairly thick nose. The fairly long jaw has square angles, a wide ramus, and strong chin. This is an interaction between Cro-Magnon-like Basic Whites and Alpines, plus some Nordic-Iranian traits—a re-segregation of many Neolithic traits from the mainland, Balkans, and Crete with enough proto-Hellenic absorption (cf. *50* and *46 Ler*) to foreshadow the Mycenaean blend as seen also in the neighboring Plain clan. Several of the males resemble each other (*23, 28, 52 Ler*), and of the females *55 Ler* could be from the Forest and *45 Ler* from the Central clan.

The equally infertile Plain clan next door shows no hyperostosis and is less variable than the preceding one, and is generally later than it in date. The stature is rather short and the very small skull (Plate XV) tends to be long and high, with swept-back forehead and long occiput. The intermediate face has a prominent and wide nose going with a toothy and long-jawed mouth. This Mediterranean-Iranian blend shows the same sort of back-cross recurrence of local Neolithic plus proto-Hellenic traits that appear in different form in the Eastern clan (cf. *181* and *189 Ler*) and foreshadows a frequent linear variant common not only in the Late Bronze Age Argives but also in Classical and later Greeks.

The Bay clan, like the Western clan, is very small but at the eastern rather than western end of the excavated cemetery and it dates from the Middle Helladic to Late Helladic II, roughly the period of the real rise of Mycenae and the Shaft Grave dynasties. It is quite fertile. The intermediate skull (Plate XVI) is smooth-planed and low, on the whole like the Sea clan average. These people exhibit a pre-Greek plus proto-Hellenic blend of Mediterranean traits similar to that of the average Mycenaean.

This clan analysis suggests that certain groups—Western, Northern, River, Marsh, and Sea—show closer male than female similarities, as expected in a patrilocal grouping. In other groups—Forest, Central, Spring, and Eastern—male dissimilarity with female similarities suggests a matrilocal setup. The other four groups are equivocal, though Bridge, Plain, and Bay do not seem patrilocal. It is possible, of course, that none of the groups ancestral to these Middle Bronze people were matrilineal, as various authorities have guessed, and that the appearances of matrilocality simply show that place of residence was a matter of convenience rather than an inheritance and kinship relationship. But I shall assume that the pre-Indo-European peoples were not patriarchal and that the intruders were, as indicated by language terms.

On this basis I will work out a tentative synthesis (this would be easier with a complete picture of the pre-Greek population), namely, that at least two Neolithic invading groups (F1, F2, A3, B4; and A1, B2, C2) combined with a still partially undefined but nevertheless vital Mesolithic hunting population (A2, E2, C3), and this combination was followed by an Early Bronze Age addition from the East (B1, C4, C5, A4, D3, F3). Tables 12 and 13 show no enormous change from the Early Neolithic series (from Macedonia) to the late fourth plus third millennium B.C. series (from Greece as a whole). The former is a Dinaroid, mesocrane, broad-nosed and slightly toothy combination of Dinaric-Mediterraneans, Basic Whites, and Alpines of Paleolithic background. The latter is shorter, smaller, with lower head, shallower and more orthognathous mouth area, and much narrower nose—relatively more Mediterranean and narrow-nosed Eastern Alpine, as if from Aegean intrusions from southern and central Cyclades (Angel, 1951, 1959). These pre-Greek intruders may have brought an Early Bronze Age culture from Anatolia, but the proto-Lycians at Karataş are too high-headed and long-faced to be an ideal direct source. At Lerna the Neolithic population may have been more linear, i.e., Basic White and Mediterranean, so that the Early Helladic blend, for which we lack any evidence south of Corinth, may also have been less mesocrane.

Thus at Lerna the Southern and Forest clans in large part, and the Central and Spring clans to some extent, might represent the original population, perhaps matrilineal, with Minoan and Cycladic additions. The Western and River clans might represent an eastern group of Early Bronze Age proto-Hellenic intruders (the possible destroyers of the Early Helladic II palace) bearing Iranian and some Eastern Alpine traits. The Northern and (later) Bridge clans represent to a large extent the northern intruders bringing Corded Nordic (D2), Alpine (C) and Macedonian (i.e., Early Neolithic) traits. And the Eastern clan, apparently matrilocal, combines all these, with possible Anatolian additions.

The Marsh and Sea clans represent differing combinations of all these elements possibly reinforced from Crete and Anatolia, the latter clan being especially heterogeneous. The Plain and Bay clans show a return toward the pre-Greek mode, as if the new Mycenaean blend was emerging with considerable autochthonous elements, as suggested by the fecundity and fertility analyses. The Middle Bronze skeletons from Argos and Eleusis all show parallels, but this emergence is clearer at Asine where *17*(A3), *7*(A1), *15*(A5), *23*(A3), *22*(B3), *26*(B3), and *10FA*(C4) represent presumed pre-Greek elements; where *1*(D4), *3*(D3), *12*(C5), and *20FA*(C5) represent eastern intruders; and where *4*(D2), *21*(D2), *2*(D1), *6*(D1–A2), *11*(D5), *24*(F1), and *19FA*(E3) represent northern or Balkan intruders (Furst, 1930; and further restored and restudied by Angel).

We have already seen that fecund females at Lerna (types A3, F3, D5, A1, E2, F4) as opposed to less fecund females (types A3, C2, D4, F1, C1) scarcely differ sharply enough to show any certain microevolutionary trend, except possibly selection against Alpines. The fertile clans—Southern, Central, River, Marsh, and Bay—favor Eastern Alpines (C4), Dinaroids (F2, F3, F4), and perhaps Basic Whites (A1, A3); the infertile clans—Bridge, Eastern, Plain, and Sea—show excesses of Mixed Alpine and Mediterranean; while Alpines, Iranians (D4, D3), and Nordics (D1, D2, D5) are intermediate. Thus some elements from the pre-Greek population seem to tend to outbreed part of the northern element, partly because of thalassemic protection against malaria. Possibly the matrilocal clans are less fertile than the patrilocal; but this is not a clear trend. The significant finding is that I see no clear major differential fertility effect in terms of types, of intruders versus natives, of matrilocal versus patrilocal clans, or of presence or absence of porotic hyperostosis—only a number of individual contrasts in fertility in which all the above factors play some part and this is the result one might expect from the kind of complete and persistent mixture which marks this phase in the formation of the Hellenic people.

This mixture must have been stimulating from the biological standpoint, since it promoted many new combinations and to a very small extent some hybrid vigor. But the effects of the cultural and social clash, the adjustment, and the fairly rapid growth and exploitation of new possibilities must have been far more important. The invading Indo-European speaking groups, probably coming from two difference sources and six to ten generations apart, must each have included people of determination and ingenuity, even though both groups may have come largely as refugees to an area they knew through trade. Neither group fits the archeological concept of a warrior band, in spite of the wounds affecting 10% of their descendants; the helmets, swords, shields, horse-drawn chariots do not appear clearly until middle phases of the Bronze Age. But they had the energy to conquer, settle among and marry, and to impose their probably more efficient language, their burial customs, in large part their social structure, and probably their religion on an expanding Early Bronze Age society, handicapped only by the usual prehistoric difficulties with respect to disease (malaria, etc.) and scanty food supply.

CONCLUSIONS

Ecology

The ecology of Lerna, next to the sea, the Argive plain, the then forested mountains of Arcadia, and close to its own special springs, marshes, and river, favored the raising of barley, wheat, vines, olives, and domestic animals (including the horse after 1950 B.C.), but historically and almost certainly prehistorically it also favored the Anopheles mosquito, carrier of malarial plasmodia parasitic on man.

Demography

The focus of this monograph, the Middle Bronze Age cemetery of Lerna V (plus a few burials from the end of Lerna IV and from the greater part of Lerna VI) provided 234 skeletons, of which 35% were infants, 21% children, and 44% adults over 15 years old who lived on the average to the age of 34 years (37 for males, 31 for females), and who were buried in family groups from which I have arbitrarily deduced thirteen clans. Pelvic changes suggest that the average woman might have 5.0 births (5.5 per fertile woman, assuming 10% sterility) and that 2.2 of these infants grew to adulthood, producing a population increase of 7% per generation or .3% annually. Reconstruction of the living population profile suggests that marriage might have been at 17 or 18 for girls, whose childbearing period might have lasted 12 years; that a generation might be 24 years; and that the annual birth rate might have been 44.6 and the death rate 40.5 per thousand, with natural increase up to .4% annually, allowing doubling of the population in 7½ to 10 generations. This increase, extremely rapid for a preindustrial society, was achieved despite a possible infant death rate of at least 300 per thousand and a combined stillbirth and abortion rate of at least 60 and plausibly much higher. Family size, including older relatives, might have been about 5.7 people. This allows a population estimate of close to 800 people during the central part of the Middle Bronze Age when there may have been an increase in population density from under 15 to almost 30 per square kilometer in the circum-Isthmian parts of Greece. Lerna had a notably heterogeneous population, like Asine, Argos, and Eleusis at the same time, and this suggests breakdown of isolates and considerable migration during the preceding Early Helladic III (Lerna IV) period.

HEALTH AND DISEASE

Population increased at Lerna in spite of the major handicap of malaria, plausibly falciparum malaria, as indicated by partially protective thalassemia or sicklemia seen in expansion of cranial marrow spaces (porotic hyperostosis) in 26% of juvenile and 16% of adult skeletons (12% of the total in Middle Bronze Age sites, including those away from marshes). Gene frequency for abnormal hemoglobin might have been about .20 to .25. Porotic hyperostosis was much more frequent in Early Neolithic times (it was found in 60% of adult skeletons at Nea Nikomedeia, a marsh site) and decreased steadily to 1% in Classical times, then increased to 45% in Turkish times, plausibly paralleling, with a time lag, the changes in endemic malaria, including falciparum malaria, caused by improvement and then later decline in methods of farming and swamp drainage. If other diseases, such as the dysenteries, hookworm, tetanus, variola, tuberculosis, could have been studied, they might have shown profiles generally similar but quite different in detail and in time of first occurrence.

Slight signs of seasonal malnutrition or severe childhood disease occur as growth arrest lines on tooth enamel, and the average stature, 167 cm. for men and 154 cm. for women is about 5 cm. less than that of the people from the royal shaft graves at Mycenae. Arthritis begins early in adulthood and reaches a higher frequency than in later Greeks, but is less than in such groups as Eskimo. Neck arthritis is especially striking because of its frequency. Fractures occur in at least 10% of the people, with evidence of other injuries in at least another 10%. Dental disease, at the level of 7 lesions per person (almost 25%) is quite severe, worse than in Neolithic or Classical times or among the healthier Mycenaean kings. Abscessed teeth correlate significantly with neck arthritis. Dental disease and such malformations as clubfoot tend to be particularly frequent in certain clans.

GENETICS AND MICROEVOLUTION

The following traits differ considerably in distribution between clans: porotic hyperostosis, sacral spina bifida, Carabelli's cusp, perfect dentitions, stature, skull morphology, fecundity, fertility. The more fecund females (about 25% of the total, as suggested by pelvic changes) produced almost 50% of the births and were more linear, larger-headed, and possibly taller than the less fecund. But the more fertile clans differ only slightly from the total group, partly in consonance with the direction of the change to the Late Bronze Age population (Tables 6 and 10). Clans with porotic hyperostosis tended to be very slightly more fertile. Infant skeletons did not seem malformed or small, even though they possibly may have had more anemia than adults. Among the skeletons of children, however, growth seems not to have equaled American norms. The extreme heterogeneity of the population, over 20% above average in variability, complicates any simple social selective force and this hybridization plus the increasing population makes for stability and physical and mental vigor in the next historical period.

Population Origins, Migrations

My subjective and extremely speculative survey suggests that origins of the population were mostly local, derived from the Neolithic and later pre-Greek populations, with the Near East and Upper Paleolithic Central and Eastern Europe as ultimate sources. But the altogether too sketchy data for the period before 2000 B.C. plus an analysis of the Middle Bronze Age do suggest a double intrusion of peoples who must have introduced Indo-European languages: from the east (originating in Iran and the steppe country) and from the north (also originating in the steppe country and from among Balkan mountain peoples). They seem to have been themselves mixed and newly forming groups, and they produced slight trends in Nordic-Iranian plus Eastern and European Alpine and Dinaroid directions.

Body Build and Posture

Like Classical and modern Greeks, the Lerna people were relatively robust and stocky, rather than slender, and they show the hip, knee, and ankle adaptations to a rough-country gait expected at this time and place.

General Meaning

In the broad contexts of economic change (from hunting plus collecting to settled farming to urban trade and interdependence and unification) and of evolutionary change (from Neanderthal to later varieties of *Homo sapiens*) the Middle Bronze Age people of Lerna belong to the start of proto-urban synthesis.

The invention of farming and its first spread in the immediate postglacial period clearly produced human biological shocks as population growth outstripped cultural control of disease and made it difficult to obtain a really balanced diet rich in protein. Evidences of a decline in health are seen in the reduction in body size, the lack of improvement in juvenile or adult male mortality (though there is a slight increase in female longevity), an increase in dental disease, and a huge increase in porotic hyperostosis (in groups near marshes or standing water). During the Neolithic and Early Bronze Age these challenges of poor health, expanding population, and consequent migrations called forth a major effort for more creative use of living space—a more effective farming, pottery, metallurgy, ships, carts, geometry, complex politico-military structure—the result was a slow improvement in health and increasing local stability and population growth. During the Middle Bronze Age the rate of mixture both culturally and biologically suddenly increased, probably as a spinoff from all the areas of population growth and migration. The synthesis of ideas and of genes resulting from these movements and mixtures (not least from Indo-European-speakers' migrations) reached a critical mass by the Middle Bronze Age, and there began an almost explosive creativity that continued through the later Bronze Age and into City-State times. The Lerna Middle Bronze Age focuses for us the actual limits of rate and type of population increase, the enormous heterogeneity, the social processes of mixture plus genetic selection, and the successful maintenance of health in balance with diseases such as falciparum malaria. One might compare this whole process with a slow-motion movie of the chemistry of an explosion, or see it as a micro-mirror for our own times of revolution and synthesis.

This study is in fact an attempt to see as a living social organism a past population at a critical time in the history of a people—their transformation into a creative and ongoing society. I could make this attempt at understanding the living of a prehistoric people only through a study of all of their physical remains plus, from archeologists and other experts, a knowledge of their environment, their diet, and the material objects in their culture, as well as a more or less firm structure of knowledge of hundreds of other sites made into a chronological sequence by a host of scholars and scientists. To strengthen the tradition of fullest possible analysis of the remains of our ancestors, in order to understand them and ourselves more fully, is perhaps the most important contribution of this monograph.

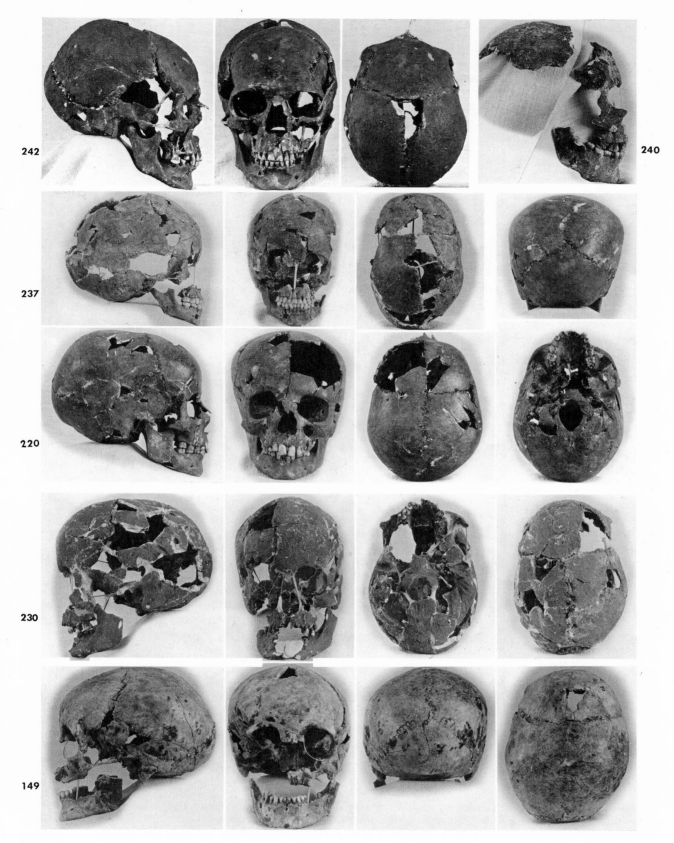

Plate I

Top: female skulls **240** and **242** are Late Neolithic, **237** (4 years old) and **220** (10 years old) are Early Neolithic; all clearly show a linear Basic White trend (A3, A3, A1, A1).   Bottom: Early Iron Age female, **230,** has Nordic-Iranian features (D2); Roman period female, **149,** is squatfaced Basic White (A4) with Alpine fullness.

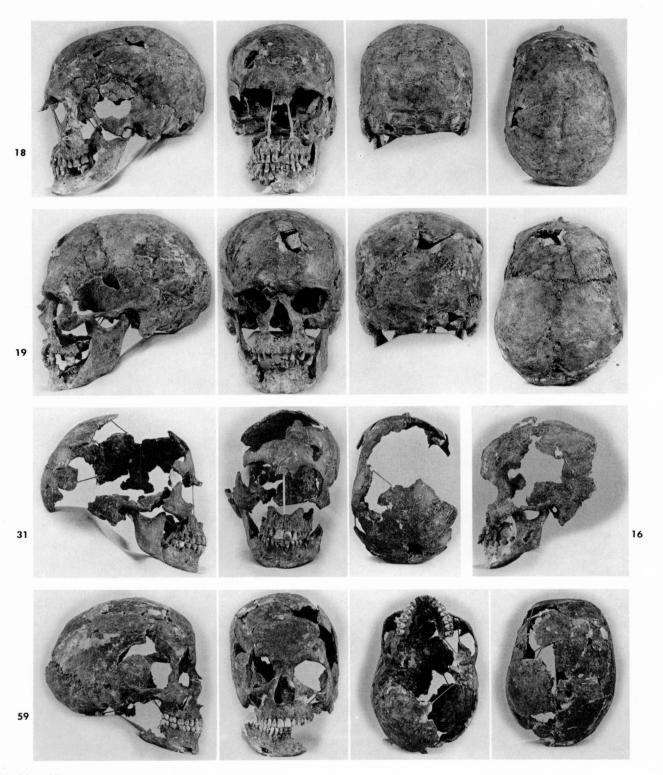

Plate II
Skulls from clan 1 (Western), Middle Bronze Age, early to middle phases: **18** and **19** are males, **31** and **59** females, and **16** an adolescent female. Except for **16** (Eastern Alpine, C4), they show variations of the Nordic-Iranian trend (D4, D2, D4, D3); all might derive from intruders from Anatolia with steppe-country genetic background.

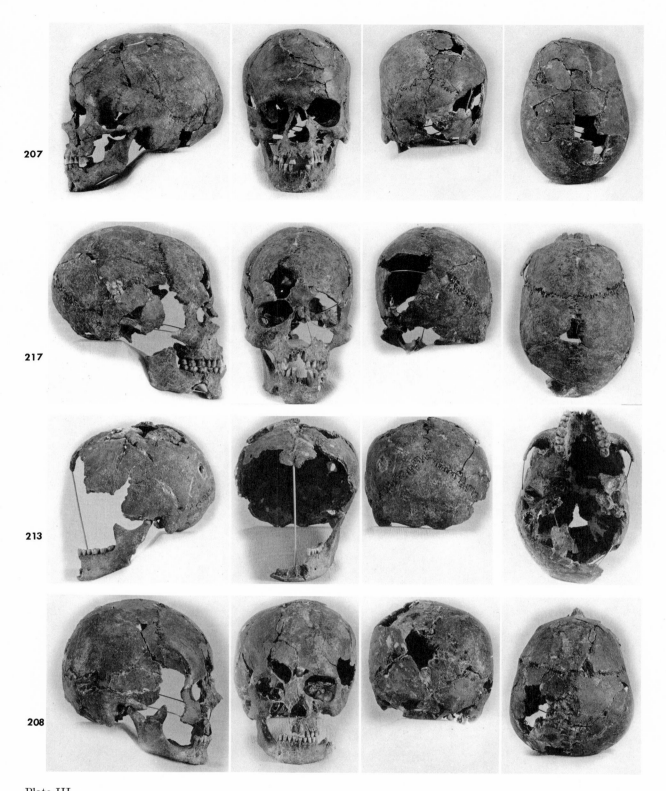

Plate III
Skulls from clan 2 (Southern), Middle Bronze Age, very early to middle phases: **207, 213,** and **208** are females and **217** is male. **207** and **217** are Basic White (A1), in contrast with the European Alpine (C3) and Eastern Alpine (C4) trends in **213** and **208;** all maintain pre-Greek traits, eventually Near Eastern, not excluding Cretan or Cypriote additions.

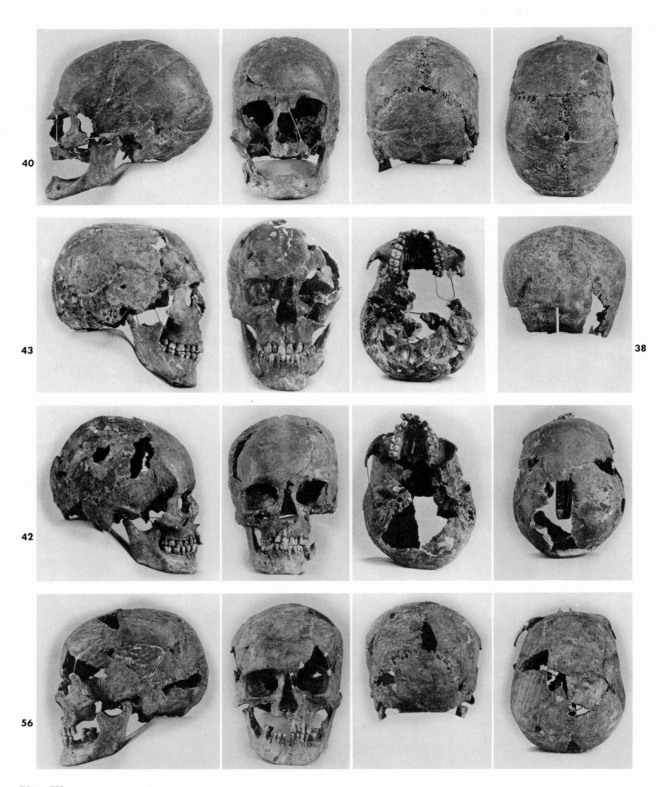

Plate IV
Skulls from clan 4 (Central), Middle Bronze Age, very early to middle phases: **40** and **43** are male, **38** (occiput only), **42**, and **56** are female. They represent, respectively, Iranian (D4), Dinaroid (F3), Alpine (C4), Basic White (A3), and Mixed Alpine (E2) trends; and suggest a connecting of northwestern Anatolian, north Greek Early Neolithic and Early Helladic backgrounds.

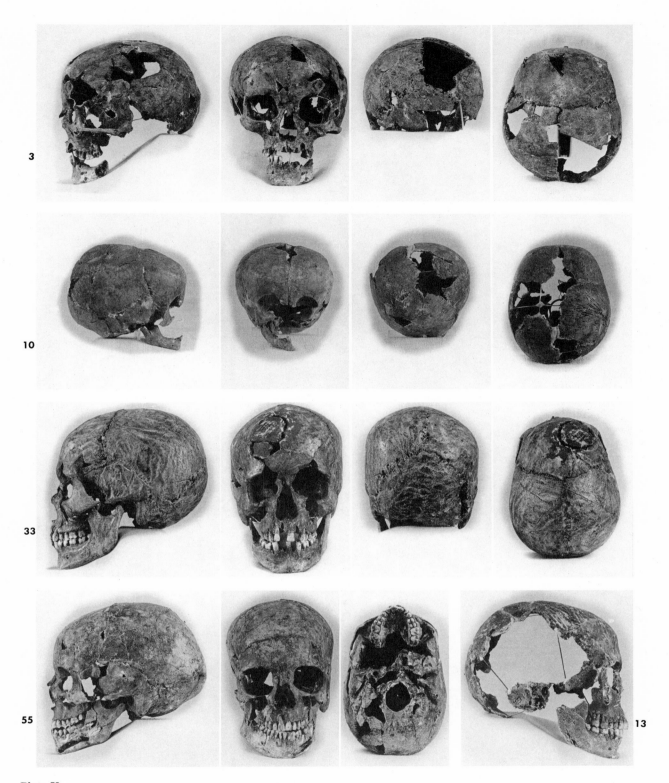

Plate V
Skulls from—clan 5 (Marsh), Middle Bronze Age, late phase (Lerna V): **3** (female, Alpine, C2) and **10** (infant suffering from porotic hyperostosis-thalassemia).—Clan 3 (Forest), very early: **33** (male, Mediterranean, B1, with traumatic trephination, conceivably a scapegoat) and **13** (female, Basic White, A1).—Clan 12 (Sea): **55** (female adolescent, Basic White, A1), continuing traits of the autochthonous population into the much later Sea clan.

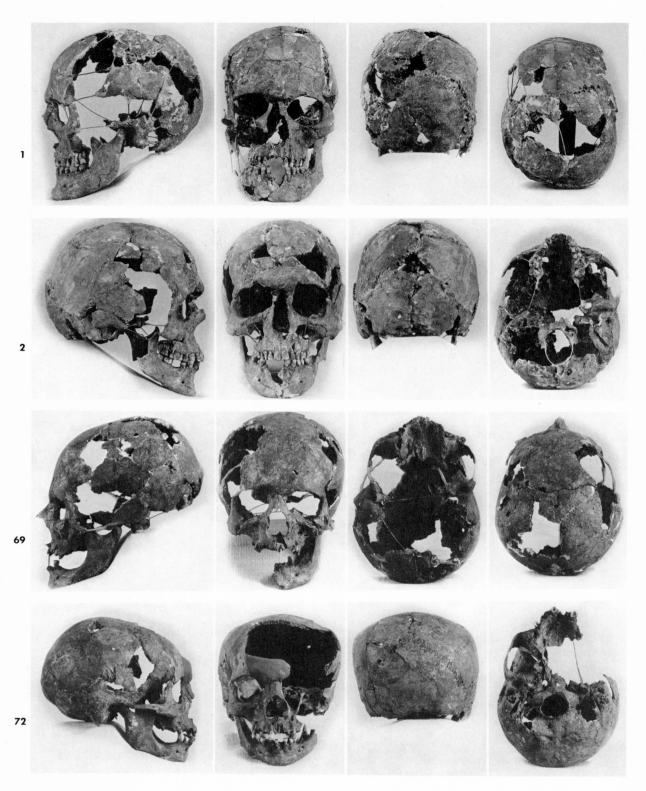

Plate VI

Skulls from clan 5 (Marsh), Middle Bronze Age, middle to late phases, superimposing on edge of clan 8: **1** and **2,** males from a single grave, are Nordic (D1) and Dinaroid (F2), respectively, and probably close relatives; **69** and **72** are males of high (C4) and squat (C5) Eastern Alpine tendency, as in Neolithic southern Cyprus and later in Anatolia and the central Cyclades.

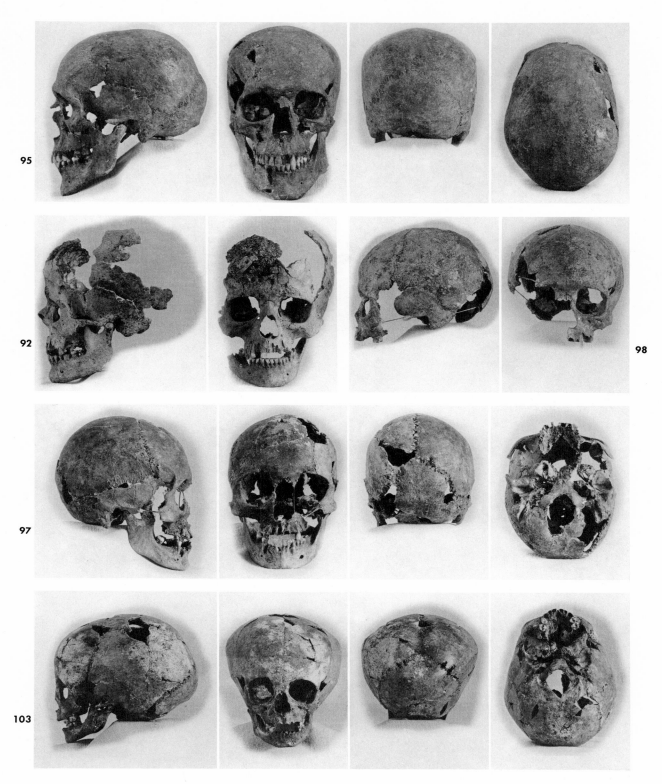

Plate VII
Skulls from clan 6 (Spring), Middle Bronze Age, early to middle phases: **95** is a male, **92** and **97** females, **98** a boy of 11, and **103** a child of 2. **95** is Iranian-Mediterranean (D3), and **92** (Mixed Alpine, E1) has similar aquilinity, comparable with southwestern Anatolia (there are no Melian skeletons for comparison); **97** has Dinaroid traits (F4).

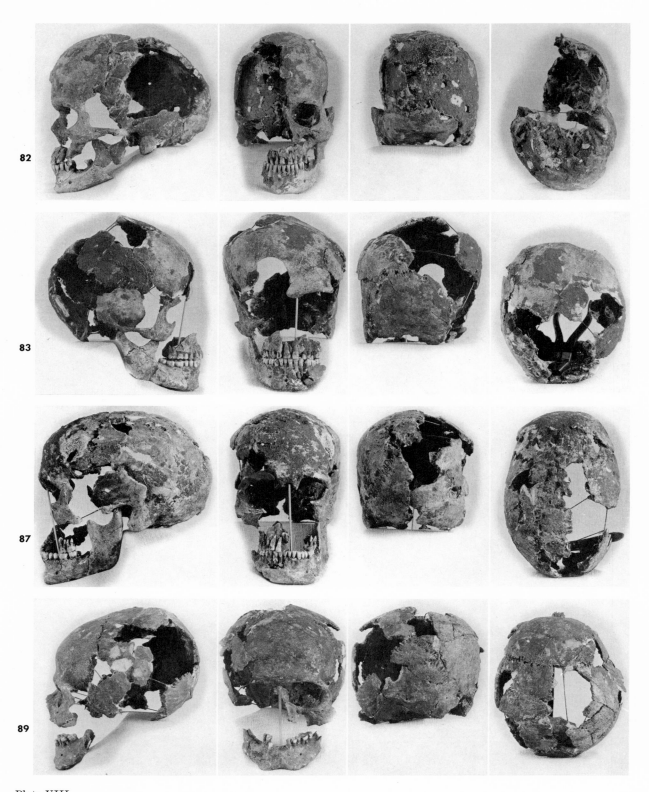

Plate VIII

Skulls from clan 7 (River), Middle Bronze Age, middle phases: **82, 83, 87,** and **89** are males, the first two from one grave. **82** and **87** resemble each other and show Corded Nordic (D2) traits; **83,** a probable close relative, is Dinaroid (F2); and **89** is Eastern Alpine (C4), suggesting trans-Anatolian origins and mixture with autochthones (as seen in Plate IX, **88** and **91**).

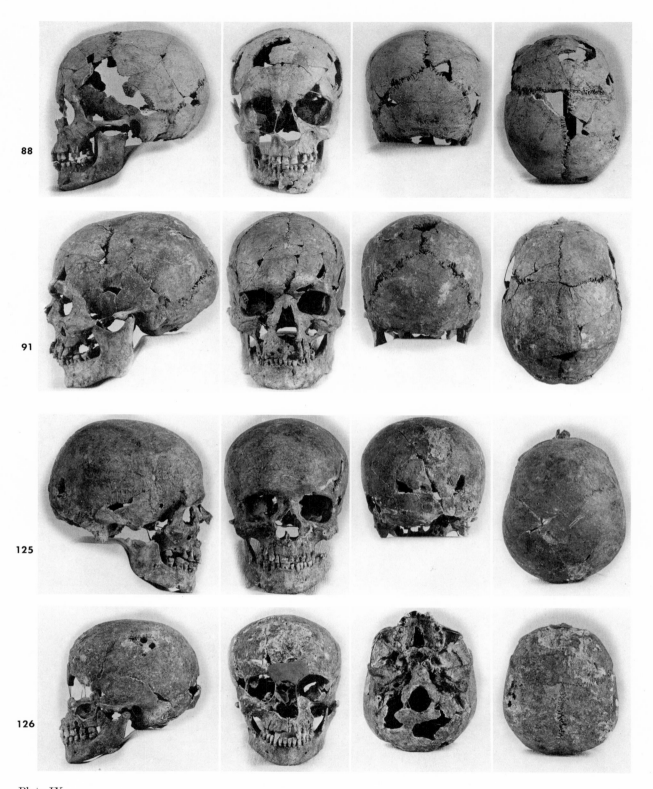

Plate IX

Skulls from—clan 7 (River): **88** and **91,** males, are Mediterranean (B3) and Basic White (A2), showing Paleolithic plus Corded traits and complete metopic suture.—Clan 8 (Northern), Middle Bronze Age, early phase: **125,** male, and **126,** female, come from one grave and show, respectively, Mixed Alpine (E2) and Alpine (C2) traits, perhaps of northern and autochthonous origin.

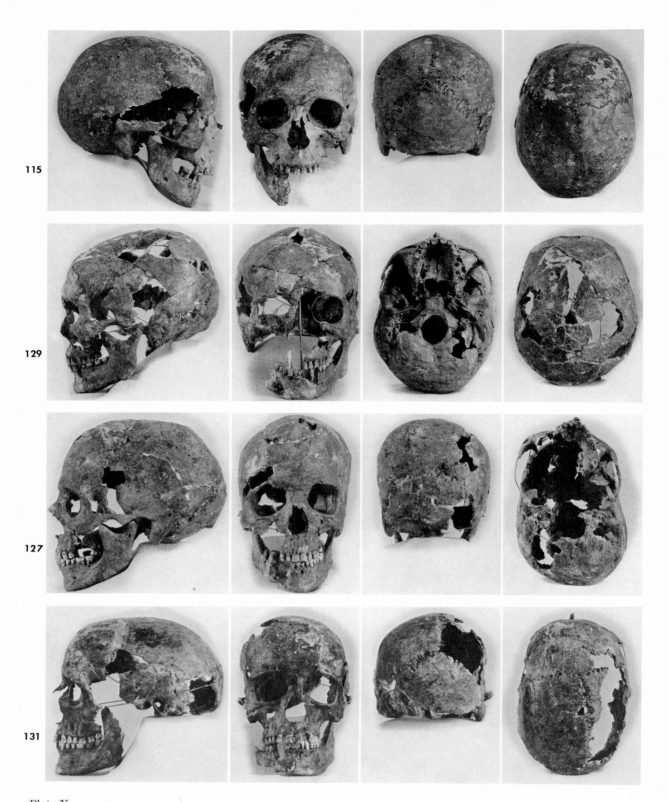

Plate X

Skulls from clan 8 (Northern), Middle Bronze Age, early phase: **115, 129, 127,** and **131** are all males. **129** (second row) has Mixed Alpine (E2) resemblances, like **125** on Plate IX, and the rest show Nordic-Iranian trends, D1, D4 (Iranian), and D5, respectively, suggesting steppe-country connections; **115** (D1) shares "family" traits with **127,** and with **125** (E2) on Plate IX, and **128** (C1) on Plate XI.

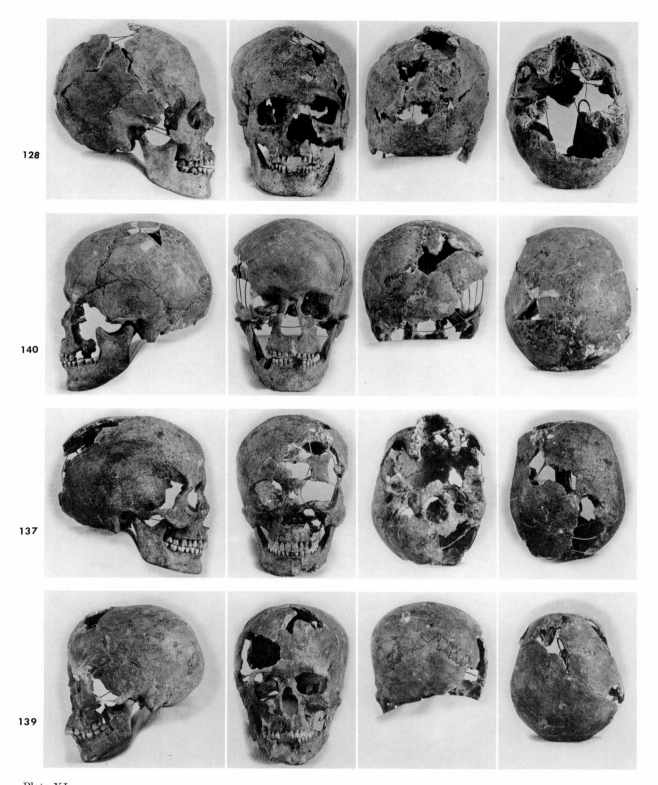

Plate XI

Skulls from clan 8 (Northern), Middle Bronze Age, early phase: **128** and **140** are both males of Alpine tendency (C1 and C3) bearing family similarities with **115** (Plate X); **137** and **139** are both females sharing a grave with **140** (also with **136** and **138**; their trends are Halstatt Nordic (D5) and Dinaric-Mediterranean (F4); **137, 138,** and **139** may be relatives; a northern connection is plausible.

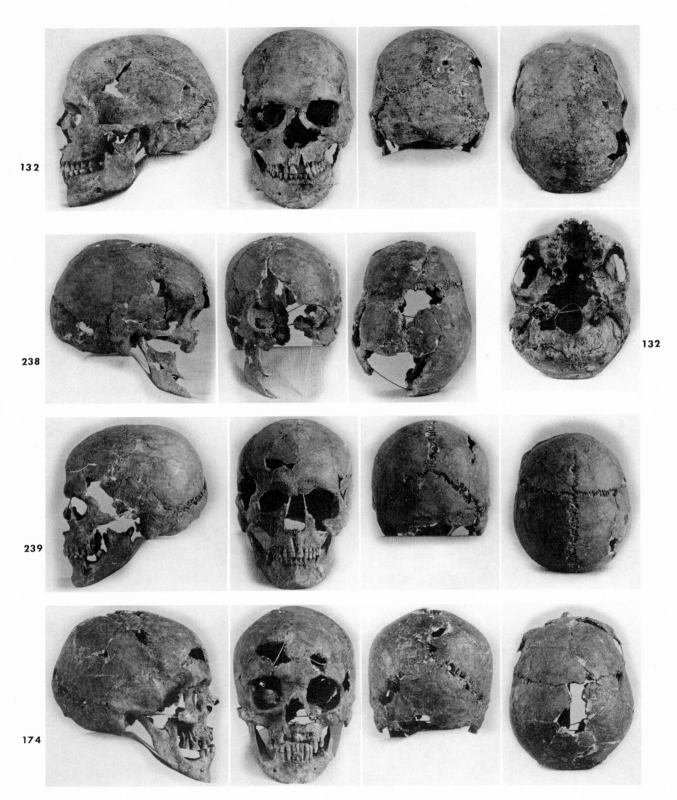

Plate XII
Skulls from—clan 8 (Northern): **132** is a male with Upper Paleolithic traits (A2) like **91** in clan 7 (Plate IX) and with facial similarities to **115** (Plate X).—Clan 9 (Bridge), Middle Bronze Age, middle phase: **238** and **239,** males, shared a double grave; **238** shows a Mediterranean trend (B1), **239** is Alpine (C1) somewhat resembling **140** (Plate XI) except for a complete metopic suture, and **174** is Mixed Alpine (E2); both **239** and **174** have Dinaroid traits.

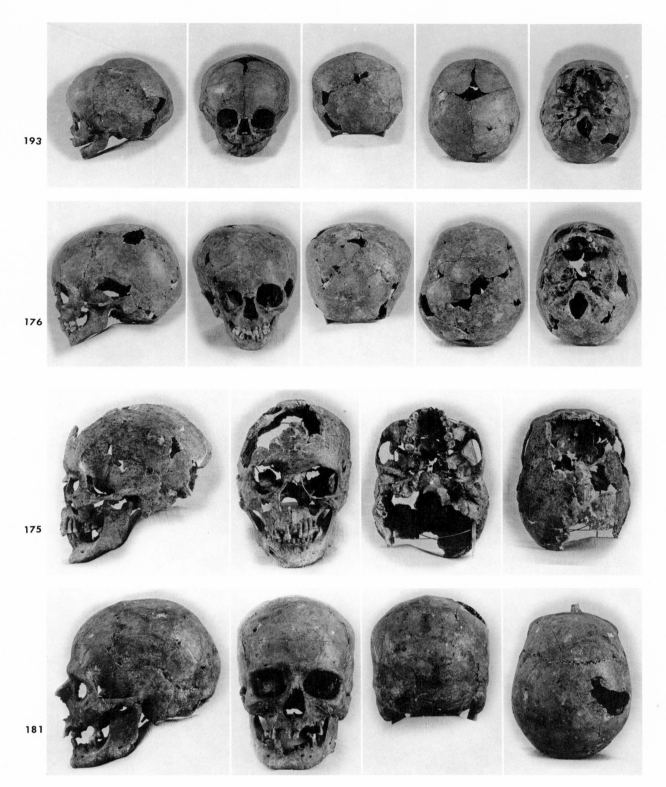

Plate XIII
Skulls from—clan 9 (Bridge), Middle phase: A young infant, **193,** and a two-year-old, **176,** both fit the intermediate Alpine-Mediterranean traits of the three adult males from clan 9 on Plate XII.—Clan 10 (Eastern), Middle Bronze Age, middle to late phases: **175** and **181,** males, show, respectively, mainly Mediterranean (B1) and Basic White (A3) traits in almost even balance with Iranian-Anatolian (D3) aquilinity; **181** shows a probable severe head-wound, unhealed.

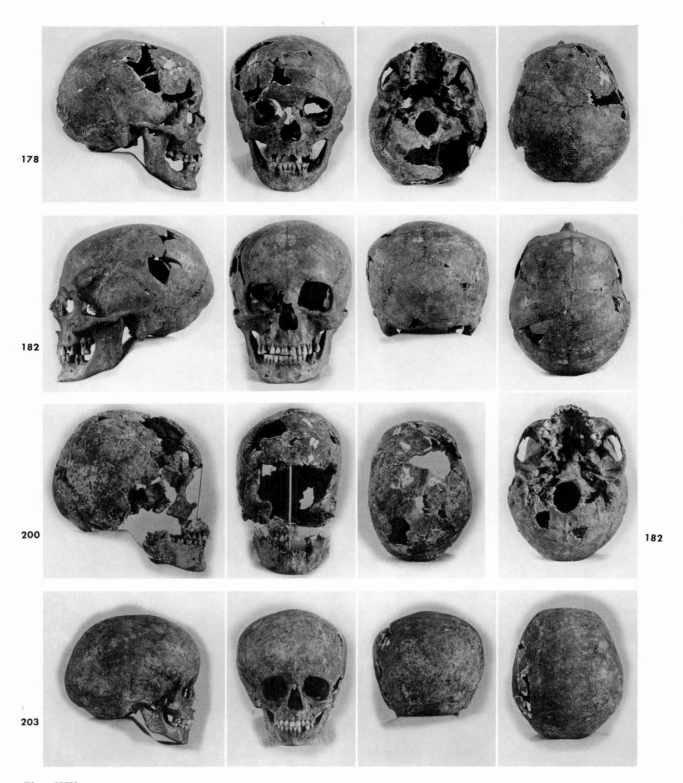

178

182

200

182

203

Plate XIV
Skulls from clan 10 (Eastern), Middle Bronze Age, middle to late phases; **178, 182,** and **200** are females and **203** is a child of four representing many dead children. **178** shows Alpine traits (C1) and also resembles **175** (Plate XIII); **182** shows Dinaroid (F3) and Iranian traits, with complete metopic suture; and **200** shows Iranian-Mediterranean (D3). Trait recombinations typify Clans 9 and 10.

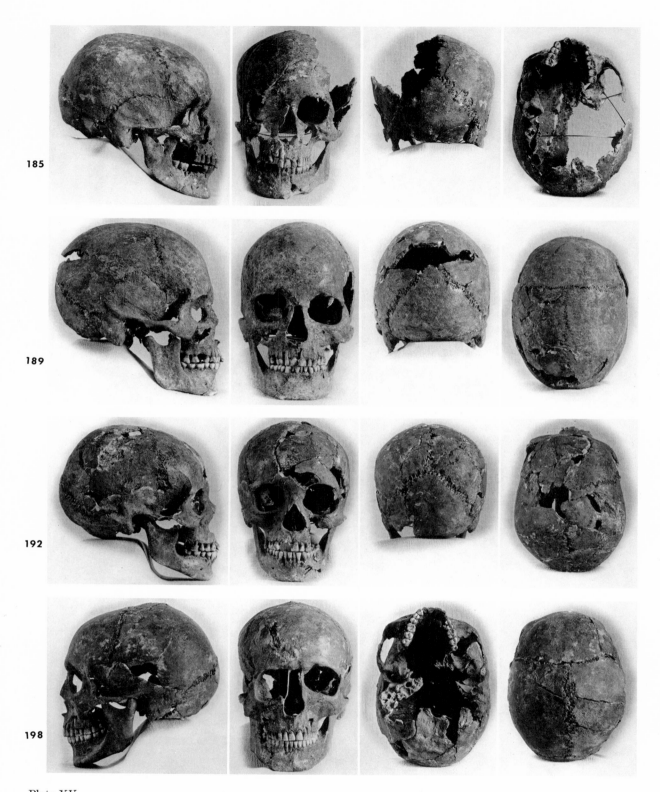

Plate XV

Skulls from clan 11 (Plain), Middle Bronze Age, late phase: **185, 189,** and **198,** males, and **192,** female, are all linear in form with minor Iranian (D4) traits. **185** shows a Mediterranean (B1) trend; **189,** Basic White (A3); **192,** Mediterranean (B2); and **198,** Iranian; forming a blend of the non-Alpine sectors of autochthones and intruders foreshadowing much of the Mycenaean population.

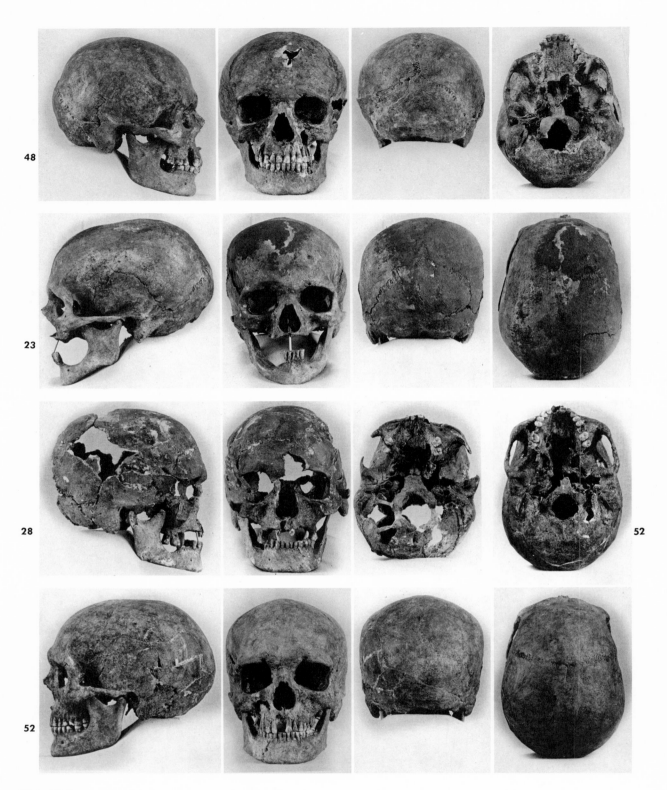

Plate XVI

Skulls from clan 12 (Sea), Middle Bronze Age, early middle to latest phases (Lerna VI): Among four males, **48** has the squat Eastern Alpine (C5) tendencies of the Central Cyclades and Anatolia; **23, 28,** and **52** have, respectively, Basic White trends, A4, A3, and A4. **52,** early enough to be ancestral, represents a squat-faced long-vaulted combination frequent in Crete and Early Helladic Greece; **55,** the adolescent girl on Plate V, exhibits similar traits.

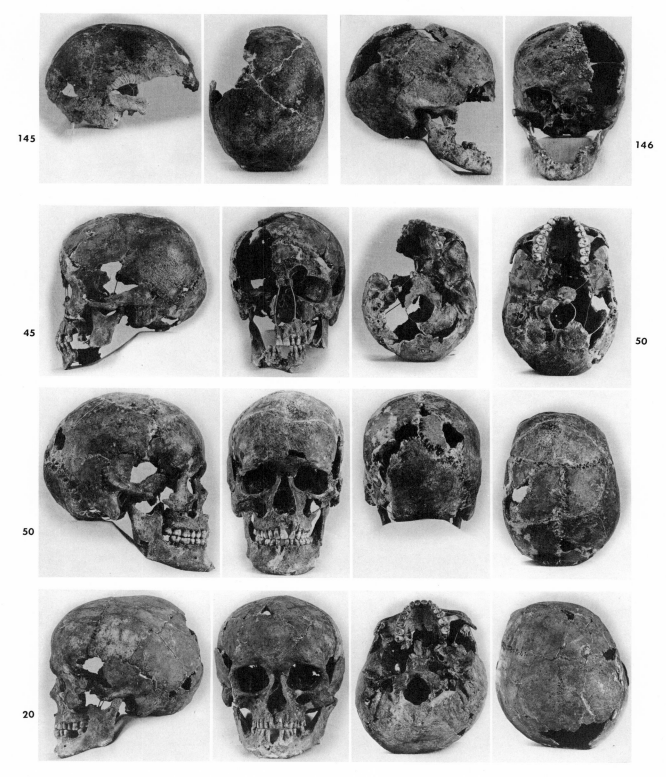

Plate XVII
Skulls from—clan 12 (Sea): **45,** a female, is Mixed Alpine (E1) with family similarity to **50,** a male with Nordic-Iranian traits (D2-4) and to **20,** also male, with clearcut Alpine traits (C1); all show recombination of pre-Greek with intrusive traits.— Clan 13 (Bay), Middle Bronze Age, very late phase: **145** (male) and **146** (female) show Mediterranean (B3) and Basic White (A3) trends, each with Iranian influence.

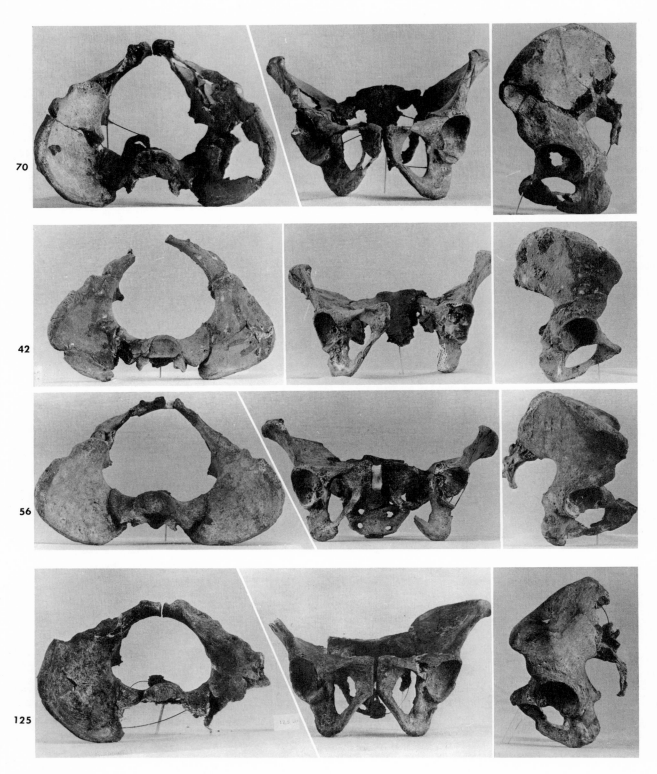

Plate XVIII

Pelves of **70** and **125** (males, clan 8) and of **42** and **56** (females, clan 4). The latter are of average and high fecundity, respectively, possibly daughter and mother; **56** is a rather short woman with large pelvis and cranial signs of porotic hyperostosis, while **42,** also short, died young, yet has a very deep pelvis.

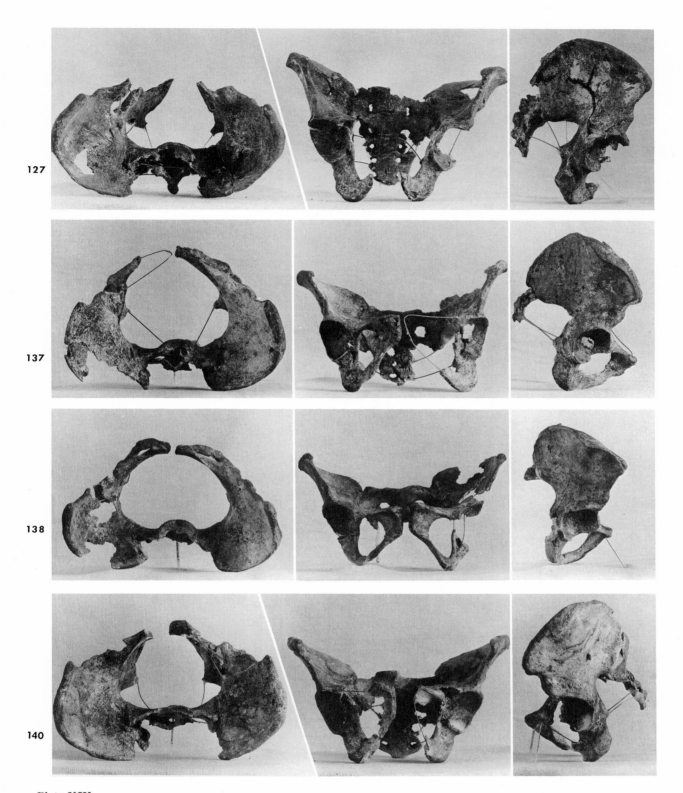

Plate XIX
Pelves of **127** and **140** (males, clan 8) and **137** and **138** (females from the same grave as **140**). Apparently the females are relatives; **137,** a fairly short woman, shows signs of great apparent fecundity and **138,** of very little; a girl who died at about 18, her pelvis is quite shallow. Fertility of clan 8 is medium.

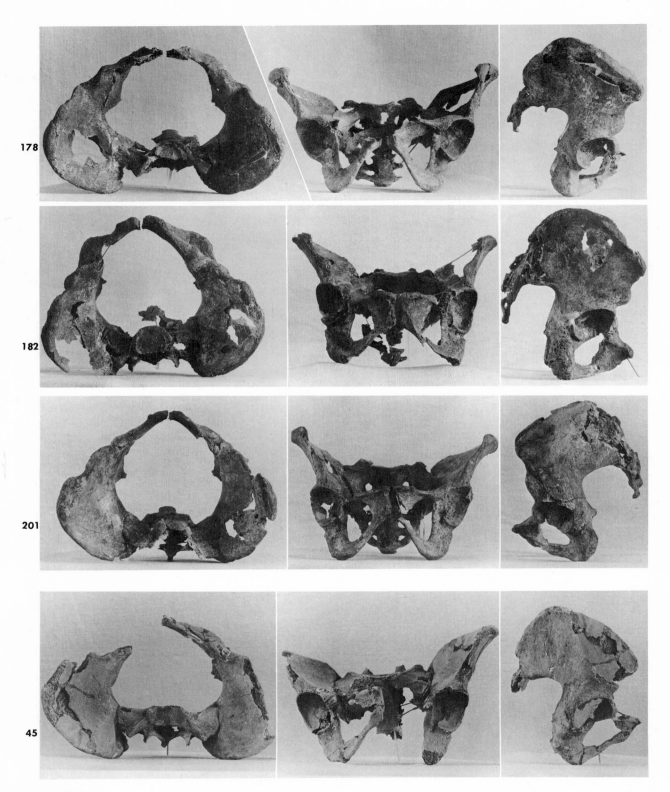

Plate XX
Pelves (female) of **178, 182,** and **201** from clan 10 and **45** from clan 12. In apparent fecundity **178** is low, **201** and **45** are medium, and **182** is very high. **182** is tall, robust, older than average, and with medium vertebral arthritis and a strikingly deep pelvis. Apparent infertility of clans 10 and 12 is a result of high juvenile mortality.

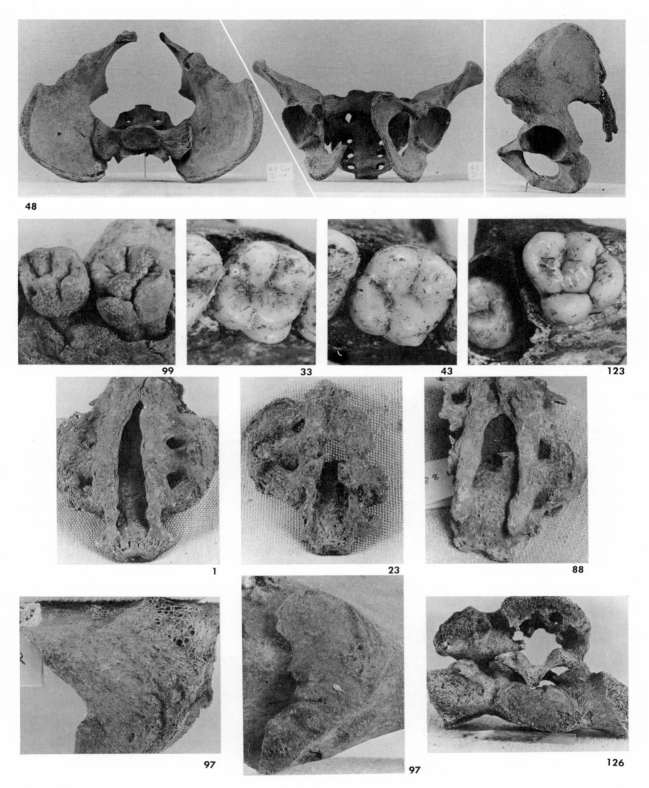

Plate XXI

Top: pelvis of **48** (male, clan 12) with epiphyses just fusing. Second row: varying development of Carabelli cusp on upper first molar of **99** (child about 7, clan 6), **33** (male, clan 3), **43** (male, clan 4), and **123** (child about 10, clan 8); Third row: partial sacral hiatus in **1** (male, clan 5), **23** (male, clan 12), and **88** (male, clan 7); hiatus and Carabelli cusp each result from single dominant genes plus modifiers and suggest family intermarriage. Bottom: childbirth effects on pubis and sacroiliac joint of fairly fecund pelvis of **97** (clan 6) and partial fusion of L_5 to S_1 in **126** (female, clan 8).

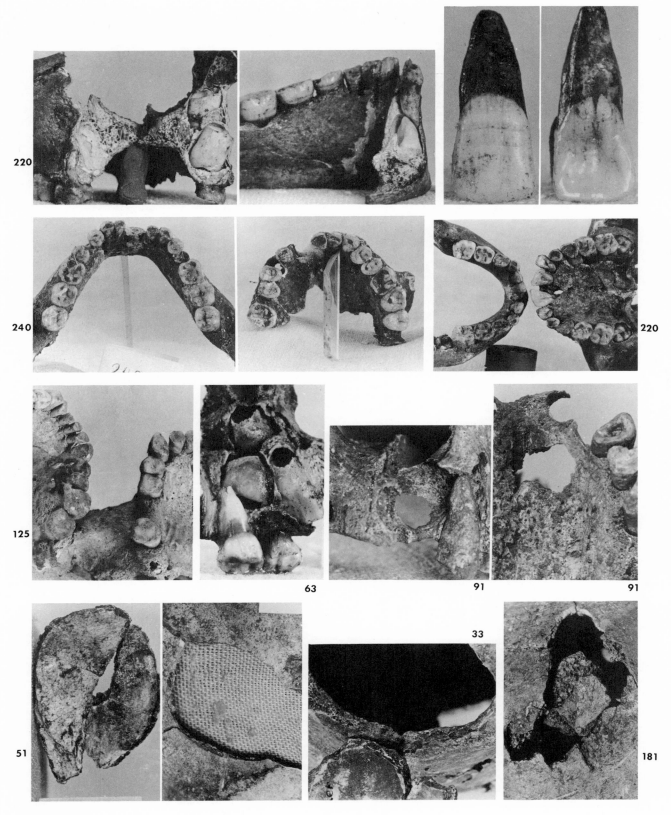

Plate XXII

Top: erupting permanent teeth and milk teeth of **220** (Early Neolithic girl about 10); note lines of arrest in formation of enamel. Second row: marked tooth wear in **240** (Late Neolithic female) and **220** (Early Neolithic child). Third row: tartar, wear, and paradontal disease in **125** (male, clan 8); incisor, canine, and premolar crowns formed in alveolus of **63** (7 or 8-year-old child, clan 5); facial and palatal views of active cyst related to roots of incisor teeth (lost) of **91** (clan 7). Bottom: cleancut trephined piece of frontal bone and skull hole of **51** Myc (male) from royal shaft grave Γ (excavated by John Papadimitriou and George Mylonas) for comparison with trephination of **33** (male, clan 3) and skull wound of **181** (male, clan 10), all possibly the result, respectively, of warfare, ceremonial *pharmakos*, or accident.

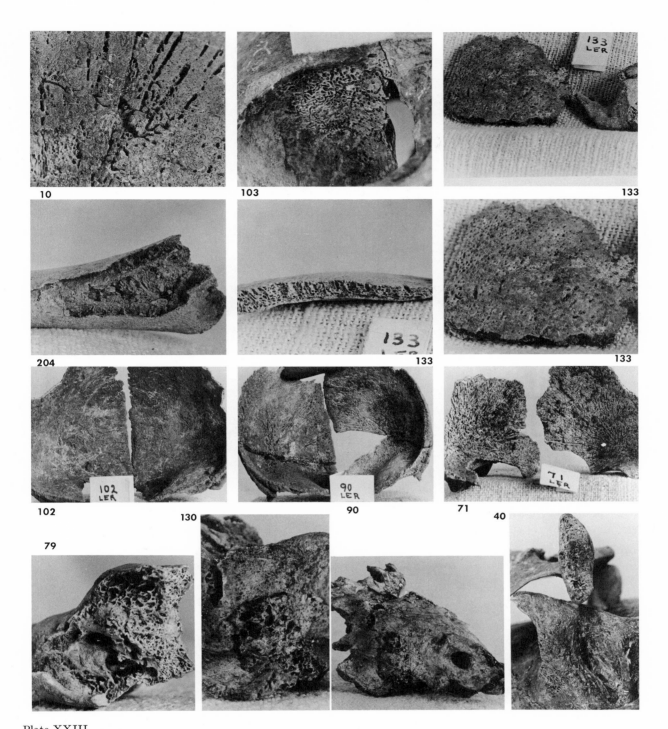

Plate XXIII

Top: porotic hyperostosis (anemia effects) on skull surfaces of **10** (1 year old, clan 5, on Plate V), showing radial gaps in outer table; **103** (2½ years old, clan 6, on Plate VII) showing "cribra orbitalia"; **133** (2½ years old, clan 8), showing parietal porosity and malar thickening.   Second row: **204** (9-month infant, clan 9), showing inner shell of completely unremodelled cortex with puffed out marrow cavity around it at lower end of humerus; and **133,** showing thickened diploic marrow space surface porosity of "stretched" outer table in marked porotic hyperostosis at an age (2½) when normally the diploë is scarcely visible. These dramatic changes of marrow space in children reflect severe anemia and probable homozygous thalassemia. Third row: Three stages of increase in blood vessel grooves on inner surfaces of frontal bones of full term (**102,** clan 6) and slightly premature infants (**90,** clan 6, and **71,** clan 5); these are probably precursor signs of homozygous thalassemia, or erythroblastosis.   Bottom: A normal left middle ear of an infant (**79,** clan 3), a possibly fatal inflammation of wall of sigmoid sinus in **130** (3½ years old, clan 8), and inflammatory arthritic bone loss in temporomandibular joint of **40** (clan 4).

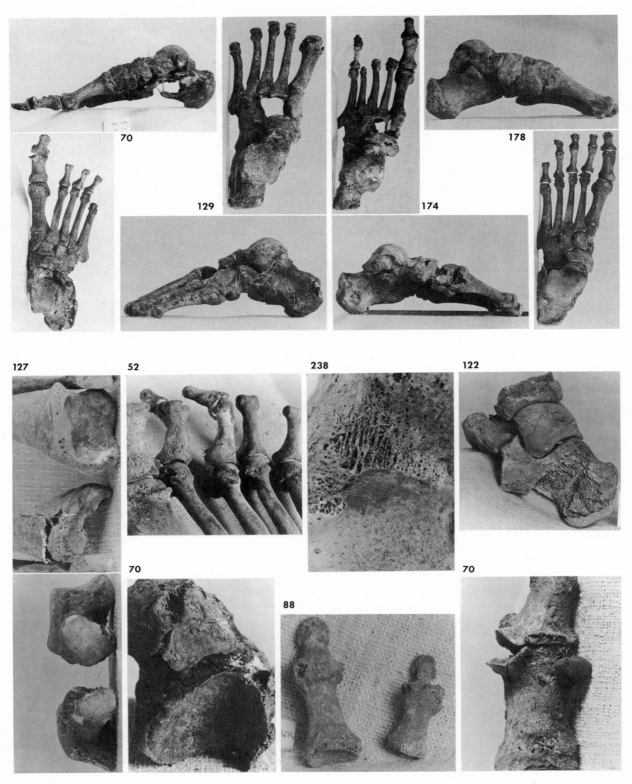

Plate XXIV

Top: feet of a man (**70,** clan 8) with apparent gout; a man (**129,** clan 8) with high arches; a man (**174,** clan 9) with slight foot arthritis, stress on bifurcating ligament and signs of a "pigeon-toed" gait; a woman (**178,** clan 10) with normal feet; lengths are, respectively, 242, 223, 220, and 197 mm.   Middle: **127** (male, clan 8), ankle joints (tibiae and tali), with the mortise structure of the right ankle rounded off, pointing to complete instability of ankle ligaments and muscles; **52** (male, clan 12), arthritic changes in hammer toes; **238** (male, clan 9), peculiar surface resorption on the calcaneus behind the subtalar joint, possibly reflecting overstress on ligaments in running on rough surfaces; **122** (adolescent male, clan 8), unusual calcaneo-navicular joint, which may go with a degree of club foot.   Bottom: arthritis on underside of talus of **70;** fused distal joints of thumb and little finger of **88** (male, clan 7), indicating tendon infection via ulnar bursa; and gouty big toe of **70.**

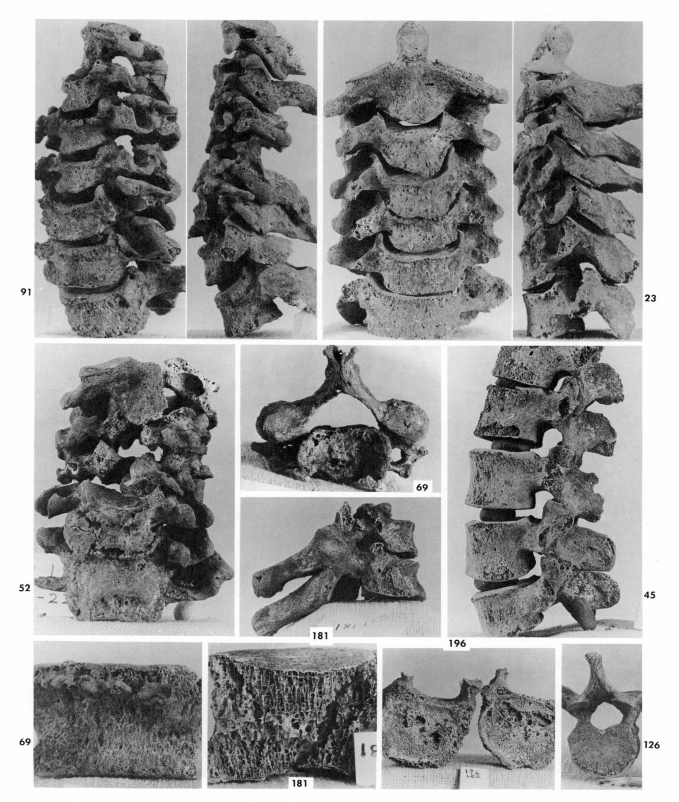

Plate XXV

Top: marked arthritic breakdown and exostoses on facets of neck vertebrae and some centra arthritis in **91** (middle-aged man, clan 7), and milder breakdown of disks more than facets in neck of **23** (old man, clan 12), showing effect of wear and tear as opposed to trauma (in **91**). Middle: slight neck arthritis in upper part of neck of **52** (male, clan 12) but complete fusion and disk loss between C_6 and C_7; upper surface of typical arthritic neck vertebra with disk injury in **69** (male, clan 5); side view of facet fusion between C_7 and T_1 in **181** (male, clan 10), in contrast with **52;** and normal lumbar vertebrae showing average arthritic change of facets in **45** (clan 12), a fecund woman at the edge of middle age. Bottom: average lumbar centrum lipping in **69** (male, clan 5); normal intravertebral spongiosa and plates in **181** (male, clan 10) for comparison with Schmorl herniation holes through thoracic vertebral plates in **196** (female, clan 10); incipient fusion of vertebral rim epiphysis in **126** (subadult girl, clan 8).

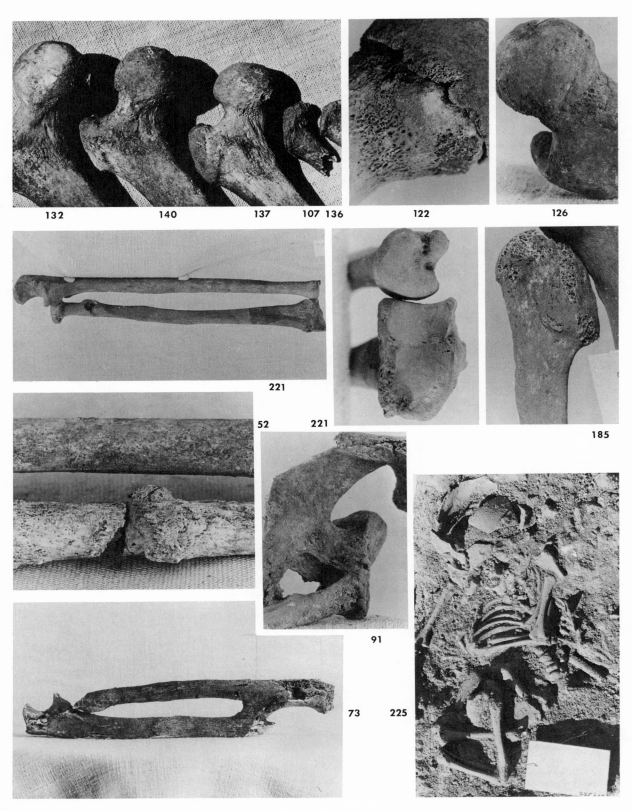

Plate XXVI

Top: examples from clan 8 showing the reaction area of the neck of the femur where crossing of iliofemoral ligament and zona orbicularis presses on it during violent extension (as in children running recklessly downhill or striding women leaning backward during pregnancy); **132** and **140** (males) show the healed hypertrophic plaque formation plus Poirier's facets caused by ilio-psoas pressure on femur head right next to the plaque; **137** (female) shows medium to marked fossae with resorption of bone cortex, as do **109** and **136** (older infants); **122** (adolescent) shows medium and marked surface "erosion," as does **126** (subadult woman). Second row: forearm of **221**, an Early Neolithic man, with slight periostitis and wrist arthritis (probably from hard use of muscles); and tumor on the fibula head of **185** (male, clan 11). Third row: radius midshaft fracture (**52**, male, clan 12) in process of healing, with callus partly formed; and "wound" in the right scapula of **91** (male, clan 7). Bottom: healed forearm fracture (**73**, male, clan 3), with a bony bridge between the bones, probably from hemorrhage into interosseous membrane; Early Neolithic infant (**225**) in the ground as discovered.

LITERATURE CITED

ALLISON, A. C.
1955. Aspects of polymorphism in man. Cold Spring Harbor Symposia on Quantitative Biology, vol. 20, pp. 239–252.
1964. Polymorphism and natural selection in human populations. Cold Spring Harbor Symposia on Quantitative Biology, vol. 29, pp. 137–149.

ANDERSON, JAMES E.
1968. Late Paleolithic skeletal remains from Nubia. Pages 996–1040 in Fred Wendorf, The prehistory of Nubia. Southern Methodist Univ., Contr. Anthropol., vol. 2, no. 2.

ANGEL, J. LAWRENCE
1945. Neolithic ancestors of the Greeks. Amer. Journ. Archaeol., vol. 49, no. 3, pp. 252–260.
1946. Social biology of Greek culture growth. Amer. Anthropol., vol. 48, no. 4.
1946a. Skeletal changes in ancient Greece. Amer. Journ. Phys. Anthropol., n.s., vol. 4, pp. 69–97.
1951. Troy. The human remains. Suppl. monograph 1 (40 pp.) in C. W. Blegen, Troy: Excavations conducted by the University of Cincinnati, 1932–1938. Princeton Univ. Press.
1951a. Population size and microevolution in Greece. Cold Spring Harbor Symposia on Quantitative Biology, vol. 15, pp. 343–351.
1952. The human skeletal remains from Hotu, Iran. Proc. Amer. Philos. Soc., vol. 96, no. 3, pp. 258–269.
1953. The human remains from Khirokitia. Appendix (pp. 416–430) in P. Dikaios, Khirokitia. London, Oxford Univ. Press.
1954. Social biology in a Cypriote village [Abstract]. Amer. Journ. Phys. Anthropol., n.s., vol. 12, p. 298.
1955. Human biology, health, and history in Greece from first settlement until now. Yearbook Amer. Philos. Soc., 1954, pp. 168–172.
1958. Human biological changes in ancient Greece, with special reference to Lerna. Yearbook Amer. Philos. Soc., 1957, pp. 266–270.
1959. Early Helladic skulls from Aghios Kosmas. Pages 167–169 in G. E. Mylonas, Aghios Kosmas. Princeton Univ. Press.
1960. Physical and psychological factors in culture growth. Fifth Internat. Congress Anthropol. and Ethnol. Sci., Philadelphia, 1956, edit. A. F. C. Wallace, pp. 666–670. Univ. Pennsylvania Press.
1961. Neolithic crania from Sotira. Appendix I (pp. 223–229) in P. Dikaios, Sotira. Museum Monographs, Univ. Museum, Univ. Pennsylvania.
1964. Osteoporosis: thalassemia? Amer. Journ. Phys. Anthropol., n.s., vol. 22, pp. 369–373.
1964a. The reaction area of the femoral neck. Clinical Orthopaedics, no. 32, pp. 130–142.
1964b. Prehistoric man. Chapter 6 (pp. 96–117) in 34th Yearbook, National Council for the Social Studies: New perspectives in world history, edit. Shirley H. Engle. Washington, National Education Association.
1966. Porotic hyperostosis, anemias, malarias, and marshes in the prehistoric Eastern Mediterranean. Science, vol. 153, no. 3737, pp. 760–763.
1966a. Appendix: Human skeletal remains at Karataş. Pages 255–257 in Machteld J. Mellink, Excavations at Karataş-Semayük in Lycia, 1965. Amer. Journ. Archaeol., vol. 70.
1967. Human biological forces in the development of civilization. Yearbook Amer. Philos. Soc., 1966, pp. 315–317.
1967a. Porotic hyperostosis or osteoporosis symmetrica. Chapter 29 (pp. 378–389) in Diseases in antiquity, edit. Don Brothwell and A. T. Sandison. Springfield, Ill., Charles C Thomas.
1968. Appendix: Human Remains at Karataş. Pages 260–263 in Machteld J. Mellink, Excavations at Karataş-Semayük in Lycia, 1967. Amer. Journ. Archaeol., vol. 72, 1 pl.

1968a. Ecological aspects of palaeodemography. Pages 263–270 *in* The skeletal biology of earlier human populations, edit. Don R. Brothwell. Symposia for the Study of Human Biology no. 8. Oxford, Pergamon Press.

1968b. Human skeletal material from Slovenia. Pages 73–108 *in* Mecklenburg Collection, Part I, edit. Hugh Hencken. vi + 108 pp. Cambridge, Mass., Amer. School Prehist. Res., Peabody Mus., Bull. 25.

1969. The bases of paleodemography. Amer. Journ. Phys. Anthropol., n.s., vol. 30, pp. 427–437.

1969a. Paleodemography and evolution. Amer. Journ. Phys. Anthropol., n.s., vol. 31, pp. 343–353.

1969b. Human skeletal material from Franchthi Cave. Appendix II (pp. 380–381) *in* Thomas W. Jacobsen, Excavations at Porto Cheli and vicinity, Preliminary Report II: the Franchthi Cave, 1967–1968. Hesperia, vol. 38, pp. 343–381.

1970. Human skeletal remains at Karataş. Appendix (pp. 253–259) *in* Machteld J. Mellink, Excavations at Karataş-Semayük and Elmali in Lycia, 1969. Amer. Journ. Archaeol., vol. 74.

197–. Early Neolithic people of Nea Nikomedeia. Homo, Fundamenta-Anthropologie des Neolithicums (in press).

BALFOUR, M. C.
1936. Some features of malaria in Greece and experience with its control. Rivista di Malarialogia, vol. 15, sezione 1, fasc. 2, pp. 114–131.

BELMONT, JOHN S., and RENFREW, COLIN
1964. Two prehistoric sites on Mykonos. Amer. Journ. Archaeol., vol. 68, no. 4, pp. 395–400.

BERRY, A. CAROLINE and BERRY, R. J.
1967. Epigenetic variation in the human cranium. Journ. Anat., vol. 101, no. 2, pp. 361–379.

BIALOR, PERRY A., and JAMESON, MICHAEL
1962. Paleolithic in the Argolid. Amer. Journ. Archaeol., vol. 66, pp. 181–182.

BLEGEN, CARL W.
1963. Troy and the Trojans. (Ancient Peoples and Places, edit. Glyn Daniel.) 240 pp. New York, F. A. Praeger.

BLUMBERG, B. S. [ed.]
1961. Genetic polymorphisms and geographic variations in disease. 240 pp. New York, Grune and Stratton, Inc.

BOESSNECK, JOACHIM
1956. Zu den Tierknochen aus neolithischen Siedlungen Thessaliens. 36. Bericht der Römisch-Germanischen Kommission, 1955, pp. 1–51.

BOROVANSKY, L.
1936. Pohlavní rozdíly na lebce člověka. Czech Academy of Arts and Sciences, II class. 114 pp. (Summary in English: Sexual differences in human skulls. Anthropologie (Prague), vol. 16, pp. 129–133, 1938.)

BRACE, C. LORING
1964. The fate of the "Classic" Neanderthals: a consideration of hominid catastrophism. Current Anthropol., vol. 5, no. 1, pp. 3–43.

BRAIDWOOD, ROBERT J., and HOWE, BRUCE
1960. Prehistoric investigations in Iraqi Kurdistan. Chicago Univ. Oriental Inst. Studies in Oriental Civilization, 31, 184 pp.

1962. Southwestern Asia beyond the lands of the Mediterranean littoral. Pages 132–146 *in* R. J. Braidwood and G. R. Willey, Courses toward urban life: Archeological considerations of some cultural alternates. Chicago, Aldine.

BRIGGS, L. CABOT
1955. The Stone Age races of Northwest Africa. Amer. School Prehistoric Research, Bull. 18, 98 pp., Peabody Museum, Harvard Univ.

BROOKS, C. E. P.
1949. Climate through the ages. 2 ed. (1 ed. 1926). London, Ernest Benn.

BRONEER, OSCAR
1939. A Mycenaean fountain on the Athenian Acropolis. Hesperia, vol. 8, pp. 317–430.

BROTHWELL, DON R.
1963. The macroscopic dental pathology of some earlier human populations. Pages 271–288 *in* Dental anthropology, edit. D. R. Brothwell. New York, Pergamon Press.

BRUCE-CHWATT, L. J.
1965. Paleogenesis and paleo-epidemiology of primate malaria. Bull. World Health Org., vol. 32, pp. 363–387.

BUCK, R. J.
1964. Middle Helladic matt-painted pottery. Hesperia, vol. 33, pp. 231–313.
BURN, A. R.
1966. The Pelican history of Greece. 415 pp. New York, Penguin Books (Pelican A792).
BUTZER, KARL W.
1964. Environment and archeology. An introduction to Pleistocene geography. 524 pp. Chicago, Aldine.

CAFFEY, JOHN
1937. The skeletal changes in the chronic hemolytic anemias. Amer. Journ. Roentgenol. and Radium Therapy, vol. 37, pp. 293–324.
CATLING, H. W.
1966. Cyprus in the Neolithic and Bronze Age periods. No. 43 (vol. 1, chs. 9c, 26b; vol. 2, chs. 4c, 22b) *in* The Cambridge Ancient History. 44 pp. Cambridge Univ. Press.
CASKEY, JOHN L.
1954. Excavations at Lerna, 1952–53. Hesperia, vol. 23, pp. 3–30.
1955. Excavations at Lerna, 1954. Hesperia, vol. 24, pp. 25–49.
1956. Excavations at Lerna, 1955. Hesperia, vol. 25, pp. 147–173.
1957. Excavations at Lerna, 1956. Hesperia, vol. 26, pp. 142–162.
1958. Excavations at Lerna, 1957. Hesperia, vol. 27, pp. 125–144.
1959. Excavations at Lerna, 1958. Hesperia, vol. 28, pp. 202–207.
1960. The Early Helladic period in the Argolid. Hesperia, vol. 29, pp. 285–303.
1962. Excavations in Keos, 1960–61. Hesperia, vol. 31, pp. 263–283.
1964. Excavations in Keos, 1963. Hesperia, vol. 33, pp. 314–335.
1965. Houses of the fourth settlement at Lerna. Pages 144–152 *in* Memorial volume for Anastasias K. Orlandos [Title in Greek]. Athens, The Archeological Society in Athens.
1965a. Greece, Crete, and the Aegean Islands in the Early Bronze Age. No. 24 (vol. 1, ch. 36a) *in* The Cambridge Ancient History. 44 pp. Cambridge Univ. Press.
1966. Greece and the Aegean Islands in the Middle Bronze Age. No. 45 (vol. 2, ch. 4a) *in* The Cambridge Ancient History. 32 pp. Cambridge Univ. Press.
1966a. Excavations in Keos, 1964–1965. Hesperia, vol. 35, pp. 363–376.
CASKEY, JOHN L., and CASKEY, ELIZABETH G.
1960. The earliest settlements at Eutresis. Supplementary excavations, 1958. Hesperia, vol. 29, pp. 126–167.
CHARLES, J. A.
1967. Early arsenical bronzes—a metallurgical view. Amer. Journ. Archaeol., vol. 71, pp. 21–26.
CHILDE, GORDON
1946. What happened in history. 280 pp. New York, Penguin Books (Pelican A108).
CLARK, GRAHAME
1952. Prehistoric Europe. The economic basis. 349 pp. New York, Philosophical Library.
CLARK, GRAHAME, and PIGGOTT, STUART
1965. Prehistoric societies. (Vol. *in* The history of human society, edit. J. H. Plumb.) 356 pp. New York, Knopf.
COCKBURN, AIDAN
1963. The evolution and eradication of infectious diseases. 255 pp. Baltimore, Johns Hopkins Press.
COON, CARLETON S.
1939. The races of Europe. 739 pp. New York, Macmillan.
1951. Cave explorations in Iran, 1949. Museum Monographs, Univ. Museum, Univ. Pennsylvania, 125 pp.
1952. The excavations at Hotu Cave. Trans. New York Acad. Sci., ser. 2, vol. 14, no. 4, pp. 179–180.
1962. The origin of races. 724 pp. New York, Knopf.
COUTTS, MALCOLM B., and WOODWARD, E. PAUL
1965. Surgery and sprained ankles. Clinical Orthopaedics, no. 42, pp. 81–90.

DEBETS, G. F.
1948. Palaeoanthropology of the U.S.S.R. [In Russian]. Trudy Institut Antropologii, Arkheologii i Etnografii, Akademii Nauk SSSR, n.s., vol. 4, 389 pp. Moscow.
1955. Skulls in epipaleolithic cemetery near site Voloschkoyo [in Russian]. Sovetskaya Ethnographiya, vol. 3, pp. 62–73.

DEEVEY, EDWARD S.
  1960. The human population.   Scientific American, vol. 203, no. 3, pp. 194–204.
DIKAIOS, P.
  1953. Khirokitia. Final report on the excavation of a Neolithic settlement in Cyprus on behalf of the
      Department of Antiquities 1936–46.   447 pp.   London, Oxford Univ. Press.
  1961. A guide to the Cyprus Museum.   3 ed., 238 pp.   Nicosia, Chr. Nikolaou & Sons, Ltd.
DILLER, AUBREY
  1937. Race mixture among the Greeks before Alexander.   Univ. Illinois, Studies in Language and
      Literature, vol. 20, nos. 1–2, 187 pp.
DIXON, ROLAND
  1923. The racial history of man.   583 pp.   New York, Charles Scribner Sons.
DOBZHANSKY, TH.
  1951. Genetics and the origin of species.   3 ed. (1 ed., 1937), 364 pp.   New York, Columbia Univ. Press.
DORIGNY, A. S.
  1908. Rustica res.   Vol. 4, pt. 2, pp. 899–927, in Dictionnaire des antiquités grecques et romaines, edit.
      E. Saglio and E. Pottier (Daremberg-Saglio).   Paris.
DRACHMANN, A. G.
  1938. Pflug.   In Pauly-Wissowa, Real-encyclopädie der Classischen Altertumswissenschaft, vol. 19, pt. 2,
      pp. 1461–1471.
DUBLIN, LOUIS I.; LOTKA, A. J.; and SPIEGELMAN, MORTIMER
  1949. Length of life.   Rev. ed. (1 ed. 1936).   New York, Ronald Press.
DUCKWORTH, W. L. H.
  1913. Archeological and ethnological researches in Crete.   Pages 224–268 in British Assoc. for Adv. Sci.,
      82nd Meeting, Dundee, 1912. London.
DUNN, FREDERICK L.
  1965. On the antiquity of malaria in the Western Hemisphere.   Human Biology, vol. 37, no. 4, pp. 385–393.

EDMUNSON, MUNRO S.
  1961. Neolithic diffusion rates.   Current Anthropol., vol. 2, pp. 70–102.
EHRICH, ROBERT W.
  1940. Preliminary notes on Tarsus crania.   Amer. Journ. Archaeol., vol. 44, no. 1, pp. 87–92.
  1965. Geographical and chronological patterns in East Central Europe.   Pages 403–458 in Chronologies
      in Old World Archaeology, edit. R. W. Ehrich.   Univ. Chicago Press.
ESIN, UFUK, and BENEDICT, PETER
  1963. Recent developments in the prehistory of Anatolia.   Current Anthropol., vol. 4, no. 4, pp. 339–346.
EWING, GEORGE H.
  1966. Functional implications of the morphology of Mesolithic crania from Nubia [Abstract].   Amer.
      Journ. Phys. Anthropol., n.s., vol. 25, no. 2, p. 214.

FALLS, HAROLD F.
  1953. Skeletal system, including joints.   Chapter 14 (pp. 236–286) in Clinical genetics, edit. Arnold Sorsby.
      London, Butterworth.
FARRAND, W. R.
  1964. Geology and physiography of the Beyşehir-Suğla depression, western Taurus lake district, Turkey.
      Türk Arkeoloji Derglisi, vol. 13, no. 1, pp. 149–154.
FARRINGTON, BENJAMIN
  1944. Greek science. Vol. 1, Thales to Aristotle.   154 pp.   New York, Penguin Books (Pelican A142).
  1949. Greek science. Vol. 2, Theophrastus to Galen.   181 pp.   New York, Penguin Books (Pelican A192).
FEREMBACH, DENISE
  1962. La nécropole épipaléolithique de Taforalt (Maroc Oriental). Étude des squelettes humains.   175 pp.
      Rabat, Centre National de la Recherche Scientifique.
FIENNES, RICHARD
  1965. Man, nature and disease.   268 pp.   New York, New American Library (Signet T2653).
FLANNERY, KENT V.
  1965. The ecology of early food production in Mesopotamia.   Science, vol. 147, pp. 1247–1256.
FOLTINY, STEPHEN
  1959. The oldest representations of wheeled vehicles in Central and Southeastern Europe.   Amer. Journ.
      Archaeol., vol. 63, no. 1, pp. 53–58.

FRENCH, DAVID H.
1963. Excavations at Can Hasan: Second preliminary report, 1962. Anatolian Studies, vol. 13, pp. 29–42.

FÜRST, CARL M.
1930. Zur Anthropologie der Prähistorischen Griechen in Argolis. Lunds Universitets Årsskrift, n.f. Avd. 2, Bd. 26, Nr. 8; Kungl. Fysiografiska Sälskapets Handlingar, n.f. Bd. 41, Nr. 8, 130 pp., 40 pl.

GARN, STANLEY M.; LEWIS, A. B.; KOSKI, K.; and POLACHEK, D. L.
1958. The sex difference in tooth calcification. Journ. Dental Research, vol. 37, pp. 561–567.

GARROD, DOROTHY A. E., and BATE, D. M. A.
1937. The Stone Age of Mt. Carmel. Vol. 1. Oxford, Clarendon Press.

GAUL, JAMES H.
1948. The Neolithic period in Bulgaria. Amer. School of Prehistoric Res., Bull. 16, 252 pp., Peabody Museum, Harvard Univ.

GENOVES, SANTIAGO
1963. Estimation of age and mortality. Chapter 35 (pp. 353–364) in Don Brothwell and Eric Higgs, Science in archaeology. New York, Basic Books.

GEJVALL, NILS-GUSTAF
1960. Westerhus. Medieval population and church in the light of skeletal remains. 144 pp. Lund, Håkan Ohlssons Boktryckeri.
1969. Lerna. A preclassical site in the Argolid, volume 1, the Fauna. xvi+107 pp., 25 pl. Princeton, N.J., Amer. School of Classical Studies at Athens.

GILES, EUGENE
1964. Sex determination by discriminant function analysis of the mandible. Amer. Journ. Phys. Anthropol., n.s., vol. 22, pp. 129–136.

GILES, EUGENE, and ELLIOT, ORVILLE
1963. Sex determination by discriminant function analysis of crania. Amer. Journ. Phys. Anthropol., n.s., vol. 21, pp. 53–68.

GIMBUTAS, MARIJA
1963. The Indo-Europeans: Archaeological problems. Amer. Anthropol., vol. 65, pp. 815–836.

GINSBURG, B. B.
1956. Anthropological characteristics of Kazakhstan people in the Bronze Age [in Russian]. Trudy Instituta Istorii, Arkheologii i Etnografii Akad. Nauk Kazakhskoi SSR, Alma-Ata, 1, pp. 159–171.

GLESNER, JAMES R., and DAVIS, GERALD L.
1966. Bilateral calcaneo-navicular coalition occurring in twin boys. Clinical Orthopaedics, no. 47, pp. 173–176.

GLOTZ, G. [transl. M. R. Dobie]
1926. Ancient Greece at work. 2 vols. New York, Knopf.

GOMME, A. W.
1933. The population of Athens in the fifth and fourth centuries B.C. Oxford, Blackwell.

GRACE, VIRGINIA
1961. Amphoras and the ancient wine trade. 32 pp. Amer. School of Classical Studies at Athens.

GRAVES, WILLIAM W.
1922. Observations on age changes in the scapula. Amer. Journ. Phys. Anthropol., vol. 5, pp. 21–33.

GREULICH, W. W., and THOMS, H.
1938. The dimensions of the pelvic inlet of 789 white females. Anat. Record, vol. 72, pp. 45–51.

GULICK, CHARLES BURTON
1902. The life of the ancient Greeks: With special reference to Athens. New York, D. Appleton and Co.

GURNEY, O. R.
1965. Anatolia, c. 1750–1600 B.C. No. 11 (vol. 2, ch. 6) in The Cambridge Ancient History. Rev. ed., 32 pp. Cambridge Univ. Press.
1966. Anatolia, c. 1600–1380 B.C. No. 44 (vol. 2, ch. 15a) in The Cambridge Ancient History. 30 pp. Cambridge Univ. Press.

HACKETT, L. W.
1937. Malaria in Europe; an ecological study. London, Oxford Univ. Press.

HAMPERL, H., and WEISS, P.
1955. Über die spongiose Hyperostose an Schädeln aus Alt-Peru. Virchow's Archiv, vol. 327, no. 6, pp. 629–642.

HARLAN, JACK R., and ZOHARY, D.
   1966. Distribution of wild wheats and barley.   Science, vol. 153, pp. 1074–1080.
HARRISON, JANE
   1922. Prolegomena to the study of Greek religion.   682 pp.   Cambridge Univ. Press (repr. 1955: New
      York, Meridian Books MG 3).
HELBAEK, HANS
   1960. The paleoethnobotany of the Near East and Europe.   Pages 99–118 in Robert J. Braidwood and
      Bruce Howe, Prehistoric investigations in Iraq: Kurdistan.   Univ. Chicago Oriental Institute,
      Studies in Oriental Civilization, no. 31.
HIGGS, E.
   1962. Part II, The biological data.   Pages 271–274 in R. J. Rodden, Excavations at the Early Neolithic
      site at Nea Nikomedeia, Greek Macedonia (1961 season).   Proc. Prehistoric Soc., n.s., vol. 28.
   1963. A Middle Paleolithic industry in Greece: preliminary report.   Man, vol. 63, pp. 2–3.
   1964. A hand-axe from Greece.   Antiquity, vol. 38, p. 54.
HIGGINS, CHARLES G.
   1966. Possible disappearance of Mycenaean coastal settlements of the Messenian Peninsula.   Amer. Journ.
      Archeol., vol. 70, pp. 23–29.
HJORTSJÖ, CARL-HERMAN
   1947. To the knowledge of the prehistoric craniology of Cyprus.   Särtryck ur Kungl. Hum. Vetenskapssam-
      fundets: Lund Arsberättelse 1946–47, 77 pp.
HOPF, MARIA
   1962. Nutzpflanzen vom Lernäischen Golf.   Jahrb. Römisch-Germanischen Zentralmuseums Mainz,
      vol. 9, pp. 1–19.
HOOTON, ERNEST A.
   1930. Indians of Pecos. A study of their skeletal remains.   391 pp.   New Haven, Yale Univ. Press.
HOWELL, F. CLARK
   1958. Upper Pleistocene man of the southwest Asian Mousterian.   Pages 185–198 in Hundert Jahre
      Neanderthaler [Neanderthal Centenary] 1856–1956, edit. G. H. R. von Koenigswald.   New York,
      Wenner-Gren Foundation.
HOWELLS, WILLIAM W.
   1941. The early Christian Irish: The skeletons at Gallen Priory.   Proc. Roy. Irish Acad., sec. C, vol. 46,
      pp. 103–219.
HRDLIČKA, ALEŠ
   1939. Important Paleolithic find in Central Asia.   Science, vol. 90, pp. 296–298.
HUNTINGTON, ELLSWORTH
   1910. The burial of Olympia.   Geographical Journ., vol. 36, pp. 657–672.
HURME, V. O.
   1957. Time and sequence of tooth eruption. Symposium on the human dentition in forensic medicine.
      Journ. Forensic Sci., vol. 2, pp. 377–388.

JACOBSEN, THOMAS W.
   1969. Excavations at Porto Cheli and vicinity, Preliminary Report II: the Franchthi Cave, 1967–1968.
      Hesperia, vol. 38, pp. 343–381.
JARDÉ, AUGUSTE
   1925. Les Céréales dans l'antiquité grecque. I., La Production.   Paris.
JARONOFF, DMITRI
   1948. Anthropometric material and racial affinities of Neolithic Bulgaria.   Chapter 8 (pp. 220–228) in
      James H. Gaul, the Neolithic period in Bulgaria, Amer. School of Prehistoric Res., Bull. 16,
      Peabody Museum, Harvard Univ.
JASNY, NAUM
   1944. The wheats of Classical antiquity.   The Johns Hopkins University Studies in Historical and Political
      Science, ser. 62, no. 3, 176 pp.
JONES, W. H. S.
   1907. Malaria: A neglected factor in the history of Greece and Rome.   Cambridge, England, Macmillan
      and Bowes.
   1909. Malaria and Greek history.   Univ. Manchester Publ. 43 (Historical Series no. 8).

KEITH, SIR ARTHUR
1931. New discoveries relating to the antiquity of man. 512 pp. London, Williams and Norgate.

KENYON, KATHLEEN M.
1959. Some observations on the beginnings of settlement in the Near East. Journ. Roy. Anthropol. Inst., vol. 89, pp. 5–9.
1959a. Earliest Jericho. Antiquity, vol. 33, pp. 5–9.

KITTO, H. D. F.
1951. The Greeks. 256 pp. New York, Penguin Books (Pelican A2220).

KLEIN, H.; PALMER, C. E.; and KRAMER, M.
1937. Studies on dental caries, II. The use of the normal probability curve for expressing the age distribution of eruption of the permanent teeth. Growth, vol. 1, pp. 385–394.

KLIMA, BOHUSLAV
1962. The first ground plan of an Upper Paleolithic loess settlement in Middle Europe and its meaning. Pages 193–210 in R. J. Braidwood and G. R. Willey, Courses toward urban life: Archaeological considerations of some cultural alternatives. Chicago, Aldine.

KOKKOROS, P., and KANELLIS, A.
1960. Découverte d'un crâne d'homme paléolithique dans la péninsule chalcidique. L'Anthropologie, vol. 64, pp. 438–446.

KÖKTEN, I. KILIÇ
1963. Die Stellung von Karain innerhalb der Türkischen Vorgeschichte. Anatolia, vol. 7, pp. 59–86.

KROGMAN, WILTON M.
1937. Cranial types from Alişar Hüyük and their relations to other racial types, ancient and modern, of Europe and Western Asia. Pages 213–293 in H. H. Von der Osten, The Alishar Hüyük, Seasons of 1930–32. Part 3. Univ. Chicago Oriental Institute, publ. 30.
1939. A guide to the identification of human skeletal material. F.B.I. Law Enforcement Bull., vol. 8, no. 8, pp. 3–31.
1940. Racial types from Tepe Hissar, Iran, from the Late Fifth to Early Second Millennium, B.C. Verhandelingen der Koninklijke Nederlandsche Akademie van Wetenschappen, Afdeeling Natuurkunde, Tweede Sectie, vol. 39, no. 2, 87 pp.
1949. Ancient cranial types at Chatal Hüyük and Tell Al-Judaidah, Syria, from the late fifth millenium B.C. to the mid-seventh century, A.D. Türk Tarih Kurumu Basimevi Belleten, vol. 13, no. 51 (July 1949), pp. 407–477, 23 tables, 26 figs.
1962. The human skeleton in forensic medicine. 337 pp. Springfield, Charles C Thomas.

LASKER, GABRIEL W.
1960. Variances of bodily measurements in the offspring of native and immigrants to three Peruvian towns. Amer. Journ. Phys. Anthropol., n.s., vol. 18, pp. 257–261.

LAUGHLIN, W. S., and JØRGENSEN, J. B.
1956. Isolate variation in Greenlandic Eskimo crania. Acta Genet. Stat. Medica, vol. 6, pp. 3–12.

LEHMANN, H.
1959. The maintenance of the haemoglobinopathies at high frequency. Pages 307–321 in J. H. P. Jonxis and J. F. Delafresnaye, Abnormal hemoglobins. Oxford, Blackwell.

LIVINGSTONE, FRANK G.
1958. Anthropological implication of sickle cell gene distribution in West Africa. Amer. Anthropol., vol. 60, no. 3, pp. 533–562.

MAINLAND, DONALD
1945. Anatomy as a basis for medical and dental practice. 863 pp. New York, Paul B. Hoeber.

MARCOVITS, ADALBERT
1929. Concerning the finds of Stone Age in Greece made up to the present time [in Greek]. Greek Anthropol. Soc. Proc., vol. 7, pp. 114–134. Athens.
1931. Recherches sur la période de la pierre en Grèce [Abstract in French of above]. Rev. Anthr. Comptes Recherches de la Societé Hellénique d'Anthropologie, vol. 41, pp. 7–8.

MARESH, MARION M.
1955. Linear growth of long bones of extremities from infancy through adolescence. Amer. Journ. Diseases of Children, vol. 89, pp. 725–742.

MARKHAM, S. F.
1947. Climate and the energy of nations. 2 ed., 240 pp. New York, Oxford University Press.
MARTIN, R., and SALLER, K.
1959. Lehrbuch der Anthropologie. 3 ed. (2 ed., 1928), 3 vols., 2416 pp. Stuttgart, Gustav Fischer.
MAULL, OTTO
1922. Griechisches Mittelmeergebiet. 132 pp. Breslau, Ferdinand Hirt.
MAYR, ERNST
1963. Animal species and evolution. 797 pp. Cambridge, Harvard Univ. Press.
MacDONNELL, W. R.
1913. On the expectation of life in ancient Rome, and in the provinces of Hispania and Lusitania.
Biometrika, vol. 9, pp. 366–380.
McCOWN, T. D.
1939. [Unpublished] The Natufian crania from Mt. Carmel, Palestine, and their interrelationships. Ph. D.
Thesis, Univ. California at Berkeley.
McCOWN, T. D., and KEITH, SIR ARTHUR
1939. The Stone Age of Mt. Carmel. Volume 2. The fossil remains from the Levalloiso-Mousterian. 390 pp.
Oxford, Clarendon Press.
McDONALD, WILLIAM A., and SIMPSON, RICHARD HOPE
1961. Prehistoric habitation in southwestern Peloponnese. Amer. Journ. Archaeol., vol. 65, pp. 221–260.
1969. Further explorations in southwestern Peloponnese, 1964–68. Amer. Journ. Archaeol., vol. 73,
pp. 123–177.
McKERN, T. W., and STEWART, T. DALE
1957. Skeletal age changes in young American males, analysed from the standpoint of age identification.
Quartermaster Res. & Dev. Command (Natick, Mass.), Environ. Protection Res. Div., Techn.
Report EP-45, 179 pp.
MELLAART, JAMES
1958. The end of the Early Bronze Age in Anatolia and Aegean. Amer. Journ. Archaeol., vol. 62, pp. 9–33.
1963. Çatal Hüyük in Anatolia: Excavations which revolutionise the history of the earliest civilisations.
Illust. London News: Part I (Jan. 26, 1963), pp. 118–121; Part II (Feb. 2, 1963), pp. 160–164;
Part III (Feb. 9, 1963), pp. 196–198.
1965. Earliest civilizations of the Near East. (Library of the Early Civilizations.) 143 pp. New York,
McGraw-Hill.
1967. Çatal Hüyük. A Neolithic town in Anatolia. New aspects of archaeology, edit. Sir Mortimer
Wheeler. New York, McGraw-Hill Book Co.
MELLINK, MACHTELD J.
1965. Anatolian chronology. Pages 101–131, in Chronologies in Old World archaeology, edit. R. W.
Ehrich. Univ. Chicago Press.
1965a. Excavations at Karataş-Semayük in Lycia, 1964. Amer. Journ. Archaeol., vol. 69, pp. 241–251.
1966. Archaeology in Asia Minor. Amer. Journ. Archaeol., vol. 70, no. 2, pp. 139–159, and addenda in
no. 3, pp. 279–282.
1969. Excavations at Karataş-Semayük in Lycia, 1968. Amer. Journ. Archaeol., vol. 73, pp. 319–331,
pls. 71–78.
MEREDITH, HOWARD V.
1943. Physical growth from birth to two years: I. Stature. Univ. Iowa Studies: Studies in Child Welfare
19. 255 pp. Iowa City, Univ. Iowa Press.
MICHELL, H.
1940. The economics of Ancient Greece. Cambridge University Press.
MILOJČIČ, VLADIMIR
1956. Die erste präkeramische bäuerliche Siedlung der Jungsteinzeit in Europa. Germania, vol. 34,
pp. 208–210.
1960. Hauptergebnisse der Deutschen Ausgrabungen in Thessalien 1953–1958. 56 pp. Bonn, Rudolf
Habelt Verlag.
MILOJČIČ, VLADIMIR; BOESSNECK, JOACHIM; and HOPF, MARIA
1962. Die deutschen Ausgrabungen auf der Argissa-Magula in Thessalien, I. Beiträge zur ur- und früh-
geschichtlichen Archäologie des Mittelmeer Kulturraumes, Band 2. Bonn.
MORANT, G. M.
1925. A study of Egyptian craniology from Prehistoric to Roman times. Biometrika, vol. 17, pp. 1–52.

Moseley, John E.
1965. The paleopathologic riddle of "symmetrical osteoporosis." Amer. Journ. Roentgenol., Radium Therapy and Nuclear Med., vol. 95, pp. 135–142.

Motulsky, Arno G.
1960. Metabolic polymorphisms and the role of infectious diseases in human evolution. Human Biology, vol. 32, pp. 28–62.

Moulder, James W.
1962. The biochemistry of intracellular parasitism. 172 pp. Univ. Chicago Press.

Mylonas, George E.
1959. Aghios Kosmas. An Early Bronze Age settlement and cemetery in Attica. 191 pp. Princeton Univ. Press.

Myres, J. L.
1930. Who were the Greeks? 634 pp. Berkeley, Univ. California Press.

Nathan, Hilel
1959. Spondylolysis. Its anatomy and mechanism of development. Journ. Bone and Joint Surgery, vol. 41A, pp. 303–320.

Necrasov, Olga, and Cristescu, Maria
1957. Contribuçie la studiul antropologic al scheletelor din complexul mormintelor cu ocru de la Holboca-Iași. Probleme de Antropologie, vol. 3, pp. 73–147.
1959. Les Premiers Brachycéphales néolithiques et énéolithiques sur le territoire de la R. P. Roumaine. Bericht über die 6. Tagung der Deutschen Ges. für Anthropologie, Kiel 1958, pp. 152–159.
1959 a. Étude anthropologique des squelettes énéolithiques de Dolheştii Mari. Analele Ştiinçifice ale Universitäçii "Al. i. Cuza" din Iaşi, n.s. (sect. 3, St. nat.), vol. 5, pp. 47–60.
1965. Données anthropologiques sur les populations de l'âge de la pierre en Roumanie. Homo (Göttingen), vol. 16, no. 3, pp. 129–161.

Neel, James V.
1951. The population genetics of two inherited blood dyscrasias in man. Cold Spring Harbor Symposia on Quantitative Biology, vol. 15, pp. 141–158.
1953. Haemopoietic system. Chapter 24 (pp. 446–475) in Clinical Genetics, edit. Arnold Sorsby. London, Butterworth.
1958. The study of natural selection in primitive and civilized human populations. Human Biol., vol. 30, pp. 43–72.
1959. Genetic aspects of abnormal hemoglobins. Pages 158–180 in J. H. P. Jonxis and J. F. Delafresnaye, Abnormal hemoglobins. Oxford, Blackwell.

Neel, James V.; Salzano, F. M.; Junqueira, P. C.; Keiter, F.; and Maybury-Lewis, D.
1964. Studies on the Xavante Indians of the Brazilian Mato Grosso. Amer. Journ. Human Genetics, vol. 16, pp. 52–140.

Nemeskéri, János; Harsányi, László; and Acsádi, György
1960. Methoden zur Diagnose des Lebensalters von Skelettfunden. Anthropologischer Anzeiger, vol. 24, pp. 70–95.

Nicholson, G.
1945. The two main diameters at the brim of the female pelvis. Journ. Anat., vol. 79, part 3, pp. 131–135.

Notestein, Frank W. [Ed.]
1960. On population: Three essays—by Thomas Malthus, Julian Huxley, and Frederick Osborn. 144 pp. New York, New American Library (Mentor MD295).

Oliver, Douglas L., and Howells, W. W.
1957. Micro-evolution: Cultural elements in physical variation. Amer. Anthropol., vol. 59, pp. 965–978.

Pendergrass, Eugene P.; Schaeffer, J. Parsons; and Hodes, Philip J.
1956. The head and neck in Roentgen diagnosis. 2 ed., 2 vols., 1759 pp. Springfield, Charles C Thomas.

Perkins, Dexter, Jr.
1964. Prehistoric fauna from Shanidar, Iraq. Science, vol. 144, no. 3626, pp. 1565–1566.

Perrot, Jean
1962. Palestine-Syria-Cilicia. Pages 147–164 in R. J. Braidwood and G. R. Willey, Courses toward urban life: Archeological considerations of some cultural alternatives. Chicago, Aldine.

PIGGOTT, STUART
   1965. Ancient Europe from the beginnings of agriculture to classical antiquity. 343 pp. Chicago, Aldine.
POTTER, R. G.; WYON, J. B.; NEW, M.; and GORDON, J. E.
   1965. Fetal wastage in eleven Punjab villages. Human Biol., vol. 37, no. 3, pp. 262–273.

RADULESCU, C., and SAMSON, P.
   1962. Sur un centre de domestication du mouton dans la Mésolithique de la grotte "La Adam" en Dobrogea.
      Zeitschr. für Tierzüchtung und Züchtungbiol., vol. 76, pp. 282–320.
REED, CHARLES A.
   1960. Animal domestication in the prehistoric Near East. Pages 119–145 in Robert J. Braidwood and
      Bruce Howe, Prehistoric investigations in Iraqui Kurdistan. Univ. Chicago Oriental Institute,
      Studies in Oriental Civilization, no. 31.
RENAULT, MARY
   1956. The last of the wine. New York, Pantheon Books, Inc. (Pocket Books, no. 72025, 1964).
RENFREW, COLIN
   1967. Cycladic metallurgy and the Aegean Early Bronze Age. Amer. Journ. Archaeol., vol. 71, no. 1,
      pp. 1–20.
REYNOLDS, EARLE L.
   1945. The bony pelvic girdle in early infancy. Amer. Journ. Phys. Anthropol., n.s., vol. 3, pp. 32–354.
ROBINOW, M.; RICHARDS, T. W.; and ANDERSON, MARGARET
   1942. The eruption of deciduous teeth. Growth, vol. 6, pp. 127–133.
ROBINSON, DAVID M.
   1942. Excavations at Olynthus, XI. Necrolynthia, a study in Greek burial customs and anthropology.
      Johns Hopkins Studies in Archeology, no. 32.
ROBINSON, D. M., and GRAHAM, J. W.
   1938. Excavations at Olynthus, VIII. The Hellenic house. Johns Hopkins Studies in Archaeology,
      no. 25.
RODDEN, ROBERT J.
   1962. Excavations at the Early Neolithic site at Nea Nikomedeia, Greek Macedonia (1961 season). Proc.
      Prehistoric Soc., n.s., vol. 28, pp. 267–288.
   1964. Recent discoveries from prehistoric Macedonia. An interim report. Balkan Studies (Thessalonike),
      vol. 5, pp. 109–124.
   1965. An early Neolithic village in Greece. Scientific American, vol. 212, no. 4, pp. 82–90.
RODDEN, R. J., and RODDEN, J. M.
   1964. A European link with Çatal Hüyük: the 7th millennium settlement of Nea Nikomedeia in Macedonia.
      Illustr. London News, Part I (April 11), pp. 564–567 (Site and pottery); Part II (April 18), pp.
      604–607 (Burials and the shrine).
RUNGE, CARL F.
   1954. Roentgenographic examination of the lumbosacral spine in routine pre-employment examinations.
      Journ. Bone and Joint Surgery, vol. 36A, pp. 75–84.

SCHMIDT, ERICH F.
   1937. Excavations at Tepe Hissar Damghan. 478 pp. Philadelphia, Univ. Pennsylvania Press.
SCHMORL, GEORG, and JUNGHANNS, H.
   1957. Die gesunde und die kranke Wirbelsäule in Röntgenbild und Klinik. 4 ed., 332 pp. Stuttgart,
      Georg Thieme Verlag.
ŞENYÜREK, M. S.
   1950. A note on three skulls from Alaca Höyük. Türk Tarih Kurumu Basimevi Belleten, vol. 14, no. 53,
      pp. 57–84.
   1951. A note on the human skeletons in the Alaca Höyük Museum. Ankara Universitesi Dil ve Tarih-
      Coğrafya Fakültesi Dergisi, vol. 9, nos. 1–2, pp. 43–61.
SERVICE, ELMAN R.
   1962. Primitive social organization. An evolutionary perspective. 211 pp. New York, Random House.
SEYMOUR, THOMAS D.
   1908. Life in the Homeric Age. 704 pp. New York, Macmillan.

SHEAR, T. LESLIE

1928. Excavations in the theatre district and tombs of Corinth in 1928.   Amer. Journ. Archaeol., vol. 32, pp. 474–495.

1929. Excavations in the theatre district and tombs of Corinth in 1929.   Amer. Journ. Archaeol., vol. 33, pp. 515–546.

SIMPSON, GEORGE G.

1952. The meaning of evolution.   New Haven, Yale University Press.

1958. The study of evolution: methods and present status of theory.   Chapter 1 (pp. 7–26) *in* Behavior and evolution, edit. G. G. Simpson and A. Roe.   New Haven, Yale Univ. Press.

SOGNNAES, REIDAR F.

1950. Is the susceptibility to dental caries influenced by factors operating during the period of tooth development?   Pages 37–52 *in* Sugar and dental caries, a symposium.   Journ. Calif. State Dental Assoc., vol. 26, no. 3.

SOLECKI, RALPH S.

1963. Prehistory in Shanidar Valley, northern Iraq.   Science, vol. 139, no. 1551, pp. 179–193.

1964. An archaeological reconnaissance in the Beyşehir Suğla area of south western Turkey.   Türk Arkeoloji Dergisi, vol. 13, no. 1, pp. 129–148.

SORSBY, ARNOLD [Ed.]

1953. Clinical genetics.   580 pp.   London, Butterworth.

STÉPHANOS, CLON

1884. Grèce. Géographie médicale. I. Orographie, hydrographie, pp. 363–370; III. Géologie, pp. 388–397; IV. Flore, pp. 397–401; VI. Ethnologie, pp. 406–432; VII. Anthropologie, pp. 432–440; VIII. Démographie, pp. 440–479; IX. Hygiène, pp. 479–488; X. Pathologie, pp. 488–551.   *In* Dict. Enc. des Sci. Méd., edit. A. Dechambre, ser. 4, vol. 10.   Paris.

STEWART, T. DALE

1943. Relative variability of Indian and white cranial series.   Amer. Journ. Phys. Anthropol., n.s., vol. 1, pp. 261–270.

1954. Evaualtion of evidence from the skeleton.   Chapter 17 (pp. 407–450) *in* Legal medicine, edit. R. B. H. Gradwohl.   St. Louis, Mosby.

1956. Examination of the possibility that certain skeletal characters predispose to defects in the lumbar neural arches.   Clinical Orthopaedics, vol. 8, pp. 44–60.   Philadelphia.

1957. Distortion of the pubic symphyseal surface in females and its effect on age determination.   Amer. Journ. Phys. Anthrop., n.s., vol. 15, no. 1, pp. 9–18.

1959. Restoration and study of the Shanidar I Neanderthal skeleton in Baghdad, Iraq.   Yearbook Amer. Philos. Soc., 1958, pp. 274–278.

1959a. The restored Shanidar I skull.   Ann. Rep. Smithsonian Inst. for Year Ended June 30, 1958 (publ. 4369), pp. 473–480.

1968. Identification by the skeletal structures.   Chapter 11 (pp. 123–154) *in* Gradwohl's Legal Medicine, edit. Francis E. Camps.   Bristol, John Wright & Sons Ltd.

STUBBINGS, FRANK H.

1963. The rise of Mycenaean civilization.   No. 18 (vol. 2, ch. 14) *in* The Cambridge Ancient History. 37 pp.   Cambridge Univ. Press.

TANNER, JAMES M.

1962. Growth at adolescence.   2 ed., 324 pp.   Oxford, Blackwell.

TARN, W. W.

1930. Hellenistic civilisation.   334 pp.   London, Arnold.

THEOCHARIS, D.

1958. Pre-ceramic Thessaly [in Greek].   Thessalika (Volos), no. 1, pp. 70–86.

THIEME, F. P., and SCHULL, W. J.

1957. Sex determination from the skeleton.   Human Biol., vol. 29, pp. 242–273.

THOMAS, ELIZABETH MARSHALL

1958. The harmless people.   266 pp.   New York, Random House (Vintage Books V289).

THOMPSON, WARREN S.

1942. Population problems.   3 ed., 471 pp.   New York, McGraw-Hill.

TOBIN, WILLIAM J., and STEWART, T. DALE

1953. Gross osteopathology of arthritis.   Clinical Orthopaedics, vol. 2, pp. 167–183.

TODD, T. W.
  1920. Age changes in the pubic bone. Part I, The male white pubis. Amer. Journ. Phys. Anthropol., vol. 3, pp. 285–334.
TODD, T. W., and LYON, D. W., JR.
  1924. Endocranial suture closure, its progress and age relationship. Part I. Adult males of white stock. Amer. Journ. Phys. Anthropol., vol. 7, pp. 325–384.
TROTTER, MILDRED, and GLESER, GOLDINE C.
  1958. A re-evaluation of estimation of stature based on measurements of stature taken during life and of long bones after death. Amer. Journ. Phys. Anthropol., n.s., vol. 16, pp. 79–124.

VALLOIS, H. V.
  1936. Les Ossements natoufiens d'Erg-el-Ahmar (Palestine). L'Anthropologie, vol. 46, pp. 529–543.
  1939. Les Ossements humains de Sialk. Contribution à l'étude de l'histoire raciale de l'Iran ancien. Pages 113–192 in Fouilles de Sialk, 1933, 1934, 1937, II. Louvre, Dept. des Antiquités Orientales, Série Archéol. 5.
VANDERPOOL, EUGENE
  1965. News letter from Greece. Amer. Journ. Archaeol., vol. 69, pp. 353–357.
VAN LOON, MAURITS N.
  1966. Mureybat: An early village in inland Syria. Archaeology, vol. 19, no. 3, pp. 215–216.
VAN ZEIST, WILLEM, and WRIGHT, H. E., JR.
  1963. Preliminary pollen studies at Lake Zeribar, Zagros Mountains, Southwestern Iran. Science, vol. 140, no. 3562, pp. 65–67.
VENTRIS, M., and CHADWICK, J.
  1953. Evidence for Greek dialect in the Mycenaean archives. Journ. Hellenic Studies (London), vol. 73, pp. 84–103.
VICKERY, K. F.
  1936. Food in early Greece. University of Illinois Studies in the Social Sciences, vol. 20, no. 3, 97 pp.

WASHBURN, S. L.
  1948. Sex differences in the pubic bone. Amer. Journ. Phys. Anthropol., n.s., vol. 6, no. 2, pp. 199–208.
WEIDENREICH, FRANZ
  1945. The Paleolithic child from the Teshik-Tash cave in southern Uzbekistan (Central Asia). Amer. Journ. Phys. Anthropol., n.s., vol. 3, no. 2, pp. 151–163.
WEINBERG, SAUL S.
  1961. Halafian and Ubaidian influence in Neolithic Greece. Fifth International Congress of Prehistoric and Protohistoric Sciences, Hamburg, 1958. Berlin.
  1962. Excavations at prehistoric Elateia, 1959. Hesperia, vol. 31, pp. 158–209.
  1962a. Solving a prehistoric puzzle. Archaeology, vol. 15, pp. 262–266.
  1965. The Aegean in the Stone and Early Bronze Ages. Pages 285–320 in Chronologies in Old World Archaeology, edit. R. W. Ehrich. Univ. Chicago Press.
  1965a. The Stone Age in the Aegean. No. 36 (vol. 1, ch. 10) in The Cambridge Ancient History. 68 pp. Cambridge Univ. Press.
WINTROBE, M. W.
  1951. Clinical hematology. 3 ed., 1048 pp. Philadelphia, Lea and Febiger.
WOO, T. L.
  1930. A study of seventy-one Ninth Dynasty Egyptian skulls from Sedment. Biometrika, vol. 22, pp. 65–93.
WRIGHT, SEWALL
  1931. Evolution in Mendelian populations. Genetics, vol. 16, pp. 97–159.

YOUNG, MATTHEW, and INCE, J. G. H.
  1940. A radiographic comparison of the male and female pelvis. Journ. Anat., vol. 74, pp. 374–385.

APPENDIX

NOTE: In the tables under each clan the order of listing is adult males, adult females, adolescents, children, and infants.

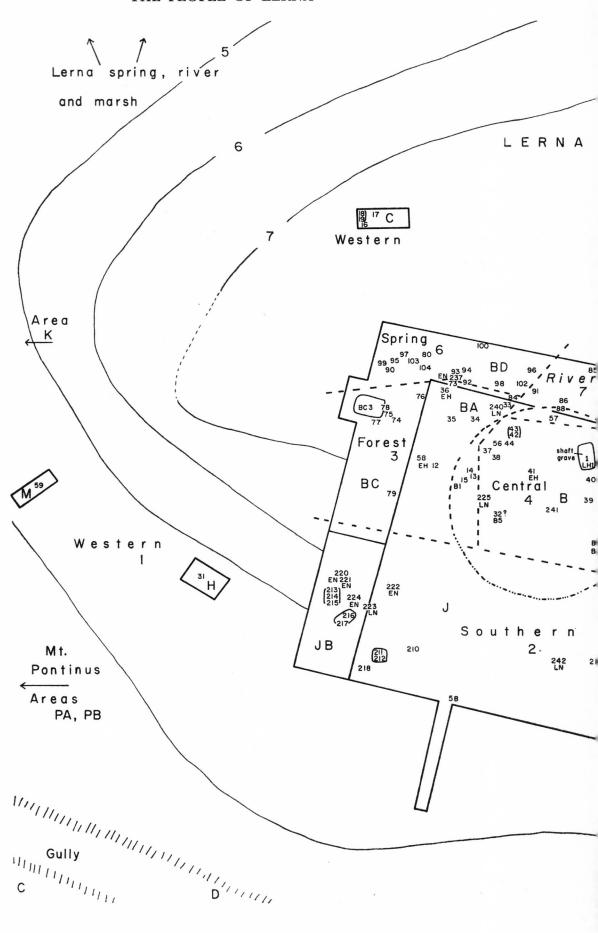

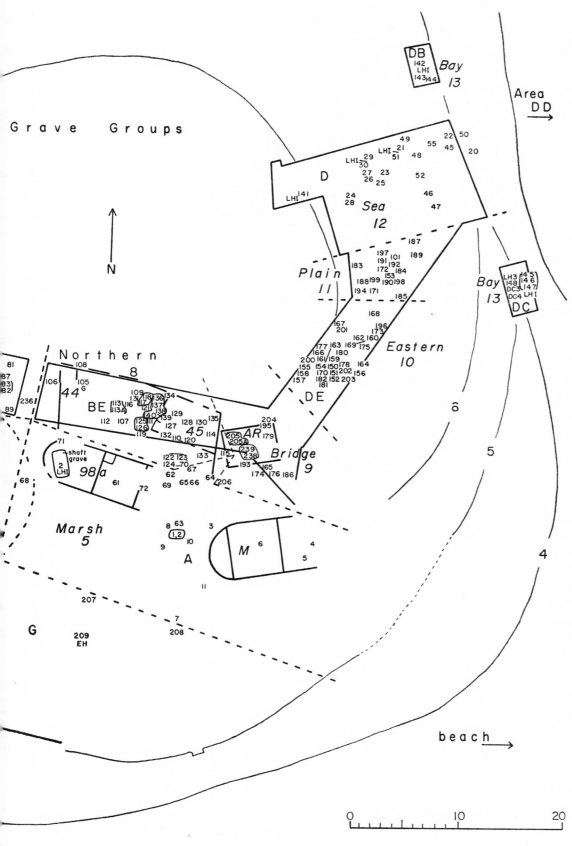

Figure 5. Plan of burials at Lerna based on Tucker Blackburn's careful coordination of John L. Caskey's excavation records. Contour lines are in meters above sea level. Continuous lines mark the excavation trenches (C, BC, DE, etc.) and areas (B, J, G, A, etc.) and a few of the houses (98 a, M, 44, 45, and AR). The central tumulus (dotted outline) appears on the plan but not the E.H. III palace or House of the Tiles (whose burnt ruins the tumulus partly covers). Dotted lines separate the grave groupings, or clans, of Middle Bronze times (late Lerna IV, Lerna V, and Lerna VI). Burials from any period other than strict Middle Helladic (Lerna V) are marked EN (Early Neolithic), LN (Late Neolithic), EH (end of Early Helladic III), LH I and II (beginning of Late Helladic), and G (Geometric). Areas K, PA and PB (Early Iron Age Geometric burials), and DD (Roman period burial) are off the plan in the direction shown by the arrows.

TABLE 14. MEASUREMENTS, ANGLES, AND INDICES OF INDIVIDUAL SKELETONS FROM LERNA

Clan and period	Early Neolithic				Late Neolithic					
Grave and area or trench	JA-JB J6 West		JA-JB 1.5 W. of AX 2.8		HTN-1		JC-1		HTJ-1	
Number	220		224		240		242		225	
Sex and age Pubic symphysis phase	F 10– –		F?? 0– – b		F 26 –		F 26 –		F?? 0+ –	
	L.	R.	L.	R.	L.	R.	L.	R.	L.	R.
Humerus: Max. length	197	197[a]		66	289?	–	283		72	72–
Vert. head diam.	–	28	–	–	–	–	38	41?	–	–
Max. midshaft diam.	12	13	–	–	19	–	20	20+	–	–
Min. midshaft diam.	10+	11	–	–	13	–	17	16	–	–
Biepicondylar breadth	–	–	–	–	(54)	–	55	55	–	–
Radius: Max. length	147	149	–	52	–	(229)	(223)	221	58–	58–
Ulna: Max. length	161	164	–	–	–	–	239?	–	64+	64+
Clavicle: Max. length	– 95? –		–	(40)	–	–	136	130	–	49
Scapula: Breadth	67	–	–	–	–	–	–	–	–	–
Femur: Max. length	–	306[b]	77	76+	–	410??	402?	–	82	83
Max. head diam.	29+	29	–	–	–	49	–	40	–	–
Subtrochanteric a-p diam.	16	16	–	–	20	21	24	23	–	–
Subtrochanteric transv. diam.	20	21	–	–	28	29	34	33	–	–
Midshaft a-p diam.	16	16+	–	–	24	24	28	28	–	–
Midshaft transv. diam.	17	17+	–	–	25	26	26	25	–	–
Neck torsion angle (°)	–	+	–	–	–	(0)	25?	–	–	–
Platymeric index	80.0	76.2	–	–	71.4	72.4	70.6	69.7	–	–
Pilastric index	94.1	94.1	–	–	96.0	92.3	107.7	112.0	–	–
Robusticity index	–	11.2	–	–	–	12.2?	13.6	–	–	–
Tibia: Length, lat. cond.-mall.	–	229[c]	–	–	–	–	340	–	70	70
Nutr. foramen level a-p diam.	22	22	–	–	–	–	33	34	–	–
Nutr. foramen level transv. diam.	15	16+	–	–	–	–	23	22	–	–
Head retroversion angle (°)	–	22	–	–	–	–	17	–	–	–
Cnemic index	71.4	72.7	–	–	–	–	69.7	–	–	–
Fibula: Max. length	218	221	–	–	–	–	–	–	–	–
Stature estimate (cm., Trotter)	128.3?		–		158.0?		156.3		–	
Brachial index	–	–	–	–	(79.2)		78.1		–	–
Lumbar vertebrae height (Ant. & post.)	–	–			–		–		–	
Sacrum (Height & breadth)	–	(74)	–	–	–	–	–	120	–	–
Innominate: Height	140	143	–	–	–	–	–	–	–	–
Iliac breadth	98	100	34	33	–	–	–	158	–	(36)
Ischial length	54	55	–	–	–	–	(80)	–	–	–
Pubic length	–	45?	–	–	–	–	–	–	–	–
Pelvis: Bi-iliac breadth	–		–		–		–		–	
Inlet diam. (A-p & transv.)	–	–	–	–	–	–	–	–	–	–
Inlet angle with horizontal (°)	–		–		–		–		–	
Brim index	–		–		–		–			
Talus: Length	–	40	–	–	–	–	47	46	–	–
Breadth	–	33	–	–	–	–	38	38	–	–
Mid-trochlear height	–	21	–	–	–	–	27	28	–	–
Neck diversion angle (°)	–	39	–	–	–	–	14	14	–	–
Calcaneus: Max. length	–	51	–	–	–	–	–	78	–	–

[a] with epiphyses, 212.   [b] with epiphyses.   [c] with epiphyses, 243.

	1. WESTERN (Mid. Br. Age, early to mid. ph.)								2. SOUTHERN (Middle Bronze Age, very early to middle phases)									
	C-M		H-1		M-1		C-H		JA-J2B		JB-J4A		JB-J4B		GP-G2		GQ-G3	
	19		31		59		17		212		216		217		207		208	
	M 42 VIII		F 18– –		F 26 –		F? 8 –		M 33 VI		M 37 –		M 24? –		F 30 V		F 38 –	
	L.	R.	L.	R.	L.	R.	L.	R.	L.	R.	L.	R.	L.	R.	L.	R.	L.	R.
	318	320	–	292+	281	284–	189	–	–	(310)	–	–	–	(310) –	269?	(272)	(274)	–
	44	–	–	40	41	40	–	–	–	–	–	–	–	–	–	–	40?	–
	23	24	20	20	18	19	16	–	–	23	–	21?	20	–	20	21	20	20
	18	19	15	15	15	14	12	–	–	20+	–	20?	17	–	14	15–	16	16
	63?	–	–	55	54	–	–	–	–	–	–	–	–	–	55	55	51–	–
	247	–	225	–	205	–	144	146	(240)	–	–	–	(240)	–	(191)?	197	203	–
	267	–	–	–	–	–	159	–	–	–	–	–	–	–	(212)?	218	221	–
	– (145) –		–	–	–	–	–	–	–	–	–	(135)	–	–	–	130	(128)	
	450?	–	403?	–	–	(390)	261	–	–	–	–	(425)	(435)	–	–	(370)	–	–
	45	–	41	40	–	40	–	31	–	–	–	–	41+	–	(40+)	–	–	–
	–	–	22	24	23	22	19	17	–	–	–	21	–	–	23	23	–	–
	–	–	28	30	27	26	23	22	–	–	–	34	–	–	27	28–	–	–
	31	31	27	26	22	22	20+	20	–	–	–	28	28	–	25	24	–	–
	28	28	23	23	22	22	16+	16+	–	–	–	28	25	–	23+	24	–	–
	–	–	–	–	–	–	+		–	–	–	–	–	–	–	–	–	–
	–	–	78.6	80.0	85.2	84.6	–	–	–	–	–	61.8	–	–	85.2	82.1	–	–
	110.7	110.7	117.4	113.0	100.0	100.0	–	–	–	–	–	100.0	112.0	–	108.7	100.0	–	–
	13.2?	–	12.5?	–	–	(11.4)	–	–	–	–	–	–	–	–	–	–	–	–
	–	–	– (305)		– (320)		209	–	– (355) –		–	–	(340)	–	(312)	–	–	–
	–	38	31	–	–	26	25	–	38	–	–	–	34	–	30	32	–	–
	–	25	21	–	–	20	19	–	25	–	–	–	23–	–	20	20	–	–
	–	–	–	–	–	–	s.	–	–	–	–	–	–	–	–	–	–	–
	–	65.8	67.7	–	–	76.9	–	–	65.8	–	–	–	67.6	–	66.7	62.5	–	–
	–	–	–	–	–	–	–	–	353?	–	–	–	–	–	304?	–	–	–
	170.4		154.2		152.5		–		167.3		(164.1)		(166.5)		148.2		151.2	
	77.7	–	–	77.0	73.0	–	–	–	–	–	–	–	–	–	71.0	–	–	–
	–	–	–	–	–	–	–	–	–	–	–	–	–	–	–	–	–	–
	–	–	–	–	–	–	–	–	–	–	–	–	–	–	–	–	–	–
	–	–	–	–	–	–	–	–	–	–	–	–	–	–	–	–	–	–
	–	–	–	–	–	–	–	–	–	–	–	–	–	–	–	–	–	–
	–	–	83?	–	–	–	–	–	–	–	–	–	–	–	–	–	–	–
	–	–	–	–	–	–	–	–	–	–	–	–	–	–	–	–	–	–
	–		–		–		–		–		–		–		–		–	
	–		–		–		–		–		–		–		–		–	
	–		–		–		–		–		–		–		–		–	
	–	–	47	–	49	48	–	–	55	–	–	–	51	51	52	52	–	–
	–	–	41	–	37	38	–	–	45	–	–	–	(37+)	40	40	40+	–	–
	–	–	41	–	26	26–	–	–	89	–	–	–	(28–)	30	28–	27+	–	–
	–	–	28	–	27	24	–	–	30?	–	–	–	27	27	36	37	–	–
	–	–	69	63?	–	74	–	–	– (79) –		–	–	81	80	–	73	–	–

TABLE 14 .Measurements, Angles, and Indices of Individual Skeletons from Lerna

Clan and period	2. Southern (Middle Bronze Age, very early to middle phases) cont.											
Grave and area or trench	JA-J1		JA-J2A		JB-J3A		JA-J5		JB-J3B		JB-J3C	
Number	210		211		213		218		214		215	
Sex and age	F 30		F 31		F 26		F? 38?		?M 13		M?? 4	
Pubic symphysis phase	–		VI		IV?		–		–		–	
	L.	R.	L.	R.	L.	R.	L.	R.	L.	R.	L.	R.
Humerus: Max. length	–	(290)	–	299	305	–	–	(265)	260+	–	–	(125)
Vert. head diam.	–	–	–	40+	40	–	–	–	38	–	–	–
Max. midshaft diam.	–	20+	21	22–	21–	21	–	22	16+	–	–	11
Min. midshaft diam.	–	15	17	17	16	16	–	18	13	–	–	9
Biepicondylar breadth	–	–	–	55?	–	58	55	–	45?	45+	–	–
Radius: Max. length	–	(236)	–	220?	(235)	–	–	–	–	(190)	–	–
Ulna: Max. length	–	–	–	239	(252)	–	–	–	–	–	–	–
Clavicle: Max. length	–	–	–	133	–	–	–	–	(115)	–	–	74?–
Scapula: Breadth	–	–	–	–	–	–	–	–	–	–	–	–
Femur: Max. length	–	–	–	–	–	–	–	–	(380)	–	–	170
Max. head diam.	–	–	41	41	–	40	–	–	–	–	–	–
Subtrochanteric a-p diam.	–	–	–	24	24	–	25	–	22	–	–	13
Subtrochanteric transv. diam.	–	–	–	32	28	–	30	–	27	–	–	18
Midshaft a-p diam.	–	27	–	27	26	–	28	–	23	–	–	14
Midshaft transv. diam.	–	29	–	24	25	–	24	–	22	–	–	14
Neck torsion angle (⁰)	–	–	–	–	–	–	–	–	–	–	–	–
Platymeric index	–	–	–	75.0	85.7	–	83.3	–	–	–	–	–
Pilastric index	–	93.1	–	112.5	104.0	–	116.7	–	–	–	–	–
Robusticity index	–	–	–	–	–	–	–	–	–	–	–	–
Tibia: length, lat. cond.–mall.	–	–	–	–	–	–	(320)	–	–	–	140	–
Nutr. foramen level a-p diam.	–	–	–	–	–	21	34–	–	29	–	15	–
Nutr. foramen level transv. diam.	–	–	–	–	–	29	22–	–	21	–	13	–
Head retroversion angle (⁰)	–	–	–	–	–	–	–	–	–	–	–	–
Cnemic index	–	–	–	–	–	72.4	64.7	–	–	–	–	–
Fibula: Max. length	–	–	–	–	–	–	–	–	–	–	–	–
Stature estimate (cm., Trotter)	(155.4)		158.7		160.5		(154.5)		146		–	
Brachial index	–	–	–	73.6	–	–	–	–	–	–	–	–
Lumbar vertebrae height (Ant. & post.)	–	–	–	–	–	–	–	–	–	–	–	–
Sacrum (Height & breadth)	–	–	109	(115)	–	–	–	–	–	–	–	–
Innominate: Height	–	–	–	–	–	–	–	–	–	–	–	–
Iliac breadth	–	–	–	–	–	–	–	–	–	–	–	–
Ischial length	–	–	–	–	–	–	–	–	–	–	–	–
Pubic length	–	–	–	81	–	–	–	–	–	–	–	–
Pelvis: Bi-iliac breadth	–		–		–		–		–		–	
Inlet diam. (A-p & transv.)	–	–	–	–	–	–	–	–	–	–	–	–
Inlet angle with horizontal (⁰)	–		–		–		–		–		–	
Brim index	–		–		–		–		–		–	
Talus: Length	–	–	48	49	46	46+	47	47	52	–	–	–
Breadth	–	–	39	40–	36–	36	36	37	38	–	–	–
Mid-trochlear height	–	–	28	27	25+	26–	28	27	26+	–	–	–
Neck diversion angle (⁰)	–	–	43	(31+)	34	34	–	54	34	–	–	–
Calcaneus: Max. length	–	–	–	72	70	70+	74	–	68?	–	–	–

3. FOREST (Middle Bronze Age, very early to middle phases)

AD-1		GP-G4		BA-4		BC-4		B-2		BC-5		BC-2		BA-5		BB-3	
60		209		73		76		12		77		75		36		58	
F 0– —		F 0 —		M 50? —		M 40 VIII		F 45 —		F 28 V		M 12 —		F 0– —		F 0– —	
L.	R.	L.	R.	L.	R.	L.	R.	L.	R.	L.	R.	L.	R.	L.	R.	L.	R.
65	—	64+	64	—	—	—	—	(263)	—	286?	288?	—	237	62	62	62+	62+
—	—	—	—	—	—	—	—	—	—	—	—	—	—	—	—	—	—
—	—	—	—	—	—	21	—	20	—	19	19	18	19	—	—	—	—
—	—	—	—	—	—	18	—	17	—	14	14	14	14	—	—	—	—
—	—	—	—	—	(62)	63?	63	—	—	—	51	—	35–	—	—	—	—
51	51+	50+	50+	—	242?	232?	—	—	201	—	213	(186)	—	48	48	51	51+
57	—	—	58	—	255?	253	—	—	—	—	—	(204)	—	55	—	59	59+
45	—	41	—	—	—	—	—	—	—	124?	(124)	—	—	—	—	—	—
—	28	28+	28	—	—	—	—	—	—	—	—	—	—	—	26	—	—
(69)	(68)	74+	75	—	—	(425)	—	—	—	388?	—	—	—	71	—	73–	73
—	—	—	—	51	—	—	—	—	—	36	37–	—	—	—	—	—	—
—	—	6	—	—	—	—	—	23	—	22	—	—	—	—	—	—	—
—	—	6	—	—	—	—	—	31	—	27	—	—	—	—	—	—	—
—	—	—	—	35	—	29	—	22	—	26	24	—	—	—	—	—	—
—	—	—	—	31	—	28	—	24	—	23	22	—	—	—	—	—	—
—	—	—	—	—	—	—	—	—	—	—	3	—	—	—	—	—	—
—	—	—	—	—	—	—	—	74.2	—	81.5	—	—	—	—	—	—	—
—	—	—	—	112.9	—	103.6	—	91.7	—	113.0	109.1	—	—	—	—	—	—
—	—	—	—	—	—	—	—	—	—	12.7	—	—	—	—	—	—	—
(62)	—	65	64?	—	—	—	—	—	—	—	(315)	—	—	62	62	—	66+
—	—	—	—	—	—	—	36?	—	—	—	30	—	—	—	—	—	—
—	—	—	—	—	—	—	25?	—	—	—	21	—	—	—	—	—	—
—	—	—	—	—	—	16	—	—	—	—	—	—	—	—	—	—	—
—	—	—	—	—	—	—	69.4	—	—	—	70.0	—	—	—	—	—	—
59	—	—	—	—	—	—	—	—	—	—	—	—	—	—	—	—	—
—		—		170.1		167.9		150.2		153.2		—		—		—	
—	—	—	—	—	—	—	—	—	—	—	74.0	—	—	—	—	—	—
—	—	—	—	—	—	—	—	—	—	119?	117?	—	—	—	—	—	—
—	—	—	—	—	—	—	—	—	—	—	—	—	—	—	—	—	—
—	—	35	—	—	—	—	—	—	—	—	—	(138)	—	—	—	—	—
—	—	—	—	—	—	—	—	—	—	—	—	(116)	—	33	32	—	33
—	—	—	—	—	—	—	—	—	—	—	69	(60)	—	—	—	—	—
—	—	—	—	—	—	—	—	—	—	—	(76)	—	—	—	—	—	—
—		—		—		—		—		—		—		—		—	
—		—		—		—		—		—		—		—		—	
—		—		—		—		—		—		—		—		—	
—	—	—	—	—	57?	(52)	—	—	—	—	—	47	—	—	—	—	—
—	—	—	—	—	41?	(38)	—	—	—	—	—	38	—	—	—	—	—
—	—	—	—	—	31?	35–	—	—	—	—	—	26	—	—	—	—	—
—	—	—	—	—	27	(+)	—	—	—	—	—	28	—	—	—	—	—
—	—	—	—	—	—	—	—	—	—	—	—	—	—	—	—	—	—

Table 14. Measurements, Angles, and Indices of Individual Skeletons from Lerna

Clan and period	4. Central (Middle Bronze Age, very early to middle phases)											
Grave and area or trench	B7-9		B8-12B		B8-13		B7-7		B8-12A		B8-14	
Number	40		43		44		39		42		56	
Sex and age	M 48		M 21		M 25		F 30?		F 20		F 37	
Pubic symphysis phase	–		II		IV		–		II		VIII	
	L.	R.	L.	R.	L.	R.	L.	R.	L.	R.	L.	R.
Humerus: Max. length	310	–	–	309	302	–	–	–	–	(268)	269	274
Vert. head diam.	–	–	–	46?	42	–	–	–	–	–	38	36
Max. midshaft diam.	21	–	22	23	20	–	–	–	20	20	20	20
Min. midshaft diam.	16	–	17	18	18	–	–	–	15	15	16+	16+
Biepicondylar breadth	62	(60)	61+	64	60	–	–	–	–	56	54	54
Radius: Max. length	–	–	(230)	(230)	236	–	–	–	–	(215)	–	202
Ulna: Max. length	–	–	251?	(255)	255	–	–	–	–	–	217	–
Clavicle: Max. length	157?	157?	134	–	–	133?	–	–	–	(120)	120	–
Scapula: Breadth	–	–	97?	–	–	–	–	–	–	–	–	90
Femur: Max. length	–	458?	426?	–	439	–	–	(433)	–	388	–	393
Max. head diam.	–	49	47	–	44	–	41	43	38	40	40	39
Subtrochanteric a-p diam.	26	25	28	–	26	–	23	26	22	22	23	24
Subtrochanteric transv. diam.	36	32	34	–	34	–	29?	22	30	30	30	29
Midshaft a-p diam.	31	30	30	29	29	–	26	27	23	24	26	27
Midshaft transv. diam.	28	26	27	28	27	–	24	25	22+	23+	26	25
Neck torsion angle (°)	–	–	–	–	16+	–	–	–	–	0	–	–
Platymeric index	72.2	78.1	82.4	–	76.5	–	79.3	–	73.3	73.3	76.7	82.8
Pilastric index	110.7	115.4	111.1	103.6	107.4	–	108.3	108.0	104.6	104.4	100.0	108.0
Robusticity index	13.0?	12.3?	13.5?	–	13.0	–	–	(12.1)	–	12.2?	–	13.4
Tibia: Length, lat. cond.–mall.	(370)	–	362?	–	354	–	–	360	–	(320)	–	–
Nutr. foramen level a-p diam.	35	–	37	36	38	–	–	31	29	30	33	–
Nutr. foramen level transv. diam.	21	–	24	23	24	–	–	23	21	24	24	–
Head retroversion angle (°)	11	–	–	11	17	–	–	–	–	10	–	–
Cnemic index	60.0	–	64.9	63.9	63.2	–	–	74.2	72.4	80.0	72.7	–
Fibula: Max. length	–	–	–	–	–	–	–	–	–	–	–	–
Stature estimate (cm., Trotter)	169.7		466.5		166.5		165.9		149.9		150.7	
Brachial index	–	–	–	74.4)–	78.1	–	–	–	–	–	–	73.7
Lumbar vertebrae height (Ant. & post.)	–	–	(126)	?	–	–	–	–	124	125	126	124
Sacrum (Height & breadth)	–	–	–	–	112	114	–	–	–	113	93	111–
Innominate: Height	–	–	–	–	–	210?	–	–	(176)	191	185	185
Iliac breadth	–	–	–	–	–	–	–	–	–	147?	145+	148?
Ischial length	–	–	–	–	–	85?	–	–	71	73	79?	76
Pubic length	–	–	–	–	–	–	–	–	–	74	–	76
Pelvis: Bi-iliac breadth	–		–		–		–		254		281	
Inlet diam. (A-p & transv.)	–	–	–	–	–	–	–	–	117	123	101	137
Inlet angle with horizontal (°)	–		–		–		–		61		62	
Brim index	–		–		–		–		95.1		73.7	
Talus: Length	55?	54	54	55	52	52	–	52	?	48	–	–
Breadth	47	46	48	47	45	43	–	44	40	39	–	–
Mid-trochlear height	30	29?	33	32	27?	27	–	29	–	28	–	–
Neck diversion angle (°)	32	34	35	33	++?	32	–	19?	–	26	–	–
Calcaneus: Max. length	82	–	83	84	81	82	–	–	76	16	–	–

				5. MARSH (Middle Bronze Age, middle to late phases)											
B-8?		B7-10		A-1 north		A-1 south		B9-23		B10-24		A-8		B9-16	
241		41		1		2		68		69		7		61	
M??0		M 0		M 26–		M 34		M 30?		M 40		F 45		F 19	
–		–		IV		VI		–		VIII		IX		–	
L.	R.	L.	R.	L.	R.	L.	R.	L.	R.	L.	R.	L.	R.	L.	R.
61	61	69	–	–	320?	305–	–	–	–	293?	–	–(301)	–	275	–
–	–	–	–	–	–	44	–	–	–	–	–	–	38?	–	–
–	–	–	–	22	24	24	–	–	–	22	25	20	20	16	–
–	–	–	–	18+	18+	20–	–	–	–	19–	18+	16	15	12	–
–	–	–	–	61	–	64	65	55	–	63–	–	–	53+	–	–
50	50	56	55	244	(244)	234?	237?	–	–	215?	217?	–	(220)	(205)	–
57–	57	64	–	– (275) –		(355)	–	(250)	–	235?	–	–	(235)	–	–
–	46	46	46	155?	–	– (155) –		–	–	(150)	(145)	–	144	–	–
28	28	29	–	–	–	–	–	–	–	95	–	–	–	–	–
71	71	80	80	466?	463?	–	(428)	450	–	(396)	–	–	–	(375)	–
–	–	–	–	–	–	47	–	–	–	–	–	–	–	(36)	–
5+	6–	–	–	28	28	–	30	28	–	27	27	–	–	–	–
6–	6	–	–	34	31+	–	34	35	–	32	32	–	–	–	–
–	–	–	–	30	29	–	32	–	29	28	29	–	–	27	–
–	–	–	–	27	27	–	28	–	30	25	26	–	–	21	–
–	–	–	–	12?	8	–	0?	–	–	–	–	–	–	–	–
–	–	–	–	82.4	90.3	–	88.2	80.0	–	84.4	84.4	–	–	–	–
–	–	–	–	111.1	107.4	–	114.3	–	96.7	112.0	111.5	–	–	128.6	–
–	–	–	–	12.3?	12.2?	–	(14.1)	–	13.2?	–	–	–	–	–	–
61	61	69	68	353	(352)	–	(355)	–	350	– (309) –		–	(325)	(300)	–
–	–	–	–	38	37	–	38	35	–	32	–	–	31	(23)	–
–	–	–	–	24–	23	–	26	24	–	22+	–	–	20	(22)	–
–	–	–	–	10	10	–	–	8	–	–	–	–	–	–	–
–	–	–	–	63.2	62.2	–	68.4	68.6	–	68.6	–	–	64.5	–	–
56+	57	–	–	–	–	–	–	–	–	321	–	–	–	–	–
–		–		170.1		166.3		167.9		159.4		158.0?		150.0?	
–	–	–	–	– 76.2 –		76.7	–	–	–	73.4?	–	– (73.1) –		–	–
–	–	–	–	–	–	–	–	–	–	–	–	(127)	?	–	–
–	–	–	–	115	121ª?	–	–	–	–	–	–	–	–	–	–
–	–	–	–	–	(213)	–	–	–	–	–	196?	–	–	–	–
34–	34	36	–	–	–	–	–	–	–	–	(145)	–	–	–	–
19	–	–	–	88?	–	–	–	–	–	–	(83)	–	–	–	–
–	–	–	–	64?	–	–	–	–	–	–	(62)	–	78?	–	–
–		–		–		–		–		–		–		–	
–	–	–	–	(100)	(130)	–	–	–	–	–	–	–	–	–	–
–		–		(76.9)		–		–		–		–		–	
–	–	–	–	55	35	54	54	51	–	–	51	–	49	42	–
–	–	–	–	47	45?	43	44+	40	–	–	44?	–	39	31	–
–	–	–	–	33+	32	31	30	31+	–	–	31	–	28	25–	–
–	–	–	–	30	30	25	23	27–	–	–	24	–	18	24	–
–	–	–	–	82	–	86	85	74?	–	76	76	–	–	–	–

ª Six segments.

TABLE 14. MEASUREMENTS, ANGLES, AND INDICES OF INDIVIDUAL SKELETONS FROM LERNA

Clan and period	5. MARSH (Middle Bronze Age, middle to late phases) cont.													
Grave and area or trench	B10-21		A-9		A-10		B10-18		A-7		A-11		A-12	
Number	67		8		9		63		6		10		11	
Sex and age / Pubic symphysis phase	F 30 / –		M? 5½ / –		F 6½ / –		M 8 / –		F? 0 / –		M? 1 / –		F? 1– / –	
	L.	R.	L.	R.	L.	R.	L.	R.	L.	R.	L.	R.	L.	R.
Humerus: Max. length	277–	(281)	142	–	–	–	(168)	–	–	70	81	81	–	–
Vert. head diam.	39	–	–	–	–	–	–	–	–	–	–	–	–	–
Max. midshaft diam.	20	21	13	–	–	–	12	12	–	6	7.5	8	–	–
Min. midshaft diam.	14+	14+	11	–	–	–	11	11	–	5.5	6.5	6	–	–
Biepicondylar breadth	–	53	32	–	–	–	–	–	–	17	20	20	–	–
Radius: Max. length	–	–	–	113	–	128?	125	126	56?	–	–	65–	75	–
Ulna: Max. length	–	–	–	–	–	–	(141)	–	–	–	–	–	82	–
Clavicle: Max. length	(130)	–	–	–	–	–	–	80??	48	48–	–	53?	–	–
Scapula: Breadth	–	–	–	–	–	–	–	–	31	30+	–	31	–	–
Femur: Max. length	–	–	(200)	–	242	–	–	–	–	80–	92	–	–	–
Max. head diam.	41	–	–	–	24	–	24?	–	–	–	–	–	–	–
Subtrochanteric a-p diam.	–	–	16	–	16	–	18	–	–	8+	9	–	–	–
Subtrochanteric transv. diam.	–	–	18–	–	20	–	21	–	–	9+	10.5	–	–	–
Midshaft a-p diam.	–	–	15	–	16	–	17	17	–	7	8	–	–	–
Midshaft transv diam.	–	–	15	–	16	–	14	14+	–	7	9	–	–	–
Neck torsion angle (°)	–	–	–	–	25?	–	sl.	–	–	–	–	–	–	–
Platymeric index	–	–	–	–	–	–	–	–	–	–	–	–	–	–
Pilastric index	–	–	–	–	–	–	–	–	–	–	–	–	–	–
Robusticity index	–	–	–	–	–	–	–	–	–	–	–	–	–	–
Tibia: Length, lat. cond.–mall.	–	–	(150)	–	189?	–	190	–	–	70?	82	–	101	
Nutr. foramen level a-p diam.	31	–	16	–	19	–	20	–	–	7.5	–	–	12	
Nutr. foramen level transv. diam.	?	–	14	–	17–	–	16	–	–	8	–	–	11+	
Head retroversion angle (°)	–	?	+	–	0	–	14	–	–	–	–	–	v.sl.	
Cnemic index	–	–	–	–	–	–	80.0	–	–	–	–	–	–	–
Fibula: Max. length	–	–	–	–	–	–	184	–	–	66	79	–	–	–
Stature estimate (cm., Trotter)	151.0		–		–		–		–		–		–	
Brachial index	–		–		–		–		–		–		–	
Lumbar vertebrae height (Ant. & post.)	–		–		–		–		–		–		–	
Sacrum (Height & breadth)	–		–		–		–		–		–		–	
Innominate: Height	–	–	–	–	118+?	–	–	–	–	–	–	–	–	–
Iliac breadth	–	–	79?	–	83	–	–	–	37	–	–	–	–	–
Ischial length	–	–	–	–	48	–	–	–	–	–	–	24+	–	–
Pubic length	–	–	–	–	–	–	–	–	–	–	–	–	–	–
Pelvis: Bi-iliac breadth	–		–		–		–		–		–		–	
Inlet diam. (A-p & transv.)	–		–		–		–		–		–		–	
Inlet angle with horizontal (°)	–		–		–		–		–		–		–	
Brim index	–		–		–		–		–		–		–	
Talus: Length	–	–	–	–	32	–	(30)	–	–	–	–	–	–	–
Breadth	–	–	–	–	24	–	22?	–	–	–	–	–	–	–
Mid-trochlear height	–	–	–	–	17	–	17	–	–	–	–	–	–	–
Neck diversion angle (°)	–	–	–	–	48	–	36	–	–	–	–	–	–	–
Calcaneus: Max. length	66	–	–	–	–	–	42	–	–	–	–	–	–	–

6. SPRING (Middle Bronze Age, early to middle phases)																	
BD-19		BD-15		BD-21		BD-16		BD-27		BD-13		BD-20		BD-24		BD-26	
95		92		97		93		103		90		96		100		102	
M 39 VII		F 30 late V		F 29 V		M?12+ –		F???2+ –		F??0– –		F??0– –		F?0+ –		F?0 –	
L.	R.	L.	R.	L.	R.	L.	R.	L.	R.	L.	R.	L.	R.	L.	R.	L.	R.
315?	–	–	–	(302)	312	(220)	(240)[b]	126	126	(59)	–	–	64	–	74	67	(65+)
46+	–	–	–	–	41	–	–	–	–	–	–	–	–	–	–	–	–
23	23	–	22	20	20	–	(13)–	11	11	–	–	–	–	–	–	–	–
17	18	–	15	15	15+	–	(12)–	9	9–	–	–	–	–	–	–	–	–
–	–	–	–	–	56	–	–	27	27	–	–	–	–	–	–	–	–
245	–	–	(210)	266?	–	–	172	96	–	49	–	–	–	–	61	54–	54
260	–	–	–	–	–	–	–	–	107	54?	54+	–	–	–	71	62	61
–	152?	(128)	–	–	138	108	–	–	62–	–	–	–	–	–	–	46	44
–	–	–	–	–	–	76	–	41?	–	–	–	–	–	–	–	–	33
(445)	(435)	–	–	–	(360)	354[b]?	–	(176)	–	73	–	75+	75	–	–	72	79
–	–	40	–	42	41+	33	34	–	–	–	–	–	–	–	–	–	–
(28)[a]	28	–	–	–	22	18	–	12	–	–	–	–	–	–	–	–	–
(21–)[a]	31	–	–	–	31	23	–	12	–	–	–	–	–	–	–	–	–
(20)[a]	31	–	–	24	26	20	20	–	–	–	–	–	–	–	–	–	–
(27)[a]	29	–	–	24	24	17	16+	–	–	–	–	–	–	–	–	–	–
–	–	–	–	–	–	–	–	–	–	–	–	–	–	–	–	–	–
–	90.3	–	–	–	71.0	–	–	–	–	–	–	–	–	–	–	–	–
(74.1)[a]	106.9	–	–	100.0	108.3	–	–	–	–	–	–	–	–	–	–	–	–
(10.6)[a]	(13.9)	–	–	–	–	–	–	–	–	–	–	–	–	–	–	–	–
350	354	–	–	–	352?	–	–	122	–	–	60	–	66	–	(75)	68	68–
38	38	–	34+	30	29+	–	–	14–	–	–	–	–	–	–	–	–	–
24	29	–	23+	20+	21	–	–	12+	–	–	–	–	–	–	–	–	–
9	11	–	11	13	8	–	–	3	–	–	–	–	–	–	–	–	–
63.2	76.3	–	67.6	66.7	72.4	–	–	–	–	–	–	–	–	–	–	–	–
–	–	–	–	–	–	–	–	124	–	–	58+	–	62	–	–	–	–
168.5		(154.5)		163.0		(141)		–		–		–		–		–	
77.8	–	–	–	–	72.4	–	–	–	–	–	–	–	–	–	–	–	–
142	134?	–	–	137	(127)	–	–	60	53	–	–	–	–	–	–	–	–
–	–	–	–	?	(116)	–	–	–	–	–	–	–	–	–	–	–	–
–	(210)	(180)	–	–	–	153?	–	–	91	–	–	30	–	–	34+	33	32+
–	161?	(140)	–	160	–	112	–	–	58	–	–	–	–	–	–	–	–
–	(80)	–	81	80	(73)	60	–	36	36+	–	–	–	–	–	–	–	20
–	75	–	86	–	86?	(55)	–	–	–	–	–	–	–	–	–	–	–
–		–		–		–	–	–		–		–		–		–	
–		–		–		–		–		–		–		–		–	
–		–		–		–		–		–		–		–		–	
51	51	–	–	52	–	–	–	–	–	–	–	–	–	–	–	–	–
45	?	–	–	36	–	–	–	–	–	–	–	–	–	–	–	–	–
31	–	–	–	28+	–	–	–	–	–	–	–	–	–	–	–	–	–
33	++	–	–	28	–	–	–	–	–	–	–	–	–	–	–	–	–
84	–	–	–	–	–	–	–	32	32	–	–	–	–	–	–	–	–

[a] Pathological. [b] With epiphysis.

TABLE 14. MEASUREMENTS, ANGLES, AND INDICES OF INDIVIDUAL SKELETONS FROM LERNA

Clan and period	7. RIVER (Middle Bronze Age, middle phase)													
Grave and area or trench	BD-3 upper		BD-9		BD-11		BD-12		BD-14		B8-15		BD-6	
Number	83		87		88		89		91		57		86	
Sex and age / Pubic symphysis phase	M 33 —		M 29 —		M 34 —		M 42 —		M 45 IX		M ? 4– —		M ? ? 1– —	
	L.	R.	L.	R.	L.	R.	L.	R.	L.	R.	L.	R.	L.	R
Humerus: Max. length	–	–	(290)	–	(288)	–	285	–	(312)	–	(120)	–	(80)	82
Vert. head diam.	–	–	–	–	–	–	42	–	–	–	–	–	–	–
Max. midshaft diam.	24	–	25	–	20–	–	22	–	23	25+	–	–	–	–
Min. midshaft diam.	20	–	20–	–	18	–	18	–	19	18+	–	–	–	–
Biepicondylar breadth	–	–	–	–	64	–	58+	–	67–	–	–	–	–	–
Radius: Max. length	–	–	(232)	–	(230)	–	210	–	242	242?	–	94	–	63
Ulna: Max. length	–	–	247	–	256+	–	(230)	–	256?	260	–	–	(70)	71
Clavicle: Max. length	–	–	–	–	–	(135)	–	–	155	(148)	69	–	54–	55
Scapula: Breadth	–	–	–	–	–	–	–	–	110	–	–	–	34	
Femur: Max. length	(405+)	–	– (440)	–	405	–	–	(392)	450?	–	168	–	– 107	–
Max. head diam.	–	–	–	45?	–	–	–	–	52?	–	–	–	–	–
Subtrochanteric a-p diam.	–	22	25	–	26	23	26	24–	25	26	–	–	–	–
Subtrochanteric transv. diam.	–	37	36	–	33	31	33	33	37	35	–	–	–	–
Midshaft a-p diam.	–	30	31	29	29	29	32	31	30	30	–	–	–	–
Midshaft transv. diam.	–	28	29	28	27	27	29	28	29+	30	–	–	–	–
Neck torsion angle (°)	–	–	–	–	–	–	–	abs?	14+	–	–	–	–	–
Platymeric index	–	59.5	69.4	–	78.8	74.2	78.8	72.7	67.6	74.3	–	–	–	–
Pilastric index	–	107.1	106.9	103.6	107.4	107.4	110.3	110.7	103.4	100.0	–	–	–	–
Robusticity index	–	–	–	(13.4)–	–	13.9 –	–	(15.2)	13.2	–	–	–	–	–
Tibia: Length, lat. cond. to mall.	–	(365)	376	–	– (310)	–	(316)	–	348	–	–	–	79	79
Nutr. foramen level a-p diam.	–	35	–	44?	32	33+	37+	36	38	37	–	–	–	–
Nutr. foramen level transv. diam.	–	25	–	27?	21	22	(25)	(22)	23?	25	–	–	–	–
Head retroversion angle (°)	–	–	–	17	–	–	14	–	14	18?	–	–	–	–
Cnemic index	–	71.4	–	61.4	65.6	66.7	–	–	(60.5)	67.6	–	–	–	–
Fibula: Max. length	–	–	–	–	–	–	–	–	(335)	–	–	–	–	–
Stature estimate (cm., Trotter)	(164.1)		169.6		164.5		158.0		168.8		–		–	
Brachial index	–	–	–	–	–	–	73.7	–	–	–	–	–	–	–
Lumbar vertebrae height (Ant. & post.)	–	–	–	–	–	–	–	–	–	–	–	–	–	–
Sacrum (Height & breadth)	–	–	–	–	(99)	?	–	–	–	–	–	–	–	–
Innominate: Height	–	–	–	–	–	–	–	–	(212)	221	–	–	–	–
Iliac breadth	–	–	–	–	–	–	–	–	151?	154?	–	72	(47)	48
Ischial length	–	–	–	–	–	–	83?	–	(79)	81?	–	38+	–	27
Pubic length	–	–	–	–	–	–	–	–	(74)	–	–	29	–	–
Pelvis: Bi-iliac breadth	–		–		–		–		–		–		–	
Inlet diam. (A-p & transv.)	–	–	–	–	–	–	–	–	(115)	(124)	–	–	–	–
Inlet angle with horizontal (°)	–		–		–		–		–		–		–	
Brim index	–		–		–		–		–		–		–	
Talus: Length	52	?	50+	50+	–	51	–	–	52	52	–	–	–	–
Breadth	42	42?	41+	41–?	–	40	–	–	?	43	–	–	–	–
Mid-trochlear height	29	–	31–	30+	–	30	–	–	–	31+	–	–	–	–
Neck diversion angle (°)	31	38	28	27	–	24	–	–	–	27	–	–	–	–
Calcaneus: Max. length	–	–	–	80	79	76	–	–	–	–	–	–	–	–

8. NORTHERN (Middle Bronze Age, early phase)

BF-1		BE-11		BE-18		BE-19(1)		BE-20		BE-22		BE-23		BE-25		BE-26	
236		115		70		125		127		128		129		131		132	
F?0 –		M38 –		M35 VII		M44 VIII		M43 –		M44 VIII		M38 VII		M24 –		M48 IX	
L.	R.	L.	R.	L.	R.	L.	R.	L.	R.	L.	R.	L.	R.	L.	R.	L.	R.
67	67–	–	(320)	–	(320)	(300)	306	(305)	308?	(304)	309	–	–	333?	340?	302	–
–	–	–	–	–	–	–	–	–	–	–	42+	–	–	–	(45+)	46	–
5+	6–	–	23	21	23	22	24	25	23	21+	22	22?	–	23	23	24	24
5	5	–	18	17	19	19–	20	18	17	16–	16–	?	–	19–	19+	20	20
15	16–	–	–	–	66	64	63+?	61	61	50	54	62	–	–	–	63	–
55	–	–	–	(245)	–	235–	–	–	247	– (252) –		–	–	–	254?	239	–
61	61+	–	–	(268)	–	–	–	–	271	–	–	–	263?	–	278?	265	–
–	–	–	–	–	–	–	–	146	–	–	–	– (150) –		154??	152	148	143
31–	30+	–	–	–	–	–	–	–	–	–	–	–	–	–	–	–	–
–	77+	–	(433)	(450)	–	442	(435)	439	422[b]	–	–	450	450	(474)	(473)	(425+)	–
–	–	–	–	47	–	46	–	46	44	–	45+	45	45	47	48	46	47–
–	8–	24–	23	29	–	27	27	26	25	24	–	25	25	27	28	28	31
–	8	35–	24	33	–	34	32	35	34+	33	–	35	34	37	37	34	32
–	6–	–	27	27	–	29+	30–	29	27	26	–	27	30–	30	31	32	–
–	6+	–	27–	27	–	27	28	27	25	29	–	31	31	27	28+	29–	–
–	–	–	–	–	–	19	–	17	15	–	–	13	–	4	sl.	–	–
–	–	68.6	67.6	87.9	–	79.4	84.4	74.3	73.5	72.7	–	71.4	73.5	73.0	75.7	82.4	96.9
–	–	–	100.0	100.0	–	107.4	107.1	107.4	108.0	89.7	–	87.1	96.8	111.1	110.7	110.3	–
–	–	–	(12.6)	–	–	12.7	–	12.8	12.4	–	–	13.0	13.6	(12.1)	(12.6)	(14.4)	–
–	69	–	–	–	–	360	364	347+	339[b]	–	–	372	374	403??	–	–	–
–	7+	–	35–?	–	–	36	–	32	22+	–	–	34	35	40–	40?	–	–
–	7	–	23	–	–	26	–	22+	25–	–	–	25	24	26	25	–	–
–	–	–	–	–	–	7	10?	6	8	–	–	7?	11	11	–	–	–
–	–	–	65.7	–	–	72.2	–	68.8	78.1	–	–	73.5	68.6	–	62.5	–	–
–	68	–	–	–	–	355–	–	340–	330[b]?	–	–	362	(355)	–	–	–	–
–		(169.1)		170.8?		167.0		167.0		167.4		170.3		178.1		165.7	
–	–	–	–	(76.6)	–	–	76.8 –	–	80.2	–	–	–	–	–	75.5?–	79.1	–
–	–	–	–	–	–	142	132	137	(135)	131	–	138?	138?	–	–	130	(131)
–	–	(102)	115?	106[a]?	119	93	102	122?	111[a]	?	(118)	(105)	(112)	?	(106)	132[a]	114
–	–	–	221?	229	–	208	–	207	202	–	–	–	–	–	–	–	–
–	39	–	(150)	147	–	147?	–	140	148	–	–	–	–	–	–	–	153
–	17	–	85	80	–	74	70	(86)	90	91?	–	82?	–	–	–	(85)	–
–	–	–	–	72	–	65	62	–	(61)	–	–	67	64	–	–	(67)	–
–		–		267		(285)		264		–		–		–		–	
–	–	–	–	123[a]	127	88	118	92?	116	–	–	–	–	–	–	–	–
–		–		58		47		48?		–		–		–		–	
–		–		96.8		74.6		79.3?		–		–		–		–	
–	–	–	–	55	56	53	52	48	47[b]–	–	52	51	50+	–	51	–	–
–	–	–	–	46	46	44	43?	40–	39[b]–	–	44	42–	42	–	46	–	–
–	–	–	–	33	34–	31–	32	29	27[b]	–	30	29	29+	–	31–	–	–
–	–	–	–	25	17[b]	24	26?	23	(18)[b]	–	17	27	27	–	27	–	–
–	–	–	–	–	81	78	–	–	–	–	–	84–	82	83	–	–	(80)

[a] Six segments.   [b] Right foot pathological.

TABLE 14. MEASUREMENTS, ANGLES, AND INDICES OF INDIVIDUAL SKELETONS FROM LERNA

Clan and period	8. NORTHERN (Middle Bronze Age, early phase) cont.											
Grave and area or trench	BE-30D		BE-19(2)		BE-30A		BE-30B		BE-30C		BE-18	
Number	140		126		137		138		139		122	
Sex and age / Pubic symphysis phase	M 27 / V		F 19+ / I		F 28 / V		F 18 / I		F 28– / V		M 15	
	L.	R.	L.	R.	L.	R.	L.	R.	L.	R.	L.	R.
Humerus: Max. length	293	295	246	(248)	–	274	–	287?	277	–	–	(260)e
Vert. head diam.	40+	–	37?		–	41	–	(39)	38	–	–	–
Max. midshaft diam.	18	20	19	18??	18	18	18	18	19	19–	–	20
Min. midshaft diam.	16	16	14+	14	15	15–	11+	12	15	15–	–	15
Biepicondylar breadth	55	56–	(47–)	–	–	55	–	–	51	52	52	–
Radius: Max. length	218	221	–	(190) –	203	–	(214)c	224?	201	(195)	194	–
Ulna: Max. length	237?	241	–	(220 –	232–	–	–	241c	(220)	(223)	–	–
Clavicle: Max. length	139	–	107+?	–	–	131+	–	(122)	123	–	–	–
Scapula: Breadth	–	–	79?	75?	–	(91)	–	91?	94+	–	–	–
Femur: Max. length	423–	419–	367	(363)	385	386	412?	–	383	377	413e?	–
Max. head diam.	43	42	40	40	41	41	40	–	36–	37	41?	43
Subtrochanteric a-p diam.	25	23	(25)	22	23	24	21	–	22	22	22	22
Subtrochanteric transv. diam.	32	30	30	29	27+	27+	25	–	30	27+	26	28
Midshaft a-p diam.	29	31	22?	21	23	22	22	–	23	23	24	28–
Midshaft transv. diam.	27	25	24	22	23	23	20–	–	24	23	23	24
Neck torsion angle (°)	10	5	–	–	6	sl.	–	–	9	8	–	+?
Platymeric index	78.1	76.7	–	75.9	85.2	88.9	84.0	–	73.3	81.5	84.6	78.6
Pilastric index	107.4	124.0	91.7	95.4	100.0	95.6	110.0	–	95.8	100.0	104.4	116.7
Robusticity index	13.3	13.4	12.6	(11.9)	12.0	11.7	10.3?	–	12.5	12.4	–	12.6?
Tibia: Length, lat. cond. to mall.	–	340	(285)	–	319	315	329?	–	336	–	–	–
Nutr. foramen level a-p diam.	–	34	26?	25?	31	29–	28–	28	30	29	–	–
Nutr. foramen level transv. diam.	–	20	18	19	21	20	18	18	20	21	–	–
Head retroversion angle (°)	–	10–	–	–	+	12	–	10	11	–	–	–
Cnemic index	–	58.8	69.2	76.0	67.7	69.0	64.3	64.3	66.7	72.4	–	–
Fibula: Max. length	328	327	–	–	309	310	–	–	–	–	–	–
Stature estimate (cm., Trotter)	161.3		142.7?		150.3		155.7?		151.6		159.7?	
Brachial index	74.4	74.9	–	–	– 74.1	–	–	78.0?	72.6	–	–	–
Lumbar vertebrae height (Ant. & post.)	–	–	127	120?	–	–	119?	(114)	(132)	(122)	–	–
Sacrum (Height & breadth)	104	105	?	95	92?	107	(88)	106	?	(108)	–	–
Innominate: Height	195	192	–	–	194	189	186?	174	–	(181)	174?	–
Iliac breadth	146	138	–	–	152	150	(125)	(123)	–	–	–	–
Ischial length	75	(77)	67?	–	(75)	68	69?	65?	66–	64	73	–
Pubic length	67?	–	–	65+	–	71	66	67	76?	–	–	–
Pelvis: Bi-iliac breadth	257		–		250		251		–		–	
Inlet diam. (A-p & transv.)	92	121	–		101	129	82	132	–		–	–
Inlet angle with horizontal (°)	54		–		52		63		–		–	
Brim index	76.0		–		78.3		62.1		–		–	
Talus: Length	49	49	46	(46)	48	48+	46	–	47	–	50	–
Breadth	41+	42	37	(36)	38–	39	38	–	39	–	42	–
Mid-trochlear height	28+	29	24?	26?	27	27+	27	–	26–	–	–	–
Neck diversion angle (°)	37	38	23?	23?	26	29	29	–	37	–	–	–
Calcaneus: Max. length	74	73	64	–	–	70	66	65?	68	68	(68)	–

c Lacking lower epiphysis. e With only one epiphysis.

8. NORTHERN (Middle Bronze Age, early phase) cont.

BE-18		BE-"443"		BE-5		BE-9		BE-10		BE-13		BE-15		BE-16	
123		245		109		113		114		117		119		120	
F?10		M 13		M??1–		F 0		F??0		M??0		F??0–		M??0	
–		–		–		–		–		–		–		–	
L.	R.	L.	R.	L.	R.	L.	R.	L.	R.	L.	R.	L.	R.	L.	R.
(200)	–	103?	–	–	88	68–	–	–	66	(67)	67?	56	–	–	70
–	–	–	–	–	–	–	–	–	–	–	–	–	–	–	–
15	–	14	14–	–	9	–	–	–	–	–	–	–	–	–	–
12	–	11	11	–	8	–	–	–	–	–	–	–	–	–	–
36	–	–	36	–	–	–	–	–	–	–	–	–	–	–	–
–	(50)	–	–	–	71	–	–	52	52–	–	54–	47	–	–	(60)
–	–	–	–	–	–	60	61	61	61	–	58+	53–	–	–	64+
–	–	–	–	–	(60)	–	–	–	–	–	–	(39)	–	–	–
–	–	–	–	–	–	–	–	–	31	27	–	–	–	–	–
(270)	–	(260)f	(290)	112	–	76	76	76	77	78	77?	67	66?	80??	–
28+	–	–	–	–	–	–	–	–	–	–	–	–	–	–	–
20	–	16	–	11	10	–	–	–	–	–	–	–	–	–	–
23+	–	22	–	12	11	–	–	–	–	–	–	–	–	–	–
18	17	18	–	10–	10	–	–	7	–	–	–	–	–	–	–
17	16	17	–	11–	11	–	–	7	–	–	–	–	–	–	–
–	–	–	–	–	–	–	–	–	–	–	–	–	–	–	–
87.0	–	–	–	–	–	–	–	–	–	–	–	–	–	–	–
105.9	105.2	–	–	–	–	–	–	–	–	–	–	–	–	–	–
–	–	–	–	–	–	–	–	–	–	–	–	–	–	–	–
–	–	–	–	92?	92	–	66	67–	67+	–	–	60	61?	(69)	–
–	22	–	–	11	12–	–	–	–	–	–	–	–	–	–	–
–	17	–	–	11–	10+	–	–	–	–	–	–	–	–	–	–
–	+	–	–	+	20	–	–	–	–	–	–	–	–	–	+
–	77.3	–	–	–	–	–	–	–	–	–	–	–	–	–	–
–	–	–	–	–	–	–	–	63	–	–	–	56	–	–	–
–		–		–		–		–		–		–		–	
–	–	–	–	–	–	–	–	–	–	–	–	–	–	–	–
–	–	–	–	–	–	–	–	–	–	–	–	–	–	–	–
–	–	–	–	–	–	–	–	–	–	–	–	–	–	–	–
–	(130)	–	–	–	–	–	–	–	–	–	–	–	–	–	–
–	(85)	95?	–	–	–	–	33	37	37	40	–	30	–	–	–
–	53	–	–	–	–	–	–	16	–	–	–	–	–	–	–
–	–	–	–	–	–	–	–	13+	13+?	–	–	–	–	17	–
–		–		–		–		–		–		–		–	
–		–		–		–		–		–		–		–	
–		–		–		–		–		–		–		–	
37	–	–	–	–	–	–	–	–	–	–	–	–	–	–	–
28	–	–	–	–	–	–	–	–	–	–	–	–	–	–	–
19+	–	–	–	–	–	–	–	–	–	–	–	–	–	–	–
33	–	–	–	–	–	–	–	–	–	–	–	–	–	–	–
–	–	–	–	–	–	–	–	–	–	–	–	–	–	–	–

f Left femur without epiphysis.

TABLE 14. MEASUREMENT, ANGLES, AND INDICES OF INDIVIDUAL SKELETONS FROM LERNA

Clan and period	8. NORTHERN (Middle Bronze Age, early phase) cont.						9. BRIDGE (Middle Bronze Age, early middle phase)					
Grave and area or trench	BE-17		BE-28		BE-30		DE-28		DE-71		DE-72	
Number	121		134		136		174		238		239	
Sex and age / Pubic symphysis phase	F??0 –		F??0- –		M?1- –		M 34 VI+		M 39 VIII		M 36 VII	
	L.	R.	L.	R.	L.	R.	L.	R.	L.	R.	L.	R.
Humerus: Max. length	69–	69–	60	63	–	95	–	316?	– (290)	–	304?	308
Vert. head diam.	–	–	–	–	–	–	–	44+	–	–	–	47
Max. midshaft diam.	–	–	–	–	–	9	21	22	22	–	20	22
Min. midshaft diam.	–	–	–	–	–	8	17	18–	17	–	17	17
Biepicondylar breadth	–	–	–	–	23	–	60?	57?	–	–	58	58
Radius: Max. length	57	57	–	–	75	–	– (238)	–	(205)	–	232	234
Ulna: Max. length	67–	66	–	–	–	–	–	256?	230	–	244–	246+
Clavicle: Max. length	47	–	44	44	–	–	–	–	–	–	–	–
Scapula: Breadth	–	31	29	31?	–	–	–	–	–	–	–	–
Femur: Max. length	80+	81–	73	74	121	121	411?	413?	396?	–	(410)	–
Max. head diam.	–	–	–	–	–	–	44?	–	45	44?	47?	–
Subtrochanteric a-p diam.	–	–	–	–	10	10	23	25	24	23	24–	24
Subtrochanteric transv. diam.	–	–	–	–	11	11	34	33	33	33	31	31
Midshaft a-p diam.	–	–	–	–	9	9	33	32	25+	26+	30	31
Midshaft transv. diam.	–	–	–	–	10	10	27	27	28	26	25	24+
Neck torsion angle (°)	–	–	–	–	–	–	+15	+	–	–	–	–
Platymeric index	–	–	–	–	–	–	67.6	75.8	72.7	69.7	77.4	77.4
Pilastric index	–	–	–	–	–	–	122.2	118.5	89.3	100.0	120.0	129.2
Robusticity index	–	–	–	–	–	–	14.7?	14.4?	13.4	13.1	(13.5)	–
Tibia: Length, lat. cond. to mall.	–	71	66	66–	100	100	– (375)	–	–	(335)	346?	–
Nutr. foramen level a-p diam.	–	–	–	–	11	11	–	34	–	32	33	–
Nutr. foramen level transv. diam.	–	–	–	–	10	10	–	23	–	20	21	–
Head retroversion angle (°)	–	–	–	–	–	–	–	7	–	–	11?	–
Cnemic index	–	–	–	–	–	–	–	67.6	–	62.5	63.6	–
Fibula: Max. length	–	67+	–	–	–	–	–	(340)	–	–	–	(325)
Stature estimate (cm., Trotter)	–		–		–		165.0		158.7		165.8	
Brachial index	–		–		–		–		–		76.3	76.0
Lumbar vertebrae height (Ant. & post.)	–		–		–		–		124?	?	123	?
Sacrum (Height & breadth)	–		–		–		–		(119)	115	–	
Innominate: Height	–	–	–	51	–	–	–	191	–	209	–	–
Iliac breadth	38?	39?	–	36	48?	55	–	(150)	–	(148)	–	–
Ischial length	–	–	–	19	–	–	–	82	–	79	–	–
Pubic length	17?	–	–	16	–	–	–	70	–	–	–	–
Pelvis: Bi-iliac breadth	–		–		–		–		–		–	
Inlet diam. (A-p &-transv.)	–		–		–		–		–		–	
Inlet angle with horizontal(°)	–		–		–		–		–		–	
Brim index	–		–		–		–		–		–	
Talus: Length	–	–	–	–	–	–	51	–	48?	49–	48	50+
Breadth	–	–	–	–	–	–	42	–	40	40+	41	41
Mid-trochlear height	–	–	–	–	–	–	28	–	30	30–	29–	28
Neck diversion angle (°)	–	–	–	–	–	–	33	–	36	30	38	31
Calcaneus: Max. length	–	–	–	–	–	–	80–	–	–	82–	77	74

9. Bridge (Middle Bronze Age, early middle phase) cont.

DE-30		DE-41		DE-18		DE-33		DE-50		DE-52		DE-64	
176		186		165		179		193		195		204	
M?2		M??2+		F??0–		M 0		M??0+		F??0–		M??1–	
–		–		–		–		–		–		–	
L.	R.	L.	R.	L.	R.	L.	R.	L.	R.	L.	R.	L.	R.
109	108	–	–	66	66+	66	66?	–	76	65	66	92	92+
–	–	–	–	–	–	–	–	–	–	–	–	–	–
10	10–	–	–	–	–	–	–	–	–	–	–	10–	11
8	8	–	–	–	–	–	–	–	–	–	–	8	10
25	–	–	–	–	–	–	–	–	–	–	–	–	–
–	85	–	87	52	–	–	54+	–	59–	52	52	–	–
–	–	95	–	–	–	–	(64)	–	65+	60	60+	–	–
–	61	–	–	–	–	–	44	49+	47?	44+	45–	60?	–
45?	–	–	–	–	30?	–	27?	–	–	26?	27–	37	–
140	–	143	142+	78	68	–	(84) –	92	92	77	77+	114	113
–	–	–	–	–	–	–	–	–	–	–	–	–	–
13	–	12	11	–	–	–	–	9	9	–	–	12–	12–
15	–	14	13+	–	–	–	–	11	11	–	–	12	12
10	–	11	11	–	–	–	–	7	7	–	–	11	11
12	–	12	12	–	–	–	–	9	9	–	–	11+	12–
–	–	–	–	–	–	–	–	–	–	–	–	++?	++?
–	–	–	–	–	–	–	–	–	–	–	–	–	–
–	–	–	–	–	–	–	–	–	–	–	–	–	–
–	113?	–	–	–	–	67	67–?	78+	78	–	–	93	94–
–	13	13	–	–	–	–	–	–	–	–	–	13–	13
–	11	12	–	–	–	–	–	–	–	–	–	11	11
–	–	–	–	–	–	–	–	–	–	–	–	sl.	sl.
–	–	–	–	–	–	–	–	–	–	–	–	–	–
–	–	–	–	–	–	–	–	74+	–	62	–	88	–
–		–		–		–		–		–		–	
–	–	–	–	–	–	–	–	–	–	–	–	–	–
–	–	–	–	–	–	–	–	–	–	–	–	–	–
–	–	–	–	–	–	–	–	–	–	–	–	–	–
–	57	–	62?	37	35+	–	35–?	40?	(40)	34	36	(49)	–
–	–	–	–	–	–	–	–	24	–	18?	19	–	–
–	–	–	–	–	–	–	–	–	–	17	17+	–	25?
–		–		–		–		–		–		–	
–		–		–		–		–		–		–	
–		–		–		–		–		–		–	
–	–	–	–	–	–	–	–	–	–	–	–	–	–
–	–	–	–	–	–	–	–	–	–	–	–	–	–
–	–	–	–	–	–	–	–	–	–	–	–	–	–
–	–	–	–	–	–	–	–	–	–	–	–	–	–
–	–	–	–	–	–	–	–	–	–	–	–	–	–

Table 14. Measurements, Angles, and Indices of Individual Skeletons from Lerna

Clan and period	10. Eastern (Middle Bronze Age, middle to late phases)													
Grave and area or trench	DE-29		DE-35		DE-32		DE-36		DE-53		DE-59		DE-60	
Number	175		181		178		182		196		200		201	
Sex and age / Pubic symphysis phase	M 35 / –		M 42 / VIII		F 33 / VI		F 36 / VII		F 40+ / –		F 25 / –		F 31 / VI	
	L.	R.	L.	R.	L.	R.	L.	R.	L.	R.	L.	R.	L.	R.
Humerus: Max. length	302	–	295	–	296	–	–	301?	(280)	–	–	276	(295)	–
Vert. head diam.	46	46+	46	45?	38	37–	–	41	–	–	38?	38?	–	–
Max. midshaft diam.	23	–	21	23	20+	21?	22	22	19	–	23	24–	19	2…
Min. midshaft diam.	16	–	17	17	15	15	15	15	15	–	16+	15	13	1…
Biepicondylar breadth	61	–	64–?	66	54	53	–	59–	–	–	–	54	49	4…
Radius: Max. length	226?	–	230	231	222	–	–	229	–	–	200	201	205	–
Ulna: Max. length	–	–	250?	–	239	–	–	248	–	–	233	–	235	–
Clavicle: Max. length	–	144+?	134?	–	131?	133	135?	133	124	–	132	129?	129–	–
Scapula: Breadth	–	–	–	–	83	83	–	–	–	–	(83)	–	–	–
Femur: Max. length	446	–	424	423?	405	403	–	434?	–	–	379	–	399	–
Max. head diam.	46–	46–	49	48	41	–	42+	43+	–	–	38	–	41	–
Subtrochanteric a-p diam.	24	–	27	24?	23	–	–	22	23	–	24	–	22	2…
Subtrochanteric transv. diam.	31	–	33	33	30	–	–	31	27	–	29	–	28	2…
Midshaft a-p diam.	28	27	29	29	28	–	24+	26	–	–	27	–	25	2…
Midshaft transv. diam.	25	24	27	27	24	–	24	23	–	–	26	–	25	2…
Neck torsion angle (°)	–	–	26	–	9	0	–	–	–	–	5	–	6	–
Platymeric index	77.4	–	81.8	72.7	76.7	–	–	71.0	85.2	–	82.8	–	78.6	7…
Pilastric index	112.0	112.5	107.4	107.4	116.7	–	100.0	113.0	–	–	103.8	–	100.0	9…
Robusticity index	12.1	–	13.3	13.3	13.0	–	–	11.4?	–	–	14.2	–	12.6	–
Tibia: Length, lat. cond. to mall.	351	–	339?	341?	336	–	362?	–	–	–	308	310	331	33…
Nutr. foramen level a-p diam.	35	–	36	40	34	–	29+	–	–	–	31	29	29	3…
Nutr. foramen level transv. diam.	23	–	23	25	21	–	21	–	–	–	24	23	19	1…
Head retroversion angle (°)	13	–	3	5	6	–	15	–	–	–	13	12	8	–
Cnemic index	65.7	–	63.9	62.5	61.8	–	72.4	–	–	–	77.4	79.3	65.5	6…
Fibula: Max. length	350?	–	–	–	330	–	–	–	–	–	304+	302	–	–
Stature estimate (cm., Trotter)	165.7		163.5		156.2		163.0		(152.0)		148.8		154.2	
Brachial index	–	74.8–	78.0	–	75.0	–	–	76.1	–	–	–	72.8	(69.5)	–
Lumbar vertebrae height (Ant. & post.)	–	–	136?	138?	130	(127)	130?	122	–	–	–	–	132	13…
Sacrum (Height & breadth)	–	–	–	–	97	(114)	116[a]	115	–	–	–	–	109	11…
Innominate: Height	216	–	–	–	197	194	–	202	–	–	–	–	199	20…
Iliac breadth	(160)	–	(165)	–	–	152	–	153?	–	–	–	–	145?	14…
Ischial length	80?	–	–	–	74	73	78	77	–	–	76	–	76	7…
Pubic length	–	(70)	–	–	73	71	76	81	–	–	80	–	83?	8…
Pelvis: Bi-iliac breadth	–		–		270		251		–		–		251	
Inlet diam. (A-p & transv.)	–	–	–	–	96?	142	121	125–	–	–	–	–	122	12…
Inlet angle with horizontal (°)	–		–		56?		59		–		–		63	
Brim index	–		–		67.6?		96.8		–		–		96.8	
Talus: Length	–	52	?	57	46+	46	55	55	–	–	48	48	49	4…
Breadth	–	42	46?	46	40	39?	41	42?	–	–	36	37	38+	3…
Mid-trochlear height	–	30	–	31	28	27?	27	28	–	–	25	26	27	2…
Neck diversion angle (°)	–	28	22	20	24	23	32	30	–	–	36	35	23?	3…
Calcaneus: Max. length	79	79	–	–	68	67	–	85	–	–	–	70	74	7…

[a] Six segments.

10. EASTERN (Middle Bronze Age, middle to late phases) cont.

DE-10 158 F??1+ / –		DE-22 168 M?2- / –		DE-24 170 M??2+ / –		DE-27 173 M?5+ / –		DE-31 177 F?2+ / –		DE-63 203 F?4 / –		DE-1 150 M1- / –		DE-2 151 F?1- / –		DE-3 152 M??0 / –	
L.	R.	L.	R.	L.	R.	L.	R.	L.	R.	L.	R.	L.	R.	L.	R.	L.	R.
–	(100)	–	105	(110–)	110	– 142?	–	–	–	127	128	(88)	94	85	85	66	66
–	–	–	–	–	–	–	–	–	–	–	–	–	–	–	–	–	–
–	–	–	10	10	10	13	–	–	11+	10	10	–	9–	–	9	–	–
–	–	–	8	8+	9–	10	–	–	10	8	8+	–	8–	–	8	–	–
–	–	–	26	–	27	–	28?	–	–	27	–	–	–	–	22	–	–
(72)	–	– 84?	–	–	88	107	–	–	–	98?	(99)	69	69	–	69	–	54
–	(82)	–	–	–	97–	–	–	–	–	(108)	109	–	77	–	76	–	61
–	–	–	64–	66	65	–	–	–	–	66	(65)	–	–	–	–	42?	42?
–	–	–	43	–	–	53	54	–	–	(44)	–	–	–	–	–	29?	–
115	–	–	–	– 149?	–	–	–	–	137?	167	169	113?	(108)	103	103	78	79
–	–	–	–	–	–	–	–	–	–	–	–	12	11	10	10+	–	–
11	–	–	14	–	–	–	–	–	13	12	12	13	12	13	11	–	–
13	–	–	14	12	12	–	–	–	15	15	15–	9	9	9	8	–	–
10	–	–	11	14	15	–	–	12	12	12	11	10	9	9+	10	–	–
11	–	–	13	10	10	–	–	12	12	13	12	–	–	–	–	–	–
–	–	–	–	12	12	–	–	–	–	+?	+?	–	–	–	–	–	–
–	–	–	–	–	–	–	–	–	–	–	–	–	–	–	–	–	–
–	–	–	–	–	–	–	–	–	–	–	–	–	–	–	–	–	–
–	–	117	–	117	–	168	–	–	118?	137	136	–	–	–	(87)	66–	66
–	–	15	–	13	13	17	19	15	14	13	13	12	–	–	10	–	–
–	–	14	–	12	12?	15	16	13	13	11	11	10	–	–	11	–	–
–	–	–	–	–	–	–	–	–	–	sl.	sl.	–	–	–	–	–	–
–	–	–	–	–	–	–	–	–	–	–	–	–	–	–	–	–	–
–	–	112	–	112+	–	163	–	–	–	135	–	61	–	–	–	–	–
–		–		–		–		–		–		–		–		–	
–	–	–	–	–	–	–	–	–	–	–	–	–	–	–	–	–	–
–	–	–	–	–	–	–	–	–	–	–	–	–	–	–	–	–	–
–	–	–	–	–	–	–	–	–	–	–	–	–	–	–	–	–	–
–	–	–	–	–	63	–	–	–	–	98	100	–	–	47	(46)	32?	–
–	–	–	59	35	34+	–	–	–	–	(70)	73	–	–	27	27	–	–
–	–	33	33	–	–	–	–	–	–	37	39	–	–	27	–	–	–
–	–	25+	26	–	–	–	–	31	–	35	34	–	–	–	–	–	–
–		–		–		–		–		–		–		–		–	
–	–	–	–	–	–	–	–	–	–	–	–	–	–	–	–	–	–
–	–	–	–	–	–	–	–	–	–	–	–	–	–	–	–	–	–
–	–	–	–	–	–	19+	–	–	–	–	–	–	–	–	–	–	–
–	–	–	–	–	–	–	–	–	–	–	–	–	–	–	–	–	–
–	–	–	–	–	–	–	–	–	–	–	–	–	–	–	–	–	–
–	–	–	–	–	–	40	–	–	–	33	–	–	–	–	–	–	–

TABLE 14. MEASUREMENTS, ANGLES, AND INDICES OF INDIVIDUAL SKELETONS FROM LERNA

Clan and period	10. Eastern (Middle Bronze Age, middle to late phases) cont.													
Grave and area or trench	DE-11		DE-12		DE-14		DE-15		DE-19		DE-23		DE-62	
Number	159		160		162		163		166		169		202	
Sex and age / Pubic symphysis phase	F??0+ / –		M??0– / –		M??0+ / –		F 0– / –		M??0+ / –		M??0 / –		M??0+ / –	
	L.	R.	L.	R.	L.	R.	L.	R.	L.	R.	L.	R.	L.	R.
Humerus: Max. length	–	68	–	59	70+	70+	65–	65	–	69	70	70+	66	67
Vert. head diam.	–	–	–	–	–	–	–	–	–	–	–	–	–	–
Max. midshaft diam.	–	–	–	–	–	–	–	–	–	–	–	–	–	–
Min. midshaft diam.	–	–	–	–	–	–	–	–	–	–	–	–	–	–
Biepicondylar breadth	–	–	–	–	–	–	–	–	–	–	–	–	–	–
Radius: Max. length	58+	58	–	49	57	57	52	–	56	–	–	56	–	53
Ulna: Max. length	66	–	–	56	64	–	–	–	–	64+	–	45?	–	61
Clavicle: Max. length	–	–	42	41	–	–	44+	44	–	–	–	–	–	–
Scapula: Breadth	–	–	26	26	33?	32?	29+?	–	–	–	–	28–?	–	–
Femur: Max. length	82	–	71	72–	83	83–	76	76	81	80	83	–	82	–
Max. head diam.	–	–	–	–	–	–	–	–	–	–	–	–	–	–
Subtrochanteric a-p diam.	–	–	–	–	–	–	–	–	–	–	–	–	9	–
Subtrochanteric transv. diam.	–	–	–	–	–	–	–	–	–	–	–	–	9	–
Midshaft a-p diam.	–	–	–	–	–	–	–	–	–	–	–	–	6	–
Midshaft transv. diam.	–	–	–	–	–	–	–	–	–	–	–	–	8	–
Neck torsion angle (°)	–	–	–	–	–	–	–	–	–	–	–	–	–	–
Platymeric index	–	–	–	–	–	–	–	–	–	–	–	–	–	–
Pilastric index	–	–	–	–	–	–	–	–	–	–	–	–	–	–
Robusticity index	–	–	–	–	–	–	–	–	–	–	–	–	–	–
Tibia: Length, lat. cond.–mall.	–	–	62	62–	71	70+	–	–	71?	71	70	70+	68	67
Nutr. foramen level a-p diam.	–	–	–	–	–	–	–	–	–	–	–	–	–	–
Nutr. foramen level transv. diam.	–	–	–	–	–	–	–	–	–	–	–	–	–	–
Head retroversion angle (°)	–	–	–	–	–	–	–	–	–	–	–	–	–	–
Cnemic index	–	–	–	–	–	–	–	–	–	–	–	–	–	–
Fibula: Max. length	–	–	58	58–	65+	–	–	–	68	68–	66	–	64+	–
Stature estimate (cm., Trotter)	–		–		–		–		–		–		–	
Brachial index	–	–	–	–	–	–	–	–	–	–	–	–	–	–
Lumbar vertebrae height (Ant. & post.)	–	–	–	–	–	–	–	–	–	–	–	–	–	–
Sacrum (Height & breadth)	–	–	–	–	–	–	–	–	–	–	–	–	–	–
Innominate: Height	39	–	–	–	–	–	–	–	–	–	–	–	–	–
Iliac breadth	21	–	38	–	40–	41	36	26?	37	37	39+	40	39	40
Ischial length	–	–	17	–	–	22	–	–	–	–	–	22	–	–
Pubic length	–	–	–	–	–	–	–	–	–	–	–	–	–	19
Pelvis: Bi-iliac breadth	–		–		–		–		–		–		–	
Inlet diam. (A-p & transv.)	–	–	–	–	–	–	–	–	–	–	–	–	–	–
Inlet angle with horizontal (°)	–		–		–		–		–		–		–	
Brim index	–		–		–		–		–		–		–	
Talus: Length	–	–	–	–	–	–	–	–	–	–	–	–	–	–
Breadth	–	–	–	–	–	–	–	–	–	–	–	–	–	–
Mid-trochlear height	–	–	–	–	–	–	–	–	–	–	–	–	–	–
Neck diversion angle (°)	–	–	–	–	–	–	–	–	–	–	–	–	–	–
Calcaneus: Max. length	–	–	–	–	–	–	–	–	–	–	–	–	–	–

11. PLAIN (Middle Bronze Age, late phase)																	
DE-40		DE-45		DE-55		DE-48		DE-42		DE-46		DE-4		DE-25		DE-38	
185		189		198		192		187		190		153		171		183	
M 30+ −		M 38 −		M 35 VII		F 27 V		F??1+ −		M??2+ −		M??0 −		F??0 −		M??0 −	
L.	R.	L.	R.	L.	R.	L.	R.	L.	R.	L.	R.	L.	R.	L.	R.	L.	R.
275?	−	300	304	312	−	271	275?	97	−	(114)	−	−	67	68	68	66	66
−	−	49	50	45+	−	38	37?	−	−	−	−	−	−	−	−	−	−
21	22+	22−	22	21	22	20	20	10−	−	−	−	−	−	−	−	−	−
17	18	17	17	18	18	15−	14	8	−	−	−	−	−	−	−	−	−
56?	−	62−	61	61	62	51	52	−	−	−	−	−	−	−	−	−	−
−	218?	235?	−	−	254	202	205+	72?	−	−	−	−	53	−	55	−	54
−	(232)	260	262+	−	−	−	236+	−	−	(98)	−	−	−	−	62	62+	63
−	−	139	135	156	−	−	−	−	−	−	−	−	−	−	−	−	−
98	−	−	−	−	−	−	−	−	−	−	−	29?	−	30?	−	−	−
419?	−	− (425) −		451	−	394	383?	− 120 −		−	152?	77	77	78−	78−	76	76−
−	−	46	−	46	−	39	39?	−	−	−	12	−	−	−	−	−	−
26	25	24	25	27	27	19	20	−	−	−	14	−	−	−	−	−	−
34	34	33	32	33	34	29	30	10	10	−	11	−	−	−	−	−	−
29	28	26	25	28	29	25	24	13	12+	−	12	−	−	−	−	−	−
27	25	28	27	27	26+	24	25	9−	9−	−	−	−	−	−	−	−	−
6	6	−	−	14	−	12	−	11	11	−	−	−	−	−	−	−	−
76.5	73.5	72.7	78.1	81.8	79.4	65.5	66.7	−	−	−	−	−	−	−	−	−	−
107.4	112.0	92.9	92.6	103.7	111.5	104.2	96.0	−	−	−	−	−	−	−	−	−	−
13.5?	−	−	−	12.3	−	12.6	12.9	−	−	−	−	−	−	−	−	−	−
343	−	−	−	374	(362)	319	−	93	95−	128	128	−	67	68	68	66	66
35+	−	−	−	37	−	29	30−	13	12	13−	13−	−	−	−	−	−	−
24	−	−	−	26	−	20	20	10	10	11+	12	−	−	−	−	−	−
12	−	−	−	9?	−	14	13	−	−	−	−	−	−	−	−	−	−
68.6	−	−	−	70.3	−	69.0	66.7	−	−	−	−	−	−	−	−	−	−
(319)[a]	−	−	−	−	349?	−	304	−	94	−	−	−	−	−	−	61	61
160.4		165.7		170.0		150.9		−		−		−		−		−	
	79.3−?	78.3	−	− 81.4 −		74.5	74.6	−	−	−	−	−	−	−	−	−	−
−	−	−	−	135	127?	123?	117?	−	−	−	−	−	−	−	−	−	−
−	−	−	−	−	−	(81)	(102)	−	−	−	−	−	−	−	−	−	−
−	−	−	−	−	−	−	−	−	−	−	65	−	35	−	−	−	−
−	−	−	−	−	−	−	−	−	−	−	−	−	−	36	36	35	−
−	−	77	−	84?	−	−	−	−	−	−	31	−	−	−	−	−	−
−	−	(63)	−	73?	−	−	−	−	−	−	−	−	−	17	17	−	−
−		−		−		−		−		−		−		−		−	
−		−		−		−		−		−		−		−		−	
−		−		−		−		−		−		−		−		−	
50	50	−	−	−	−	−	45	−	−	−	−	−	−	−	−	−	−
41	40	−	−	−	−	−	38	−	−	−	−	−	−	−	−	−	−
29	29+	−	−	−	−	−	25	−	−	−	−	−	−	−	−	−	−
33	37	−	−	−	−	−	30	−	−	−	−	−	−	−	−	−	−
−	79	83	−	78	76	68	67	−	−	32	−	−	−	−	−	−	−

[a] tumor.

TABLE 14. MEASUREMENTS, ANGLES, AND INDICES OF INDIVIDUAL SKELETONS FROM LERNA

Clan and period[b]	11. PLAIN (Middle Bronze Age, late phase) cont.											
Grave and area or trench	DE-43		DE-47		DE-51		DE-54		DE-57		D-4	
Number	188		191		194		197		199		23	
Sex and age Pubic symphysis phase	M??0- —		F??0- —		M??0 —		M??0 		F??0 —		M 60 —	
	L.	R.	L.	R.	L.	R.	L.	R.	L.	R.	L.	R.
Humerus: Max. length	68	68–	–	–	–	70+?	70	70	66	66	(291)	291
Vert. head diam.	–	–	–	–	–	–	–	–	–	–	42	42
Max. midshaft diam.	–	–	–	–	–	–	–	–	–	–	21	23
Min. midshaft diam.	–	–	–	–	–	–	–	–	–	–	17	17
Biepicondylar breadth	–	–	–	–	–	–	–	–	–	–	–	58
Radius: Max. length	53	53	53	–	–	56	–	54	–	52+	232	234
Ulna: Max. length	61–	61	61	–	–	64	62?	62+	58	–	253?	254
Clavicle: Max. length	44	43–?	–	–	–	–	–	44	–	45–	–	141
Scapula: Breadth	–	–	–	–	–	–	–	–	–	29	95	–
Femur: Max. length	77?	77	78	78	–	(85)	82	82	80–	80–	419	411
Max. head diam.	–	–	–	–	–	–	–	–	–	–	42	41
Subtrochanteric a-p diam.	–	–	–	–	–	–	–	–	–	–	24	24
Subtrochanteric transv. diam.	–	–	–	–	–	–	–	–	–	–	32	33
Midshaft a-p diam.	–	–	–	–	–	–	–	–	–	–	30	27
Midshaft transv. diam.	–	–	–	–	–	–	–	–	–	–	27	25
Neck torsion angle (°)	–	–	–	–	–	–	–	–	–	–	+?	++
Platymeric index	–	–	–	–	–	–	–	–	–	–	75.0	72.7
Pilastric index	–	–	–	–	–	–	–	–	–	–	111.1	108.0
Robusticity index	–	–	–	–	–	–	–	–	–	–	13.7?	12.7
Tibia: Length, lat. cond. to mall.	67+	67	67–	66+	(68)	–	–	–	69–	69	– (332)	–
Nutr. foramen level a-p diam.	–	–	–	–	–	–	–	–	–	–	37	38
Nutr. foramen level transv. diam.	–	–	–	–	–	–	–	–	–	–	22	24
Head retroversion angle (°)	–	–	–	–	–	–	–	–	–	–	8	8
Cnemic index	–	–	–	–	–	–	–	–	–	–	59.5	63.2
Fibula: Max. length	–	–	63	–	–	–	–	–	(63)	–	–	–
Stature estimate (cm., Trotter)	–		–		–		–		–		162.3	
Brachial index	–	–	–	–	–	–	–	–	–	–	–	80.4
Lumbar vertebrae height (Ant. & post.)	–	–	–	–	–	–	–	–	–	–	–	–
Sacrum (Height & breadth)	–	–	–	–	–	–	–	–	–	–	–	–
Innominate: Height	–	–	–	–	–	–	–	–	–	–	–	–
Iliac breadth	37	–	36	–	41?	–	(38)	–	35	–	–	–
Ischial length	–	20	–	–	22?	–	21	–	–	–	–	–
Pubic length	–	–	–	–	–	–	18	–	16+	–	–	–
Pelvis: Bi-iliac breadth	–		–		–		–		–		–	
Inlet diam. (A-p & transv.)	–		–		–		–		–		–	
Inlet angle with horizontal (°)	–		–		–		–		–		–	
Brim index	–		–		–		–		–		–	
Talus: Length	–	–	–	–	–	–	–	–	–	–	47?	–
Breadth	–	–	–	–	–	–	–	–	–	–	38?	–
Mid-trochlear height	–	–	–	–	–	–	–	–	–	–	25?	–
Neck diversion angle (°)	–	–	–	–	–	–	–	–	–	–	32	–
Calcaneus: Max. length	–	–	–	–	–	–	–	–	–	–	–	–

12. Sea (Middle Bronze Age, middle to very late phases)															
D-9		D-18		D-20		D-22		D-15		D-14		D-16		D-17	
28		48		50		52		45		55		46		47	
M 43 VIII		M 21 II		M 27 V		M 55 X		F 33 VI		F 15 (adol.) I		M? 4+ –		M? 4 –	
L.	R.	L.	R.	L.	R.	L.	R.	L.	R.	L.	R.	L.	R.	L.	R.
(306)	(310)	300	306	–	314	301	–	–	292?	–	267	144	145	150	–
–	–	43	44	–	46+?	43	–	39	–	–	36	–	–	–	–
22	23	20	20+	22	23	20	22	–	21	16	17	11	–	11	–
17	19	18	18	18	18	17	17+	–	17	15	14	10	–	10	–
62	63	61	62	61	59	62	63–	–	55	–	48?	31	–	–	–
238	–	228	237	–	245?	251	249	–	–	184[a]	186[a]	–	108	–	126
260	260	251	258	–	268	–	271	–	(240)	209	213	–	–	–	–
–	–	136	138	–	145?	146	–	–	–	111?	–	75	73	–	–
–	–	101	–	–	–	–	–	–	–	–	–	54	53?	–	–
–	448	–	411	452+?	460	–	(439)	435?	–	404	399	198?	204	212	–
–	49	44	43	47	46+	–	(47)	41?	42–	41	41	–	–	–	–
–	27	22	22	27	27	25	26	27	24	20	20	14	13	13	–
–	36	33	34–	32	32	33	32	30	31	27	26	18	16	18	–
29	29	28	28	28	30	31	33	27	–	21	21	14	15	15	–
28–	28	26	25	28	28	28	26	26	–	22	21	18	16	14	–
–	–	–	15	35	++	–	0?	–	–	–	–	++	++	–	–
–	75.0	66.7	64.7	84.4	84.4	75.8	81.2	90.0	77.4	–	–	–	–	–	–
103.6	103.6	107.7	112.0	100.0	107.1	110.7	126.9	103.8	–	–	–	–	–	–	–
–	12.8	–	13.0	12.5	12.8	–	(13.5)	12.3	–	10.9	–	–	–	–	–
367	–	–	354	–	(378)	–	372?	339?	–	–	–	–	158	170	–
–	36	33?	34	–	37	–	36	31	–	–	27	–	16	18	16
–	28	23	23	–	24	–	24	25	–	–	21	–	15	14	13+
7	–	–	15	–	6	–	16	11	–	–	0	–	sl.?	–	–
–	77.8	69.7	67.6	–	64.9	–	66.7	80.6	–	–	–	–	–	–	–
–	–	–	–	–	–	–	347	–	–	–	–	–	–	–	–
169.7		164.5		171.0		168.5		159.9		150.9		–		–	
–	(77.3) –	76.0	77.5	–	78.0	83.4	–	–	–	–	–	–	–	–	–
127	124	131	125	135	133	131	126	135	132	104	97	76	65	–	–
–	–	109	112	?	(116)	(92)	?	(110)	121	?	94?	–	–	–	–
–	–	204	205	–	216	–	–	(203)	200?	169	167	–	–	–	–
–	–	(148)	153	–	–	–	–	147?	–	130	131	81	–	–	–
–	–	84	83	–	88	–	–	(82)	80	71	72	–	–	–	–
–	–	64	–	–	(79)	–	–	–	75?	–	–	–	–	–	–
–		274		–		–		300		–		–		–	
–	–	100	126	–	–	–	–	98?	132	?	102	–	–	–	–
–		63		–		–		55?		–		–		–	
–		79.4		–		–		74.2		–		–		–	
56	(55)	52	51	?	–	52	51	–	49	49	47	–	–	–	–
44	(43)	44	42	47?	–	42?	43+	–	40	38	39	–	–	–	–
30	30	30	29	–	–	30	29+	–	26	26	26	–	–	–	–
20	20	34	31	–	–	35	41	–	32	36	24	–	–	–	–
85	–	83	81	–	–	84	85	–	–	–	69	–	–	–	–

[a] Without epiphysis.

TABLE 14. MEASUREMENTS, ANGLES, AND INDICES OF INDIVIDUAL SKELETONS FROM LERNA

Clan and period	13. BAY (Middle Bronze Age, very late phase)									
Grave and area or trench	DC-1(1)		DB1-2		DC-1(2)		DC-1(3)		DB1-1	
Number	145		144		146		147		143	
Sex and age	M 50 ?		F?? 20		F 49		F 40		M?? 0+	
Pubic symphysis phase	–		–		IX		–		–	
	L.	R.	L.	R.	L.	R.	L.	R.	L.	R.
Humerus: Max. length	–	(320)	(300)	–	(278)	–	(275)	–	–	–
Vert. head diam.	–	–	42	–	–	–	–	–	–	–
Max. midshaft diam.	–	24	19	–	21	–	19	–	–	–
Min. midshaft diam.	–	21–	15	–	15	–	15	–	–	–
Biepicondylar breadth	–	–	53	–	–	52	55	–	–	–
Radius: Max. length	–	–	–	(232)	–	–	–	207	56+	57
Ulna: Max. length	–	261	–	–	–	–	–	–	63	–
Clavicle: Max. length	–	–	–	(135)	–	–	–	–	–	–
Scapula: Breadth	–	–	–	–	–	–	–	–	30	(29)
Femur: Max. length	–	(445)	–	400	–	–	(410)	–	82	82+
Max. head diam.	–	–	42	–	41+?	–	41	–	–	–
Subtrochanteric a-p diam.	–	26	23	22	–	–	–	–	–	–
Subtrochanteric transv. diam.	–	31	29	30	–	–	–	–	–	–
Midshaft a-p diam.	–	33	26	26	–	25	26	–	–	–
Midshaft transv. diam.	–	28	25+	26	–	24	24	–	–	–
Neck torsion angle (°)	–	–	–	–	–	–	–	–	–	–
Platymeric index	–	83.9	79.3	73.3	–	–	–	–	–	–
Pilastric index	–	117.9	104.0	100.0	–	104.2	108.3	–	–	–
Robusticity index	–	–	–	13.1	–	–	(12.3)	–	–	–
Tibia: Length, lat. cond. to mall.	–	–	–	–	– (324) –		–	–	– (75) –	
Nutr. foramen level a-p diam.	–	–	–	32	31	–	–	–	–	–
Nutr. foramen level transv. diam.	–	–	–	23	21	–	–	–	–	–
Head retroversion angle (°)	–	–	–	–	13	–	–	–	–	–
Cnemic index	–	–	–	71.9	67.7	–	–	–	–	–
Fibula: Max. length	– (325) –		–	–	–	–	–	–	– 63 –	
Stature estimate (cm., Trotter)	170.0		152.9		(153)		153.1		–	
Brachial index	–		–		–		–		–	
Lumbar vertebrae height (Ant. & post.)	–	–	–	–	–	–	–	–	–	–
Sacrum (Height & breadth)	–	–	–	–	–	–	–	–	–	–
Innominate: Height	–	–	–	–	–	173?	–	–	–	–
Iliac breadth	–	(165)	–	–	–	–	–	–	–	38
Ischial length	–	–	–	–	–	67?	–	–	–	–
Pubic length	–	–	–	–	–	70?	–	–	–	–
Pelvis: Bi-iliac breadth	–		–		–		–		–	
Inlet diam. (A-p & transv.)	–	–	–	–	–	–	–	–	–	–
Inlet angle with horizontal (°)	–		–		–		–		–	
Brim index	–		–		–		–		–	
Talus: Length	55?	56?	49	49	–	–	45	44+	–	–
Breadth	47	46?	?	36	–	–	38+	?	–	–
Mid-trochlear height	31	31?	–	(27)	–	–	25	–	–	–
Neck diversion angle (°)	23	23	23	23	–	–	27	23?	–	–
Calcaneus: Max. length	–	–	–	–	–	–	–	–	–	–

EARLY IRON AGE—GEOMETRIC												Roman			
PA3-2a		PA4-1		PB1-1		PA3-3		PA5-1a		PB1-2		DD-1		DD-1a	
226		229		232		227		230		233		149		149a	
M 35 / –		M 33 / VI?		M 25 / –		F 25– / –		F 24 / –		F 32 / VI		F 33 / –		F 30–? / –	
L.	R.	L.	R.	L.	R.	L.	R.	L.	R.	L.	R.	L.	R.	L.	R.
–	–	–	352	–	–	(250)	(255)	(285)	–	–	–	–	(285)	(285)	–
–	–	–	46	–	–	–	–	–	–	–	–	–	–	–	–
–	–	23	24	–	–	18	18	18	19	–	18	17	17+	17+	17+
–	–	17	18	–	–	15	14	13	14	–	17	13	13	14	15
–	–	63	61	–	–	–	–	–	–	–	–	–	–	50	–
–	235	261?	–	–	–	–	194	–	–	215	–	–	–	–	–
–	–	278	–	–	–	–	–	–	–	–	–	–	–	–	–
–	–	(160)	–	–	–	–	–	–	–	–	–	–	–	–	–
–	–	–	–	–	–	–	–	–	–	–	–	–	–	–	–
–	–	–	(455+)	410?	–	(360)	–	(395)	–	–	(380)	–	(375)	–	385
–	–	–	46	45	–	–	–	–	–	–	–	–	39	–	41
–	–	–	26	26	–	–	–	22	–	–	24	–	21	–	18
–	–	–	27	29	–	–	–	31	–	–	31	–	26	–	27
–	–	–	32	29	–	20	–	25	24	–	27	–	24	–	22
–	–	–	30	28	–	24	–	24	25	–	27	–	21	–	23
–	–	–	–	–	–	–	–	–	–	–	–	–	–	–	–
–	–	–	96.3	89.7	–	–	–	71.0	–	–	77.4	–	80.8	–	66.7
–	–	–	106.7	103.4	–	83.3	–	104.2	96.0	–	100.0	–	114.3	–	95.7
–	–	–	–	–	–	–	–	–	–	–	–	–	–	–	11.8
(360)	–	–	386?	–	–	–	–	–	–	–	–	–	–	–	–
35	35	–	39	–	35	–	–	–	31	34	33	–	–	27	–
24	23+	–	33	–	23	–	–	–	21	24	24	–	–	19	–
12	–	16	21	–	–	–	–	–	–	–	–	–	–	–	–
68.6	65.7	–	84.6	–	65.7	–	–	–	67.7	70.6	72.7	–	–	70.4	–
–	–	–	–	–	–	–	–	–	–	–	–	–	–	–	–
167.8		176.3		159.0??		146.9		152.7?		156.8		(147)		149.2	
–		74.2?		–		–		–		–		–		–	
–	–	148	135	–	–	–	–	–	–	–	–	134	–	–	–
–	–	–	–	–	–	–	–	–	–	–	–	–	–	–	–
–	–	–	–	–	–	–	–	–	–	–	–	–	–	–	178
–	–	–	–	–	–	–	–	–	–	–	–	76	–	–	73
–	–	–	80	–	–	–	–	–	–	–	–	–	–	–	–
–	–	–	65	–	–	–	–	–	–	–	–	–	–	–	–
–		–		–		–		–		–		–		–	
–	–	–	–	–	–	–	–	–	–	–	–	–	–	–	–
–		–		–		–		–		–		–		–	
–		–		–		–		–		–		–		–	
52–	52–	54	54–	–	–	–	–	–	–	–	–	–	–	–	–
42	42+	–	47	–	–	–	–	–	–	–	–	–	–	–	–
30	29+	(30)	31	–	–	–	–	–	–	–	–	–	–	–	–
32	30	31	30	–	–	–	–	–	–	–	–	–	–	–	–
–	–	–	80?	–	–	–	–	–	–	–	–	–	–	–	–

TABLE 15. MEASUREMENTS, ANGLES, AND INDICES OF INDIVIDUAL SKULLS FROM LERNA

Clan and period		E. Neol.	Late Neolithic			1. Western (Mid. Br. Age, early-middle phases)				
Measurement or index	Grave and area or trench / Number / Sex and age / Skull type (see Table 1, pp. 36–37)	JA-B 220 f 10– A1	HTN-1 240 f 26 A3?	JC-1 242 f 26 A3(F)	BD-27 237 f? 4 A1(D4)	C-L 18 m 49 D4(B4)	C-M 19 m 42 D2	H-1 31 f 18– D4??	M-1 59 f 26 D3	C-F 16 f 15+ C4?
23 a	Horizontal circumference	499	–	515?	442?	516	550	–	499	–
25	Sagittal arc	373	–	363–?	352?	345	(399)	–	370?	–
26	Frontal arc	120	–	119	119	125	129	–	123	–
27	Parietal arc	138	116	131?	130	110	136	–	140	–
1	Vault: Length, max.	177	(178)	184	160	191–?	200	182	178	(165)
(21)	Height, auricular-vertex	112	–	119	108	118	120	–	117+	(113)
5	Base length, basion-nasion	85	–	100?	70	(129)	(120)	–	(100)	–
8	Breadth, max.	137	128?	141+	111?	129	149	(132)	128	(145)
9	Frontal breadth, min.	98	89?	98	80	93	103	(98)	88?	(86)
45	Cheek breadth, bizygomatic	109?	–	131	(86)	118–?	134?	–	114?	(110)
66	Jowl breadth, bigonial	85	102	101	64	(94)	103	92?	–	85?
65	Jaw breadth, bicondylar	102	–	121	(83)	–	120?	–	–	104
71 a	Ramus breadth, min.	30	30?	30–	(23)	29	35	32	–	29
69	Chin height	28	32	33	23	29	35	31	28+	29
48	Upper face height, nas.-prosth.	55	–	67?	(43)	72?	72	(68)	62	(63)
55	Nose height	40	–	46	(31)	55?	52	(49)	44	(48)
54	Nose breadth	22	–	25?	15?	23	26+	(25)	23	(22)
57(2)	Upper nasalia breadth	11+	–	15	8–	12	17	–	8	–
49 a	Interorbital breadth	24?	–	26?	(17)	(23)	25	21?	22	–
51 a	Left orbit breadth, dakryon	36?	–	38^r	32	41	38	38–	40–?	–
52	Left orbit height	28	27^r	31^r	24?	35–?	30	36–?	31–?	30
60	Palate, alveolar length	46	(49)	(54)	–	57	58	55?	49	–
61	Palate, alveolar breadth	56	63?	66	43?	66	71	58?	65	(61)
*	Alveolar plane angle	6	–	7	–	5?	3	–	11	–
72	Face profile angle	83	–	87	–	94?	82	–	90	–
79	Mandibular angle	124	122	136	140	132	137	137	–	135
81	Crown length, upper molar 1	10.0	9.1	10.4	–	10.3	–	–	–	9.5
81(1)	Crown breadth, upper molar 1	10.6	10.8	11.0	–	11.5	–	–	–	10.3
	Indices:									
8 × 100/1	Cranial	77.4	(71.9)	76.6	69.4?	67.5	74.5	(72.5)	71.9	(82.4
2 × (21)/1 + 8	Mean auricular height	71.3	–	73.2	79.7?	73.8	69.0	–	76.5	–
9 × 100/8	Fronto-parietal breadth	71.5	69.5?	69.5	72.1?	72.1	69.1	(74.2)	68.8	(61.4
47 × 100/45	Facial	84.4	–	86.3	(87.2)	97.5?	86.6	–	93.0?	–
54 × 100/55	Nasal	55.0	–	54.4?	(48.4)	41.8	50.0	(51.0)	52.3	(45.8

^{r} Right

	2. Southern (Mid. Br. Age, v. early-mid. ph.)					3. Forest (Mid. Br., v. early-mid.)		4. Central (Mid. Br. Age, v. early to mid. ph.)					
JA-J2B 212 m 33 A3??	JB-J4B 217 m 24? A1	GP-G2 207 f 30 A1	GQ-G3 208 f 38 C4	JA-J2A 211 f 31 F2?	JB-J3A 213 f 26 C3	BA-1 33 m? 22 B1	B-3 13 f 25 A1	BB-1 37 m 32 C4?	B7-9 40 m 48 D4	B8-12B 43 m 21 F3	BB-2 38 f 44 C4?	B8-12A 42 f 20 A3	B8-14 56 f 37 E2
−	520	508?	514?	−	(514)	495	(503)	−	515	512?	−	488	501
−	377?	379	364	−	345	364	360?	−	379	355?	−	(352)	355
123	127	130	122	134	(120)	130	123	−	125	108?	−	113	127
(117)	141	135	123	−	125?	126	127	−	132	121?	−	126	128
−	193	180	174	−	176?	178	185	−	188	184	(170)	173	175
−	119	117	117	−	(115)	116	(104)	(125)	122	103	(113)	111	113
−	(106)	(94)	106?	−	−	104?	−	−	105?	(105)	−	−	104?
−	135	128	147	−	150	132	(130)	(145)	128	142	146	132	135
95	98	89+	94	(95)	(115)	88	(102)	−	98	99?	−	97	92?
−	128	118?	127?	−	−	116	−	−	123	122?	−	124?	128?
−	(96)	83	(101)	101?	(112)	91?	−	105	101	94+?	−	(85)	91+
−	−	108	−	−	(127)	(110)	−	−	125	(114)	−	−	111
−	33	27−?	28+	28	(31)	31	31	31	30	31	−	33	30
−	35?	29	29	(29)	32?	31	31?	34	(34)	36+	30	28	32
−	67?	61	63	−	−	65	62	−	(69)	78	−	58	62
−	49	42+	45	−	−	51	44	−	48?	55	−	39	47
−	30	24	23?	−	−	26	22?	−	28?	25	−	22	21
10	12	11	14	−	−	9	−	−	14	(14)	−	11?	9?
24	22?	21?	23	−	−	19	19?	−	24	(25)	−	22	21
41	37	36?	38	39?	−	41	41	−	40	41	−	42	38+
33?	30?	33	30	33r+	−	33	35r	−	32?	33r	−	29r	31r
−	55?	−	−	−	−	55	(51)	−	(48)	53	−	51	(48)
−	61	(59)	−	−	−	65	63	−	(48)	63	−	54	(55)
−	−1	16	(10)	−	−	10	−	−	(1)	9	−	1	(14)
−	76?	83	85	−	−	85	(84)	−	(88)	88	−	79	90
−	(111)	132	128	−	−	128	−	−	123	132?	−	122?	123
−	11.9	10.9	−	−	−	10.6	10.0	−	−	10.9	−	9.6	−
−	12.0	9.8	−	−	−	12.0	12.5	−	−	11.9	−	10.7	−
−	70.0	71.1	84.5	−	85.2?	74.2	(70.3)	−	68.1	77.2	(85.9)	76.3	77.1
−	72.6	76.0	73.1	−	(70.5)	74.8	(64.8)	−	77.2	63.2	−	73.0	77.9
−	72.6	69.5	64.0	−	76.7	66.7	(78.5)	−	76.6	69.7?	−	73.5	68.2
−	87.5	87.3	80.3	−	−	97.4	−	−	(93.5)	108.2?	−	79.0?	85.2
−	61.2	57.1	51.1	−	−	51.0	50.0	−	(58.3)	45.4	−	56.4	44.7

r Right

TABLE 15. MEASUREMENTS, ANGLES, AND INDICES OF INDIVIDUAL SKULLS FROM LERNA

Measurement or index	5. MARSH (Mid. Br. Age, mid. to late phases)							6. SPRING (Mid. Br. Age, early to mid. ph.)				
	A-1 n. 1 m 26 D1	A-1 s. 2 m 34 F2	B10-20 66 m? 33 E3	B10-24 69 m 40 C4	B10 72 m? 40 C5	A-2, 3, 4 3 f 33? C2	A-11 10 m? 1 C1	BD-19 95 m 39 D3	BD-15 92 f 30 E1?	BD-21 97 f 29 F4	BD-22 98 m? 11- C1	BD-27 103 f?? 2+ A5
23a	522?	532-?	495	520??	510	487	413	500	–	462	468?	479
25	370	353?	345	(370)	341	(330)	306	356	–	321	(324)	350
26	129	140	116	132	105	122	100	124	–	108	112	117
27	131	112	119	133	110	118	113	123	–	117	105	118
1	187	187	172	184	178n	164	137	182	(173)	160-	159	169
(21)	118	124	(109)	128	108	112	102-	108	(120)	111	109?	111
5	(108)	(120)	–	–	99n	–	70	(99)	–	92	–	82
8	133?	147	132	151	147	140	117	135	(147-)	127	137	138
9	95	102?	97	98?	93?	95?	75	86	94	100	91?	87
45	130	141?	(133)	125?	123-?	119?	–	118?	124	127?	(102)	85
66	108	102?	–	(93)	95?	–	(31)	102	85	88?	–	69
65	112?	(121)	–	(116)	(120)	–	–	117?	(118)	118?	–	79
71a	31	31	–	31	31	–	19	29	29	28	–	23
69	35	41+	–	34	31-	30	16+	37	28	27	–	21-
48	67	72	(58)	67?	62	60	–	72	61	69	56	46
55	49	51	44	51	43	46	–	50+	44	51	41	33-
54	25?	21	26?	24+	25n	21	–	24-	22	21?	(21)	18+
57(2)	13?	12	14	12	–	13	–	12	10	13-	14	7?
49a	22?	24?	23	21	23	25	(18)	19	21	24?	22	18?
51a	43-?	44?	39-	41?	38+?	34	28+	37+	37	38+	35	33
52	34-?	34r	31r+	31+	32r	30	27r	32-	29	38r	32	27-
60	(46)	52?	–	51?	(59)	50?	–	47?	53?	(48)	(43)	(40)
61	67	64?	–	(60)	(56)	56?	–	64?	(57)	(55)	(58)	48
*	2	10	–	2	5	15	–	10?	5	12?	11	16
72	94	90	–	80	82	102?	–	87	88	89	84	95
79	123	129?	–	127	128	–	138	140	113	129	–	142
81	10.4	9.8	–	–	–	–	–	10.5	10.6	–	11.2	–
81(1)	11.6	11.6	–	–	–	–	–	11.9	11.0	–	11.7	–
$8 \times 100/1$	71.1?	78.6	79.1	82.1	82.6?	85.4	85.4	74.2	(84.2-)	79.4	86.2	81.7
$2 \times (21)/1+8$	73.8	73.8	(71.7)	76.6	66.7	73.7	80.3	68.4	(75.0)	77.1	73.6	72.3
$9 \times 100/8$	71.4?	72.1?	71.3	64.9?	63.3?	67.9	64.1	63.7	(64.0)	78.7	66.4?	63.0
$47 \times 100/45$	90.8	92.2	–	88.0?	85.4?	84.9?	–	103.4?	82.3	85.8?	–	88.2
$54 \times 100/55$	51.0	41.2?	60.0	47.1?	58.1?	45.6	–	48.0	50.0	41.2	51.2	54.5

r Right   n Left orbit roof, glabella, nasion restored

	7. RIVER (Mid. Br. Age, mid. phase)						8. NORTHERN (Middle Bronze Age, early to middle phases)							
BD-31. 82 m 43 D2	BD-3u. 83 m 33 F2	BD-9 87 m 29 D2	BD-11 88 m 34 B3	BD-12 89 m 42 C4	BD-14 91 m 45 A2	BE-11 115 m 38 D1	BE-19 125 m 44 E2	BE-20 127 m 43 D4	BE-22 128 m 44 C1	BE-23 129 m 38 E2	BE-25 131 m 24 D5	BE-26 132 m 48 A2	BE-30D 140 m 27 C3
544	512?	552?	517?	504?	546	526+	520	528	504	530	520?	522	526?
(413)	(400)	(412)	(373)	363	385	383	380	391	(400)	(385)	(365)	379	(376)
136	(135)	143	123	125	132	135	132	143	125	134	121	133	138
137	145	118	130	115	137	122	135	132	(166)	131	119	138	127
188	172	205	183	174	201	189	183	198	181?	186+	189	184+	175
120-?	132?	125	114	125?	120-	116	122	120-	125?	120	105?	117-	120+
–	–	(108)	–	(88)	(115)	101	(97)	(111)	(101)	(97)	–	(107)	(86)
135?	147	138?	136?	147?	140	142	147	133	145	147	125?	135	150?
(101)	107?	96?	103	91?	102	97	102	102?	97	102	99	119	91
(134)	(135)	(120)	121	(138)	139+	135?	125?	125?	136?	141?	(135)	140	134?
(106)	(98)	(98)	92	(95)	108	(98)	98+?	104?	98	(110)	(101)	104+	92
–	–	–	(100)	–	126	–	(107)	118?	(123)	(139)	–	126?	(119)
34	35	34	30	–	37	28+	35	33	34	32	(35)	35-	32-
34	33	35	32	31	34	36?	33	35+	30-	32	31	38	36
(70)	(75)	(78)	69?	(55)	71?	73	68	73+	65	67	71	71	65
(52)	–	(63)	–	(44)	58?	51	48	51	48	(48)	52+	49	49?
(21)	–	–	48?	(22)	26	26	27	23	24	(23)	23	28	24+
(10-)	–	11?	15?	10	16	12	14	13	13	–	14?	15	12
(22)	–	25?	23	21	28	20	25+	24	23?	(23)	(21)	23+?	21
36	–	33?	41?	39	38-	40	37	41	39	39	38	38	(37)
30?	(28)r	28?	35?r	30+	27	34-	32	34+	31r	32r	33	32	31?
–	–	(50)	(50)	–	63?	56?	57?	58	48?	(49)	51	55	(49)
–	–	–	(67)	–	(67)	(66)	61?	(55)	61	(64)	65	64	(64)
–	–	–	9?	–	9?	17?	-4	4	3	–	2	9	–
(82)	–	–	82	(77)	83	91	85	86	78	93	79	85	83
(130)	120	119	119?	–	108	(135)	130?	131	125	125	–	121	125
–	9.0	10.0	9.0	–	11.0	–	9.2	–	10.0	10.8	10.0	9.4	–
–	10.2	10.9	12.0	–	12.8	–	10.3	–	11.0	11.7	11.0	11.7	–
66.2?	85.5	67.3?	74.3	84.5	69.6	75.1	80.3	67.2	80.1	79.0	66.1?	73.4	85.7
73.5	82.5	72.7	71.2	78.1	70.6	70.3	73.9	72.3	76.7	72.3	66.9	73.1	74.1
(74.8)	72.8?	67.6	75.5	61.9?	72.9	68.3	69.4	76.7	66.9	69.4	79.2?	74.1	60.7
(86.6)	(86.7)	(105.0)	94.2?	(71.7)	84.2	91.1?	88.8?	95.2?	79.4	79.4	(85.2)	85.7	82.1?
(40.4)	–	–	52.1	(50.0)	44.8	51.0	56.2	45.1	50.0	(47.9)	44.2	57.1	49.0

r Right

TABLE 15. MEASUREMENTS, ANGLES, AND INDICES OF INDIVIDUAL SKULLS FROM LERNA

Measurement or index	8. NORTHERN (Middle Bronze Age, early to middle phases) cont.				9. BRIDGE (Mid. Br. Age, early mid. ph.)					10. EASTERN (Middle Bronze Age, middle to late phases)		
	BE-19 126 f 19+ C2	BE-30A 137 f 28 D5	BE-30B 138 f 18– F1(C1)	BE-30C 139 f 28 F4	DE-28 174 m 34 E2	DE-71 238 m 39 B1	DE-72 239 m 36 C1	DE-30 176 m?2 B2	DE-50 193 m??0+ E1?	DE-29 175 m 35 B1	DE-35 181 m 42 A3	DE-32 178 f 33 C1
23a	466?	499?	–	479	532?	521?	490?	442	369	(520)	(514)	500?
25	328^n	362?	–	(356)	391?	(381)	(367)	324	266	(375)	371	366?
26	119^n	124	–	112	145	(129)	129	120	95?	(124)	126	126
27	117	128	–	119	127	140?	131	98	90?	132	125	127
1	157+^{n}	176?	–	161	188–	189	170	155	123	185?	182	174+?
(21)	104–	116	–	109	126	115	113	105	91	115	122	107
5	91^n	97?	–	(82)	(103)	–	–	89	64	98	101	87
8	133	134?	–	137	146	140	138	127	107	135?	140+	143
9	97+	102?	–	111	126	94?	93	77	72	98	103	92?
45	120+	121?	–	120	133?	121?	121?	86?	78?	129?	131	118
66	88–	81	91	95	98?	–	91	60	61	90	101	87
65	111?	104?	118?	(115)	(120)	–	(113)	(76)	73	124?	123	118
71a	29–	28	31+	(30)	28–	31	27–	22	18	29	32	24+
69	29	26+	27	31–?	39	–	36	21	7	31	31?	26
48	58	65	–	61	66	–	65	46–	34–	67	67	60
55	44^n	47	–	42	49	–	43	34	24–	47	51	42+
54	23–	24–?	–	19?	26	–	24	18	16+	27?	25	24
57(2)	–	6	–	13	8–	–	–	10?	9	16	14	11
49a	(21)	21?	–	20	28	–	(22)	16	16	24	20	20?
51a	38	39+	–	33?	39?	–	(37)	33–	26+	40?	42	36
52	31^r?	36^r	–	26?	38?	34^r	34	30–	25	33	33	33–?
60	48	51	–	45	51?	–	(50)	(28)	29	53	54?	49?
61	57	58	–	56	62?	–	58?	46?	43	58	64+?	52?
*	9	4	–	14	9?	–	4	26?	17+	8	5	10
72	83^n	88	–	84	83+	–	85	103	90	85	84–	85
79	125	124	140	130?	150?	–	139	–	145	127	120	125
81	9.3	9.0	–	9.1	10.4	–	10.4	10.8	–	10.2	–	–
81(1)	10.7	10.2	–	10.1	11.8	–	11.3	11.3	–	11.3?	–	–
8×100/1	84.7	76.1	–	85.1	77.7	74.1	81.2	81.9	87.0	73.0?	76.9	82.2
2×(21)/1+8	71.7	74.8	–	73.2	75.4	70.1	73.4	78.0	79.1	71.9	75.8	66.9
9×100/8	72.9	76.1?	–	62.8?	68.5	67.1	67.4	60.6	67.3	72.6	73.6	64.3
47×100/45	81.7?	86.0	–	86.7	89.5?	(86.8)	92.6–?	87.2	(71.8)	87.6	83.2	84.8
54×100/55	52.3?	51.1?	–	45.2?	53.1	–	55.8	52.9	66.7	57.4	49.0	57.1

^{r} Right ^{n} Nasion area restored

	10. Eastern (Middle Bronze Age, middle to late phases) cont.					11. Plain (Mid. Br. Age, late ph.)				12. Sea (Middle Bronze Age, middle to very late phases)			
DE-36	DE-53	DE-59	DE-5	DE-22	DE-63	DE-40	DE-45	DE-55	DE-48	D-1	D-4	D-9	D-18
182	196	200	154	168	203	185	189	198	192	20	23	28	48
f 36	f 40+	f 25	f??1+	m 2–	f? 4	m 30+	m 38	m 35	f 27	m 30	m 60	m 43	m 21
F3	(E?)	D3	—	—	E1	B1	A2	D4	B2	C1	A4	A3	C5
513	–	(478)	–	–	465	501?	511	507	495	540	547	521?	507
360	–	(370)	–	–	345	(372)	(398)	365	(375)	384	393	377?	347?
121	–	120	–	–	123	129	129	118	126	138	128	139	126
117	–	133	–	–	122	126	137	134	128	137	138	138	113
182	–	175	–	–	158	182	188	185	178	182	198	(187)	174
109	–	121?	–	–	109	120?	124	117	112+	120–	124	115–	110
99	–	–	–	–	78+	–	(100)	(100)	–	97	109	105	97
146	–	123	–	–	131	141?	135	135	134	156	144	143	152
97	–	(88)	–	–	86	90	100	118	92?	106	98	98	102
133	–	–	–	–	94?	125?	134	128	120	137?	136	141–?	130?
93	–	83?	60	63	69	97?	98?	96?	84?	99	95–	90	95
124?	94–	–	72?	81	(90)	115?	113?	(116)	106?	(129)	124	(120)	120
27+	28	–	21	21–	24–	32	32	29	31	31	35	30	37
26	31	33	18	20	21	33	34	33	29	27+	36	30	32–
71	63?	–	–	–	44	65?	64	75	59	63	(65)	64	64
50–	45?	–	–	–	33	48	45	54+	45	48	50	49	47
22	29	–	–	–	19–	22+?	25	24	26	23	25	26	25+
12	–	–	–	–	10	7?	12?	(10)	12	11	15	7?	12
22	–	–	–	–	17	19?	22	(21)	20	23	22	23?	24
39	–	31?r	–	–	32	35?	41	42?	38	35?	41	38	38
36	–	–	–	–	29	32	33–	32–	33?	31+	31	32	31
52?	–	–	–	–	35	51?	56	49?	(53)	50	(46)	54?	55
68	–	–	–	–	47	(60)	64	61?	(60)	61	(49)	66	63
3	–	–	–	–	12	7	6	11?	5	9	(9)	1	5
88	–	–	–	–	93	86	86	90	81	94	(99)	88	81
122	–	–	139	145	135–	115	117	123	128	122	122	118	113
11.2	–	10.6	–	–	–	10.1	9.8	10.6	10.2	9.1	–	10.1	10.2
12.0	–	11.0	–	–	–	11.4	11.8	10.7	11.3?	10.7	–	11.1	11.9
80.2	–	70.3	–	–	82.9	77.5?	71.8	73.0	75.3	85.7	72.7	76.5?	87.4
66.5	–	81.2	–	–	75.4	74.1	76.5	73.1	71.8	71.0	72.5	69.7	67.5
66.4	–	78.0	–	–	65.6	63.8?	74.1	69.6	68.7	68.0	68.1	68.5	67.1
83.5	–	–	–	–	79.8	88.0	80.6	94.5	85.8	74.4?	(83.1)	75.9?	83.1
44.0	64.4?	–	–	–	57.6	45.8	55.6	44.4	57.8	47.9	50.0	53.1	53.2

r Right

THE PEOPLE OF LERNA

TABLE 15. MEASUREMENTS, ANGLES, AND INDICES OF INDIVIDUAL SKULLS FROM LERNA

Measurement or index	12. SEA (Middle Bronze Age, middle to very late phases) cont.					13. BAY (M.B.A., v. late ph.)		EARLY IRON AGE— GEOMETRIC		Roman
	D-20 50 m 27 D2	D-22 52 m 55 A4	D-15 45 f 33 E1	D-14 55 f 15a A1	D-16 46 m?4+ D2?	DC-1(1) 145 m 50? B3	DC-1(2) 146 f 49 A3	PA4-1 229 m 33 C3?	PA5-1a 230 f 24 D2	DD-1 149 f 33 A4(E3)
23a	542	550	498?	494	—	(514)	504?	—	505	527
25	411	390	374	361	—	(362)	364+	—	385	374
26	132	134	132	122	—	120?	130	—	135	125
27	150	130	131	127	124	127	125	—	121	135
1	194+	200	171?	180	—	183	178	—	184	186
(21)	126	119	110	113	—	112-?	114+	—	121	113
5	107	115	91?	101?	—	—	97	—	108?	94
8	138	146	137	126	—	139	137	—	131	145
9	98	100	(94)	96	—	95	(99)	—	93	95
45	127?	137	121?	108	—	—	123?	—	(117)	120
66	94?	98+	—	87	71	—	71	105?	(90)	91
65	112?	116+	—	93	(93)	—	114	128	—	—
71a	35+	37	24	33?	28	—	29+	30-	31	30
69	38	33	(29)	26	25-	—	28?	35	27?	31
48	69+	67?	60?	59	—			—	69	59?
55	51	50	43?	43	—	—	—	—	52?	42?
54	27-	26	(25)	23?	—	—	—	—	24?	—
57(2)	11	17	—	10?	—	—	13	—	(10)	—
49a	21?	25	(20)	24	—	—	25?	—	(19)	25+
51a	40	41	38	36	—	—	—	—	40?	38
52	30	32	29	32	—	—	33r	—	35+	31
60	57	51	47	48?	—	—	—	—	(47)	(47)
61	67	68	(63)	56	—	—	—	—	58-	(52)
*	2?	7	9?	16?	—	—	—	—	9?	0?
72	83?	95	86?	89?	—	—	—	—	90	83?
79	126	118	—	136	130-	—	131	128	(120)	(117)
81	11.9	8.8	—	—	—	—	—	—	9.6	—
81(1)	11.3	10.8	—	—	—	—	—	—	10.8	—
8 × 100/1	71.1	73.0	80.1?	70.0	—	76.0	77.0	—	71.2	78.0
2 × (21)/1 + 8	75.9	68.8	71.4	73.9	—	69.6	72.8	—	76.6	68.3
9 × 100/8	71.0	68.5	(68.6)	76.2	—	68.4	(72.3)	—	71.0	65.5
47 × 100/45	96.1	82.5	(85.1)	91.7	—	—	(77.2)	—	(93.2)	(86.7)
54 × 100/55	52.9	52.0	(58.1)	53.5	—	—	—	—	46.2?	—

a Adolescent   r Right

INDEX

089053